The Knights

(First Half)

Henryk Sienkiewicz

Jeremiah Curtin

Alpha Editions

This edition published in 2019

ISBN : 9789389265798

Design and Setting By
Alpha Editions
email - alphaedis@gmail.com

THE KNIGHTS OF THE CROSS.

HENRYK SIENKIEWICZ AND JEREMIAH CURTIN, WARSAW, 1900.

THE

KNIGHTS OF THE CROSS.

BY

HENRYK SIENKIEWICZ,

AUTHOR OF "QUO VADIS," "WITH FIRE AND SWORD,"
"CHILDREN OF THE SOIL," ETC.

*AUTHORIZED AND UNABRIDGED TRANSLATION FROM
THE POLISH BY*

JEREMIAH CURTIN.

FIRST HALF.

BOSTON:
LITTLE, BROWN, AND COMPANY.
1901.

University Press:
John Wilson and Son, Cambridge, U.S.A.

TO

COUNTESS ANNA BRANITSKI OF VILLANOV.

———————

MADAM, — *You know the language of this translation as accurately as you know Polish; you reverence what is true and beautiful in literature as well as in life; to you therefore I beg to dedicate these volumes.*

JEREMIAH CURTIN.

WARSAW, May 1, 1900.

INTRODUCTION.

THE period embraced in "The Knights of the Cross" is one of the most dramatic and fruitful of results in European annals, — a period remarkable for work and endeavor, especially in the Slav world.

Among Western Slavs the great events were the Hussite wars and the union of Lithuania and Poland. The Hussite wars were caused by ideas of race and religion which were born in Bohemia. These ideas produced results which, beyond doubt, were among the most striking in European experience. The period of Bohemian activity began in 1403 and ended in 1434, the year of the battle of Lipan, which closed the Bohemian epoch.

The marriage in 1386 of Queen Yadviga to Yagello, Grand Prince of Lithuania, brought Poland into intimate relations with all the regions owing allegiance to the Lithuanian dynasty, and made it possible to crush at Tannenberg the Knights of the Cross, whose object was the subjection of Poland and Lithuania, and a boundless extension of German influence in eastern Europe.

Bohemian struggles made the religious movement of the next century possible in Germany. The Polish victory at Tannenburg called forth that same movement. Had the Knights of the Cross been victorious at Tannenburg and found the East open to conquest and their apostolic labor, it is not conceivable that the German princes would have taken action against Rome, for such action would not have been what we call practical politics, and the German princes were pre-eminently

practical. But when the road to the East was barred
by Polish victory there was no way for Germany to
meet Rome but with obedience or a new religion; hence
the German Reformation. Luther himself declared
that he could not have succeeded had Huss not lived
before him. Huss gave the intellectual experience
needed by the Germans while Polish victory threw
them back upon Germany and thus forced the issue
between Roman and German tendencies.

The history ending at Tannenberg is of profound
interest, whether we consider the objects sought for on
each side, or the details involved in the policy and the
acts, diplomatic and military, of the two opposing forces.

The struggle between German and Slav began long
before the Knights of the Cross were in existence.
Originating in earlier ages in what undoubtedly was
mere race opposition, it grew envenomed at the beginning of the ninth century, after the restoration, or more
correctly, perhaps, after the creation of the Western
Empire in 800, in the person of Charlemagne. This
new Roman Empire was German; there was little of
Roman in it save the claim to universal dominion.
This pretension to empire was reinforced greatly by
association with the Church, whose unbending resolve
it was to bring all men to the doctrine of Christ, that is,
to bring them within its own fold and jurisdiction.

The position of peoples outside the Empire and the
Church, that is, people independent and not Christian,
who refused the rule of the Empire and the teachings
of the Church, was that of rebels against Imperial
authority, and dupes of Satan.

The position was aggravated intensely by the fact
that those peoples were forced to accept political subjection and the new religion together. Political subjection meant that the subordinated race went into contempt
and inferiority, was thrust down to a servile condition;

the race lost land, freedom, language, race institutions, primitive ideas, and that aboriginal philosophy which all races have without exception, no matter what be their color or what territory they occupy.

North Germany from the Elbe eastward is Germanized Slav territory; the struggle to conquer the region between the Elbe and the Oder lasted till the end of the twelfth century, the process of Germanizing lasted during centuries afterward. Those of the Slav leaders in this region who were of use in managing the people and were willing to associate themselves with the invaders retained their positions and became German. The present ducal houses of Mecklenburg-Strelitz and Mecklenburg-Schwerin are of this kind, Slav in origin.

After the fall of those Slavs between the Elbe and the Oder the German (Roman) Empire and Poland stood face to face.

Omitting details for which there is no space here it suffices to state that the early leaders of the Poles saw at once the supreme need in their own case of separating religion from other questions. The first historic ruler of Poland, Miezko I., 963–992, married a Bohemian princess and introduced Christianity himself. He forestalled the Germans and deprived them of the apostolic part of their aggressive movement, and one great excuse for conquest.

Being Christianized the Poles maintained themselves against the Germans, but as they were Christian they felt obliged to extend Christianity to places embraced within their territory or connected with it.

Along the Baltic from the Vistula to the Niemen lived the Prussians, a division of the Lithuanian stock. The Lithuanians are not exactly Slavs, but they are much nearer to the Slavs than to any other people, and are among the most interesting members of the great Aryan race. In their language are preserved verbal forms which are more primitive than those retained in Sanscrit, and with the single exception of the Gaelic of Ireland and Scotland it has preserved in actual use the most primitive forms of Aryan speech, though its grammatical methods are not so primitive as some used in the Gaelic.

The Prussians had a great love for their own primitive racial religion and for their independence; this religion and this independence they considered as inseparable. They inhabited a portion, or what was considered a portion, of the territory of Konrad, Prince of Mazovia, who tried to convert them; but instead of succeeding in his attempt he met with failure, and the Prussians took revenge by invading that part of his territory which was purely Polish and Christian, and which was known as Mazovia, immediately south of and bordering on Prussia, which, as stated already, touched on the Baltic and extended from the Vistula to the Niemen. The chief town of Mazovia was Warsaw, which became afterward the capital of Poland.

Among measures taken by Konrad to convert Prussia was the formation of a military order called the Brothers of Dobryn. These Brothers the Prussians defeated terribly in 1224.

In 1226 Konrad called in the Knights of the Cross to aid in converting the stubborn Prussians, and endowed them with land outside of Prussia, reserving sovereign rights to himself, at least implicitly. The Knights, however, intended from the very first to take the territory from Konrad and erect a great German State in the east of Europe on Slav and Lithuanian ruins. They had no intention of performing apostolic labor without enjoying the highest earthly reward for it, that is, sovereign authority.

Before he had received the grant from Konrad, the Grand Master of the Order obtained a privilege from the Emperor Frederick II., who in virtue of his pretended universal dominion bestowed the land which Konrad might give for the use of the Knights, and in addition all territory which the Order could win by conquest.

The work of conquest and conversion began. A crusade against Prussia was announced throughout Europe. From Poland alone went twenty thousand men to assist in the labor.

Soon, however, Konrad wished to define his sovereign rights more explicitly. The Order insisted on complete independence. In 1234 a false[1] document was prepared and presented by the Grand Master to Pope Gregory IX. as the deed of donation from Konrad. The Pope accepted the gift, gave the territory in fief to the Order, informed Konrad, August, 1234, of the position of the Knights, and enjoined on him to aid them with all means in his power.

Konrad of Mazovia was in an awkward position. He had brought in of his own will a foreign power which had all western Europe and the Holy See to support it, which had, moreover, unbounded means of discrediting the Poles; and these means the Order never failed in using to the utmost.

In half a century after their coming the Knights, aided by volunteers and strengthened by contributions from the rest of Europe had subjugated and converted Prussia, and considered Lithuania and Poland as sure conquests, to be made at their own leisure and in great part at the expense of Western Christendom.

This was the power which fell at Tannenberg.

The German military Order of The Teutonic Knights, or Knights of the Cross, was founded in Palestine in 1190 to succeed an Order of Knight Hospitallers, also German, which was founded about 1128.

[1] Dzieje Narodu Polskiego Dr. A. Lewicki, p. 82, Warsaw, 1899,

From 1190 to 1210 there were three Grand Masters of this Order. In 1210 was elected the fourth, Hermann von Salza, who transferred the order to Europe, established it first in Hungary and later in Prussia, where he laid the foundations of its power and settled the conditions according to which it rose and fell.

The policy of the Order in Prussia was to carry on apostolic labor through military conquest, found a State, and later pull down other States to strengthen the one it had founded. When broken on the field of battle it had no principle through which it might rise again to its previous significance.

The further fate of this Order is described briefly in my introduction to "The Deluge," pages IX and X.

The Order of Knights of the Sword was founded in 1205 to spread Christianity in Livonia, east of Prussia. After a career of thirty-three years it was united with the Order of Knights of the Cross during the time of the Grand Master Hermann von Salza.

JEREMIAH CURTIN.

WARSAW, May 1, 1900.

THE

KNIGHTS OF THE CROSS.

CHAPTER I.

In Tynets, at the Savage Bull, an inn which belonged to the monastery, were sitting a number of persons, listening to the tales of a veteran warrior, who had come from distant parts, and was relating adventures through which he had passed in war and on the road.

He was a bearded man, in the vigor of life, broad shouldered, almost immense, but spare of flesh; his hair was caught up in a net ornamented with beads; he wore a leathern coat with impressions made on it by armor; his belt was formed entirely of bronze squares; under this belt was a knife in a horn sheath; at his side hung a short travelling-sword.

Right there near him, behind the table, sat a youth with long hair and a gladsome expression of eye, evidently the man's comrade, or perhaps his armor-bearer, for he was also in travelling-apparel, and wore a similar coat, on which were impressions of armor. The rest of the society was composed of two country people from the neighborhood of Cracow and three citizens in red folding caps, the sharp-pointed tops of which hung down on one side a whole yard.

The innkeeper, a German wearing a yellow cowl and collar with indented edge, was pouring to them from a pitcher into earthen tankards substantial beer, and listening with interest to the narrative of warlike adventures.

But with still greater interest did the citizens listen. In those days the hatred which, during the time of Lokietek, distinguished citizens from knightly landowners, had decreased notably; citizens held their heads higher than in later centuries. They were still called at that time " des aller durchluchtigsten Kuniges und Herren "[1] and their readi-

[1] See note at the end of Volume II.

ness "ad concessionem pecuniarum" (to pay money) was esteemed; hence it happened frequently that merchants were seen drinking in inns on the footing of lord brother with nobles. Nobles were even glad to see them, for merchants, as persons who possessed ready coin, paid usually for men with escutcheons.

So this time they sat and conversed, winking from moment to moment at the innkeeper to replenish the tankards.

"Then, noble knights," said one of the merchants, "ye have examined a piece of the world?"

"Not many of those now assembling in Cracow from all parts have seen as much," answered the knight.

"And not a few will assemble," continued the citizen. "Great feasts, and great happiness for the kingdom! They say, too, and it is certain, that the king has ordered for the queen a brocade bed embroidered with pearls, and above it a canopy. There will be festivals and tournaments within barriers, such as the world has not seen to this day."

"Interrupt not the knight, Gossip Gamroth," said a second merchant.

"I am not interrupting him, Gossip Eyertreter, but I think that he himself will be glad to know what people are saying, for surely he is going to Cracow. As it is, we shall not return to the city to-day, for the gates would be closed before us; and at night insects, hatched among chips, do not let people sleep, so we have time for everything."

"But you answer one word with twenty. You are growing old, Gamroth."

"Still I can carry a piece of damp cloth under my arm."

"Oh, indeed! but such cloth that light passes through it, as through a sieve."

Further conversation was interrupted by the warrior.

"It is sure," said he, "that I shall stop in Cracow, for I have heard of the tournaments, and shall be glad to try my strength in the lists, — and this nephew of mine here also, who, though young and beardless, has seen more than one coat of mail on the ground."

The guests looked at the youth, who smiled joyously, and, when he had put his long hair behind his ears with both hands, raised the tankard of beer to his lips.

"Even if we wished to return," added the old knight, "we have no place to which we could go."

"How is that?" asked one of the nobles. "Whence are ye, and what are your names?"

"I am called Matsko of Bogdanets, and this stripling is the son of my brother; his name is Zbyshko. Our shield is the Blunted Horseshoe, with watchword Hail!"

"Where is your Bogdanets?"

"Oh, better ask me, lord brother, where it was, for it exists no longer. Even during the wars of the Grymaliti and Nalentchi our Bogdanets was burned to its foundations, and what we had there people took from us; our serving-men fled. The place was left naked, for neighboring land-tillers went farther into the wilderness. I with my brother, the father of this stripling, built up our castle anew, but the next year water swept it away from us. After that my brother died, and then I was alone with his orphan. 'I shall not stay here,' thought I. At that time people were talking of war, and of this, that Yasko of Olesnitsa, whom King Vladislav sent to Vilno to succeed Mikolai of Moskorzov, was seeking knights diligently throughout Poland. As I knew Yanko, the worthy abbot of Tulcha, I pledged my land to him, and with borrowed money bought arms and horses. I found for myself the outfit usual in war, this lad, who was twelve then, I seated on a pony, and away to Yasko of Olesnitsa."

"With this stripling?"

"My dear, he was not even a stripling at that time, but he was a sturdy little fellow. At twelve he could put his crossbow on the ground, press with his stomach, and so turn the bow crank that no Englishman whom we saw at Vilno could do better."

"Was he so strong?"

"He carried my helmet at twelve, and when thirteen winters old he carried my shield."

"Then there was no lack of wars there?"

"Thanks to Vitold, there was not. The prince was always urging the Knights of the Cross, and every year they sent expeditions to Lithuania against Vilno. Various nations went with them: English, who are the first of bowmen, French, Germans, Bohemians, Swiss, and Burgundians. They felled forests, built fortresses on the way, and at last harried Lithuania savagely with fire and sword, so that all the people who dwelt in that land wished to leave it, and search out another, even at the end of the world, — even among sons of Belial, if only far from Germans."

"It was reported here that all Lithuanians wished to go away with their children and wives; we did not believe that."

"But I saw it. Hei! had it not been for Mikolai of Moskorzov, and Yasko of Olesnitsa, and without boasting, had it not been for us, Vilno would not now be existing."

"We know. Ye would not surrender the castle."

"And we did not. Listen, then, attentively to what I tell you; for I am a man who has served, I am a warrior of experience. People of the old time said in their day, 'Lithuania is venomous,' and they spoke truly. The Lithuanians fight well single-handed, but in the open field they cannot measure with the knighthood. When the horses of the Germans sink in swamps, or when they are in a dense forest, it is different."

"The Germans are good knights!" exclaimed the citizens.

"They stand like a wall, man to man, in iron armor, so covered that hardly is the eye of a dog brother of them to be seen through his vizor. And they go in line. It used to happen that the Lithuanians would strike them and be scattered like sand, and if they were not scattered the Germans put them down like a pavement and trampled them. But the Germans are not alone, for all nations in the world serve with the Knights of the Cross. Ah, those strangers are gallant! More than once a foreign knight would bend forward, lower his lance, and even before battle strike all alone into a whole army, like a falcon into a flock."

"Christ!" called out Gamroth. "Who is the best among the foreigners?"

"It depends on the weapon. At the crossbow the English are best; they pierce armor through and through with a shaft, and hit a dove a hundred steps distant. The Chehs cut terribly with axes. At the two-handed sword no one surpasses the German. The Swiss delight in breaking thick helmets with iron flails. But the greatest knights are those who come from the French land. They will fight with thee on foot or on horseback, and hurl terribly valiant words at thee; words which thou wilt not at all understand, for their speech is as if one were to rattle a tin plate, though these people are God-fearing. They have accused us, through German interpreters, of defending Pagans and Saracens against Knights of the Cross, and have bound themselves to prove it by a knightly duel. There is to be a judgment of God between four of their knights and four of ours; the meeting is appointed at the court of Vatslav, the Roman Emperor and King of Bohemia."

Here greater curiosity seized the country people and the

merchants, so that they stretched their necks over the tankards toward Matsko of Bogdanets and inquired, —
"And of ours who will meet the French? Tell quickly!"
Matsko raised his beer to his lips, drank, and answered:
"Ei! have no fear for our men. They are Yan of Vloshchova, castellan of Dobryn; Mikolai of Vashmuntov; Yasko of Dakov; and Yarosh of Chehov. All are knights to be proud of, deadly fellows. Whether they do battle with lance, sword, or axe — it is nothing new to them! Men's eyes will have something to look at, and their ears something to hear. I have said, put foot on the throat of a Frenchman and he will send knightly words at thee. So help me God and the Holy Cross! as the French talk, so do ours slay."

"There will be glory, if God bless us," said one of the nobles.

"And Saint Stanislav!" added another. Then, turning to Matsko, he continued: "Well, now go on! You have glorified the Germans and other knights, saying that they are brave and that they broke Lithuanians easily. But against you was it not more difficult? Did they go against you with the same willingness? How did God favor? Give praise to our side!"

Evidently Matsko was no braggart, hence he answered modestly, —

"Whoso is fresh from distant lands strikes us willingly, but after he has tried us once and a second time he has not the same courage, for our people are stubborn. We have been reproached often with this stubbornness. 'Ye despise death,' say our enemies, 'but ye help the Saracens, and for this ye will be damned!' But in us stubbornness increases, for what they say is untrue. The double kingdom baptized Lithuania, and all people there confess Christ the Lord, though not every one does so with knowledge. We know that when a devil was cast out of the cathedral in Plotsk, our gracious lord gave command to set up a candle to him, and priests had to tell the king that it was improper to do that. Well, how must it be in the case of a common man? More than one says to himself: 'The prince has given command to be christened, he has given command to bow down to Christ, so I bow down; but why should I spare a pot of curds on the ancient pagan devils, why not throw them a toasted turnip, or pour to them beer foam? Unless I do so my horses will drop dead, or my cows will be sick, or their milk will grow bloody, or there will be harm to the harvest.' Many act in this way, and fall under suspicion. But they act thus through ignorance and through fear of devils. Formerly those devils had pleasant lives. They had their groves, their houses, horses to ride on, and they received tithes. But now the groves are cut down, they have nothing to eat; bells are rung in the towns, so this vileness is confined in the deepest forests and howls there in anguish. If a Lithuanian goes to the forest among pines, one devil or another pulls him by the coat, and says 'Give!' Some give, but there are bold fellows who give nothing, and even catch the devils. One man poured roasted peas into an ox bladder, and thirteen devils crawled in right away. He shut them in with a service-wood plug and took them for sale to the Franciscan monks in Vilno, who gave him twenty groshes with gladness, so as to destroy the enemies of Christ's name. I myself saw that bladder, and a disgusting odor entered a man's nostrils at a distance from it; by such odors do foul spirits express their terror of holy water."

"But who counted the thirteen devils?" asked the merchant Gamroth, cleverly.

"A Lithuanian who saw them crawl in counted. It was evident that they were there, for that was shown by the stench, but no one would take out the plug."

"Those are wonders, wonders!" cried one of the nobles.

"I have looked my fill at great wonders not a few. We cannot say that those Lithuanian people are pleasant, everything about them is strange. They are shaggy, and hardly a prince among them curls his hair; they eat roasted turnips, preferring them to all other food, for they say that turnips increase bravery. They live in the same house with their cattle and their serpents, they know no moderation in eating and drinking. They hold married women in no esteem, but maidens they reverence highly and recognize great power in them; so if any maiden rubs a man's stomach with dried sycamore, gripes leave him that moment."

"Well, one would not be sorry to have the gripes if the maiden were shapely." called out Eyertreter.

"Ask Zbyshko," replied Matsko of Bogdanets.

Zbyshko laughed till the bench shook beneath him. "There are wonderful maidens among them!" said he. "Was not Ryngalla wonderful?"

"What Ryngalla? Some gay one? Tell us immediately."

"Have ye not heard of Ryngalla?" inquired Matsko.

"Not a word."

"Well, she is Prince Vitold's sister, and was the wife of Henryk, Prince of Mazovia."

"How is that? What Prince Henryk? There was only one Mazovian prince of that name, the bishop elect of Plotsk, but he died."

"The same man. A dispensation was to come from Rome to him, but death gave him the first dispensation; evidently he did not delight the Lord over much with his conduct. I was sent in that time with a letter from Yasko of Olesnitsa, to Prince Vitold, when Prince Henryk came from King Vladislav to Ritterswerder, as the bishop elect of Plotsk. The war had already become disagreeable to Vitold for this reason specially, that he could not take Vilno, and to our king his own brothers and their loose conduct had become disagreeable. The king, seeing then greater skill and more wisdom in Vitold than in his own brothers, sent the bishop to him with proposals to leave the Knights of the Cross and incline to obedience, for which the government of Lithuania would be given him. Vitold, always eager for change, listened to the pleasant message. There were feasts and tournaments. The bishop mounted a horse with delight, and exhibited his knightly prowess in the lists, though other bishops did not approve of this conduct. By nature all princes of Mazovia are strong, and it is notorious that even maidens of that stock break horseshoes easily. So one day the prince bishop swept three knights of ours from their saddles, another day five, and me among them, while the horse under Zbyshko he put on his haunches. He received all rewards from the hands of the marvellous Ryngalla, before whom he knelt in full armor. And they so fell in love that at feasts attendant clerics drew him away by the sleeves from her, and Vitold restrained the princess his sister. Then the prince bishop said: 'I give a dispensation to myself, and the pope will confirm it, if not the pope in Rome, he of Avignon, and we will have the marriage straightway, or I shall be consumed.' It was a great offence against God, but Vitold did not wish to offend the king's envoy. Then the young couple went to Suraj, and later to Slutsk, to the great grief of this Zbyshko here, who, in German fashion, had chosen Princess Ryngalla as the lady of his heart, and vowed fealty till death to her."

"Indeed, this is true!" broke in Zbyshko. "But after-

ward people said that Princess Ryngalla, understanding that
it was not proper for her to be married to the bishop elect
(for though married, he had no wish to abandon his spiritual
dignity), and because such a marriage could not be blessed
by the Lord, poisoned her husband. Hearing of this, I
prayed a holy hermit near Lublin to free me from my
vow."

"He was a hermit indeed," answered Matsko, with a smile,
" but I am not sure that he was holy, for we came upon him
one Friday in the forest, where he was cracking bear-bones
with an axe, and sucking out the marrow till there was
gurgling in his throat."

" But he said that marrow was not flesh, and besides that
he had a dispensation to eat it, for he had miraculous visions
in sleep after eating marrow, and could prophesy on the
morrow till mid-day."

" Well, well," replied Matsko.   "But the wonderful Ryngalla is a widow, and she may summon thee to service."

" She would summon me in vain, for I shall choose another lady to serve till death, and besides I shall find a
wife."

" First find the belt of a knight."

" Of course! but will there not be tournaments after the
queen's delivery?   Before that, or after it, the king will belt
more than one man.   I shall challenge every one.   The prince
would not have unseated me had my horse not sat on his
haunches."

"There will be better men there than thou."

Then a nobleman from near Cracow exclaimed, —

" By the dear God! in presence of the queen will appear,
not such men as thou, but the most renowned knights on
earth: Zavisha of Garbov, and Farurey and Dobko of
Olesnitsa, and Povala of Tachev, and Pashko Zlodye of Bis-
kupitsi, and Yasko Nashan, and Abdank of Gora, and
Andrei of Brohotsitsi, and Krystin of Ostrov, and Yakov of
Kobylani!   How couldst thou cope with these, with whom no
man can cope either here or at the court of Bohemia or Hungary.   What sayest thou, art thou better than they?   How
old art thou? "

" Eighteen," replied Zbyshko.

" Then each man of them could bend thee between his
fingers."

" We shall see."

" I have heard," said Matsko, "that the king rewards

bountifully knights returning from the Lithuanian war. Say ye who come from the capital if that be true?"

"True as God lives!" said one of the nobles. "The bountifulness of the king is known throughout the world, but now it will not be easy to squeeze up to him, for in Cracow it is just swarming with guests who are assembling to be there during the delivery of the queen and the christening, wishing thus to show honor and fealty to our king. The King of Hungary is to be there, and they say the Roman Emperor too, and various princes, counts, and knights as numerous as poppy seed, because each man hopes that he will not go away empty-handed. They have said, even, that Pope Boniface himself will come; he also needs the aid and favor of our lord against his enemy in Avignon. In such a throng it will not be easy to gain audience, but if it be gained, and our lord's feet embraced, he will care for a man of merit bountifully, be assured."

"Then I will embrace his feet, for I have rendered service, and if there be war I will go again. I have gained booty, and received something from Prince Vitold as reward. I feel no need, but my evening years are coming, and in old age, when strength leaves his bones, a man is glad to have a quiet corner."

"The king was rejoiced to see those who returned from Lithuania under Yasko of Olesnitsa, and they are all eating fatly at present."

"Well! I did not return at that time, I warred on; for ye should know that that peace between the king and Prince Vitold was ground out upon the Germans. The prince recovered his hostages cunningly, and then attacked the Order. He stormed and burnt castles, slew knights, cut down a multitude of people. The Germans wished to take revenge in company with Swidrygello, who fled to them. There was a great expedition again. Conrad himself, the Grand Master, went with it, leading immense forces. They besieged Vilno, strove to storm castles from great towers, tried to take them by treason, but had no success in anything! And in their retreat so many fell that not one half escaped. We took the field once more against the brother of the Grand Master, Ulrich of Jungingen, burgomaster of Sambia. But Ulrich was afraid of the prince and fled with weeping. Since that flight there is peace, and they are building up Vilno anew. A certain holy monk, who could walk on red-hot iron barefoot, prophesied that thenceforth while the world was the world Vilno would not see near its walls an armed German. But if that be true, whose hands did the work?"

Matsko of Bogdanets stretched forth his hands, which were broad and strong beyond measure; others began to nod and add, —

"Yes, yes! he is right in what he says."

But further conversation was interrupted by a noise coming through the windows, from which the panes had been taken because the night was bright and warm. From afar was heard a clinking, the voices of people, the snorting of horses, and songs. Those present were astonished, for the hour was late and the moon had risen high in the heavens. The innkeeper, a German, ran out to the court of the inn, but before the guests could drain the last tankard he returned still more hurriedly.

"Some court is coming!" exclaimed he.

A moment later at the door appeared a youth in a blue kaftan, and on his head a red folding cap. He stopped, looked at the company, and seeing the host said, —

"Wipe the tables there and trim the lights; Princess Anna Danuta will halt here to rest."

Then he turned away. In the inn there was a movement, the host called to his servants and the guests looked at one another with astonishment.

"Princess Anna Danuta!" said one of the citizens; "that is the daughter of Keistut; she is wife of Yanush of Mazovia. She has passed two weeks already in Cracow, but went out to Zator, to Prince Vatslav on a visit, and now is returning of course."

"Gossip Gamroth," said the second citizen, "let us go to the hay in the barn; this company is too high for us."

"I do not wonder that they travel at night," remarked Matsko, "for it is hot in the day-time; but why come to an inn when there is a cloister near by?"

Here he turned to Zbyshko.

"A sister, a full sister of the wonderful Ryngalla. Dost understand?"

"But there must be many Mazovian damsels with her, hei!" said Zbyshko.

CHAPTER II.

MEANWHILE the princess passed in. She was a smiling-faced, middle-aged lady, dressed in a red mantle and a green, closely fitting robe; at her hips was a golden girdle, which dropped downward in front and was fastened low with a great clasp. Behind the lady walked damsels of her court, some older, others not full-grown yet; most of them had garlands of roses and lilies on their heads, and lutes in their hands. Some carried whole bunches of fresh flowers, evidently plucked along the road. The room was filled, for after the damsels came a number of courtiers and young boys. All entered briskly, with gladness in their faces, conversing loudly, or singing, as if intoxicated with the beautiful evening and bright moonlight. Among the courtiers were two choristers, one with a lute, the other with a guitar at his girdle. One of the damsels, quite young yet, perhaps twelve years of age, carried behind the princess a lute adorned with brass nails.

"May Jesus Christ be praised!" said the princess, halting in the middle of the room.

"For the ages of ages. Amen!" answered those present, making low bows as they spoke.

"But where is the host?"

The German, hearing the summons, pushed forward and knelt in German fashion.

"We shall stop here for rest and refreshment," said the lady. "But move about briskly, for we are hungry."

The citizens had departed already, but now the two city nobles, and Matsko of Bogdanets with young Zbyshko, unwilling to disturb the court, bowed a second time with the intention of leaving the room; but the princess detained them.

"Ye are nobles, ye will not interrupt! Make the acquaintance of our courtiers. Whence is God conducting you?"

At once they announced their names, their escutcheons, their service, and the villages by which they entitled themselves. It was only when the lady heard from Matsko whence he was returning that she clapped her hands, and said, —

"See, here is luck! Tell us of Vilno; tell of my brother and sister. Will Prince Vitold come to the delivery of the queen and to the christening?"

"He would like to come, but not knowing whether he will be able, he has sent a silver cradle in advance by priests and boyars, as a gift to the queen. I and my nephew have come to guard this cradle on the road."

"Then is the cradle here? I should like to see it. Is it all silver?"

"All silver, but it is not here. They have taken it to Cracow."

"But what are ye doing in Tynets?"

"We have turned back to visit the procurator of the cloister, our relative, and confide to the care of the worthy monks what war has given us, and what the Prince has bestowed."

"Then God has shown favor? Was the booty considerable? But tell us why my brother was uncertain of coming."

"Because he is preparing an expedition against the Tartars."

"I know that, but it troubles me, since the queen has prophesied an unhappy end to it, and what she prophesies always comes true."

Matsko smiled.

"Our lady is saintly, there is no denying that," said he, "but a host of our knighthood will go with Prince Vitold, splendid men; to meet them will not be easy for any force."

"And ye will not go?"

"No, for I was sent with others to take the cradle; besides I have not taken armor from my body for five years," said Matsko, pointing to the impressions of the armor on his elkskin coat. "Only let me rest, then I will go; and if I should not go I will give Zbyshko, this nephew of mine, to Pan Spytek of Melshtyn, under whose lead all our knights will enroll themselves."

Princess Anna looked at the stately figure of Zbyshko, but further conversation was interrupted by the arrival of a monk from the cloister, who, when he had greeted the princess, began humbly to reproach her for not having sent a courier with the announcement of her coming, and for not halting at the monastery instead of a common inn, which was unworthy of her dignity. There was no lack in the monastery of houses and edifices in which even an ordinary person could find entertainment, and what would be done in case of majesty, especially that of the spouse of a prince from whose ancestors and relatives the abbey had received so many benefactions?

"We have stopped only to rest our limbs," said the princess, good-humoredly; "in the morning we must go to Cracow. We have slept enough in the day, and are travelling at night, because it is cool; and as it was past cock-crow I did not wish to rouse the pious monks, especially with a company which has singing and dancing more in mind than rest."

But when the monk continued to insist, she added, —

"No. We will remain here. A good hour will pass in listening to worldly songs; we shall be at the church for morning mass, to begin the day with God."

"There will be a mass for the prosperity of the gracious prince and princess," said the monk.

"The prince, my consort, will come only after four or five days."

"The Lord God has power to send fortune from afar; but meanwhile let it be permitted us poor people to bring even wine from the cloister."

"We shall thank you for it gladly," said the princess.

"Hei! Danusia, Danusia!" called she, when the monk had gone; "come out on the bench and rejoice our heart with that same song which thou gavest us in Zator."

Thereupon the courtiers placed a bench quickly in the middle of the room. The choristers sat, one at each end of it, between them stood that young girl who had borne behind the princess the lute adorned with brass nails. On her head was a garland, her hair was flowing over her shoulders; her robe was blue, her shoes red, with long tips. Standing on the bench she seemed a child, but at the same time a wonderful child, — a church statue, as it were, or a marionette. It was evident also that this was not the first time that she stood up and sang to the princess, for not the slightest confusion was evident in her.

"Go on, Danusia, go on!" cried the damsels.

She held the lute in front of her, raised her head like a bird about to sing, and closing her eyes, began in her silvery voice, —

> "Oh had I wings as a wild goose,
> I would fly after Yasek,
> I would fly after him to Silesia!"

The choristers accompanied her promptly, one on a guitar, the other on a large lute ; the princess, who loved worldly songs beyond everything, swayed her head from side to side, and the little maiden sang on in a thin, childlike, fresh voice. It was like the singing of birds in a forest in springtime.

> "I would sit on a fence in Silesia,
> Look at me, Yasek dear,
> Look at the poor little orphan."

And again the choristers accompanied.

Young Zbyshko of Bogdanets, accustomed from childhood to war and its stern images, had never seen anything like that in his life. He nudged in the shoulder a Mazovian standing near by, and inquired, —

"Who is she?"

"She is a maiden of Princess Anna's suite. There is no lack of choristers with us who amuse the court; but she is the dearest little chorister of all, and the princess listens to no person's songs with such eagerness as to hers."

"That is no wonder to me. I thought her a real angel, and I cannot gaze at her sufficiently. What is her name?"

"But have you not heard? — Danusia. Her father is Yurand of Spyhov, a wealthy and valiant count, who is of those in advance of the banner."

"Hei! human eyes have not seen the like of her."

"All love her, for her singing, and her beauty."

"But who is her knight?"

"She is a child yet."

Conversation was interrupted a second time by Danusia's singing.

From one side Zbyshko gazed at her, — at her bright hair, her raised head, her half-closed eyes, and at her whole figure, illuminated both by the light of the wax candles and the light of the moon-rays coming in through the open window; and he was more and more astonished. It seemed to him that he had seen her sometime, but he could not remember where, — in a dream, or at Cracow, in a church window. Then he pushed the courtier, and asked in a low voice, —

"Is she of your court, then?"

"Her mother came from Lithuania with Princess Anna Danuta, who gave her in marriage to Yurand of Spyhov. She was beautiful and of a great family, beloved of the princess beyond other damsels, and loving the princess herself. For this reason she named her daughter Anna Danuta. Five years ago, when the Germans fell upon our court at Zlotoria, she died of fright. Princess Anna took the little girl at that time, and is rearing her. Her father comes often to the court, and is glad when he sees his child in good health and beloved of the princess. But, as often as he looks at her, he sheds tears thinking of his dead one; and then he turns against the Germans, to seek vengeance for the terrible wrong which they wrought on him. No man loved his own wife more than he up to that time in all Mazovia, and he has slain a host of Germans already in revenge for her."

Zbyshko's eyes gleamed in one moment, and the veins thickened on his forehead.

"Then did the Germans kill her mother?" asked he.

"They killed her, and they did not kill her. She died of fright. Five years ago there was peace; no one was thinking of war, and each man went about with no feeling of danger. The prince went to build a castle in Zlotoria, without troops, but with his court, as is usual in peace time. Just then the German traitors attacked us without declaration of war, without cause. Forgetting the fear of God, and all the benefactions which they had received from his ancestors, they lashed the prince to a horse, bore him away, and slew his people. The prince sat long in captivity among them, and only when King Vladislav threatened war did they set him free, out of fear; but during that attack Danusia's mother died, for her heart rose in her throat, and it choked her."

"And you were present? What is your name? I have forgotten."

"I am Mikolai of Dlugolyas; my surname is Obuh. I was present at the attack. I saw a German, with peacock-plumes on his helmet, strap Danusia's mother to his saddle, and saw her grow white before his eyes. They cut me down with a halberd, the mark of which I bear yet."

Then he showed a deep scar which extended from beneath his hair to his brow.

A moment of silence followed. Zbyshko fell to gazing at Danusia again, and inquired, —

"And you say that she has no knight?"

But he did not await the answer, for at that moment the singing ceased. One of the choristers, a large, weighty man, stood up on a sudden; by this the bench tipped at one end; Danusia tottered, spread out her arms; but before she could fall, or jump off, Zbyshko sprang forward with the speed of a wildcat, and caught her in his arms. The princess, who at

the first moment screamed out from fear, began at once to laugh, and said, —
"Here is Danusia's knight! Come hither, young knight, and give us our dear little songstress!"
"He caught her gallantly!" cried voices among the courtiers.

Zbyshko went toward the princess, holding Danusia at his breast; she, clinging to his neck with one arm, raised the lute high with the other, fearing lest she might break it. Her face was smiling and gladdened, though she was somewhat frightened.

Meanwhile the youth, on reaching the princess, placed Danusia before her; then kneeling and raising his head, he said, with a boldness marvellous at his age, —
"Let it be according to your words, gracious lady! It is time for this charming maiden to have her knight; and it is time, too, for me to have my lady, whose beauty and virtue I shall recognize; so with your leave I will make vows to this one, and be faithful to her unto death in all trials."

Astonishment shot over the face of the princess, not because of Zbyshko's words, but because all had happened so suddenly. The custom of knightly vows was not Polish, it is true; but Mazovia, being on the German boundary, and seeing knights frequently from even distant lands, was acquainted with that custom better than other provinces, and accepted it rather early. The princess had heard of it also still earlier, at the court of her renowned father, where all Western customs were looked on as law, and as models for the noblest warriors. For these reasons she did not find in Zbyshko's wish anything to offend her or Danusia. On the contrary, she was glad that this little girl, who was dear to her, should begin to attract the hearts and eyes of knights. So with delighted face she turned to the little maid.

"Danusia, Danusia! dost wish to have thy knight?"

The blond-haired Danusia sprang up three times in her red shoes, and then, seizing the princess by the neck, began to cry, with as much delight as if they had offered her a plaything permitted only to older persons for amusement:
"I do, I do, I do!"

The princess laughed till her eyes were filled with tears, but at last the lady, freeing herself from Danusia's arms, said to Zbyshko, —
"Well! make the vow! make the vow! What dost thou vow to her?"

Zbyshko, who amidst the laughter had preserved an un-
shaken dignity, spoke up with equal seriousness, without rising from his knee,—
"I vow to her that when I reach Cracow I will hang my
shield in front of an inn, and on it a declaration, which a
cleric learned in letters will write for me: that Panna Danusia,
daughter of Yurand, is the most beautiful and virtuous among
the damsels who inhabit all kingdoms. And should any man
deny this I will do battle with him till I perish or he perishes,
unless he should prefer to go into slavery."
"Well done! It is clear that thou knowest knightly
customs. And what more?"
"And, since I have learned from Pan Mikolai that Panna
Danusia's mother yielded her last breath through the act of a
German with peacock-plumes on his helmet, I vow to gird
my body with a hempen cord, and, though it should eat me
to the bone, I will not remove the cord till I have slain three
German knights, torn three such plumes from their helmets,
and placed them at the feet of my lady."
At this the princess grew serious and inquired,—
"Art thou not making this vow to raise laughter?"
"So help me God and the Holy Cross," answered Zbyshko,
"I will repeat this vow in the church before priests."
"It is praiseworthy to give battle to the fierce enemy of
our race, but I grieve for thee, since thou art young and
mayst perish easily."
Then pushed forward Matsko of Bogdanets. Till that
moment, like a man of past times he had merely shrugged
his shoulders; now he thought fit to speak.
"As to that be not troubled, gracious lady. Death in
battle may meet any man, and to a noble, whether old or
young, this is even praiseworthy. But war is no wonder to
this lad, for though years are lacking him, it has happened him more than once to fight on horseback and on
foot with lance or axe, with a long or a short sword, with
a shield or without one. For a knight to make vows to a
damsel whom he looks on with gladness is a novel custom, but as Zbyshko has promised his three peacock-plumes
I make no reproach. He has harried the Germans, let
him harry them again; and if from that harrying a pair
of German heads should burst, he will have only the more
glory."
"I see that the affair is not with some common youth,"
said the princess, and she turned to Danusia. "Sit thou in

my place, as the first person at present, but do not laugh, for it is not becoming."

Danusia took Princess Anna's place and wished to feign seriousness, but her blue eyes laughed at the kneeling Zbyshko, and she was unable to restrain herself from moving her feet through delight.

" Give him thy gloves," said the princess.

Danusia drew off her gloves which she gave to Zbyshko, who took them with great respect.

" I will fasten these to my helmet," said he, pressing them to his lips, " and whoso tries to get them, woe to him." Then he kissed Danusia's hands, and after the hands her feet, and rose. But that moment his former seriousness deserted him, and great joy filled his heart because thenceforth he would pass as a mature man before all that court; so, shaking Danusia's gloves, he cried, half in joy, half in anger,—

" Come on, dog brothers with your peacock-plumes! Come on!"

But at that moment the same monk entered the inn who had been there before; and with him two others, older than he. Behind them monastery servants bore wicker baskets, and in them vessels of wine, and various dainties collected quickly. Those two fell to greeting the princess and reproaching her for not having gone to the monastery; but she explained a second time that, since she had slept and the whole court had slept in the daytime, they were travelling at night, hence needed no sleep; and not wishing to rouse the distinguished abbot, or the worthy monks, she preferred to halt at the inn and rest their limbs there.

After many courteous phrases they decided finally on this: that after matins and early mass the princess and her court would accept a meal and rest in the monastery. Besides the Mazovians, the hospitable monks invited the landowners of Cracow, and Matsko of Bogdanets, who intended in every case to go to the monastery and leave there the property which he had won in war, or had received as gifts from the bountiful Vitold, and which was intended to free Bogdanets from pledge. Young Zbyshko had not heard the invitations, for he had run to his own and his uncle's wagons, which were under guard of their attendants, so as to dress and stand in more befitting costume before Danusia and the princess. Taking his boxes from the wagon, he commanded to bear them to the servants' room, and he dressed there. First he arranged his hair hurriedly and thrust it into a silk net, in which were interwoven amber beads with real pearls in front. Then he put on a "jacket" of white silk embroidered with gold griffins, and at the bottom with ornamented border; above this he girded himself with a double gilded girdle, from which depended a small sword in a scabbard inlaid with silver and ivory. All this was new, gleaming, and not stained with any blood, though taken as booty from a young Frisian knight, serving with the Knights of the Cross. Next, Zbyshko put on very beautiful trousers, one leg of which was striped red and green, the other yellow and violet: both ended above in many-colored squares. When he had put on purple shoes with long, pointed toes, splendid and fresh, he betook himself to the general room.

When he stood on the threshold the sight of him made indeed a strong impression on all. The princess, when she saw what a beautiful knight had made vows to Danusia, was delighted still more, and Danusia at the first moment sprang toward him like a deer. But, whether she was restrained by the beauty of the youth, or the voices of admiration from the courtiers, she stopped before she had run to him; so that, halting a step distant from Zbyshko, she dropped her eyes suddenly, and clasping her hands began, blushing and confused, to twist her fingers.

But after her came up others: the princess herself, the courtiers, the damsels, the choristers and the monks; for all wished to look at him more closely. The Mazovian maidens gazed at Zbyshko as at a rainbow, each regretting that he had not chosen her. The elder ones admired the costliness of the dress; and round him was formed a circle of the curious; Zbyshko stood in the centre with a boastful smile on his face, turning somewhat on the spot where he stood, so that they might look at him better.

"Who is that?" asked one of the monks.

"That is a young knight, the nephew of this lord here," replied the princess, pointing to Matsko; "he has just now made a vow to Danusia."

The monks showed no astonishment, since such vows bound to nothing. Vows were made frequently to married ladies, and in notable families, among whom Western customs were known, almost every lady had her knight. If a knight made vows to a damsel, he did not become her betrothed thereby; on the contrary, she took another for husband most frequently; but he, in so far as he possessed

the virtue of constancy, did not cease in fealty to her, but
he married another.

Danusia's youth astonished the monks somewhat more,
but not over much, for in that age youths of sixteen became
castellans. The great queen Yadviga herself was only
fifteen when she came from Hungary, and girls of thirteen
were given in marriage. Besides, they were looking more in
that moment at Zbyshko than Danusia, and were listening to
Matsko, who, proud of his nephew, had begun to relate how
the young man had come to possess such famous apparel.

" A year and nine weeks ago," said he, " we were invited
to feasts by Saxon knights; and with them as guest was a
certain knight from the distant nation of the Frisians, who
dwell far away at the edge of the ocean, and he had with
him his son, three years older than Zbyshko. Once at a
feast that son told Zbyshko .unbecomingly that he had
neither beard nor moustache. Zbyshko, being quick-tempered, would not listen to this calmly, but seizing him at
once by the lips plucked out all the hair from them, for
which afterward we fought for death or servitude."

" How is that? Did you fight? " asked Mikolai.

" I did, for the father took his son's part, and I Zbyshko's; so we fought, four of us, in presence of the guests,
on a space of trampled earth. We made an agreement of
this sort, that whoso conquered should take the wagons and
horses and servants of the conquered. And God favored
us. We slew those Frisians, though with no little toil, for
they lacked neither courage nor strength; and we took
famous booty. There were four wagons, for each wagon a
pair of draught-horses four immense stallions, nine servants,
and two excellent suits of armor, such as one might find
rarely with our people. The head-pieces we broke, it is
true, in the battle, but the Lord Jesus consoled us with
other things, for in a box bound famously with iron were
suits of costly apparel, and that suit in which Zbyshko has
now arrayed himself was with them."

At this the two nobles from Cracow, and all the Mazovians
looked with greater respect on the uncle and nephew, and
Mikolai, surnamed Obuh, said, —

" Ye are, I see, unyielding, stern men."

" We believe now that this young man will get the three
peacock-plumes."

Matsko smiled, wherewith in his stern face there was
something quite predatory.

Meanwhile the monastery servants had drawn forth from the wicker baskets wine and tidbits, and from the servants' quarters girls had begun to bring plates full of smoking fried eggs flanked with sausages from which went forth a pronounced and savory odor of wild-boar flesh. At sight of this a desire to eat seized all, and they moved toward the tables.

No one, however, took a place earlier than the princess. When she had sat down at the middle of the table she commanded Danusia and Zbyshko to sit side by side, and then said to Zbyshko, —

"It is proper that thou eat from one dish with Danusia, but act not as other knights do with their ladies, bring not thy foot to hers under the table, touch not her knees, for she is too young."

"I will not, gracious lady," replied he, "unless after two or three years, when the Lord Jesus will permit me to perform my vow, and when this berry will ripen; and as to treading on her feet, I could not do that if I wished, for they are hanging in the air."

"True!" answered the princess, "and it is pleasant to see that thou hast decent manners."

Then followed silence, for all had begun to eat. Zbyshko cut the fattest bits of sausage and gave them to Danusia, or put them directly into her mouth, and she, glad that so stately a knight was serving her, ate with full cheeks, blinking and smiling, now at him, now at the princess.

After the plates had been cleared the monastery servants poured out sweet, fragrant wine, to men in abundance, to women sparingly; but Zbyshko's knightliness appeared specially when they brought in full measures of nuts from the monastery; native wild nuts, and, rare in that time, Italian nuts brought from afar, which the company seized very eagerly, so that after a while throughout the whole room nothing was heard save the noise of nutshells cracked between jaws. It would be vain to suppose that Zbyshko thought only of himself, for he preferred to show the princess and Danusia his knightly strength and abstinence rather than lower himself in their eyes through greed for dainties. Taking from moment to moment a handful of nuts, whether Italian or native, he did not put them between his teeth as did others, but squeezed them with his iron fingers, cracked the shells, and gave clean kernels to Danusia. He invented even an amusement for her. After he had

removed the kernels he put his hand to his lips and blew the
shells suddenly with his mighty breath to the ceiling.
Danusia laughed so much that the princess, fearing lest
the girl might choke herself, commanded him to abandon
the amusement. Seeing, however, Danusia's delight, she
asked, —

" Well, Danusia, is it nice to have thy knight?"

" Oi, nice!" answered the maiden. And putting forth a
rosy finger she touched Zbyshko's white silk jacket, withdrew the finger suddenly, and asked, —

" And will he be mine to-morrow?"

" To-morrow, in a week, and till death," answered Zbyshko.

The supper came to an end when, after the nuts, sweet
pancakes full of berries were brought to them. Some of the
courtiers wished to dance, others preferred to hear the
singing of the choristers, or of Danusia; but toward the end
of the supper Danusia's eyelids began to grow heavy; her
head dropped first to one side, then to the other; once and
a second time she looked at the princess, then at Zbyshko;
again she rubbed her eyes with her fists and immediately
rested with great confidence against the knight's shoulder,
and fell asleep.

" Is she asleep?" asked the princess. " Now thou hast
thy 'lady.' "

" She is dearer to me sleeping than another in a dance,"
answered Zbyshko, sitting erect and motionless so as not to
rouse the maiden.

But not even the playing and singing of the choristers
roused her. Some kept time to the music with their feet,
others accompanied by beating the dishes, but the greater the
noise the better she slept, with her mouth open, like a little
fish. She woke only when, at cock-crow and the sound of
church bells, all moved from the table crying, —

" To matins! to matins!"

" We will go on foot to praise God," said the princess.

And taking the awakened Danusia by her hand, she went
forth first from the inn, and after her the whole court. The
night had grown pale. On the eastern sky a slight brightness was visible. green at the top, rosy below that, and under
all a narrow golden ribbon as it were, which widened as one
looked at it. On the west the moon seemed to withdraw
before that brightness. The dawn became rosier and clearer
each instant. The world awoke wet from abundant dew,
refreshed and joyful.

"God has given fine weather, but the heat will be violent," said the courtiers.

"That is no harm," answered Pan Mikolai, quieting them, "we shall take a sleep at the cloister and reach Cracow about evening."

"For another feast, surely."

"There are feasts every day now in Cracow, and after the tournaments there will be greater ones."

"We shall see how Danusia's knight will exhibit himself."

"Ei! They are in some sort men of oak! Have ye heard what they said of that battle of four?"

"Perhaps they will join our court, for they are counselling together about something."

And really they were counselling, for Matsko was not greatly rejoiced over what had happened; moving, there-fore, in the rear of the retinue, and lingering purposely, so as to speak more at freedom, he said, —

"In truth there is no profit for thee in this. I shall push up to the king somehow, even with this court, and mayhap I shall gain something. I should like wonderfully to get some little castle or town. Well, we shall see. In good time we shall redeem Bogdanets from pledge, for what thy fathers possessed we must possess also. But whence are we to get men? Those whom the abbot settled he will take back again; land without men has no value, so mark what I say: Make vows to whom it may please thee, or make them not, but go with Pan Melshtyn to Prince Vitold against the Tartars. Should the expedition be summoned before the queen's delivery, wait not for delivery or tournaments, but go, for there may be profit. Thou knowest how bountiful Prince Vitold is, and he knows thee already; acquit thyself manfully, he will reward thee well. And above all, if God favor, thou mayst get captives beyond number. The Tartars are like ants in the world. In case of victory there will be sixty for each warrior."

Here Matsko, who was greedy for land and labor, began to imagine, —

"God give me a blessing to drive in about fifty men and settle them in Bogdanets. We should open a strip of wilder-ness and increase, both of us. And knowest thou, that no-where wilt thou collect so many men as thou mayst collect there."

But Zbyshko shook his head.

"Oh, I should find horse boys who live on horse carrion, people unused to land work! What good would they be in Bogdanets? Besides, I have vowed to get three German peacock-plumes. Where should I find them among Tartars?"

"Thou hast vowed, for thou art stupid, and so are the vows."

"But my noble and knightly honor, how with that?"

"How was it with Ryngalla?"

"Ryngalla poisoned the prince, and the hermit absolved me."

"The abbot in Tynets will absolve thee. An abbot is better than a hermit; that man looked more like a robber than a monk."

"I want no absolution."

Matsko stopped, and asked with evident anger, —

"Well, how will it be?"

"Go yourself to Vitold, for I will not go."

"Thou knecht! But who will bow down before the king? And art thou not sorry for my bones?"

"A tree might fall on your bones and not break them. But even were I sorry for you I am unwilling to go to Vitold."

"What wilt thou do? Wilt thou be a falconer, or a chorister at the Mazovian court?"

"Is a falconer something evil? Since it is your wish to grumble rather than listen, then grumble."

"Where wilt thou go? Is Bogdanets nothing to thee? Wilt thou plow in it with thy nails, without men?"

"Not true! you have argued bravely with your Tartars. Have you heard what the people of Rus say, — 'Thou wilt find as many Tartars as there are corpses of them on the field, but no man will seize a captive, for no man can overtake a Tartar in the steppe.' On what could I overtake one! On those heavy stallions which we took from the Frisians? And what booty could I find? Mangy sheepskin coats, nothing else! And only when I return rich to Bogdanets will they call me comes (count)."

Matsko was silent, for there was much justice in Zbyshko's words, and only after a while did he say, —

"But Prince Vitold would reward thee."

"Oh yes! you know; he rewards one man too much and gives another nothing."

"Then tell me, whither art thou going?"

"To Yurand, of Spyhov."

Matsko twisted the belt of his skin kaftan with anger, and said, —

"God daze thy eyes!"

"Listen," answered Zbyshko, calmly. "I have talked with Pan Mikolai, and he says that Yurand is seeking vengeance on the Germans for his wife. I will go and assist him. You have said, first of all, that it is nothing wonderful for me to fight with Germans, for I know them, and I know methods against them. Secondly, I shall find the peacock-plumes there at the boundary more quickly, and third, you know that no common man wears a peacock-plume above his head, so that if the Lord Jesus will grant the crests, he will grant booty at the same time. Finally, a captive taken there is not a Tartar. To settle such a one in the forest is not the same as — Pity me, O God!"

"What! hast lost thy reason, boy? There is no war now, and God knows when there will be."

"Oh, simplicity! The bears have made peace with the bee-keepers; bears injure no bee-nests now, they eat no honey. Ha! ha! But is it news to you that, though great armies are not warring, and though the king and the Grand Master have put their seals to parchment, there is always a terrible uproar on the boundary? If some one takes cattle, a number of villages will be burnt for each cow, and castles will be attacked. But what as to seizing boys and maidens and merchants on the highways? Do you remember earlier times, of which you yourself have told me? Was it hard for that Nalench who seized forty men who were going to the Knights of the Cross? He put them under the ground and would not let them out till the Grand Master sent him a wagon full of coin. Yurand of Spyhov does nothing else but seize Germans, and near the boundary there is work at hand always."

For a while they walked on in silence; meanwhile the daylight came, and bright sun-rays lighted the cliffs on which the monastery was built.

"God can give luck everywhere," said Matsko at last, with a satisfied voice. "Pray that He give it thee."

"It is sure that His favor is everything!"

"And think of Bogdanets, for thou wilt not persuade me that thou hast the wish to go to Bogdanets, and not to Yurand of Spyhov, for that chatterer."

"Speak not in that way, or I shall be angry. I look on her with gladness and do not deny it; that is a different vow

from the one to Ryngalla. Hast thou met a more beautiful
maiden?"

"What is her beauty to me? Take her when she grows
up, if she is the daughter of a great comes."

Zbyshko's face grew bright with a kindly smile.

"That may happen too. No other lady, no other wife.
When your bones grow weak you will nurse my grandchildren
and hers."

Then Matsko smiled in turn, and he said, entirely pacified:

"Hail! Hail! Storms of them, and let them be like hail!
Joy for old age, and salvation after death. Give that to us,
O Jesus."

CHAPTER III.

PRINCESS Anna Danuta, Matsko, and Zbyshko, had been in Tynets before, but in the retinue were courtiers who saw it for the first time, and these, when they raised their eyes, looked with astonishment on the magnificent abbey, on the indented walls running along cliffs above precipices, on edifices standing now on the slopes of the mountain, now within battlements piled up, lofty, and shining in gold from the rising sun. By these noble walls, edifices, houses, and buildings destined for various uses, and the gardens lying at the foot of the mountain, and carefully cultivated fields which the eye took in from above, it was possible at the first glance to recognize ancient inexhaustible wealth, to which people from poor Mazovia were not accustomed, and at which they must unavoidably be astonished. There existed, it is true, old and wealthy Benedictine monasteries in other parts of the kingdom, as, for example, in Lubush on the Odra, in Plotsk, in Great Poland, in Mogilno, and other places, but none could compare with Tynets, whose possessions exceeded not only dependent principalities, but whose incomes might rouse envy even in kings at that period.

Among the courtiers, therefore, astonishment increased, and some of them were almost unwilling to believe their own eyes. Meanwhile the princess, wishing to shorten the road for herself, and rouse the curiosity of her attendant damsels, fell to begging one of the monks to relate the old and terrible tale of Valger the Charming, which had been told her in Cracow, though not with much detail.

Hearing this, the damsels gathered in a close flock around the lady and walked up the mountain-side slowly in the early rays of the sun, looking like a troop of moving flowers.

"Let the tale of Valger be told by Brother Hidulf, to whom he appeared on a certain night," said one monk, looking at another, a man of gray years already, who with a body somewhat bent walked at the side of Pan Mikolai.

"Have you seen him with your own eyes, pious father?" asked the princess.

"I have seen him," replied the monk, gloomily; "for times are granted when God's will permits him to leave his hellish underground dwelling and show himself in the light."
" When does this happen? "

The monk glanced at the other two and was silent, for there was a tradition that Valger's ghost was to appear when the morals of the Knights of the Cross should become lax and the monks think more than was proper of worldly pleasures and wealth. No one wished to confess aloud that it was said also that the ghost foretold war or other misfortunes; so Brother Hidulf, after a moment's silence, said, —

" His ghost heralds nothing good."

" I should not like to see him," said the princess, making the sign of the cross on herself; " but why is he in hell? — since, as I hear, he only avenged too severely a personal wrong."

"Though during his whole life he had been virtuous," answered the monk, sternly, " he would have been damned in every case, for he lived during pagan times, and was not cleansed by holy baptism."

At these words the brows of the princess contracted with pain, for she remembered that her mighty father, whom she had loved with her whole soul, had died also in pagan error, and must burn through all eternity.

" We are listening," said she after a moment of silence.

Brother Hidulf began his narrative, —

" There lived in pagan times a wealthy count, who because of great beauty was called Valger the Charming. This country, as far as the eye sees, belonged to him, and on expeditions, besides footmen he led forth a hundred spearmen, for all nobles on the west to Opole and on the east to Sandomir were his vassals. No man could count his cattle, and in Tynets he had a fortress filled with coin, just as the Knights of the Cross have in Malborg at present."

" I know they have! " interrupted Princess Anna.

" And he was like a giant," continued the monk, — " he tore up oak trees by the roots; and in beauty, in playing on the lute, and in singing, no man on earth could compare with him. But once, when he was at the court of the King of France, the king's daughter, Helgunda, fell in love with him. Her father had wished to give her to a convent for the glory of God, but she fled with Valger to Tynets, where they lived in vileness, for no priest would give them Christian marriage. In Vislitsa lived Vislav the Beautiful, of the race of King Popiel. Once this Vislav, during the absence of Valger, fell to ravaging the lands of Tynets. Valger conquered him and brought him to Tynets, not remembering that every woman who looked on Vislav was ready straightway to desert father, mother, and husband, so be it that she could satisfy her desire. And so it happened with Helgunda. She invented such bonds for Valger that though he was a giant, though he tore up oak trees, he was not able to break the bonds, and she delivered him to Vislav, who took him to Vislitsa. But Vislav had a sister named Rynga. When she heard Valger singing in an underground dungeon she fell in love with him straightway, and freed him from under the earth. When he had slain Helgunda and Vislav with a sword, Valger left their bodies to the crows and returned to Tynets with Rynga."

" Did not he do what was right? " inquired the princess.

" If he had received baptism, and given Tynets to the Benedictines," answered Hidulf, " perhaps God would have remitted his sins, but since he did not do that the earth swallowed him."

" Were the Benedictines in this kingdom at that time? "

" The Benedictines were not in this kingdom, for pagans alone lived here then."

" In such case how could he receive baptism, or give away Tynets? "

" He could not, and for that very reason he is condemned to endless torments in hell," replied the monk, with dignity.

" Surely he speaks the truth! " said a number of voices.

They were now approaching the main gate of the monastery, in which the abbot at the head of a numerous retinue of monks and nobles was waiting for the princess. There were always many laymen, " messengers, advocates, procurators," and monastery officials there. Many landholders, even great nobles, held countless cloister lands by feudal tenure, rather exceptional in Poland, and these, as vassals, were glad to appear at the court of the " suzerain," where near the high altar it was easy to receive a grant, an abatement, and every kind of benefaction, — dependent frequently on some small service, clever word, or a moment of good-humor in the mighty abbot. While preparing for solemnities in the capital many also of such vassals assembled from distant places; those of them for whom it was difficult, be-

cause of the throng, to find an inn in Cracow, found lodg-
ings in Tynets.   For these reasons the *Abbas centum
villarum* (abbot of a hundred villas) might greet the princess
with a retinue still more numerous than common.

He was a man of lofty stature, with an austere and wise
face, with a head shaven on the crown, but lower down,
above the ears, encircled by a garland of hair growing gray.
On his forehead was a scar from a wound received evidently
during years of young knighthood; eyes penetrating, haughty,
looked out from beneath dark brows.   He was dressed in
a habit like other monks, but over it was a black mantle
lined with purple, and on his neck a gold chain from the end
of which depended a cross, also gold and inlaid with precious
stones, the emblem of his dignity as abbot.   His whole
bearing indicated a man haughty, accustomed to command,
and self-confident.   But he greeted the princess cordially,
and even with humility, for he remembered that her husband
came of that stock of Mazovian princes from which King
Vladislav and Kazimir the Great were descended on the
female side, and at present the reigning queen was the
mistress of one of the broadest realms on earth.   He
passed the threshold of the gate, therefore, inclined his
head low, and, when he had made the sign of the cross
over Anna Danuta and the whole court, with a golden tube
which he held in the fingers of his right hand, he said, —

"Be greeted, gracious lady, at the poor threshold of
monks.   May Saint Benedict of Murcia, Saint Maurice,
Saint Boniface, and Saint Benedict of Anagni, and also
Saint John of Ptolomeus, our patrons who dwell in eternal
light, endow thee with health and with happiness; may they
bless thee seven times daily through every period of thy
life."

"They would have to be deaf not to hear the words of so
great an abbot," said the princess, courteously; "all the
more since we have come here to mass, during which we
shall place ourselves under their protection."

Then she extended her hand to him, which he, kneeling
with courtliness on one knee, kissed in knightly fashion;
after that they passed in through the gateway without delay.
Those inside were waiting evidently for mass to begin, for
at that moment the bells great and small were rung, trum-
peters sounded shrill trumpets at the church door, in honor of
the princess, while others beat enormous kettle-drums made
of ruddy copper and covered with rawhide; these gave forth

a roaring sound. On the princess, who was not born in a
Christian country, every church had thus far produced a deep
impression, but that church of Tynets produced it all the
more, since in respect of grandeur there were few others to
compare with it. Gloom filled the depth of the sanctuary.
Only at the high altar were trembling rows of various lights
mingled with the glitter of candles, illuminating the gilding
and the carving. A monk in full vestments came out with
the chalice, bowed to the princess, and began mass. Directly
rose the smoke of abundant incense, which, hiding the priest
and the altar, went upward in quiet clusters, increasing the
mysterious solemnity of the church.

Anna Danuta bent her head backward, and spreading her
hands at the height of her face began to pray earnestly.
But when the organ — organs were rare in churches at that
time — shook the whole nave with majestic thunder, filled it
with angels' voices, scattering as it were the song of the
nightingale, the eyes of the princess were uplifted, on her
face besides devotion and awe was depicted delight beyond
limit, and it might seem to one looking at her that she was
some blessed one, gazing at heaven opened in miraculous
vision.

Thus prayed the daughter of Keistut, born in paganism.
Though in daily life, like all people of that period, she mentioned the name of God in a friendly and intimate manner,
in the house of the Lord she raised her eyes in childlike
dread, and in subjection to a mysterious and infinite power.

In a like pious manner, though with less awe, did the
whole court pray. Zbyshko knelt outside the stalls among
the Mazovians, for only the princess and her damsels were
inside, and he committed himself to the guardianship of
God, and at moments looked at Danusia, who sat with
closed eyes near the princess; and he thought that in truth
there was worth in becoming the knight of such a maiden,
but also that he had promised her no common thing. Under
the "jacket" which he had won, he had girded on the hempen
rope, but that was only one part of the vow, after which he
had to accomplish the other, which was incomparably more
difficult. So now, when the wine and beer which he had
drunk in the inn had gone from his head, he was troubled in
no slight degree as to the manner in which he should accomplish it. There was no war. In the disturbance on the
boundary it was indeed easy for him to meet an armed German, break his skull, or lay down his own head. This he

had told Matsko also. "But," thought he, "not every German wears peacock or ostrich plumes on his helmet:" of guests of the Knights of the Cross only certain counts, and of the Knights of the Cross themselves only comturs, and then not every one. If there should be no war, years might pass before he could find his three plumes. This too came to his head, that not being belted, he could only challenge unbelted men to combat in battle. He hoped, it is true, to receive the belt of a knight from the king in time of the tournaments which were promised after the christening, for he had earned it long before — but what next? He would go to Yurand of Spyhov, and assist him; he would crush warriors as far as possible, and that would be the end. But common warriors were not knights with peacock-plumes on their helmets.

In this suffering and uncertainty, seeing that without the special favor of God he would not do much, he began to pray: "Grant, O Jesus, war with the Knights of the Cross, and the Germans who are the enemies of this kingdom and of us all; and rub out those men who are more ready to serve the chieftain of hell than they are to serve Thee, bearing in their hearts hatred against us, most angry of all that our king and queen, having baptized Lithuania, prevent them from cutting down Thy servants with the sword. For which anger chastise them.

"And I, sinful Zbyshko, am penitent before Thee and implore aid from Thy five wounds to send me, at the earliest, three noted Germans with peacock-plumes on their helmets, and permit me in Thy mercy to slay them, because I have vowed those plumes to Panna Danusia, the daughter of Yurand; she is Thy servant, and I have sworn on my knightly honor. And of what is found on the slain I will bestow the tenth part on Thy church faithfully, so that Thou, sweet Jesus, may receive profit and honor from me; and know Thou that I promise with a sincere heart, and not idly. And as this is true, so help me. Amen."

But as he prayed, his heart melted more and more from devotion, and he added a new promise, that after freeing Bogdanets from pledge he would give to the church all the wax which the bees should make during a whole year. He hoped that his uncle Matsko would not oppose this, and the Lord Jesus especially would be rejoiced at having wax for candles, and from wishing to receive it at the earliest would help him the sooner. This thought seemed so just that delight filled Zbyshko's soul thoroughly. He was almost certain now that he would be heard, that war would come soon, and even should it not come he would get his own in every case. He felt in his hands and feet a strength so great that he would at that moment have attacked a whole company. He thought, even, that when he had made the promises to God he might have added two more Germans to Danusia. The young man's impulsiveness urged him to this, but prudence gained the victory, for he feared to weary God's patience by excessive demand.

His confidence, however, increased when, after mass and a long repose, to which the whole court gave itself, he heard a conversation which the abbot held with Anna Danuta at breakfast.

The wives of princes and kings in that age, through devotion, and because of lordly gifts, which the Order did not spare on them, showed the Knights of the Cross great friendship. Even the saintly Yadviga restrained, while her life lasted, the hand of her powerful husband raised above them. Anna Danuta alone, having experienced the Order's cruel injustice in her family, hated the Knights from her whole soul. So when the abbot inquired about Mazovia and its affairs she fell to accusing the Knights of the Cross bitterly.

"What is to be done in a principality which has such neighbors? There is peace, as it were; embassies and messages pass, but still we cannot be sure of the day or the hour. The man at the border who lies down to sleep in the evening never knows but he may wake up in bonds, or with a sword-edge at his throat, or a burning roof above his head. Oaths, seals, and parchments give no security against betrayal. It was not otherwise at Zlotoria, when in time of profound peace the prince was snatched away into captivity. The Knights of the Cross declared that his castle might become a threat to them. But castles are made for defence, not attack; and what prince is there who has not the right to build castles on his own land, or repair them? Neither weak nor strong are respected by the Knights of the Cross; the weak they despise, and they strive to bring the strong down to ruin. To him who does them good they return evil. Is there in the world an Order which has received in other kingdoms such benefactions as they have received from Polish princes? And how have they paid for them? With hatred, with ravaging of lands, with war and betrayal. As to complaint, it is useless. It is useless to complain to the Apos-

tolic See itself, for living in pride and malice they disobey
the Pope of Rome even. They have sent now, as it were,
an embassy on the occasion of the queen's delivery, and for
the coming christening, but only because they wish to turn
away the wrath of the powerful king, which has been roused
by their deeds in Lithuania. In their hearts, however, they
are always meditating the ruin of this kingdom and the
whole Polish race."

The abbot listened attentively and agreed, but said afterward, —

"I know that the comtur, Lichtenstein, has come to Cracow at the head of an embassy; he is a brother highly esteemed in the Order for his distinguished family, his bravery,
and his wisdom. Perhaps you will see him here soon, gracious lady, for he sent me notice yesterday that, wishing to
pray before our relics, he would come on a visit to Tynets."

When she heard this the princess began to raise new
complaints.

"People declare, and God grant with truth, that a great
war will come soon, — a war in which there will be on one side
the Polish kingdom and all peoples whose speech resembles
ours, and on the other all Germans and the Knights of the
Cross. Very likely there is a prophecy of some saint touching this."

"Of Saint Bridget," interrupted the learned abbot; "eight
years ago she was reckoned among the saints. The pious
Peter of Alvaster, and Mathew of Linköping wrote down her
visions, in which a great war is really predicted."

Zbyshko quivered with delight at these words, and unable
to restrain himself asked, —

"And is it to come soon?"

The abbot, occupied with the princess, did not hear, or
perhaps feigned not to hear, this question.

"Young knights among us," continued the princess, "are
delighted with this war, but those who are older and more
sober of judgment speak thus: 'Not the Germans do we
fear, though great is their pride and strength; not swords
and lances, but the relics which the Knights have do we fear,
for against them the strength of man is as nothing.'"

Here Princess Anna looked with fear at the abbot and
added in a low voice: "Likely they have the true wood of
the Holy Cross: how, then, is it possible to war with them?"

"The King of the French sent it to them," answered the
abbot.

A moment of silence followed, after which was heard the voice of Mikolai, surnamed Obuh, a man of experience and training.

"I was in captivity among the Knights," said he, "and I saw processions at which that great sacred relic was carried. But besides, there is in the cloister at Oliva a number of others most important, without which the Order would not have risen to such power."

At this the Benedictines stretched their necks toward the speaker, and asked with great curiosity, —

"Will you tell us what they are?"

"There is a border from the robe of the Most Holy Virgin, there is a back tooth of Mary Magdalen, and branches from the fiery bush in which God the Father appeared to Moses; there is a hand of Saint Liberius; and as to bones of other saints, a man could not count them on his toes and fingers."

"How war with them?" repeated the princess, with a sigh.

The abbot wrinkled his lofty forehead, stopped for a moment, then said, —

"It is difficult to war with them, if only for the reason that they are monks and bear the cross on their mantles; but if they have exceeded the measure in sin, residence among them may become hateful to those relics, and in that hour not only will the relics not add, but they will detract from them, so as to fall into more pious hands. May God spare Christian blood, but should a great war come there are relics also in our kingdom which will act on our side. The voice in the vision of Saint Bridget said: ' I have placed them as bees of usefulness and fixed them on the border of Christian lands. But behold they have risen against me, they care not for souls and spare not the bodies of people who, out of error, turned to the Catholic faith, and to me. They have made slaves of these people and fail to teach them God's commands; depriving them of the holy sacraments, they condemn them to greater torments of hell than if they had remained in paganism. And they make war to satisfy their greed.' Therefore have confidence in God, gracious lady, for their days are numbered rather than yours; but meanwhile receive with thankful heart this tube here, in which is a toe of Saint Ptolomeus, one of our patrons."

The princess stretched forth her hand trembling from delight, and on her knees received the tube, which she pressed to her lips immediately. The delight of the lady was shared by the courtiers and the damsels, for no one doubted that blessing and prosperity would be diffused over all, and perhaps over the whole principality from such a gift. Zbyshko also felt happy, for it seemed to him that war ought to follow straightway after the Cracow festivities.

CHAPTER IV.

IT was well on in the afternoon when the princess with her retinue moved out of hospitable Tynets for Cracow. Knights of that period, before entering the larger cities or castles to visit notable personages, arrayed themselves frequently in full battle armor. It was the custom, it is true, to remove this immediately after passing the gates. At castles the host himself invited them with the time-honored words, " Remove your armor, noble lords, for ye have come to friends; " none the less, however, the " war" entrance was considered the most showy, and enhanced the significance of the knight. In accordance with this showiness, Matsko and Zbyshko arrayed themselves in their excellent mail and shoulder-pieces which they had won from the Frisian knights, — bright, gleaming, and adorned on the edges with an inlaid thread of gold. Pan Mikolai, who had seen much of the world and many knights in his life, and who was no common judge of military matters, saw at once that that mail was forged by armorers of Milan, the most famous in the world, — mail of such quality that only the richest knights could afford it; a suit was equal in value to a good estate. He inferred from this that those Frisians must have been famous knights in their nation, and he looked with increased respect at Matsko and Zbyshko. Their helmets, though also not of the poorest, were less rich; but their gigantic stallions, beautifully caparisoned, roused admiration and envy among the courtiers. Matsko and Zbyshko, sitting on immensely high saddles, looked down on the whole court. Each held a long lance in his hand; each had a sword at his side, and an axe at his saddle. They had sent their shields, it is true, for convenience, to the wagons; but even without them, they looked as if marching to battle, not to the city.

Both rode near the carriage, in which, on the rear seat, was the princess with Danusia. In front, the stately lady Ofka, the widow of Krystin of Yarzambek, and old Pan Mikolai. Danusia looked with great interest at the iron knights; and the princess, taking from her bosom repeatedly the tube with the relic of St. Ptolomeus, raised it to her lips.

"I am terribly curious to know what bones are inside," said she at last; "but I will not open it myself, through fear of offending the saint. Let the bishop open it in Cracow."

"Oh, better not let it out of your hands," said the cautious Pan Mikolai; "it is too desirable."

"Mayhap you speak justly," said the princess, after a moment's hesitation; then she added: "No one has given me such consolation for a long time as that worthy abbot, — first with this gift, and second because he allayed my fear of the Knights of the Cross."

"He speaks wisely and justly," said Matsko. "The Germans had at Vilno various relics, especially because they wished to convince their guests that the war was against pagans. Well, and what came of this? Our people saw that if they spat on their hands and struck out with the axe straight from the ear, a helmet and a head fell. The saints give aid; it would be a sin to say otherwise; but they aid only the honest who go in a right cause to do battle in God's name. So I think, gracious lady, that when it comes to a great war, though all other Germans were to help the Knights, we shall beat them to the earth, since our people are more numerous; and the Lord Jesus has put greater strength in our bones. And as to relics, have we not in the monastery of the Holy Cross the wood of the Holy Cross?"

"True, as God is dear to me!" answered the princess. "But it will remain in the monastery, and they will take theirs to the field with them."

"It is all one! Nothing is far from God's power."

"Is that true? Will you tell how it is?" asked the princess, turning to the wise Mikolai.

"Every bishop will bear witness to this," answered he. "It is far to Rome, but the pope governs the world, — what must it be in the case of God!"

These words calmed the princess completely; so she turned the conversation to Tynets and its magnificence. In general the Mazovians were astonished, not only by the wealth of the cloister, but by the wealth and also the beauty of the whole country through which they were passing. Round about were large and wealthy villages: at the sides of these, gardens full of fruit trees. linden groves, with storks' nests on the lindens, and on the ground beehives with straw covers. Along the road on one side and the other extended grain fields of all sorts. At moments the wind bent a sea of wheat ears still partly green; among these, thick as stars in the sky, twinkled heads

of the blue-star thistle and the bright red poppy. Here and
there, far beyond the fields, darkened a pine wood; here and
there, bathed in sunlight, oak and alder groves rejoiced the
eye; here and there were damp, grassy meadows, and wet
places above which mews were circling; next were hills occupied by cottages, and then fields. Clearly, that country was
inhabited by a numerous and industrious people enamoured of
land; and as far as the eye saw, the region seemed to be not
only flowing with milk and honey, but happy and peaceful.

"This is the royal management of Kazimir," said the princess; "one would like to live here, and never die."

"The Lord Jesus smiles on this land," said Mikolai; "and
the blessing of God is upon it. How could it be otherwise,
since here, when they begin to ring bells, there is no corner
to which the sound does not penetrate? It is known, indeed,
that evil spirits, unable to endure this, must flee to the
Hungarian boundary, into deep fir woods."

"Then it is a wonder to me," said Pani Ofka, "that
Valger the Charming, of whom the monks have been telling
us, can appear in Tynets, for they ring the bells there seven
times daily."

This remark troubled Mikolai for a moment, and he answered
only after some meditation, —

"First, the decisions of God are inscrutable; and second,
consider for yourselves that Valger receives a special permission each time."

"Be that as it may, I am glad that we shall not pass a night
in the cloister. I should die of terror if such a hellish giant
appeared to me."

"Ei! that is not known, for they say that he is wonderfully charming."

"Though he were the most beautiful, I would not have a
kiss from one whose mouth is breathing sulphur."

"Ah, even when devils are mentioned, kissing is in your
head."

At these words the princess, and with her Pan Mikolai and
the two nobles from Bogdanets, fell to laughing. Danusia,
following the example of others, laughed without knowing
why; for this reason Ofka turned an angry face to Mikolai,
and said, —

"I would prefer him to you."

"Ei! do not call the wolf from the forest," answered the
Mazovian, joyfully, "for a hellish fury drags along the road
frequently between Cracow and Tynets; and especially toward

evening he may hear you, and appear the next moment in the form of the giant."

" The charm on a dog!" answered Ofka.

But at that moment Matsko, who, sitting on his lofty stallion, could see farther than those in the carriage, reined in his steed, and said, —

" Oh, as God is dear to me! What is that? "

" What? "

" Some giant is rising from behind the hill before us."

" The word has become flesh!" cried the princess. " Do not say anything!"

But Zbyshko rose in his stirrups, and said: " As I am alive, the giant Valger, no one else!"

From terror the driver stopped the horses, and, without letting the reins out of his hands, fell to making the sign of the cross; for now he too saw from his seat the gigantic figure of a horseman on the opposite eminence.

The princess stood up, but sat down immediately with a face changed by fear. Danusia hid her head in the folds of the princess's robe. The courtiers, the damsels, and the choristers, who rode behind, when they heard the ominous name, began to gather closely around the carriage. The men feigned laughter yet, but alarm was in their eyes; the damsels grew pale; but Mikolai, who had eaten bread from more than one oven, preserved a calm countenance; and, wishing to pacify the princess, he said, —

" Fear not, gracious lady. The sun has not set, and even were it night Saint Ptolomeus could hold his own against Valger."

Meanwhile the unknown horseman, having ascended the prolonged summit of the hill, reined in his horse and stood motionless. He was perfectly visible in the rays of the setting sun, and really his form seemed to exceed the usual dimensions of men. The distance between him and the princess's retinue was not more than three hundred yards.

" Why has he stopped?" asked one of the choristers.

" Because we too have stopped," answered Matsko.

" He is looking toward us, as if to take his choice," remarked the second chorister. " If I knew that he was a man, and not the evil one. I would go and strike him on the head with my lute."

The women, now thoroughly terrified, began to pray aloud, but Zbyshko. wishing to exhibit his courage before the princess and Danusia, said, —

" I will go anyhow. What is Valger to me?"

At this Danusia began to call, half in tears: "Zbyshko! Zbyshko!" but he had ridden forward and was advancing more quickly, confident that, even should he find the real Valger, he would pierce him with his lance.

" He seems a giant," said Matsko, who had a quick eye, "because he stands on the hilltop. He is large indeed, but an ordinary man — nothing more. I will go, and not let a quarrel spring up between him and Zbyshko."

Zbyshko, advancing at a trot, was thinking whether to lower his lance at once, or only see, when near by, how that man on the eminence looked. He decided to see first, and soon convinced himself that that thought was better, for as he approached the unknown lost his uncommon proportions. The man rode a gigantic steed, larger than Zbyshko's stallion, and was immense himself, but he did not surpass human measure. Besides, he was without armor; he wore a velvet, bell-shaped cap and a white linen mantle, which kept away dust; from under the mantle peeped forth green apparel. Standing on the hilltop the knight's head was raised and he was praying. Evidently he had halted to finish his evening prayer.

"Ei, what kind of a Valger is he?" thought the young man.

He had ridden up so near that he could reach the unknown with a lance. The stranger, seeing before him a splendidly armed knight, smiled kindly, and said, —

"Praised be Jesus Christ."

"For the ages of ages."

"Is not that the court of the Princess of Mazovia down there?"

"It is."

"Then ye are coming from Tynets?"

But there was no answer to that question, for Zbyshko was so astonished that he did not even hear it. He stood for a moment as if turned to stone, not believing his own eyes. About twenty-five rods beyond the unknown man he saw between ten and twenty mounted warriors, at the head of whom, but considerably in advance, rode a knight in complete shining armor and a white mantle, on which was a black cross; on his head was a steel helmet with a splendid peacock-plume on the crest of it.

"A Knight of the Cross!" muttered Zbyshko.

And he thought that his prayer had been heard; that

God in His mercy had sent him such a German as he had prayed for in Tynets; that he ought to take advantage of God's favor. Hence, without hesitating an instant, before all this had flashed through his head, before he had time to recover from his astonishment, he bent in the saddle, lowered his lance half the distance to his horse's ear, and giving his family watchword "Hail! hail!" rushed against the Knight of the Cross as fast as his horse could spring.

The knight was astonished also; he reined in his steed and without lowering the lance which was standing in his stirrup, looked forward, uncertain whether the attack was on him.

"Lower your lance!" shouted Zbyshko, striking the iron points of his stirrups into the flanks of his stallion. "Hail! hail!"

The distance between them was decreasing. The Knight, seeing that the attack was really against him, reined in his steed, presented his weapon, and Zbyshko's lance was just about to strike his breast when that instant some mighty hand broke it right near the part which Zbyshko held, as if it had been a dried reed; then that same hand pulled back the reins of the young man's stallion with such force that the beast buried his forefeet in the earth and stood as if fixed there.

"Madman, what art thou doing?" called a deep, threatening voice. "Thou art attacking an envoy, insulting the king!"

Zbyshko looked and recognized that same gigantic man who, mistaken for Valger, had frightened a while before Princess Anna's court ladies.

"Let me go against the German! Who art thou?" cried he, grasping at the handle of his axe.

"Away with the axe! — by the dear God! Away with the axe, I say, or I will whirl thee from the horse!" cried the unknown, still more threateningly. "Thou hast insulted the majesty of the king, thou wilt be tried."

Then he turned to the people who were following the knight and shouted, —

"Come hither!"

Meanwhile Matsko had ridden up with an alarmed and ominous face. He understood clearly that Zbyshko had acted like a madman, and that deadly results might come of the affair; still, he was ready for battle. The entire retinue of the unknown knight and of the Knight of the Cross were barely fifteen persons, armed some with darts and some with crossbows. Two men in complete armor might meet them, and not without hope of victory. Matsko thought, therefore, that if judgment were awaiting them in the sequel it might be better to avoid it, break through those people, and hide somewhere till the storm had passed. So his face contracted at once, like the snout of a wolf which is ready to bite, and thrusting his horse in between Zbyshko and the unknown, he inquired, grasping his sword at the same time, —

"Who are you? Whence is your right?"

"My right is from this," answered the unknown, "that the king has commanded me to guard the peace of the region about here; people call me Povala of Tachev."

At these words Matsko and Zbyshko looked at the knight, sheathed their weapons, already half drawn, and dropped their heads. It was not that fear flew around them, but they inclined their foreheads before a loudly mentioned and widely known name; for Povala of Tachev was a noble of renowned stock and a wealthy lord, possessing many lands around Radom; he was also one of the most famous knights of the kingdom. Choristers celebrated him in songs, as a pattern of honor and bravery, exalting his name equally with that of Zavisha of Garbov, and Farurey, and Skarbek of Gora, and Dobko of Olesnitsa, and Yasko Nanshan, and Mikolai of Moskorzov, and Zyndram of Mashkovitse. At that moment he represented the person of the king; hence for a man to attack him was the same as to put his head under the axe of an executioner.

So Matsko, when he had recovered, said, in a voice full of respect, —

"Honor and obeisance to you, O lord, to your glory and bravery."

"Obeisance to you also, O lord, though I should prefer not to make acquaintance with you on such an unpleasant occasion," replied Povala.

"How is that?" inquired Matsko.

But Povala turned to Zbyshko: "What is the best that thou hast done, young lad? On the public highway thou hast attacked an envoy near the king! Knowest thou what awaits thee for that?"

"He attacked an envoy because he is young and foolish; for that reason it is easier for him to act than consider," said Matsko. "But judge him not severely, for I will tell the whole story."

" It is not I who will judge him. My part is merely to put bonds on him."

" How is that?" asked Matsko casting a gloomy glance at the whole assembly of people.

" According to the king's command."

At these words silence came on them.

" He is a noble," said Matsko at length.

" Then let him swear on his knightly honor that he will appear before any court."

" I will swear on my honor!" cried Zbyshko.

" That is well. What is thy name?"

Matsko mentioned his name and escutcheon.

" If of the court of the princess, pray her to intercede for thee before the king."

" We are not of the court. We are journeying from Lithuania, from Prince Vitold. Would to God that we had not met any court! From the meeting misfortune has come to this youth."

Here Matsko began to relate what had happened in the inn; hence he spoke of the meeting with the court of the princess, and Zbyshko's vow, but at last he was seized by sudden anger against Zbyshko, through whose thoughtlessness they had fallen into such a grievous position, and turning to him he cried, —

" Would to God that thou hadst fallen at Vilno! What wert thou thinking of, young wild boar?"

" Oh," said Zbyshko, "after the vow, I prayed to the Lord Jesus to grant me Germans, and I promised Him gifts; so when I saw peacock-plumes, and under them a mantle with a black cross, straightway some voice in me cried: 'Strike the German, for this is a miracle!' Well, I rushed forward — who would not have rushed forward?"

" Hear me," interrupted Povala, "I do not wish you evil, for I see clearly that this youth has offended more through giddiness peculiar to his age than through malice. I should be glad to take no note of his act, and go on as if nothing had happened. But I can do so only in case this comtur should promise not to complain to the king. Pray him on that point; mayhap he will take compassion on the youth."

" I should rather go to judgment than bow before a Knight of the Cross; it does not become my honor as a noble."

Povala looked at him severely and said: " Thou art acting ill. Thy elders know better than thou what is proper, and

what is not proper, for the honor of a knight. People have
heard of me also, and I will say this to thee, that had I done
a deed like thine I should not be ashamed to beg forgiveness for it."

Zbyshko blushed, but casting his eyes around, he said:
"The ground is even here, if it were a little trampled.
Rather than pray the German, I should prefer to meet him
on horseback or on foot to the death, or to slavery."

"Thou art stupid!" said Matsko. "How couldst thou
do battle with an envoy? It is not for thee to do battle with
him, or him with thee, a beardless youth."

"Forgive, noble lord," said he, turning to Povala. "The
boy has become insolent because of the war. Better not let
him talk to the German, for he would offend him a second
time. I will beg, and if after his mission is ended that
comtur wishes to fight in an inclosure, man against man, I
will meet him."

"He is a knight of great family, who will not meet everyone," answered Povala.

"Is he? But do I not wear a belt and spurs? A prince
might meet me."

"That is true, but speak not to him of battle unless he
mentions it himself; I fear lest he might grow malignant
against you. Well, may God aid you!"

"I will go to take thy trouble on myself," said Matsko
to his nephew, "but wait here."

Then he approached the Knight of the Cross, who, having
halted some yards distant, was sitting motionless on his
horse, which was as large as a camel. The man himself looked
like a cast-iron statue, and listened with supreme indifference
to the above conversation. Matsko, during long years of
war, had learned German; so now he began to explain to the
comtur in that language what had happened. He laid blame
on the youth and impulsive character of the young man to
whom it had seemed that God himself had sent a knight
with a peacock-plume, and finally began to beg forgiveness
for Zbyshko.

But the comtur's face did not quiver. Stiff and erect,
with raised head, he looked with his steel eyes at the speaking Matsko with as much indifference and at the same time
with as much unconcern as if he were not looking at the
knight or even at a man, but at a stake or a fence. Matsko
noted this, and though his words did not cease to be polite,
the soul in him began evidently to storm; he spoke with

increasing constraint, and on his sunburnt cheeks a flush appeared. It was evident that in presence of that cool insolence he struggled not to grit his teeth and burst out in awful anger.

Povala saw this, and, having a good heart, resolved to give aid. He too, during the years of his youth, had sought various knightly adventures at the Hungarian, Austrian, Burgundian, and Bohemian courts, — adventures which made his name widely famous; he had learned German, so now he spoke to Matsko in that language, in a voice conciliatory and purposely facetious, —

" You see, gentlemen, that the noble comtur considers the whole affair as not worth one word. Not only in our kingdom, but everywhere, striplings are without perfect reason; such a knight as he will not war against children, either with the sword or the law."

Lichtenstein, in answer, pouted with his yellow moustaches, and without saying a word urged his horse forward, passing Matsko and Zbyshko; but wild anger began to raise the hair under their helmets, and their hands quivered toward their swords.

" Wait, son of the Order! " said the elder master of Bogdanets through his set teeth, " I make the vow now, and will find thee when thou hast ceased to be an envoy."

" That will come later," said Povala, whose heart had begun also to be filled with blood. " Let the princess speak for you now, otherwise woe to the young man."

Then he rode after Lichtenstein, stopped him, and for some time they conversed with animation. Matsko and Zbyshko noticed that the German did not look on Povala with such a haughty face as on them, and this brought them to still greater anger. After a time Povala turned toward the two men, and waiting a while till the Knight of the Cross had gone forward, he said, —

" I have spoken on your behalf, but that is an unrelenting man. He says that he will refrain from making complaint only in case you do what he wishes."

" What does he wish ? "

" ' I will stop to greet the princess of Mazovia,' said he ; ' let them ride up to where we are, come down from their horses, take off their helmets, and on the ground, with bare heads, beg of me.' " Here Povala looked quickly at Zbyshko, and added : " This is difficult for men of noble birth — I understand, but I must forewarn thee that if thou wilt not do this it is unknown what awaits thee, perhaps the sword of the executioner."

The faces of Matsko and Zbyshko became as of stone. Silence followed a second time.

"Well, and what?" asked Povala.

"Only this," answered Zbyshko, calmly, and with such dignity as if in one moment twenty years had been added to his age: "The power of God is above people."

"What does that mean?"

"This, that even had I two heads, and were the executioner to cut off both, I have one honor, which I am not free to disgrace."

At this Povala grew serious, and turning to Matsko inquired, —

"What do you say?"

"I say," answered Matsko, gloomily, "that I have reared this lad from infancy; besides, our whole family is in him, for I am old; but he cannot do that, even if he had to die."

Here his stern face quivered, and all at once love for his nephew burst forth in him with such strength that he seized the youth in his iron inclosed arms and cried, —

"Zbyshko! Zbyshko!"

The young knight was astonished, and said, yielding to the embrace of his uncle, —

"Oh, I did not think that you loved me so!"

"I see that you are true knights," said Povala, with emotion, "and since the young man has sworn on his honor to appear, I will not bind him; such people as you may be trusted. Be of good cheer. The German will stay a day in Tynets; so I shall see the king first, and will so explain the affair as to offend him least. It is fortunate that I was able to break the lance — very fortunate!"

"If I must give my head," said Zbyshko, "I ought at least to have had the pleasure of breaking the bones of that German."

"Thou wishest to defend thy honor, but this thou dost not understand, that thou wouldst have disgraced our whole nation," answered Povala, impatiently.

"I understand that, and therefore I am sorry."

"Do you know," continued Povala, turning to Matsko, "that if this stripling escapes in any way you will have to hood him as falcons are hooded; otherwise he will not die his own death."

"He might escape if you gentlemen would conceal from the king what has happened."

"But what shall we do with the German? I cannot tie his tongue in a knot, of course."

"True! true!"

Thus speaking they advanced toward the retinue of the princess. Povala's attendants, who before mixed with Lichtenstein's people, now rode behind them. From afar were visible among Mazovian caps the waving peacock-plumes of the Knight of the Cross, and his bright helmet gleaming in the sun.

"The Knights of the Cross have a wonderful nature," said Povala of Tachev, as if roused from meditation. "When a Knight of the Cross is in trouble he is as reasonable as a Franciscan, as mild as a lamb, and as sweet as honey, so that a better man thou wilt not find in the world; but let him once feel strength behind him, none is more swollen with pride, with none wilt thou find less mercy. It is evident that the Lord Jesus gave them flint instead of hearts. I have observed very many nations, and more than once have I seen a true knight spare the weaker, saying to himself, 'My honor will not be increased if I trample on the prostrate.' But just when the weaker is down the Knight of the Cross is most unbending. Hold him by the head and he will not be proud; if thou act otherwise woe to thee. Take this envoy; he required right away, not merely your prayer for pardon, but your disgrace. I am glad that that will not happen."

"There is no waiting for it!" called out Zbyshko.

After these words they rode up to the retinue and joined the court of the princess.

The envoy of the Knights of the Cross, when he saw them, assumed immediately an expression of pride and contempt. But they feigned not to see him. Zbyshko halted at Danusia's side and told her joyfully that Cracow was clearly visible from the hill. Matsko began to tell a chorister of the uncommon strength of Povala, the lord of Tachev, who broke a spear in Zbyshko's hand as if it had been a dry reed.

"But why did he break it?" asked the chorister.

"Because the young man had levelled it at the German, but only in jest."

The chorister, who was a noble and a man of experience, did not think such a jest very becoming, but seeing that

Matsko spoke of it lightly he did not look on the matter with
seriousness. Meanwhile such bearing began to annoy the
German. He looked once and a second time at Zbyshko,
then at Matsko; at last he understood that they would not
dismount, and paid no attention to him purposely. Then
something, as it were steel, glittered in his eyes, and straightway he took leave. At the moment when he started Povala
could not restrain himself, and said to him at parting, —
"Advance without fear, brave knight. This country is in
peace and no one will attack you, unless some boy in a jest."
"Though manners are strange in this country, I have
sought not your protection, but your society," answered
Lichtenstein; "indeed I think that we shall meet again, both
at this court and elsewhere."
In the last words sounded a hidden threat; therefore
Povala answered seriously, —
"God grant." Then he inclined and turned away; afterward he shrugged his shoulders and said in an undertone,
but still loud enough to be heard by those nearest him, —
"Dry bones! I could sweep thee from the saddle with the
point of my lance, and hold thee in the air during three
'Our Fathers.'"
Then he began to converse with the princess, whom he
knew well. Anna Danuta asked what he was doing on the
highway, and he informed her that he was riding at command of the king to maintain order in the neighborhood,
where, because of the great number of guests coming from
all parts to Cracow, a dispute might arise very easily. And
as a proof he related that of which he had been himself a
witness a little while earlier. Thinking, however, that there
would be time enough to beg the intercession of the princess
for Zbyshko when the need came, he did not attach too much
significance to the event, not wishing to interrupt gladsome-
ness. In fact, the princess even laughed at Zbyshko for his
haste to get peacock-plumes. Others, learning of the broken
lance, admired the lord of Tachev because he had broken it
so easily with one hand.
Povala, being a little boastful, was pleased in his heart
that they were glorifying him, and at last began to tell of the
deeds which had made him famous, especially in Burgundy
at the court of Philip the Bold. Once in time of a tournament, after he had broken the spear of a knight of the
Ardennes, he caught him by the waist, drew him from his
saddle and hurled him up a spear's length in the air, though the

man of Ardennes was clad from head to foot in iron armor.
Philip the Bold presented him with a gold chain for the deed,
and the princess gave him a velvet slipper, which he wore on
his helmet thenceforward.

On hearing this narrative all were greatly astonished,
except Pan Mikolai, who said, —

" There are no such men in these effeminate days as during
my youth, or men like those of whom my father told me. If
a noble at present succeeds in tearing open a breastplate, or
stretching a crossbow without a crank, or twisting an iron
cutlass between sticks he is called a man of might and exalts
himself above others. But formerly young girls used to do
those things."

"I will not deny that formerly people were stronger,"
answered Povala, " but even to-day strong men may be
found. The Lord Jesus was not sparing of strength in my
bones, still I will not say that I am the strongest in the kingdom. Have you ever seen Zavisha of Garbov? He could
overcome me."

" I have seen him. He has shoulders as broad as the
bell of Cracow."

" And Dobko of Olesnitsa? Once he was at a tournament
which the Knights of the Cross held in Torun ; he stretched
out twelve knights with great glory to himself and our
nation."

" But our Mazovian, Stashko Tsolek was stronger than
you, or Zavisha, or Dobko. It was said that he took a
green stick in his hand and squeezed sap from it."

" I will squeeze sap from one too ! " exclaimed Zbyshko.

And before any one could ask him for a trial, he sprang to
the roadside, broke off a good twig from a tree, and there,
before the eyes of the princess and Danusia, he pressed it
near one end with such force that the sap began really to
fall in drops on the road.

" Ei! " cried Pani Ofka at sight of this, " do not go to war;
it would be a pity for such a man to die before marriage."

" It would be a pity," repeated Matsko, growing gloomy
on a sudden.

But Pan Mikolai began to laugh, and the princess joined
him. Others, however, praised Zbyshko's strength aloud,
and since in those times an iron hand was esteemed above all
other qualities, the damsels cried to Danusia : " Be glad ! "
And she was glad, though she did not understand well what
she could gain from that morsel of squeezed wood. Zbyshko,

forgetting the Knight of the Cross altogether, had such a lofty look that Mikolai, wishing to bring him to moderation, said, —

"It is useless to plume thyself with strength, for there are stronger than thou. I have not seen what thou hast done, but my father was witness of something better which happened at the court of Carolus, the Roman Emperor. King Kazimir went on a visit to him with many courtiers, among whom was this Stashko Tsolek, famous for strength and son of the voevoda Andrei. The emperor boasted that among his men he had a certain Cheh who could grasp a bear around the body and smother him immediately. Then they had a spectacle and the Cheh smothered two bears, one after the other. Our king was greatly mortified, and not to go away shamefaced he said: 'But my Tsolek will not let himself be put to shame.' They appointed a wrestling match to come three days later. Knights and ladies assembled, and after three days the Cheh grappled with Tsolek in the courtyard of the castle; but the struggle did not last long, for barely had they embraced when Tsolek broke the Cheh's back, crushed in all his ribs and only let him out of his arms when dead, to the great glory of our king. Tsolek, surnamed Bonebreaker from that day, once carried up into a tower a great bell which twenty townspeople could not stir from the earth."

"But how many years old was he?" inquired Zbyshko.

"He was young."

Meanwhile Povala, riding at the right near the princess, bent at last toward her ear and told her the whole truth concerning the seriousness of what had happened, and at the same time begged her to support him, for he would take the part of Zbyshko, who might have to answer grievously for his act. The princess, whom Zbyshko pleased, received the intelligence with sadness, and was greatly alarmed.

"The bishop of Cracow has a liking for me," said Povala. "I can implore him, and the queen too, for the more intercessors there are, the better for the young man."

"Should the queen take his part a hair will not fall from his head," said Anna Danuta; "the king honors her greatly for her saintliness and her dower, especially now when the reproach of sterility is taken from her. But in Cracow is also the beloved sister of the king, Princess Alexandra; go to her. I too will do what I can, but she is his sister while I am a cousin."

" The king loves you also, gracious lady."

" Ei, not as her," replied the princess, with a certain
sadness; " for me one link of a chain, for her a whole chain;
for me a fox skin, for her a sable. The king loves none of
his relatives as he does Alexandra. There is no day when
she goes away empty-handed."

Thus conversing they approached Cracow. The road,
crowded beginning with Tynets, was still more crowded.
They met landholders going to the city at the head of their
men; some were in armor, others in summer garments and
straw hats; some on horseback, others in wagons with their
wives and daughters, who wished to see the long promised
tournaments. In places the entire road was crowded with the
wagons of merchants, who were not permitted to pass Cracow,
and thus deprive the city of numerous toll dues. In those
wagons were carried salt, wax, wheat, fish, oxhides, hemp,
wood. Others leaving the city were laden with cloth, kegs
of beer, and the most various merchandise of the city.
Cracow was now quite visible; the gardens of the king, of
lords and of townspeople surrounded the city on all sides;
beyond them were the walls and the church towers. The
nearer they came, the greater the movement, and at the gates
it was difficult to pass amid the universal activity.

" This is the city! there is not in the world another such,"
said Matsko.

" It is always like a fair," said one of the choristers. " Is
it long since you were here?"

" Long. And I wonder at Cracow as if I were looking at
it for the first time, as we come now from wild countries."

" They say that Cracow has grown immensely through
King Yagello."

" That is true. From the time that the Grand Prince of
Lithuania ascended the throne, the vast regions of Lithuania
and Rus have become open to the traffic of Cracow; because
of this the city has increased day by day in population, in
wealth, and in buildings; it has become one of the most
important in the world."

" The cities of the Knights of the Cross are respectable
too," said the weighty chorister again.

" If we could only get at them!" said Matsko. " There
would be a respectable booty!"

But Povala was thinking of something else, namely, that
young Zbyshko, who had offended only through stupid impulsiveness, was going into the jaws of the wolf as it were.

The lord of Tachev, stern and stubborn in time of war, had a real dovelike heart in his mighty breast; since he knew better than others what was waiting for the offender, pity for the youth seized the knight.

"I am meditating and meditating," said he to the princess, "whether to tell the king what has happened, or not tell him. If the German knight does not complain, there will be no case, but if he is to complain it would be better to tell earlier, so that our lord should not flame up in sudden anger."

"If the Knight of the Cross can ruin any man, he will ruin him," said the princess. "But I first of all will tell the young man to join our court. Perhaps the king will not punish a courtier of ours so severely."

Then she called Zbyshko, who, learning what the question was, sprang from his horse, seized her feet, and with the utmost delight agreed to be her attendant, not only because of greater safety, but because he could in that way remain near Danusia.

"Where are you to lodge?" asked Povala of Matsko.

"In an inn."

"There is no room in the inns this long time."

"Then I will go to a merchant, an acquaintance, Amyley. Perhaps he will shelter us for the night."

"But I say to you, come as guests to me. Your nephew might lodge in the castle with the courtiers of the princess, but it will be better for him not to be under the hand of the king. What the king would do in his first anger, he would not do in his second. It is certain also that you will divide your property, wagons, and servants, and to do that, time is needed. With me, as it is known to you, you will be safe and comfortable."

Matsko, though troubled a little that Povala was thinking so much of their safety, thanked him with gratitude, and they entered the city. But there he and Zbyshko forgot again for a time their troubles at sight of the wonders surrounding them. In Lithuania and on the boundary they had seen only single castles, and of more considerable towns only Vilno, — badly built, and burnt, all in ashes and ruins. In Cracow the stone houses of merchants were often more splendid than the castle of the Grand Prince in Lithuania. Many houses were of wood, it is true, but many of those astonished the beholder by the loftiness of the walls and the roofs, with windows of glass, the panes fitted into lead sashes, panes which so reflected the rays of the setting sun

that one might suppose the house burning. But along
streets near the market were large houses of red brick, or
entirely of stone, lofty, ornamented with plates and the cross
charm on the walls. They stood one at the side of the
other, like soldiers in line, some wide, others narrow, as
narrow as nine ells, but erect, with arched ceiling — often
with the picture of the Passion, or with the image of the
Most Holy Virgin over the gate. On some streets were two
rows of houses, above them a strip of sky, below a street
entirely paved with stones, and on both sides as far as the
eye could see, shops and shops, rich, full of the most excellent, ofttimes wonderful or wholly unknown goods, on
which Matsko, accustomed to continual war and taking of
booty, looked with an eye somewhat greedy. But the public
buildings brought both to still greater astonishment; the
church of the Virgin Mary in the square, then other churches,
the cloth market, the city hall with an enormous " cellar "
in which they sold Schweidnitz beer, cloth shops, the
immense *mercatorium* intended for foreign merchants, also
a building in which the city weights were kept, barber-shops,
baths, places for smelting copper, wax, gold, and silver,
breweries, whole mountains of kegs around the so-called
Schrotamt, — in a word, plenty and wealth, which a man
unacquainted with the city, even though the wealthy owner of
a " town," could not imagine to himself.

Povala conducted Matsko and Zbyshko to his house on
Saint Ann Street, commanded to give them a spacious room,
intrusted them to attendants, and went himself to the castle;
from which he returned for supper rather late in the evening
with a number of his friends. They used meat and wine in
abundance and supped joyously; but the host himself was
somehow anxious, and when at last the guests went away
he said to Matsko, —

" I have spoken to a canon skilled in writing and in
law; he tells me that insult to an envoy is a capital
offence. Pray to God, therefore, that Lichtenstein make no
complaint."

When they heard this both knights, though at supper they
had in some degree passed the measure, went to rest with
hearts that were not so joyous. Matsko could not sleep,
and some time after they had lain down he called to his
nephew, —

" Zbyshko ! "

" But what ? "

" Well, taking everything into account, I think that they will cut off thy head."

" Do you think so? " asked Zbyshko, with a drowsy voice. And turning to the wall he fell asleep sweetly, for he was wearied by the road.

Next day the two owners of Bogdanets together with Povala went to early mass in the Cathedral, through piety and to see the guests who had assembled at the castle. Indeed Povala had met a multitude of acquaintances on the road, and among them many knights famous at home and abroad; on these young Zbyshko looked with admiration, promising himself in spirit that if the affair with Lichtenstein should leave him unharmed, he would strive to equal them in bravery and every virtue. One of those knights, Toporchyk, a relative of the castellan of Cracow told him about the return from Rome of Voitseh Yastrembets, a scholastic, who had gone with a letter from the king to Pope Boniface IX., inviting him to Cracow. Boniface accepted the invitation, and though he expressed doubt as to whether he could come in person, he empowered his ambassador to hold in his name the infant at the font, and begged at the same time, as a proof of his love for both kingdoms, to name the child Bonifacius or Bonifacia.

They spoke also of the approaching arrival of Sigismond of Hungary, and expected it surely; for Sigismond, whether invited or not, went always to places where there was a chance of feasts, visits, and tournaments, in which he took part with delight, desiring to be renowned universally as a ruler, a singer, and one of the first of knights. Povala, Zavisha of Garbov, Dobko of Olesnitsa, Nashan, and other men of similar measure remembered with a smile how, during former visits of Sigismond, King Vladislav had begged them in secret not to push too hard in the tournament, and to spare the " Hungarian guest," whose vanity, known throughout the world, was so great that in case of failure it brought tears from his eyes. But the greatest attention among the knighthood was roused by the affair of Vitold. Wonders were related of the splendor of that cradle of pure silver, which princes and boyars of Lithuania had brought from Vitold and his wife Anna. Before divine service groups of people were formed as is usual; these related news to each other. In one of those groups Matsko, when he heard of the cradle, described the richness of the gift, but still more Vitold's intended immense expedition against the Tartars; he was covered with questions about it. The expedition was nearly ready, for great armies had moved to Eastern Rus, and in case of success it would extend the supremacy of King Yagello over almost half the earth, to the unknown depths of Asia, — to the boundaries of Persia, and the banks of the Aral. Matsko, who formerly had been near the person of Vitold, and who was able to know his plans therefore, knew how to tell them in detail, and even so eloquently that before the bell had sounded for mass a crowd of the curious had formed around him in front of the cathedral. " It was a question," he said, "of an expedition in favor of the Cross. Vitold himself, though called Grand Prince, rules Lithuania by appointment of Yagello, and is merely viceroy. His merit, therefore, will fall on the king. And what glory for newly baptized Lithuania, and for Polish power, if their united armies shall carry the Cross to regions in which if the name of the Saviour has ever been mentioned, it was only to be blasphemed, regions in which the foot of a Pole or Lithuanian has never stood up to this time! The expelled Tohtamysh, if Polish and Lithuanian troops seat him again on the last Kipchak throne, will call himself ' son ' of King Vladislav and, as he has promised, will bow down to the Cross together with the whole Golden Horde."

They listened to these words with attention, but many did not know well what the question was, — whom was Vitold to assist? against whom was he to war? Hence some said: " Tell us clearly, with whom is the war?"

" With Timur the Lame," answered Matsko.

A moment of silence followed. The ears of Western knighthood had been struck more than once, it is true, by the names of the Golden, Blue, and Azoff Hordes, as well as various others, but Tartar questions and domestic wars between individual Hordes were not clearly known to them. On the other hand, one could not find a single man in Europe of that day who had not heard of the awful Timur the Lame, or Tamerlane, whose name was repeated with not less dread than the name of Attila aforetime. Was he not " lord of the world" and " lord of times," ruler of twenty-seven conquered kingdoms, ruler of Muscovite Rus, ruler of Siberia, China to India, Bagdad, Ispahan, Aleppo, Damascus, — a man whose shadow fell across the sands of Arabia onto Egypt, and across the Bosphorus onto the Byzantine Empire, destroyer of the human race, monstrous builder of pyramids made of human skulls, victor in all battles, defeated in none, "master of souls and bodies"?

Tohtamysh had been seated by Tamerlane on the throne of the Blue and the Golden Hordes, and recognized as "son." But when Tohtamysh's lordship extended from the Aral to the Crimea, over more lands than there were in all remaining Europe, the "son" wished to be independent; therefore, deprived of his throne by "one finger" of the terrible father, he fled to the Lithuanian prince imploring aid. It was this man precisely whom Vitold intended to conduct back to his kingdom, but to do so he would have first to measure strength with the world-ruling Limper. For this reason his name produced a powerful impression on the listeners, and after a time of silence one of the oldest knights, Kazko of Yaglov, said, —

"It is not a dispute with some trifling man."

"But it is about some trifling thing," said Pan Mikolai, prudently. "What profit to us if far off there beyond the tenth land a Tohtamysh, instead of a Kutluk, rules the sons of Belial?"

"Tohtamysh would receive the Christian faith," answered Matsko.

"He would receive it, but he has not received it. Is it possible to believe dog brothers, who do not confess Christ?"

"But it is a worthy deed to lay down one's life for the name of Christ," replied Povala.

"And for the honor of knighthood," added Toporchyk; "among us are men who will go. Pan Spytko of Melshtyn has a young and beloved wife, but he has gone to Prince Vitold for the expedition."

"And no wonder," put in Yasko Nashan; "though a man had the foulest sin on his soul, he would receive sure forgiveness for his part in such a war, and certain salvation."

"And glory for the ages of ages," said Povala. "If there is to be a war, let it be a war, and that it is not with some common person is all the better. Timur conquered the world and has twenty-seven kingdoms under him. What a glory for our people to rub him out."

"Why should we not?" answered Toporchyk, "even if he possessed a hundred kingdoms, let others fear him, not we! Ye speak worthily! Only call together ten thousand good lancers — we will ride through the world."

"What people should finish the Limper if not ours?"

So spoke the knights, and Zbyshko wondered why the
desire had not come to him earlier of going into the wild
steppes with Vitold.   During his stay in Vilno he had wished
to see Cracow, the court, take part in knightly tournaments,
but now he thought that here he might find condemnation
and infamy, while there, at the worst, he would find a death
full of glory. But Kazko of Yaglov, a hundred years old,
whose neck was trembling from age, and who had a mind
answering to his age, cast cold water on the willingness
of the knighthood.

"Ye are foolish." said he.   "Has no one of you heard
that the image of Christ has spoken to the queen?   And if
the Saviour himself admits her to such confidence, why should
the Holy Ghost, the third person of the Trinity, be less
gracious.   For this reason she sees future things, as if they
were happening in her presence, and she said this — "

Here he stopped, shook his head for a moment, and then
continued, —

"I have forgotten what she did say, but I will recall it
directly."

And he began to think; they waited with attention, for
the opinion was universal that the queen saw future events.

"Aha! I have it!" said he at last.   "The queen said
that if all the knighthood of this country should go with
Prince Vitold against the Limper, pagan power might be
crushed. But that cannot be, because of the dishonesty of
Christians. It is necessary to guard our boundaries against
Chehs, and Hungarians, and against the Knights of the
Cross, for it is not possible to trust any one.   And if only a
handful of Poles go with Vitold, Timur will finish them, or
his voevodas will, for they command countless legions."

"But there is peace at present," said Toporchyk, "and
the Order itself will give some aid, perhaps, to Vitold.
The Knights of the Cross cannot act otherwise, even for
shame's sake; they must show the holy father that they are
ready to fight against pagans. People say at court that
Kuno Lichtenstein is here not only for the christening, but
also to counsel with the king."

"Ah, here he is!" exclaimed Matsko, with astonishment.

"True!" said Povala, looking around. "As God lives,
it is he! He stayed a short time with the abbot; he must
have left Tynets before daybreak."

"He was in haste for some reason." said Matsko, gloomily.
Meanwhile Kuno Lichtenstein passed near them. Matsko

recognized him by the cross embroidered on his mantle, but
the envoy knew neither him nor Zbyshko, because the first
time he had seen them they were in helmets, and in a helmet, even with raised vizor, it was possible to see only a
small part of the face. While passing he nodded toward
Povala and Toporchyk, then, with his attendants, he ascended the steps of the cathedral, with an important and
majestic tread.

Just at that moment the bells sounded, announcing that
mass would begin soon, and frightening a flock of daws and
doves gathered in the towers. Matsko and Zbyshko, somewhat disturbed by the quick return of Lichtenstein, entered
the church with others. But the old man was now the more
disturbed, for the king's court took all the young knight's
attention. Never in his life had Zbyshko seen anything
so imposing as that church and that assembly. On the
right and on the left he was surrounded by the most famous
men of the kingdom, renowned in counsel, or in war.
Many of those whose wisdom had effected the marriage of
the Grand Prince of Lithuania with the marvellous young
Queen of Poland had died, but some were still living, and
on them people looked with uncommon respect. The youthful knight could not gaze enough at the noble figure of
Yasko of Tenchyn, the castellan of Cracow, in which se-
verity and dignity were blended with uprightness; he
admired the wise and dignified faces of other counsellors,
and the strong visages of knights with hair cut straight
above their brows and falling in long locks at the sides of
their heads and behind. Some wore nets, others only
ribbons holding the hair in order. Foreign guests, envoys
of the King of Rome, Bohemians, Hungarians, Austrians,
with their attendants, astonished with the great elegance
of their dresses; the princes and boyars of Lithuania, standing near the side of the king, in spite of the summer and
the burning days, for show's sake wore shubas lined with
costly fur; the Russian princes, in stiff and broad garments,
looked, on the background of the walls and the gilding of
the church, like Byzantine pictures.

But Zbyshko waited with the greatest curiosity for the
entrance of the king and queen, and forced his way up as
much as possible toward the stalls, beyond which, near the
altar, were two velvet cushions, — for the royal couple
always heard mass on their knees. Indeed, people did not
wait long; the king entered first, by the door of the sacristy,

and before he had come in front of the altar it was possible
to observe him well.   He had black hair, dishevelled and
growing somewhat thin above his forehead; at the sides it
was put back over his ears; his face was dark, entirely
shaven, nose aquiline and rather pointed; around his mouth
there were wrinkles; his eyes were black, small, and glittering.   He looked on every side, as if he wished before reaching the front of the altar to make estimate of all people in
the church.   His countenance had a kindly expression, but
also the watchful one of a man who, elevated by fortune
beyond his own hopes, has to think continually whether his
acts correspond to his office, and who fears malicious blame.
But for this reason specially there was in his face and his
movements a certain impatience.   It was easy to divine that
his anger must be sudden, and that he was always that same
prince who, roused by the wiles of the Knights of the Cross,
had cried to their envoys: "Thou strikest at me with a
parchment, but I at thee with a dart!"

Now, however, a great and sincere piety restrained his
native quick temper.   Not only the newly converted princes
of Lithuania, but also Polish magnates, pious from the example of grandfather and great-grandfather, were edified at sight
of the king in the church.   Often he put the cushion aside,
and knelt, for greater mortification, on the bare stones; often
he raised his hands, and held them raised till they fell of themselves from fatigue.   He heard at least three masses daily,
and heard them almost with eagerness.   The exposure of the
chalice and the sound of the bell at the Elevation always filled
his soul with ecstasy, enthusiasm, and awe.   At the end of
mass he went forth from the church as if he had been roused
from sleep, calmed and mild; soon courtiers discovered that
that was the best time to beg him for gifts or forgiveness.

Yadviga entered by the sacristy door.   Knights nearest
the stalls, when they saw her, though mass had not begun,
knelt at once, yielding involuntary honor to her, as to a saint.
Zbyshko did the same, for in all that congregation no one
doubted that he had really before him a saint, whose image
would in time adorn the altars of churches.   More especially
during recent years the severe penitential life of Yadviga
had caused this, that besides the honor due a queen, they
rendered her honor well-nigh religious.   From mouth to mouth
among lords and people passed reports of miracles wrought
by her.   It was said that the touch of her hand cured the
sick; that people deprived of strength in their members

recovered it by putting on old robes of the queen. Trust-worthy witnesses affirmed that with their own ears they had heard Christ speaking to her from the altar. Foreign monarchs gave her honor on their knees; even the insolent Knights of the Cross respected her, and feared to offend her. Pope Boniface IX. called her a saint and the chosen daughter of the Church. The world considered her acts, and remembered that that was a child of the house of Anjou and of the Polish Piasts; that she was a daughter of the powerful Ludvik; that she was reared at the most brilliant of courts; that she was the most beautiful of maidens in the kingdom; that she had renounced happiness, renounced a maiden's first love, and married as queen the "wild" prince of Lithuania, so as to bend with him to the foot of the Cross the last pagan people in Europe. What the power of all the Germans, the power of the Knights of the Cross, their crusading expeditions, and a sea of blood had not effected, her single word had effected. Never had apostolic labor been joined with such devotion; never had woman's beauty been illuminated by such angelic goodness and such quiet sorrow.

Therefore minstrels in all the courts of Europe celebrated her; knights from the most remote lands came to Cracow to see that "Polish Queen;" her own people, whose strength and glory she had increased by her alliance with Yagello, loved her as the sight of their eyes. Only one great grief had weighed upon her and the nation, — God through long years had refused posterity to this His chosen one.

But when at last that misfortune had passed, the news of the implored blessing spread like lightning from the Baltic to the Black Sea, to the Carpathians, and filled all people of the immense commonwealth with delight. It was received joyfully even at foreign courts, but not at the capital of the Knights of the Cross. In Rome they sang a "Te Deum." In Poland the final conviction was reached that whatever the "holy lady" might ask of God would be given beyond doubt.

So people came to implore her to ask health for them; deputations came from provinces and districts, begging that in proportion as the need might be she would pray for rain, for good weather, for crops, for a favorable harvest, a good yield of honey, for abundance of fish in the lakes, and beasts in the forests. Terrible knights from border castles and towns, who, according to customs received from the Germans, toiled at robbery or war among themselves, at one reminder from her sheathed their swords; freed prisoners without ransom; returned stolen herds; and gave hands to one another in concord. Every misfortune, every poverty hurried to the gates of the castle of Cracow. Her pure spirit penetrated the hearts of men, softened the lot of subjects, the pride of lords, the harshness of judges, and soared like the light of happiness, like an angel of justice and peace above the whole country.

All were waiting then with beating hearts for the day of blessing.

The knights looked diligently at the form of the queen, so as to infer how long they would have to wait for the coming heir or heiress to the throne. Vysh, the bishop of Cracow, who was besides the most skilful physician in the country, and even celebrated abroad, did not predict yet a quick delivery. If they were making preparations, it was because it was the custom of the age to begin every solemnity at the earliest, and continue it whole weeks. In fact, the lady's form, though somewhat more pronounced, preserved so far its usual outlines. She wore robes that were even too simple. Reared in a brilliant court, and being the most beautiful of contemporary princesses, she had been enamoured of costly materials, — chains, pearls, gold bracelets and rings; but at this time, and even for some years, not only did she wear the robes of a nun, but she covered her face, lest the thought of her beauty might rouse worldly pride in her. In vain did Yagello, when he learned of her changed condition, recommend, in the ecstasy of his delight, to adorn the bedchamber with cloth of gold, brocade, and precious stones. She answered that, having renounced show long before, she remembered that the time of birth was often the time of death; and hence it was not amidst jewels, but with silent humility, that she ought to receive the favor with which God was visiting her.

The gold and precious stones went meanwhile to the Academy or to the work of sending newly baptized Lithuanian youths to foreign universities.

The queen agreed to change her religious appearance only in this, that from the time when the hope of motherhood had become perfect certainty she would not hide her face, considering justly that the dress of a penitent did not befit her from that moment forward.

And in fact all eyes rested now in love on that wonderful face, to which neither gold nor precious stones could add ornament. The queen walked slowly from the sacristy to the altar with her eyes uplifted, in one hand a book, in the other a rosary. Zbyshko saw the lily-colored face, the blue eyes, the features simply angelic, full of peace, goodness, mercy, and his heart began to beat like a hammer. He knew that by command of God he ought to love his king and his queen, and he had loved them in his own way, but now his heart seethed up in him on a sudden with great love, which comes not of command, but which bursts forth of itself, like a flame, and is at once both the greatest honor and humility, and a wish for sacrifice. Zbyshko was young and impulsive; hence a desire seized him to show that love and faithfulness of a subject knight, to do something for her, to fly somewhere, to slay some one, to capture something, and lay down his head at the same time. "I will go even with Prince Vitold," said he to himself, "for how else can I serve the saintly lady, if there is no war near at hand?" It did not even come to his head that he could serve otherwise than with a sword, or a javelin, or an axe, but to make up for that he was ready to go alone against the whole power of Timur the Lame. He wanted to mount his horse immediately after mass and begin — what? He himself did not know. He knew only that he could not restrain himself, that his hands were burning, that his whole soul within him was burning.

So again he forgot altogether the danger which was threatening him. He forgot even Danusia for a while, and when she came to his mind because of the childlike singing which was heard all at once in the church, he had a feeling that that was "something else." To Danusia he had promised faithfulness, he had promised three Germans, and he would keep that promise; but the queen was above all women, and when he thought how many he would like to kill for the queen he saw in front of him whole legions of breastplates, helmets, ostrich and peacock plumes, and felt that according to his wish that was still too little.

Meanwhile he did not take his eyes from her, asking in his swollen heart, "With what prayer can I honor her?" for he judged that it was not possible to pray for the queen in common fashion. He knew how to say, "*Pater noster, qui es in coelis, sanctificetur nomen Tuum*," for a certain Franciscan in Vilno had taught him those words; perhaps the monk himself did not know more, perhaps Zbyshko had forgotten the rest; it is enough that he was unable to say the whole Pater noster (Our Father), so he began to repeat in succes-

sion those few words which in his soul meant, "Give our
beloved lady health, and life, and happiness — and think
more of her than of all others." And since this was said by
a man over whose head judgment and punishment were hanging, there was not in that whole church a more sincere
prayer.

At the end of mass Zbyshko thought that if it were permitted him to stand before the queen, fall on his face and
embrace her feet, then even let the end of the world come.
But the first mass was followed by a second, and then a
third; after that the lady went to her apartments, for usually
she fasted till mid-day, and took no part in joyful break-
fasts at which, for the amusement of the king and guests,
jesters and jugglers appeared. But old Pan Mikolai came
and summoned him to the princess.

"At the table thou wilt serve me and Danusia, as my
attendant," said the princess; "and may it be granted thee
to please the king with some amusing word or act, by which
thou wilt win his heart to thyself. If the German knight
recognizes thee, perhaps he will not make a complaint, seeing
that at the king's table thou art serving me."

Zbyshko kissed the princess's hand, then turned to Danusia,
and though he was more used to war and battles than to
courtly customs, he knew evidently what a knight ought to
do on seeing the lady of his thoughts in the morning, for he
stepped back and assuming an expression of surprise exclaimed, while making the sign of the cross, —

"In the name of the Father, Son, and Holy Ghost!"

"But why does Zbyshko make the sign of the cross?"
inquired Danusia, raising her blue eyes to him.

"Because, lovely damsel, so much beauty has been added
to thee that I wonder."

But Pan Mikolai, as an old man, did not like new foreign
knightly customs, hence he shrugged his shoulders, and
said, —

"Why wilt thou lose time for nothing and talk about her
beauty? That is a chit which has hardly risen above the
earth."

Zbyshko looked at him immediately with indignation.

"You are mad to call her that," said he, growing pale
from anger. "Know this, that if your years were less I
would command at once to trample earth behind the castle,
and let my death or yours come!"

"Be quiet, stripling! I could manage thee even to-day!"

"Be quiet!" repeated the princess. "Instead of thinking of thy own head, thou art looking for other quarrels! I ought to have found a more sedate knight for Danusia. But I tell thee this, if thou hast a wish to quarrel move hence to whatever place may please thee, for here such men are not needed."

Zbyshko, put to shame by the words of the princess, began to beg her pardon, thinking, meanwhile, that if Pan Mikolai had a grown-up son he would challenge him to a combat sometime, on foot or on horseback, unless the word were forgiven. He determined, however, to deport himself like a dove in the king's chambers, and not to challenge any one unless knightly honor commanded it absolutely.

The sound of trumpets announced that the meal was ready; so Princess Anna, taking Danusia by the hand, withdrew to the king's apartments, before which lay dignitaries and knights stood awaiting her arrival. The Princess Alexandra had entered first, for as sister of the king she occupied a higher place at the table. Straightway the room was filled with foreign guests, invited local dignitaries, and knights. The king sat at the head of the table, having at his side the bishop of Cracow and Voitseh Yastrembets, who, though lower in dignity than mitred persons, sat as ambassador of the pope, at the right hand of the king. The two princesses occupied the succeeding places. Beyond Anna Danuta in a broad arm-chair, Yan, the former archbishop of Gnesen, had disposed himself comfortably. He was a prince descended from the Piasts of Silesia, a son of Bolko III., Prince of Opole. Zbyshko had heard of him at the court of Vitold, and now, standing behind the princess and Danusia, he recognized the man at once by his immensely abundant hair, twisted in rolls like a holy-water sprinkler. At the courts of Polish princes they called him Kropidlo, and even the Knights of the Cross gave him the name "Grapidla." [1] He was famed for joyfulness and frivolity. Having received the pallium for the archbishopric of Gnesen against the will of the king he wished to occupy it with armed hand; expelled from the office for this and exiled, he connected himself with the Knights of the Cross, who gave him the poor bishopric of Kamen. Understanding at last that it was better to be in accord with a powerful king, he implored Yagello's forgiveness, returned to the country, and was wait-

[1] This is a German mispronunciation of *Kropidlo*, a sprinkler. *Kropidlo* is derived from *kropic*, to sprinkle.

ing till a see should be vacant, hoping to receive it from
the hands of his kindly lord. In fact he was not deceived;
meanwhile he was endeavoring to win the king's heart
with pleasant jests. But the former inclination towards
the Knights of the Cross had remained with him, and
even then, at the court of Yagello, though not looked
upon too favorably by knights and dignitaries, he sought
the society of Lichtenstein, and was glad to sit next him at
table.

Zbyshko, standing behind Princess Anna's chair, found
himself so near the Knight of the Cross that he could touch
him with his hand. In fact his hands began to itch immediately and to move; but that was involuntary, for he restrained
his impulsiveness, and did not permit himself any erratic
thought. Still he could not refrain from casting occasional
glances that were somewhat greedy at Lichtenstein's flax-
colored head, which was growing bald behind, at his neck,
his shoulders, and his arms, wishing to estimate at once
whether he would have much work were he to meet him
either in battle or in single combat. It seemed to him that
he would not have overmuch, for, though the shoulder-blades
of the knight were rather powerful in outline, under his
closely fitting garment of thin gray cloth, he was still a skel-
eton in comparison with Povala, or Pashko Zlodye, or the
two renowned Sulimchiks, or Kron of Koziglove, and many
other knights sitting at the king's table.

On them indeed Zbyshko looked with admiration and
envy, but his main attention was turned toward the king,
who, casting glances on all sides, gathered in, from moment
to moment, his hair behind his ears, as if made impatient by
this, that the meal had not begun yet. His glance rested for
the twinkle of an eye on Zbyshko also, and then the young
knight experienced the feeling of a certain fear; and at the
thought that surely he would have to stand before the angry
face of the king a terrible alarm mastered him. At first he
thought, it is true, of the responsibility and the punishment
which might fall on him, for up to that moment all this had
seemed to him distant, indefinite, hence not worthy of
thought.

But the German did not divine that the knight who had
attacked him insolently on the road was so near. The meal
began. They brought in caudle, so strongly seasoned with
eggs, cinnamon, cloves, ginger, and saffron, that the odor
went through the entire hall. At the same time the jester,

Tsarushek, sitting in the doorway on a stool, began to imitate the singing of a nightingale, which evidently delighted the king. After him another jester passed around the table with the servants who were carrying food; he stood behind the chairs without being noticed, and imitated the buzzing of a bee so accurately that this man and that laid down his spoon and defended his head with his hand. At sight of this, others burst into laughter.

Zbyshko served the princess and Danusia diligently, but when Lichtenstein in his turn began to slap his head, which was growing bald, he forgot his danger again and laughed till the tears came. A young Lithuanian prince, son of the viceroy of Smolensk, helped him in this so sincerely that he dropped food from the tray.

The Knight of the Cross, noting his error at last, reached to his hanging pocket, and turning to bishop Kropidlo, said something to him in German which the bishop repeated immediately in Polish.

"The noble lord declares," said he, turning to the jester, "that thou wilt receive two coins; but buzz not too near, for bees are driven out and drones are killed."

The jester pocketed the two coins which the knight had given him, and using the freedom accorded to jesters at all courts, he answered, —

"There is much honey in the land of Dobryn; that is why the drones have settled on it. Kill them, O King Vladislav!"

"Ha! here is a coin from me too, for thou hast answered well," said Kropidlo; "but remember that when a ladder falls the bee-keeper breaks his neck. Those Malborg drones which have settled on Dobryn have stings, and it is dangerous to climb to their nests."

"Oh!" cried Zyndram of Mashkov, the sword-bearer of Cracow, "we can smoke them out."

"With what?"

"With powder."

"Or cut their nests with an axe!" said the gigantic Pashko Zlodye.

Zbyshko's heart rose, for he thought that such words heralded war. But Kuno Lichtenstein understood the words too, for having lived long in Torun and in Helmno he had learned Polish speech, and he failed to use it only through pride. But now, roused by Zyndram's words, he fixed his gray eyes on him and answered, —

"We shall see."

"Our fathers saw at Plovtsi, and we have seen at Vilno," answered Zyndram.

"*Pax vobiscum! Pax, pax!*" exclaimed Kropidlo. "Only let the reverend Mikolai of Kurov leave the bishopric of Kuyav, and the gracious king appoint me in his place, I will give you such a beautiful sermon on love among nations, that I will crush you completely, for what is hatred if not *ignis* (fire), and besides *ignis infernalis* (hell fire), — a fire so terrible that water has no effect on it, and it can be quenched only with wine. With wine, then! We will go to the ops! as the late bishop Zbisha said."

"And from the ops to hell, as the devil said," added the jester.

"May he take thee!"

"It will be more interesting when he takes you; the devil has not been seen yet with a Kropidlo (holy-water sprinkler), but I think that all will have that pleasure."

"I will sprinkle thee first," said Kropidlo. "Give us wine, and long life to love among Christians!"

"Among real Christians!" repeated Lichtenstein, with emphasis.

"How is that?" asked the bishop of Cracow, raising his head. "Are you not in an old-time Christian kingdom? Are not the churches older here than in Malborg?"

"I know not," answered the Knight of the Cross.

The king was especially sensitive on the question of Christianity. It seemed to him that perhaps the Knight of the Cross wished to reproach him; so his prominent cheeks were covered at once with red spots, and his eyes began to flash.

"What," asked he in a loud voice. "Am I not a Christian king?"

"The kingdom calls itself Christian," answered Lichtenstein coldly, "but the customs in it are pagan."

At this, terrible knights rose from their seats, — Martsin Vrotsimovitse, Floryan of Korytnitsa, Bartosh of Vodzinek, Domarat of Kobylany, Povala of Tachev, Pashko Zlodye, Zyndram of Mashkovitse, Yasha of Targovisko, Kron of Koziglove, Zygmunt of Bobova, and Stashko of Harbimovitse, powerful, renowned, victors in many battles and in many tournaments; at one instant they were flushing with anger, at another pale, at another gritting their teeth they exclaimed, one interrupting another, —

"Woe to us! for he is a guest and cannot be challenged!"

But Zavisha Charny, the most renowned among the renowned, the "model of knights," turned his frowning brows to Lichtenstein, and said, —

"Kuno, I do not recognize thee. How canst thou, a knight, shame a noble people among whom thou, being an envoy, art threatened by no punishment?"

But Kuno endured calmly his terrible looks and answered slowly and emphatically, —

"Our Order before coming to Prussia warred in Palestine, but there even Saracens respected envoys. Ye alone do not respect them, and for this reason I have called your customs pagan."

At this the uproar became still greater. Around the table were heard again the cries of "Woe! woe!"

They grew silent, however, when the king, on whose face anger was boiling, clapped his hands a number of times in Lithuanian fashion. Then old Yasko Topor of Tenchyn, the castellan of Cracow, rose, — he was gray, dignified, rousing fear by the truthfulness of his rule, — and said, —

"Noble knight of Lichtenstein, if any insult has met you as an envoy, speak, there will be satisfaction and stern justice quickly."

"This would not have happened to me in any other christian land," answered Kuno. "Yesterday, on the road to Tynets, one of your knights fell upon me, and though from the cross on my mantle it was easy to see who I was, he attempted my life."

Zbyshko, when he heard these words grew deathly pale and looked involuntarily at the king whose face was simply terrible. Yasko of Tenchyn was astounded, and said, —

"Can that be?"

"Ask the lord of Tachev, who was a witness of the deed."

All eyes turned to Povala who stood for a while gloomy, with drooping eyelids, and then said, —

"It is true!"

When the knights heard this they called out: "Shame! shame! The ground should open under such a one." And from shame some struck their thighs and their breasts with their hands, others twisted the pewter plates on the table between their fingers, not knowing where to cast their eyes.

"Why did'st thou not kill him?" thundered the king.

"I did not because his head belongs to judgment," replied Povala.

"Did you imprison him?" asked the Castellan of Cracow.

"No. He is a noble, who swore on his knightly honor that he would appear."

"And he will not appear! " said Lichtenstein, with a sneer and raising his head.

With that a plaintive youthful voice called out not far from the shoulders of the Knight of the Cross, —

"May God never grant that I should prefer shame to death. It was I who did that, I, Zbyshko of Bogdanets."

At these words the knights sprang toward the hapless Zbyshko, but they were stopped by a threatening beck of the king, who rose with flashing eyes, and called in a voice panting from anger, a voice which was like the sound of a wagon jolting over stones, —

"Cut off his head! cut off his head! Let the Knight of the Cross send his head to the Grand Master at Malborg!"

Then he cried to the young Lithuanian prince, son of the viceroy of Smolensk, —

"Hold him, Yamont!"

Terrified by the king's anger, Yamont laid his trembling hand on the shoulder of Zbyshko, who, turning a pallid face toward him, said, —

"I will not flee."

But the white-bearded castellan of Cracow raised his hand in sign that he wished to speak, and when there was silence, he said, .

"Gracious king! Let that comtur be convinced that not thy anger, but our laws punish with death an attack on the person of an envoy. Otherwise he might think the more justly that there are no Christian laws in this kingdom. I will hold judgment on the accused to-morrow!"

He pronounced the last words in a high key, and evidently not admitting even the thought that that voice would be disobeyed, he beckoned to Yamont, and said, —

"Confine him in the tower. And you, lord of Tachev, will give witness."

"I will tell the whole fault of that stripling, which no mature man among us would have ever committed," said Povala, looking gloomily at Lichtenstein.

"He speaks justly," said others at once; "he is a lad yet; why should we all be put to shame through him?"

Then came a moment of silence and of unfriendly glances at the Knight of the Cross; meanwhile Yamont led away Zbyshko, to give him into the hands of the bowmen standing in the courtyard of the castle. In his young heart he felt pity for the prisoner; this pity was increased by his innate hatred for the Germans. But as a Lithuanian he was accustomed to accomplish blindly the will of the grand prince; and, terrified by the anger of the king, he whispered to Zbyshko in friendly persuasion, —

"Knowst what I will say to thee? hang thyself! The best is to hang thyself right away. The king is angry, — and they will cut off thy head. Why not make him glad? Hang thyself, friend! with us it is the custom."

Zbyshko, half unconscious from shame and fear, seemed at first not to understand the words of the little prince; but at last he understood, and stood still from astonishment.

"What dost thou say?"

"Hang thyself! Why should they judge thee? Thou wilt gladden the king!" repeated Yamont.

"Hang thyself, if thou wish!" cried Zbyshko. "They baptized thee in form, but the skin on thee has remained pagan; and thou dost not even understand that it is a sin for a Christian to do such a thing."

"But it would not be of free will," answered the prince, shrugging his shoulders. "If thou dost not do this, they will cut off thy head."

It shot through Zbyshko's mind that for such words it would be proper to challenge the young boyarin at once to a conflict on foot or on horseback, with swords or with axes; but he stifled that idea, remembering that there would be no time for such action. So, dropping his head gloomily and in silence, he let himself be delivered into the hands of the leader of the palace bowmen.

Meanwhile, in the dining-hall universal attention was turned in another direction. Danusia, seeing what was taking place, was so frightened at first that the breath was stopped in her breast. Her face became as pale as linen; her eyes grew round from terror, and, as motionless as a wax figure in a church, she gazed at the king. But when at last she heard that they were to cut off her Zbyshko's head, when they seized him and led him forth from the hall, measureless sorrow took possession of her; her lips and brows began to quiver; nothing was of effect, — neither fear of the king nor biting her lips with her teeth; and on a sudden she burst into weeping so pitiful and shrill that all faces turned to her, and the king himself asked, —

"What is this?"

"Gracious king!" exclaimed Princess Anna, "this is the

daughter of Yurand of Spyhov, to whom this ill-fated young knight made a vow. He vowed to obtain for her three peacock-plumes from helmets; and seeing such a plume on the helmet of this comtur, he thought that God himself had sent it to him. Not through malice did he do this, lord, but through folly; for this reason be merciful, and do not punish him; for this we beg thee on bended knees."

Then she rose, and taking Danusia by the hand, hurried with her to the king, who, seeing them, began to draw back. But they knelt before him, and Danusia, embracing the king's feet with her little hands, cried, —

"Forgive Zbyshko, O king; forgive Zbyshko!"

And, carried away at the same time by fear, she hid her bright head in the folds of the gray mantle of the king, kissing his knees, and quivering like a leaf. Princess Anna knelt on the other side, and, putting her palms together, looked imploringly at Yagello, on whose face was expressed great perplexity. He drew back, it is true, with his chair, but he did not repulse Danusia with force; he merely pushed the air with both hands, as if defending himself from flies.

"Give me peace!" said he; "he is at fault, he has shamed the whole kingdom! let them cut off his head!"

But the little hands squeezed the more tightly around his knees, and the childlike voice called still more pitifully, —

"Forgive Zbyshko, O king; forgive Zbyshko!"

Then the voices of knights were heard.

"Yurand of Spyhov is a renowned knight, a terror to Germans."

"And that stripling has done much service at Vilno," added Povala.

The king, however, continued to defend himself, though he was moved at sight of Danusia.

"Leave me in peace! He has not offended me, and I cannot forgive him. Let the envoy of the Order forgive him, then I will pardon; if he will not forgive, let them cut off his head."

"Forgive him, Kuno," said Zavisha Charny; "the Grand Master himself will not blame thee."

"Forgive him, lord!" exclaimed the two princesses.

"Forgive him, forgive him!" repeated voices of knights.

Kuno closed his eyes, and sat with forehead erect, as if delighted that the two princesses and such renowned knights were imploring him. All at once, in the twinkle of an eye, he changed; he dropped his head, and crossed his arms on his breast; from being insolent, he became humble, and said, in a low, mild voice, —

"Christ, our Saviour, forgave the thief on the cross, and also his own enemies."

"A true knight utters that!" exclaimed the bishop of Cracow.

"A true knight, a true knight!"

"Why should I not forgive him," continued Kuno, — "I, who am not only a Christian, but a monk? Hence, as a servant of Christ, and a monk, I forgive him from the soul of my heart."

"Glory to him!" thundered Povala of Tachev.

"Glory to him!" repeated others.

"But," added the Knight of the Cross, "I am here among you as an envoy, and I bear in my person the majesty of the whole Order, which is Christ's Order. Whoso offends me as an envoy, offends the Order; and whoso offends the Order offends Christ himself; such a wrong I before God and man cannot pardon. If, therefore, your law pardons it, let all the rulers of Christendom know of the matter."

These words were followed by a dead silence. But after a while were heard here and there the gritting of teeth, the deep breathing of restrained rage, and the sobbing of Danusia.

Before evening all hearts were turned to Zbyshko. The same knights who in the morning would have been ready at one beck of the king to bear Zbyshko apart on their swords were exerting their wits then to see how to aid him. The princesses resolved to go with a prayer to the queen, asking her to persuade Lichtenstein to drop his complaint altogether. or in case of need to write to the Grand Master of the Order, begging that he command Kuno to drop the affair. The way seemed sure, for such uncommon honor surrounded Yadviga that the Grand Master would bring on himself the anger of the pope and the blame of all Christian princes if he refused her such a request. It was not likely that he would, and for this reason, that Conrad Von Jungingen was a calm man, and far milder than his predecessors. Unfortunately the bishop of Cracow, who was also chief physician of the queen, forbade most strictly to mention even one word to her touching the matter. "She is never pleased to hear of death sentences," said he, "and though the question be one of a simple robber, she takes it to heart at once; and what would it be now, when the life of a young man is at stake, — a young man who might justly expect her

mercy. Any excitement may easily bring her to grievous
illness; her health means more for the whole kingdom than
the lives of ten knights." He declared, finally, that if any
one dared to disturb the lady in spite of his words, he
would bring down on that person the terrible wrath of
the king, and lay also the curse of the Church on him or
her.

Both princesses feared this declaration, and resolved to
be silent before the queen, but to implore the king until he
showed some favor. The whole court and all the knights
were on the side of Zbyshko. Povala asserted that he
would confess the whole truth, but would give testimony
favorable to the young man, and would represent the entire
affair as the impulsiveness of a boy. Still, every one foresaw, and the castellan of Cracow declared openly, that, if the
German insisted, stern justice must have its own.

The hearts of knights rose with growing indignation
against Lichtenstein, and more than one thought, or even
said openly: "He is an envoy and cannot be summoned to
the barriers, but when he returns to Malborg, may God not
grant him to die his own death." And those were no idle
threats, for it was not permitted belted knights to drop a
vain word; whoso said a thing must show its truth or perish.
The terrible Povala proved the most stubborn, for he had
in Tachev a beloved little daughter of Danusia's age; there
fore Danusia's tears crushed the heart in him utterly.

In fact, he visited Zbyshko that very day in the dungeon,
commanded him to be of good cheer, told him of the prayers
of both princesses and the tears of Danusia. Zbyshko,
when he heard that the girl had thrown herself at the feet
of the king, was moved to tears, and not knowing how to
express his gratitude and his longing, said, wiping his eyelids with the back of his hand, —

"Oh, may God bless her, and grant me a struggle on
foot or on horseback for her sake as soon as possible. I
promised her too few Germans, — for to such a one was
due a number equal to her years. If the Lord Jesus will
rescue me from these straits I will not be stingy with her;"
and he raised his eyes full of gratitude.

"First vow something to a church," said the lord of
Tachev, "for if thy vow be pleasing to God thou wilt be
free of a certainty. And second, listen: Thy uncle has
gone to Lichtenstein, and I will go too. There would be no
shame for thee to ask forgiveness, for thou art at fault; and

thou wouldst beg, not Lichtenstein, but an envoy. Art thou willing?"

"Since such a knight as your Grace says that it is proper, I will do so, but if he wishes me to beg him as he wanted on the road to Tynets, then let them cut my head off. My uncle will remain, and my uncle will pay him when his mission is ended."

"We shall see what he will answer to Matsko," replied Povala.

Matsko had really visited the German, but went from his presence as gloomy as night, and betook himself directly to the king, to whom the castellan himself conducted him. The king, who had become perfectly calm, received him kindly. When Matsko knelt, Yagello commanded him at once to rise, and inquired what he wanted.

"Gracious lord," said Matsko, "there has been offence, there must be punishment; otherwise law would cease in the world; but the offence is mine, for not only did I not restrain the natural passionateness of this stripling, but I praised it. I reared him in that way, and from childhood war reared him. It is my offence, gracious king, for more than once did I say to him: 'Strike first, and see afterward whom thou hast struck.' That was well in war, but ill at court. Still, the lad is like pure gold; he is the last of our race, and I grieve for him dreadfully."

"He has disgraced me, he has disgraced the kingdom," said the king. "Am I to rub honey on him for such deeds?"

Matsko was silent, for at remembrance of Zbyshko sorrow pressed his throat suddenly, and only after a long time did he speak again, with a moved voice, —

"I knew not that I loved him so much, and only now is it shown, after misfortune has come. I am old, and he is the last of our family. When he is gone — we shall be gone. Gracious king and lord, take pity on us!"

Here Matsko knelt again, and stretching forth hands that were wearied from war, he said, with tears, —

"We defended Vilno. God gave booty; to whom shall I leave it? The German wants punishment; let there be punishment, but let me yield my head. What is life to me without Zbyshko? He is young; let him free his land and beget posterity as God commands men to do. The Knight of the Cross will not even inquire whose head has fallen, if only one falls. Neither will any disgrace come on the

family for that. It is hard for a man to meet death, but,
when we look at the matter more carefully, it is better that one
man should die than that a family should be extinguished."

Thus speaking he embraced the feet of the king. Yagello
blinked, which with him was a sign of emotion, and finally
he said, —

"I shall never command to behead a belted knight! —
never, never!"

"And there would be no justice in doing so," added the
castellan. "Law punishes the guilty, but it is not a dragon
which sees not whose blood it is gulping. Consider what
disgrace would fall on your family; for were your nephew
to consent to what you propose all would hold him and his
descendants disgraced."

"He would not consent. But if it were done without his
knowledge he would avenge me afterward, as I should
avenge him."

"Bring the German to abandon his complaint," said the
castellan.

"I have been with him already."

"And what," inquired the king, stretching his neck,
"what did he say?"

"He spoke thus: ' Ye should have prayed for pardon on
the Tynets road; ye had no wish then, I have no wish
now.'"

"And why did ye not wish?"

"For he commanded us to come down from our horses
and beg him for pardon on foot."

The king put his hair behind his ears and wished to say
something, when an attendant came in with the announcement that the knight of Lichtenstein begged for an audience.

Yagello looked at the castellan, then at Matsko, but
commanded them to remain, perhaps in the hope that on
this occasion he would soften the affair by his kingly office.

Meanwhile the Knight of the Cross entered, bowed to
the king, and said, —

"Gracious lord, here is a written complaint touching the
insult which met me in your kingdom."

"Complain to him," answered the king, pointing to the
castellan.

"I know neither your laws nor your courts, but I know
this: that the envoy of the Order can make complaint only
to the king himself," said the knight, looking straight into
Yagello's face.

Yagello's small eyes glittered with impatience; but he stretched forth his hand, took the complaint, and gave it to the castellan. The castellan unrolled it and began to read, but as he read his face grew more vexed and gloomy.

"Lord," said he at length, "you insist on taking the life of that youth, as if he were a terror to the whole Order. Do you Knights of the Cross fear children?"

"We Knights of the Cross fear no one," replied the comtur, haughtily.

"Especially God," added the old castellan, in a low voice.

Next day Povala of Tachev did all that was in his power before the court to diminish Zbyshko's guilt. But in vain did he ascribe the deed to youth and inexperience, in vain did he say that even if some one who was older had made a vow to give three peacock-plumes, and had prayed to have them sent to him, and afterward had seen such a plume before him on a sudden, he too might have thought that to be a dispensation of God.

The honorable knight did not deny that had it not been for him Zbyshko's lance would have struck the German's breast. Kuno on his part had caused to be brought into court the armor worn by him that day, and it was found to be of thin plate, worn only on ceremonial visits, and so frail that, considering Zbyshko's uncommon strength, the point of the lance would have passed through the envoy's body and deprived him of life. Then they asked Zbyshko if he had intended to kill the knight.

Zbyshko would not deny. "I called to him from a distance," said he, "to lower his lance; of course he would not have let the helmet be torn from his head while alive, but if he had called from a distance that he was an envoy I should have left him in peace."

These words pleased the knights, who through good-will for the youth had assembled numerously at the court, and straightway many voices were raised. "True! why did he not cry out?" But the castellan's face remained stern and gloomy. Enjoining silence on those present he was silent himself for a while, then he fastened an inquiring eye on Zbyshko, and asked, —

"Canst thou swear, on the Passion of the Lord, that thou didst not see the mantle and the cross?"

"I cannot!" answered Zbyshko; "if I had not seen the cross I should have thought him one of our knights, and I should not have aimed at one of our men."

"But how could a Knight of the Cross be near Cracow unless as an envoy, or in the retinue of an envoy?"

To this Zbyshko made no answer, for he had nothing to say. It was too clear to all that, had it not been for the lord of Tachev, not the armor of the envoy would be before the court then, but the envoy himself with breast pierced, to the eternal shame of the Polish people; hence even those who from their whole souls were friendly to Zbyshko understood that the decision could not be favorable. In fact, after a time the castellan said, —

"In thy excitement thou didst not think whom thou wert striking, and didst act without malice. Our Saviour will reckon that in thy favor and forgive thee; but commend thyself, hapless man, to the Most Holy Virgin, for the law can not pardon thee."

Though he had expected such words, Zbyshko grew somewhat pale when he heard them, but soon he shook back his long hair, made the sign of the cross on himself, and said:

"The will of God! Still, it is difficult."

Then he turned to Matsko and indicated Lichtenstein with his eyes, as if leaving the German to his uncle's memory; and Matsko motioned with his head in sign that he understood and would remember. Lichtenstein too understood that look and that motion, and though there beat in his breast both a brave and stubborn heart, a quiver ran through him at that moment, so terrible and ill-omened was the face of the old warrior. The Knight of the Cross saw that between him and that knight there would be thenceforth a struggle for life and death; that even if he wanted to hide from him he could not, and when he ceased to be an envoy they must meet, even at Malborg.

The castellan withdrew to the adjoining chamber to dictate the sentence against Zbyshko to his secretary skilled in writing. This one and that of the knighthood approached the envoy during this interval, saying, —

"God grant thee to be judged with more mercy at the last judgment! Thou art glad of blood!"

But Lichtenstein valued only the opinion of Zavisha, for he, because of his deeds in battle, his knowledge of the rules of knighthood, and his uncommon strictness in observing them, was widely known throughout the world. In the most complicated questions in which the point was of knightly honor, men came to him frequently from a very great distance, and no one ever dared to oppose, not only because single combat with him was impossible, but also because men esteemed him as the "mirror of honor." One word of praise or of blame from his lips passed quickly among the knighthood of Poland, Hungary, Bohemia, Germany, and sufficed to establish the good or evil fame of a knight.

Lichtenstein therefore approached him and said, as if wishing to justify his stubbornness, —

"Only the Grand Master himself with the Chapter could grant him grace — I cannot."

"Your Grand Master has nothing to do with our laws' not he, but our king has power to show grace here."

"I, as an envoy, must demand punishment."

"Thou wert a knight, Lichtenstein, before becoming an envoy."

"Dost thou think that I have failed in honor?"

"Thou knowest our books of knighthood, and thou knowest that a knight is commanded to imitate two beasts, the lion and the lamb. Which hast thou imitated in this affair?"

"Thou art not my judge."

"Thou hast asked if thou hast failed in honor, and I have answered as I think."

"Thou hast answered badly, for I cannot swallow this."

"Thou wilt choke with thy own anger, not mine."

"Christ will account it to me that I have thought more of the majesty of the Order than of thy praise."

"He too will judge us all."

Further conversation was interrupted by the entrance of the castellan and the secretary. Those present knew that the sentence would be unfavorable, still a dead silence set in. The castellan took his place at the table and grasping a crucifix in his hand, commanded Zbyshko to kneel.

The secretary read the sentence in Latin. Neither Zbyshko nor the knights present understood it, still all divined that that was a death sentence. Zbyshko, when the reading was finished, struck his breast with his closed hand a number of times, repeating: "O God, be merciful to me a sinner!" Then he rose and cast himself into the arms of Matsko, who in silence kissed his head and his eyes.

On the evening of that day, the herald proclaimed, with sound of trumpets, to knights, guests, and citizens, at the four corners of the square, that the noble Zbyshko of Bogdanets was condemned by the sentence of the castellan to be beheaded with a sword.

But Matsko prayed that the execution should not take

place immediately. This prayer was granted the more easily since people of that age, fond of minute disposition of their property, were given time generally for negotiations with their families, and also to make peace with God. Lichtenstein himself did not care to insist on the speedy execution of the sentence, since satisfaction had been given the majesty of the Order; moreover, it was not proper to offend a powerful monarch to whom he had been sent, not only to take part in the solemnities of the christening, but also for negotiations touching the land of Dobryn. But the most important consideration was the health of the queen. The bishop of Cracow would not hear of an execution before her delivery, thinking rightly that it would be impossible to hide such an event from the lady, that should she hear of it she would fall into a "distress" which might injure her grievously. In this way a few weeks of life, and perhaps more, remained to Zbyshko, before the last arrangement and parting with his acquaintances.

Matsko visited him daily and comforted him as best he could. They spoke sadly of Zbyshko's unavoidable death, and still more sadly of this, that the family would disappear.

"It cannot be but you must marry," said Zbyshko once.

"I should prefer to adopt some relative, even if distant," replied Matsko, with emotion. "How can I think of marrying when they are going to cut off thy head. And even should it come to this that I must take a wife, I could not do so till I had sent Lichtenstein the challenge of a knight, till I had exacted my vengeance. I shall do that, have no fear!"

"God reward you! Let me have even that consolation! But I knew that you would not forgive him. How will you do it?"

"When his office of envoy is at an end, there will be either war or peace — dost understand? If war comes I will send him a challenge to meet me in single combat before battle."

"On trampled earth?"

"On trampled earth, on horseback or on foot, but to the death, not to slavery. If there be peace, I will go to Malborg, strike the castle gate with my lance and command a trumpeter to announce that I challenge him to the death. He will not hide, be assured."

"Of course he will not hide. And you will handle him in a way that I should like to see."

"Shall I handle him? I could not handle Zavisha, or Pashko, or Povala; but without boasting, I can handle two like him. His mother, the Order, will witness that! Was not the Frisian knight stronger? And when I cut from above through his helmet, where did my axe stop? It stopped in his teeth, did it not?"

Zbyshko drew breath at this with great consolation, and said, —

"He will die more easily than the Frisian."

The two men sighed; then the old noble said with emotion, —

"Be not troubled. Thy bones will not be seeking one another at the day of resurrection. I will have an oaken coffin made for thee of such kind that the canonesses of the church of the Virgin Mary have not a better. Thou wilt not die like a peasant, or like a nobleman created by patent. Nay! I will not even permit that thou be beheaded on the same cloth on which they behead citizens. I have agreed already with Amyley for entirely new stuff, from which a king's coat might be made. And I shall not spare masses on thee — never fear!"

Zbyshko's heart was delighted by this, so grasping his uncle's hand he repeated, —

"God reward you!"

But at times, despite every consolation, dreadful yearning seized him; hence another day, when Matsko had come on a visit, and they had scarcely exchanged greetings, he asked while looking through the grating in the wall, —

"But what is there outside?"

"Weather like gold," replied the warrior, "and warmth of the sun makes the whole world lovely."

Then Zbyshko put both hands on his uncle's shoulders and bending back his head, said, —

"O mighty God! To have a horse under one and ride over fields, over broad fields. It is sad for a young man to die — awfully sad!"

"People die even on horseback," said Matsko.

"Yes. But how many do they kill before dying!"

And he began to inquire about the knights whom he had seen at the court of the king: about Zavisha, Farurey, Povala, Lis, and all the others, — what were they doing, how did they amuse themselves, in what honorable exercises did their time pass? And he listened eagerly to the narrative of Matsko, who said that in the morning they jumped in full

armor over a horse, that they pulled ropes, fought with
swords and leaden-edged axes, and finally that they feasted,
and sang songs. Zbyshko desired with his whole heart and
soul to fly to them, and when he learned that immediately
after the christening Zavisha would go far away somewhere
to Lower Hungary against the Turks, he could not restrain
himself from weeping.

"They might let me go with him! and let me lay down
my life against pagans."

But that could not be. Meanwhile something else took
place: The two Mazovian princesses continued to think of
Zbyshko, who interested them with his youth and beauty;
finally Princess Alexandra resolved to send a letter to the
Grand Master. The Master could not, it is true, change
the sentence pronounced by the castellan, but he could intercede for Zbyshko before the king. It was not proper for
Yagello to grant pardon, since the question was of an attack
on an envoy; it seemed, however, undoubted that he would
be glad to grant it at the intercession of the Grand Master.
Hence hope entered the hearts of both ladies anew. Princess
Alexandra herself, having a weakness for the polished
Knights of the Cross, was uncommonly esteemed by them.
More than once rich gifts went to her from Malborg, and
letters in which the Master declared her venerated, saintly,
a benefactress, and special patroness of the Order. Her
words might effect much, and it was very likely that they
would not meet a refusal. The only question was to find a
courier who would show all diligence in delivering the letter
at the earliest, and in returning with an answer. When
he heard of this, old Matsko undertook the task without
hesitation.

The castellan, on being petitioned, appointed a time up to
which he promised to restrain the execution of the sentence.
Matsko, full of consolation, busied himself that very day
with his departure; later he went to Zbyshko to announce
the happy tidings.

At the first moment Zbyshko burst out in great delight,
as if the doors of the prison were open before him already;
later, however, he grew thoughtful, and soon he became sad
and gloomy.

"Who can receive any good from Germans? Lichtenstein might have asked the king for pardon, — and he
would have done well, for he would have guarded himself
from revenge, — but he would not do anything."

"He grew stubborn because we would not beg him on the Tynets road. Of Conrad, the Master, people do not speak ill. Besides, as to losing, thou wilt not lose anything."

"True," said Zbyshko, "but do not bow down low to him."

"How bow down? I carry a letter from Princess Alexandra — nothing more."

"Then if you are so good, may the Lord God assist you." All at once he looked quickly at his uncle, and said: "If the king forgives me, Lichtenstein will be mine, not yours. Remember."

"Thy head is not sure; make no promises. Thou hast had enough of those stupid vows," said the old man, in anger.

Then they threw themselves into each other's arms — and Zbyshko remained alone. Hope and uncertainty in turn shook his soul, but when night came, and with it a storm in the sky, when the barred windows were illuminated with the ominous blaze of lightning, and the walls quivered from thunder, when at last the whirlwind struck the tower with its whistle, and the dim candle went out at his bedside, Zbyshko, sunk in darkness, lost every hope again, and the whole night he could not close his eyes for a moment.

"I shall not escape death," thought he, "and nothing will help me in any way."

But next morning the worthy Princess Anna came to visit him, and with her Danusia, having a lute at her girdle. Zbyshko fell at the feet of one and then the other; though he was suffering after the sleepless night, in misfortune and uncertainty, he did not so far forget the duty of a knight as not to show Danusia his astonishment at her beauty. But the princess raised to him eyes full of sadness.

"Do not admire her," said she, "for if Matsko brings back no good answer, or if he does not return at all, poor fellow, thou wilt soon admire something better in heaven."

Then she shed tears, thinking of the uncertain lot of the young knight, and Danusia accompanied her forthwith. Zbyshko bent again to their feet, for his heart grew as soft as heated wax at those tears. He did not love Danusia as a man loves a woman, but he felt that he loved her with all his soul, and at sight of her something took place in his breast, as if there were in it another man, less harsh, less impulsive, breathing war less, and at the same time thirsting for sweet love. Finally, immense sorrow seized him because he would

have to leave her and not be able to keep the promise which
he had made.

"Now, poor girl, I shall not place the peacock-plumes at
thy feet," said he.   "But if I stand before the face of God,
I will say : ' Pardon my sins, O God, but whatever there is of
good in all the world, give it to no one else but Danusia,
daughter of Yurand of Spyhov '."

"Ye became acquainted not long ago," said the princess.
"May God grant that it was not in vain."

Zbyshko remembered all that had taken place at the inn
of Tynets, and was filled with emotion.   At last he begged
Danusia to sing for him that same song which she sang when
he had seized her from the bench and borne her to the
princess.

Danusia, though she had no mind for singing, raised her
head at once toward the arch, and closing her eyes like a
bird, she began,—

> " Oh, had I wings like a wild goose
> I would fly after Yasek,
> I would fly after him to Silesia!
> I would sit on a fence in Silesia.
> Look at me Yasek dear — "

But on a sudden from beneath her closed eyelids abundant
tears flowed forth; she could sing no longer.   Then Zbyshko
seized her in his arms in the same way that he had at the inn
in Tynets, and began to carry her through the room, repeating
in ecstasy, —

"No, but I would seek thee.   Let God rescue me, grow
up thou, let thy father permit, then I will take thee, O maiden !
Hei !"

Danusia, encircling his neck, hid her face wet with tears on
his shoulder, and in him sorrow rose more and more, sorrow
which, flowing from the depth of the sylvan Slav nature,
changed in that simple soul almost into the pastoral song :

> " Thee would I take, maiden !
> Thee would I take ! "

Meanwhile came an event in view of which other affairs
lost all significance in people's eyes.   Toward the evening of
June 21. news went around the castle of a sudden weakness
of the queen.   The physicians who were summoned, together
with the bishop of Cracow, remained in her chamber all night,

and it was learned soon from servants that premature labor
threatened the lady. The castellan of Cracow sent couriers
that same night to the absent king. Early next morning the
news thundered throughout the city and the country. Hence
all the churches were filled with people, on whom the priests
enjoined prayers for the recovery of the queen. All doubt
ceased after services. Knightly guests, who had assembled
for the approaching solemnity, nobles, deputations of merchants repaired to the castle; guilds and brotherhoods
appeared with their banners. Beginning with mid-day the
castle of Vavel was surrounded by numberless swarms of
people, among whom the king's bowmen maintained order,
enforcing peace and quiet. The city was almost depopulated,
but from time to time there passed through the deserted
streets peasants of the neighborhood, who also had heard of
the illness of the idolized lady, and were hastening toward
the castle.

Finally, in the main gate appeared the bishop and the
castellan, accompanied by the canons of the cathedral, the
counsellors of the king, and also knights. They went along
the walls, among the people, and, with faces announcing news,
began with a stern command to refrain from all outcries, for
shouts might injure the sick lady. Then they declared to all
in general that the queen had given birth to a daughter.

The news filled the hearts of all with delight, especially
since it was known at the time that, though the birth was
premature, there was no evident danger for the child or the
mother. The crowds began to separate, as it was not permitted to shout near the castle, and each one wished to give
way to his delight. Indeed, when the streets leading to the
square were filled, songs were heard and joyful shouts.
People were not even grieved that a daughter had come to
the world. "Was it bad," said they, "that King Louis had
no sons, and that the kingdom came to Yadviga? Through
her marriage with Yagello the power of the kingdom has
been doubled. So will it be this time. Where can such an
heiress be found as our king's daughter, since neither the
Roman Cæsar, nor any king is master of such a great State,
such broad lands, such a numerous knighthood! The most
powerful monarchs of the earth will strive for her hand, they
will bow down to the king and the queen, they will visit Cracow, and from this, profit will come to us merchants; besides,
some new kingdom, the Bohemian or the Hungarian, will be
joined to ours." Thus spoke the merchants among themselves,

and joy increased every moment. People feasted in private houses and in inns. The market square was full of lanterns and torches. In the suburbs country people from the regions around Cracow (more of these drew near the city continually) camped by their wagons. The Jews held council in their synagogue near the Kazimir. The square was crowded till late at night, almost till daybreak, especially near the City Hall and the weighing-house, as in time of great fairs. People gave news to one and another; they sent to the castle and crowded around those who returned with news.

The worst information was that the bishop had christened the child the night of its birth, from which people inferred that it must be very weak. Experienced citizens, however, quoted examples showing that children born half dead received power of life just after baptism. So they were strengthened with hope, which was increased even by the name given the infant. It was said that no Bonifacius or Bonifacia could die immediately after birth, for it was pre-destined them to do something good, and in the first years, and all the more in the first months of life, a child could do neither good nor evil.

On the morrow, however, came news unfavorable for child and mother; this roused the city. All day there was a throng in the churches as in time of indulgence. There were numberless votive offerings for the health of the queen and the infant. People saw with emotion poor villagers offering, one a measure of wheat, another a lamb, a third a hen, a fourth a string of dried mushrooms, or a basket of nuts. Considerable offerings came from knights, merchants, and handicraftsmen. Couriers were sent to miracle-working places. Astrologers questioned the stars. In Cracow itself solemn processions were ordered. All the guilds and brotherhoods appeared. There was a procession also of children, for people thought that innocent creatures would obtain God's favor more easily. Through the gates of the city entered new crowds from the surrounding country.

And thus day followed day amid the continual tolling of bells, the noise in the churches, the processions, and the masses. But when a week had passed and the child and the patient were alive yet, consolation began to enter hearts. It seemed to people an improbable thing that God would take prematurely the ruler of a realm who having done so much for Him would have to leave an immense work unfinished, and the apostolic woman whose sacrifice of her own happiness had brought to Christianity the last pagan people in Europe. The learned called to mind how much she had done for the Academy; the clergy, how much for the glory of God; statesmen, how much she had done for peace among Christian monarchs; Jurists, how much for justice; the poor, how much for their poverty; and it could not find place in the heads of any that a life so needful to the kingdom and the whole world might be cut down untimely.

Meanwhile on the 13th of July the bells announced sadly the death of the child. The city seethed up again, and alarm seized people; crowds besieged Vavel a second time, inquiring for the health of the queen.

But this time no one came out with good news. On the contrary, the faces of lords entering the castle or going out through the gates were gloomy, and every day more gloomy. It was said that the priest, Stanislav of Skarbimir, a master of liberal sciences in Cracow, did not leave the queen, who received communion daily. It was said also that immediately after each communion her room was filled with a heavenly light, — some even saw it through the window; this sight, however, rather terrified hearts devoted to the lady, as a sign that, for her, life beyond the earth had begun already.

Some did not believe that a thing so dreadful could happen, and those strengthened themselves with the thought that the just heavens would stop with one sacrifice. But on Friday morning, July 17th, it was thundered among people that the queen was dying. Every person living hastened to the castle. The city was deserted to the degree that only cripples remained in it, for even mothers with infants hurried to the gates. Cellars were closed, no food was prepared. All affairs stopped, and under the castle of Vavel there was one dark sea of people — disquieted, terrified, but silent.

About one o'clock in the afternoon a bell sounded on the tower of the cathedral. People knew not at once what that meant, but fear raised the hair on their heads. All faces, all eyes were turned to the tower, to the bell moving with increasing swing, — the bell, the complaining groan of which others in the city began to accompany; bells were tolled in the church of the Franciscans, the Holy Trinity, and the Virgin Mary, and throughout the length and the breadth of the city.

The city understood at last what those groans meant; the souls of men were filled with terror and with such pain as **if**

the bronze hearts of those bells were striking directly into
the hearts of all present.

Suddenly there appeared on the tower a black flag with a
great skull in the middle, under which in white were two
human shank-bones placed crosswise. Every doubt vanished that moment. The queen had given her soul to God.

Roars burst forth at the foot of the castle, the wails of a
hundred thousand persons, and they mingled with the dis-
mal sound of the bells. Some threw themselves on the
ground; others rent the clothing on their bodies, or tore
their faces; others looked at the walls in dumb bewilderment;
some groaned with deep and dull sound; some, stretching
their hands to the church and the chamber of the queen,
called for a miracle and the mercy of God. There were
heard also angry voices which in frenzy and despair went to
blasphemy. "Why was our beloved one taken from us?
To what profit were our processions, our prayers, and our
imploring? The gold and the silver offerings were dear, but
is there nothing in return for them? To take, they were
taken; but as to giving, nothing was given back!" Others,
however, repeated, with floods of tears and with groaning,
"Jesus! Jesus! Jesus!"

Throngs wished to enter the castle, to look once again on
the beloved face of the lady. They were not admitted, but
the promise was given that the body would be exposed
in the church; then every one would be able to look at it,
and to pray near it.

Later, toward evening, gloomy crowds began to return to
the city, telling one another of the last moments of the
queen, and of the coming burial, as well as of the miracles
which would be performed near her body and around her
tomb; of the miracles, all were perfectly convinced. It was
said also that the queen would be canonized immediately
after her death; when some doubted whether this could be
done, others grew impatient and threatened with Avignon.

Gloomy sadness fell on the city and on the whole country;
it seemed, not merely to common people, but to all, that with
the queen the lucky star of the kingdom was quenched.

Even among the lords of Cracow there were some who saw
the future in darkness. They began to ask themselves and
others: "What will come now? Will Yagello, after the
death of the queen, have the right to reign in the kingdom;
or will he return to his own Lithuania, and be satisfied there
with the throne of Grand Prince?" Some foresaw, and not

without reason, that he would desire to withdraw, and that in such case broad lands would fall away from the crown; attacks would begin again from the side of Lithuania, and bloody reprisals from the stubborn citizens of the kingdom; the Knights of the Cross would grow more powerful, the Roman Cæsar would increase, and also Hungary; while the Polish kingdom, yesterday one of the strongest on earth, would come to fall and to shame.

Merchants, for whom the extensive regions of Lithuania and Rus had been opened, foreseeing losses, made pious offerings to the end that Yagello might remain in the kingdom, but in such a case again they predicted a sudden war with the Order. It was known that only the queen restrained Yagello. People remembered how once, when indignant at the greed and rapacity of the Knights of the Cross, she said to them in prophetic vision : " While I live, I shall restrain the hand and just wrath of my husband, but remember that after my death punishment will fall on you for your sins."

They in their pride and blindness had no fear of war, it is true, considering that after the death of the queen the charm of her holiness would not stop the influx of volunteers from Western kingdoms. Thousands of warriors from Germany, Burgundy, France, and yet more remote countries, would come to aid them. Still, the death of Yadviga was such a far-reaching event that the envoy Lichtenstein, without waiting for the return of the absent king, hurried away with all speed to Malborg, to lay before the Grand Master and the Chapter the important, and, in some sense, terrible news.

The Hungarian, Austrian, Roman, and Bohemian envoys departed a little later, or sent couriers to their monarchs. Yagello came to Cracow in grievous despair. At the first moment he declared that he had no wish to reign without the queen, and that he would go to his inheritance in Lithuania. Then from grief he fell into torpor ; he would not decide any affair nor answer any question; at times he grew terribly angry at himself because he had gone from Cracow, because he had not been present at the death of Yadviga, because he had not taken farewell of her, because he had not heard her last words and advice.

In vain did Stanislav of Skarbimir and the bishop of Cracow explain to him that the queen's illness had happened unexpectedly, that according to human reckoning he had had time to return had the birth taken place in its own proper season. This brought no relief to him, and mildened no sorrow.

"I am not a king without her," said he to the bishop, " but a penitent sinner who will never know solace." Then he fixed his eyes on the floor, and no one could win another word from him.

Meanwhile all thoughts were occupied with the funeral of the queen. From every part of the country new crowds of lords, nobles, and people began to assemble; especially came the indigent, who hoped for abundant profit from alms at the funeral, which was to last a whole month. The queen's body was placed in the cathedral on an elevation, and placed in such manner that the wider part of the coffin, in which rested the head of the deceased, was considerably higher than the narrower part. This was done purposely, so that people might see the queen's face.

In the cathedral masses were celebrated continually; at the catafalque thousands of wax candles were burning, and amid those gleams and amid flowers she lay calm, smiling, like a white mystic rose, with her hands crossed on laurel cloth. The people saw in her a saint; they brought to her people who were possessed, cripples, sick children; and time after time, in the middle of the church was heard the cry, now of some mother who noted on the face of her sick child a flush, the herald of health, now of some paralytic who on a sudden recovered strength in his helpless limbs. Then a quiver seized the hearts of people, news of the miracle flew through church, castle, and city, then ever increasing crowds of human wretchedness appeared, wretchedness which could hope for help only through a miracle.

Meanwhile Zbyshko was entirely forgotten, for who, in face of such a gigantic misfortune, could think of an ordinary noble youth and his imprisonment in a bastion of the castle! Zbyshko, however, knew from the prison guards of the queen's death. he had heard the uproar of the people around the castle, and when he heard their weeping and the tolling of bells he cast himself on his knees, and calling to mind his own lot, mourned with his whole soul the death of the idolized lady. It seemed to him that with her something that was his had been quenched also, and that in view of such a death it was not worth while for any one to live in the world.

The echo of the funeral. the church bells, the singing of processions, and the movement of crowds, reached him for whole weeks. During this time he grew gloomy, he lost desire for food, for sleep, and walked up and down in his dungeon like a wild beast in a cage. Loneliness weighed on him, for there were days when even the prison guard did not bring him fresh food and water, so far were all people occupied by the funeral of the queen. From the time of her death no one had visited him, neither the princess nor Danusia, nor Povala, they who a little while before showed him so much good will, nor Matsko's acquaintance, the merchant Amyley. Zbyshko thought with bitterness that were Matsko to die all would forget him. At moments it came to his head that perhaps justice too would forget him, and that he would rot to death in that prison; he prayed then to die.

At last, when a month had passed after the queen's funeral and a second month had begun, he fell to despairing of his uncle's return; for Matsko had promised to come quickly and not spare his horse. Malborg was not at the end of the earth. It was possible to go and return in twelve weeks, especially if one were in a hurry. "But mayhap he is not in a hurry," thought Zbyshko with grief. "Mayhap he has found a wife on the road for himself, and will take her with gladness to Bogdanets, and wait for posterity himself, while I shall stay here forever, expecting God's mercy."

At last he lost reckoning of time, he ceased to speak with the guard, and only from the cobwebs which covered abundantly the iron grating in the window did he note that autumn was in the world. He sat for whole hours on the bed, with his elbows on his knees and his fingers in his hair, which reached now far below his shoulders, and half in sleep, half in torpor, he did not even raise his head when the guard, bringing food, spoke to him. But on a certain day the hinges squeaked, and a known voice called from the threshold, —

"Zbyshko!"

"Uncle dear!" cried Zbyshko, springing from his plank bed.

Matsko seized him by the shoulders, then embraced his bright head with his hands, and began to kiss it. Grief, bitterness, and longing, so rose in the heart of the young man that he cried on his uncle's breast like a little child.

"I thought that you would never return," said he, sobbing.

"Well, I came near that," answered Matsko.

Only then did Zbyshko raise his head and looking at him cry, —

"But what has happened you?" And he gazed with astonishment at the emaciated face of the old warrior, which had fallen in and was as pale as linen; he looked on his bent figure and on his iron gray hair.

"What has happened?" repeated he.

Matsko seated himself on the plank bed, and for a while breathed heavily.

"What has happened!" said he at last. "Barely had I passed the boundary when Germans shot me in a forest, from a crossbow. Robber knights! knowest thou? It is hard yet for me to breathe. God sent me aid, or thou wouldst not see me here."

"Who saved you?"

"Yurand of Spyhov," answered Matsko.

A moment of silence followed; then Matsko said, —

"They attacked me, and half a day later he attacked them. Hardly one half of them escaped. He took me to his castle, and there in Spyhov I wrestled three weeks with death. God did not let me die, and though suffering yet, I am here."

"Then you have not been at Malborg?"

"What had I to take there? The Germans stripped me naked, and with other things seized the letter. I returned to implore Princess Alexandra for a second one, but missed her on the road; whether I can overtake her, I know not, for I must also make ready for the other world."

Then he spat on his hand, which he stretched out toward Zbyshko and showed unmixed blood on it.

"Dost see? Clearly the will of God," added he, after a while.

Under the weight of gloomy thoughts both were silent some time, then Zbyshko inquired, —

"Do you spit blood all the time?"

"Why not, with an arrow-head fastened half a span deep between my ribs? Thou wouldst spit also — never fear! But I grew better in Yurand's castle, though now I suffer terribly, for the road was long and I travelled fast."

"Oh! why did you hurry?"

"I wished to find Princess Alexandra here and get another letter. 'Go,' said Yurand to me, 'and bring back a letter. I shall have Germans here under the floor; I will let out one on his knightly word, and he will take the letter to the Grand Master.' Yurand keeps a number of Germans there always, and listens gladly when they groan in the night-time and rattle their chains, for he is a stern man. Dost understand?"

"I understand. But this astonishes me, that you lost the first letter, for as Yurand caught the men who attacked you they must have had the letter."

"He did not catch all; something like five escaped. Such is our luck!"

Matsko coughed, spat blood again, and groaned some from pain in his breast.

"They wounded you badly," said Zbyshko. "How was it? From an ambush?"

"From a thicket so dense that a yard away nothing was visible. I was travelling without armor, since merchants had said that the road was safe — and the weather was hot."

"Who commanded the robbers? A Knight of the Cross?"

"Not a monk, but a man from Helmno who lives in Lentz, a German notorious for robbing and plundering."

"What happened to him?"

"Yurand has him in chains. But he has also two nobles of Mazovia in his dungeon; these he wishes to exchange for thee."

Again there was silence.

"Dear Jesus!" said Zbyshko, at length. "Lichtenstein will live, and he of Lentz also, while we must die unavenged. They will cut off my head, and you will not live through the winter."

"More than that, I shall not live until winter. If only I could save thee in some way!"

"Have you seen any one?"

"I have been with the castellan of Cracow; for when I heard that Lichtenstein had gone I thought that the castellan would favor thee."

"Has Lichtenstein gone?"

"He went to Malborg immediately after the queen's death. I was with the castellan, and he said: 'Your nephew's head will be cut off, not to please Lichtenstein, but because of the sentence; and whether Lichtenstein be present or absent, it is all one. Even were he to die, that would change nothing; for,' said he, 'law is according to justice, — not like a coat which may be turned inside out. The king,' said he, 'may pardon, but no one else.'"

"And where is the king?"

"After the funeral he went to Rus."

"Then there is no escape?"

"None. The castellan added: 'I am sorry for him; Princess Anna too entreats in his favor, but since I can do nothing, I am powerless.'"

"Then is Princess Anna here yet?"

"May God reward her! She is a kindly lady. She is here yet, for Yurand's daughter is ill, and the princess loves her as if she were her own child."

"Oh, for God's sake! And sickness has fallen on Danusia! What is the matter with her?"

"Do I know? The princess says that some one has bewitched her."

"Surely Lichtenstein! no one else except Lichtenstein — a dog is his mother!"

"Perhaps it was he. But what canst thou do to him? Nothing!"

"Since Danusia is sick all here have forgotten me —"

Zbyshko walked with great strides through the room, then he grasped Matsko's hand and said, after kissing it, —

"God reward you for everything! You will die for my sake; but since you have gone to Prussia, before you lose the rest of your strength do one other thing. Go to the castellan; beg him to let me out, on the word of a knight, for twelve weeks even. I will return then and let them cut off my head. But it cannot be that we should die unavenged. You know — I will go to Malborg and straightway challenge Lichtenstein. It cannot be otherwise. His death, or mine!"

Matsko fell to rubbing his forehead.

"As to going, I will go; but will the castellan grant permission?"

"I will give the word of a knight. Twelve weeks — I need no more."

"It is easy to say twelve weeks. But if thou art wounded and cannot return, what will they say of thee?"

"I will return even on my hands and feet. Have no fear! Besides, the king may come back from Rus by that time; it will be possible then to bow down to him for pardon."

"True!" answered Matsko; but after a while he added: "The castellan told me this also: 'We forgot your nephew because the queen died, but now let the affair be finished.'"

"Ei! he will permit," said Zbyshko, with consolation. "He knows well that a noble will keep his word, and whether they cut off my head now or after Saint Michael's, it is all one to the castellan."

"I will go this day."

" Go to Amyley's house to-day and lie down a little. Let them put some cure on your wound; to-morrow you will go to the castellan."

" Well, then, with God!"

They embraced and Matsko turned to the door; but he stopped on the threshold and wrinkled his brow as if thinking of something on a sudden.

" Well, but thou dost not wear a knight's belt yet. Lichtenstein will answer that he cannot fight with an unbelted man, and what wilt thou do? "

Zbyshko was perplexed for a while, and then asked, —

" But how is it in war? Must belted men choose only belted men as opponents? "

" War is war, but a duel is different."

" True — but — wait — There is need to arrange this. Yes, you see, — there is a way! Prince Yanush of Mazovia will give me a belt. When the princess and Danusia beg him, he will gird me. And on the road I will fight right away with the son of Mikolai of Dlugolyas."

" What for? "

" Because Pan Mikolai — he who is with the princess and whom they call Obuh — said that Danusia was a chit."

Matsko looked at him with astonishment. Zbyshko, wishing evidently to explain better what the question was, continued, —

" I cannot forgive him that, you know; but with Mikolai I will not fight, for he is about eighty years old."

" Listen, boy! " said Matsko. " I am sorry for thy head, but not for thy sense; thou art as stupid as a hornless he-goat."

" But what are you angry about? "

Matsko said nothing, and wanted to go; but Zbyshko sprang up once more to him.

" And how is Danusia? Is she well? Be not angry for a trifle. Besides, you were absent so long."

And he bent again to the old man's hand. Matsko shrugged his shoulders and said, " Yurand's daughter is in good health, but they do not let her out of the room. Farewell."

Zbyshko was left alone, but reborn, as it were, in soul and body. It was pleasant for him to think that he would have three months more of life, that he would go to distant lands, seek out Lichtenstein, and fight a mortal battle with him. At the very thought of this, delight filled his breast.

It was pleasant to feel that even for twelve weeks he would have a horse under him, ride through the broad world, fight, and not die unavenged. And then, let happen what might. Besides, that was an immense stretch of time; the king might return from Rus and pardon his offence; perhaps the war would break out which all had been predicting a long time; perhaps the castellan himself, when after three months he would see him victorious over the haughty Lichtenstein, would say, " Go now to the forests! " Zbyshko felt clearly that no one cherished hatred against him save the Knight of the Cross, and that only through constraint had the stern castellan condemned him.

So hope entered his breast more and more, because he doubted not that those three months would be granted. Nay, he thought that they would give him even more; for that a noble who had sworn on the honor of a knight should not keep his word would not even come to the head of the old castellan. Therefore, when Matsko came to the prison next day about nightfall, Zbyshko, who could hardly remain sitting, sprang to him at the threshold and asked, —

" Has he permitted? "

Matsko sat on the plank bed; he could not stand because of weakness; he breathed awhile heavily, and said at last:

" The castellan answered in this way: ' If you need to divide land or property, I will let out your nephew, on the word of a knight, for one or two weeks, but not longer.' "

Zbyshko was so astonished that for some time he could not utter a word.

" For two weeks? " asked he, at length. " But in one week I could not even go to the boundary! What is that? Did you tell the castellan my reason for going to Malborg? "

" Not only did I beg for thee, but Princess Anna begged also — "

" Well, and what? "

" The old man told her that he did not want your head, and that he himself grieves for you. ' If I could find some law on his side,' said the castellan, ' nay, some pretext, I would let him out altogether; but as I cannot find it, I cannot free the man. It will not be well,' said he, ' in this kingdom, when people close their eyes to law and show favor through friendship; this I will not do, even were it a question of my relative, Toporchyk, or even of my brother.' So stern is the man! And he added besides: ' We need not consider the Knights of the Cross too much, but we are not permitted to disgrace ourselves before them. What would they think, and their guests, who assemble from the whole world, if I should let out a noble condemned to death because he wants to go to them for a duel? Would they believe that punishment would touch him, or that there is justice in our kingdom? I would rather cut off one head than yield the king and the kingdom to death." To this the princess replied that justice which did not allow a relative of the king to get pardon for a man seemed to her strange justice. 'Mercy serves the king, but lack of justice serves him not,' said the castellan. At last they fell to disputing, for the princess was borne away by her anger. 'Then do not let him rot in prison!' said she. 'To-morrow I will give the order to make a scaffold on the square,' replied the castellan. With that they parted. Poor boy, the Lord Jesus alone can save thee!"

A long silence followed.

"How?" asked Zbyshko, in a low voice. "Then it will be right away?"

"In two or three days. When there is no help, there is no help; I have done all I could. I fell at the castellan's feet, I begged for pardon, but he held to his position: 'Find a law or a pretext.' But what could I find? I went to Father Stanislav of Skarbimir to bring the Lord God to thee. Let even that glory be thine, that the man confessed thee who confessed the queen. But I did not find him at home; he was with Princess Anna."

"Perhaps with Danusia?"

"Oh, pray to the Lord for thyself. That girl is better and better. I will go to the priest before daybreak to-morrow. They say that after confessing to him, salvation is as sure to thee as if thou hadst it tied up in a bag."

Zbyshko sat down, rested his elbows on his knees, and bent his head so that the hair covered his face altogether. The old man looked at him a long time, and said at last in a low voice, —

"Zbyshko! Zbyshko!"

The youth raised his face, which was angry and filled with cold stubbornness rather than pain.

"Well, what is it?"

"Listen carefully, for I may have found something." He pushed up nearer and spoke almost in a whisper: "Thou hast heard of Prince Vitold, how formerly he was imprisoned in Krev by Yagello, our present king; he escaped from con-

finement in the dress of a woman. No woman will stay
here in thy place, but take thou my coat, take my cowl,
and go forth. Dost understand? They will not notice
thee, be sure. That is certain. Beyond the doors it is
dark. They will not look into thy eyes. They saw me yesterday as I went out; no one looked at me. Be quiet, and
listen. They will find me to-morrow — Well, what? Will
they cut off my head? That would be a pleasure to them,
when as it is my death is appointed for a time two or three
weeks distant. But as soon as thou art out, mount thy
horse and ride straight to Vitold. Name thyself, bow down
to him; he will receive thee, and with him thou wilt be as
with the Lord God behind a stove. Here people say that
the armies of the prince have been swept away by the Tartar. It is unknown if that be true; it may be, for the late
queen prophesied that the expedition would end thus. If it
be true, the prince will need knights all the more, and will
be glad to see thee. But do thou adhere to him, for there is
not in the world a better service than his. If another king
loses a war, it is all over with him; but in Prince Vitold
there is such deftness that after defeat he is stronger than
ever. He is bountiful, and he loves us immensely. Tell
him everything as it happened. Tell him that it was thy
wish to go with him against the Tartar, but that thou wert
confined in the tower. God grant that he will present thee
with land and men, make a belted knight of thee, and take
thy part before the king. He is a good advocate."

Zbyshko listened in silence, and Matsko, as if urged by
his own words, continued, —

"It is not for thee to die in youth, but to return to
Bogdanets. When there, take a wife at once, so that our
race may not perish. Only when thou hast children wilt
thou be free to challenge Lichtenstein to mortal combat;
but before that see that thou keep from revenge, for they
would shoot thee somewhere in Prussia, as they did me, —
then there would be no help for thee. Take the coat, take
the cowl, and move in God's name."

Matsko rose and began to undress, but Zbyshko rose also,
seized his hand, and cried, —

"What do you wish of me? I will not do that! so help
me God and the Holy Cross!"

"Why?" asked Matsko, with astonishment.

"Because I will not."

Matsko grew pale from emotion and anger.

" Would to God thou hadst not been born ! "

" You have told the castellan that you would give your head for mine."

" Whence knowest thou? "

" Povala of Tachev told me."

" Well, what of that? "

"The castellan told you that disgrace would fall on me, and on our whole race. Would it not be a still greater disgrace were I to flee hence and leave you to the law's vengeance? "

" What vengeance? What can the law do to me when I shall die anyhow ? For God's sake, have reason."

" But have it you all the more. May God punish me if I desert you, a man sick and old. Pfu ! shame ! "

Silence followed; nothing was to be heard but the heavy, rattling breath of Matsko, and the call of the bowmen standing on guard at the gate. It was dark night now outside.

" Hear me," said Matsko at last, in a broken voice. " It was no shame for Prince Vitold to flee in disguise, it will be no shame for thee — "

" Hei ! " answered Zbyshko, with a certain sadness. " Vitold is a great prince. He has a crown from the king's hands ; he has wealth and dominion ; but I, a poor noble, have nothing — save honor."

After a while he cried, as if in a sudden outburst of anger, —

" But can you not understand this, that I so love you that I will not give your head for mine? "

Matsko rose on trembling feet, stretched forth his hand, and, though the nature of people in that age was as firm as if forged out of iron, he bellowed on a sudden in a heart-rending voice, —

" Zbyshko ! "

On the following day court servants began to draw beams to the square for a scaffold which was to be erected before the main gate of the city hall.

Still Princess Anna continued to take counsel with Yastrembets, and Father Stanislav of Skarbimir, and other learned canons skilled equally in written and customary law. She was encouraged to these efforts by the words of the castellan, who declared that, should they find "law, or pretext," he would not be slow in releasing Zbyshko. They counselled long and earnestly as to whether it was possible to find something; and though Father Stanislav prepared Zbyshko for death, and gave the last sacraments to him, he went straight from the dungeon to a consultation which lasted almost till daybreak.

Meanwhile the day of execution had come. From early morning crowds had been gathering on the square, for the head of a noble roused more curiosity than that of a common man, and besides this the weather was wonderful. Among women the news had spread also of the youthful years and uncommon beauty of Zbyshko; hence the whole road leading from the castle was blooming as with flowers from whole myriads of comely women of the citizen class. In the windows on the square, and in outbulging balconies were to be seen also caps, gold and velvet head-dresses, or the bare heads of maidens ornamented only with garlands of lilies and roses. The city counsellors, though the affair did not pertain to them really, had all come to lend themselves importance, and had taken their places just behind the knights, who, wishing to show sympathy with the young man, had appeared next the scaffold in a body. Behind the counsellors stood a many-colored crowd, composed of the smaller merchants and handicraftsmen, in the colors of their guilds. Students and children, who had been pushed back, circled about like dissatisfied flies in the midst of the multitude, crowding in wherever there appeared even a little free space. Above that dense mass of human heads was seen the scaffold covered with new cloth, on which were three persons: one the executioner, broad-shouldered and terrible, a German in a red coat and a cowl of the same stuff, with a heavy double-edged sword in his hand, — with him two assistants, their arms bared, and ropes around their loins. At their feet was a block, and a coffin, covered also with cloth; on the towers of the church of the Virgin Mary bells were tolling, filling the place with metallic sound, and frightening flocks of daws and doves.

People looked now at the road leading from the castle, now at the scaffold and the executioner standing upon it with his sword gleaming in the sunlight; then, finally, at the knights, on whom citizens looked always with respect and eagerness. This time there was something to look at, for the most famous were standing in a square near the scaffold. So they admired the breadth of shoulders and the dignity of Zavisha Charny, his raven hair falling to his shoulders. They admired the square stalwart form and the column-like legs of Zyndram of Mashkovitse, and the gigantic, almost preterhuman stature of Pashko Zlodye, the stern face of Voitseh of Vodzinka, and the beauty of Dobko of Olesnitsa, who in the tournament at Torun had finished twelve German knights, and Zygmunt of Bobova, who made himself famous in like manner in Hungary at Koshytse, and Kron of Koziglove, and Lis of Targovisko, terrible in hand-to-hand combat, and Stashko of Harbimovitse, who could overtake a horse at full speed. General attention was roused also by Matsko of Bogdanets with his pallid face; he was supported by Floryan of Korytnitse, and Martsin of Vrotsimovitse. It was supposed generally that he was the father of the condemned.

But the greatest curiosity was roused by Povala of Tachev, who, standing in the first rank, held on his powerful arm Danusia, dressed in white altogether, with a garland of rue around her bright hair. People did not understand what that meant, and why that maiden dressed in white was to witness the execution. Some said that she was Zbyshko's sister, others divined in her the lady of his thoughts; but even those could not explain to themselves her dress, or her presence at the scaffold. But in all hearts her face, like a blushing apple, though it was covered with tears, roused emotion and sympathy. In the dense throng of people they began to murmur at the unbendingness of the castellan, and the sternness of the law; these murmurs passed gradually into a roar which was simply terrible. At last here and there voices rose, saying that if the scaffold were torn away the execution would be deferred of necessity.

The crowd became animated and swayed. From mouth to mouth the statement was sent that, were the king present, beyond doubt he would pardon the youth, who, as men affirmed, was not guilty of any crime.

But all became silent, for distant shouts announced the approach of the bowmen and the king's halberdiers, in the midst of whom marched the condemned. Indeed the retinue appeared soon on the square. The procession was opened by the funeral brotherhood dressed in black robes which reached the ground, and with face coverings of similar material with openings for their eyes. People feared those gloomy figures, and at sight of them became silent. Behind those marched a detachment of crossbowmen formed of select Lithuanians, wearing coats of elkskin untanned. That was a detachment of the royal guard. Behind this were seen the halberds of another detachment; in the centre of this, between the court secretary, who had read the sentence, and Father Stanislav of Skarbimir, who bore a crucifix, walked Zbyshko.

All eyes were turned to him; from every window and balcony female forms bent forward. Zbyshko advanced dressed in the white jacket which he had won; it was embroidered with gold griffins and adorned at the bottom with a beautiful gold fringe. In this brilliant attire he seemed to the eyes of the audience a prince, or a youth of some lofty house. From his stature, his shoulders, evident under the closely fitting dress, from his strong limbs and broad breast, he seemed a man quite mature, but above that stature of a man rose a head almost childlike, and a youthful face, with the first down on its lips, which was at the same time the face of a royal page, with golden hair cut evenly above his brows and let down long on his shoulders.

Zbyshko advanced with even and springy tread, but with a pallid face. At moments he looked at the throng, as if at something in a dream; at moments he raised his eyes to the towers of the churches, to the flocks of doves, and to the swinging bells, which were sounding out his last hour to him; at moments also there was reflected on his face, as it were, wonderment that those sounds and the sobs of women, and all that solemnity were intended for him. Finally he saw on the square from afar the scaffold, and on it the red outline of the executioner. He quivered and made the sign of the cross on himself; at that moment the priest gave him the crucifix to kiss. A few steps farther on a bunch of star thistles, thrown by a young maiden, fell at his feet. Zbyshko bent down, raised it, and smiled at the maiden, who burst into loud weeping. But he thought evidently that in presence of those crowds, and in presence of women waving handkerchiefs from the windows, he ought to die bravely, and leave behind the memory of a "valiant youth" at the least. So he exerted all his courage and will; with a sudden movement he threw back his hair, raised his head higher, and advanced haughtily, almost like a victor in knightly tournaments which he had finished, a victor whom men were conducting to receive his reward.

The advance was slow, for in front the throng became denser and denser, and gave way unwillingly. In vain did the Lithuanian crossbowmen, who moved in the first rank, cry continually: "Eyk shalin! Eyk shalin!" (Out of the road!). People had no wish to know what those words meant — and crowded the more. Though the citizens of

Cracow at that time were two-thirds of them German, still round about were heard dreadful curses against the Knights of the Cross. "Shame! shame! May the German wolves perish if children must die to please them. It is a shame for the king and the kingdom!" The Lithuanians, seeing this resistance, took their bows, already drawn, from their shoulders, and looked frowningly at the people; they dared not, however, shoot into the crowd without orders. But the captain sent halberdiers in advance, for it was easier to open the road with halberds. In that way they reached the knights standing in the square around the scaffold.

These opened without resistance. First the halberdiers entered, after them came Zbyshko with the priest and the secretary, after that something took place which no one had expected.

Suddenly from among the knights stepped forth Povala, with Danusia on his arm, and cried "Stop!" with such a thundering voice that the whole retinue halted as if fastened to the earth. Neither the captain nor any of the soldiers dared oppose a lord and a belted knight whom they saw daily in the castle, and often talking with the king confidentially. Finally others, also renowned, cried with commanding voices: "Stop! stop!" Povala approached Zbyshko and gave him Danusia dressed in white.

Zbyshko, thinking that that was the farewell, seized her, embraced her, and pressed her to his bosom; but Danusia, instead of nestling up to him and throwing her arms around his neck, pulled as quickly as possible from her bright hair and from under the garland of rue a white veil and covered Zbyshko's head with it entirely, crying at the same time, —

"He is mine! he is mine!"

"He is hers!" repeated the powerful voices of the knights. "To the castellan!"

"To the castellan! To the castellan!" answered a shout from the people which was like thunder.

The priest raised his eyes, the court secretary was confused, the captain and the halberdiers dropped their weapons, for all understood what had happened.

It was an old Polish and Slav custom, as valid as law, known in Podhale, in Cracow, and even farther, that when an innocent maiden threw her veil over a man on the way to execution, as a sign that she wanted to marry him, she saved the man from death and punishment by that act. The knights knew this custom, yeomen knew it, the Polish people

of the city knew it, and Germans inhabiting from remote
times Polish cities and towns knew its force. Old Matsko
grew weak from emotion at that sight, the knights, pushing
back the crossbowmen promptly, surrounded Zbyshko and
Danusia; the people were moved, and in their delight cried
with still louder voices: "To the castellan! to the castellan!"
The crowd rose suddenly like gigantic waves of the sea.
The executioner and his assistants fled with all haste from
the scaffold. There was a disturbance, for it had become
clear to everyone that if the castellan wished to oppose the
sacred custom a terrible uproar would rise in the city. In
fact a column of people rushed at the scaffold. In the
twinkle of an eye they dragged off the cloth and tore it to
pieces, then the planks and beams, pulled away with strong
hands, or cut with axes, bent, cracked, broke — and a few
Our Fathers later there was no trace of the scaffold on that
square.

Zbyshko, holding Danusia in his arms, returned to the
castle, but this time as a real conquering triumphator; for
around him, with joyful faces, advanced the first knights of
the kingdom, at the sides, in front, and behind, crowded
thousands of men, women, and children, crying in heaven-
piercing voices, singing, stretching out their hands to
Danusia and glorifying the courage and the beauty of both.
From the windows the white hands of ladies clapped applause
to them; everywhere were visible eyes filled with tears of
rapture. A shower of garlands of roses and lilies, a shower
of ribbons, and even of gold belts and knots fell at the feet
of the happy youth, and he, radiant as the sun, his heart
filled with gratitude, raised aloft his white little lady from
moment to moment; sometimes he kissed her knees with
delight, and that sight melted young maidens to the degree
that some threw themselves into the arms of their lovers,
declaring that should these lovers incur death they would be
freed in like manner.

Zbyshko and Danusia had become, as it were, the beloved
children of knights, of citizens, and of the great multitude.
Old Matsko, whom Floryan and Martsin supported on either
side, almost went out of his mind from delight, — and from
astonishment also, that such a means of saving his nephew
had not even occurred to him.

In the general uproar Povala of Tachev told the knights
in his powerful voice how Yastrembets and Stanislav of
Skarbimir, skilled in written and customary law, had in-

vented, or rather remembered, this method while advising
with the princess. The knights wondered at its simplicity,
saying among themselves that except those two, no one else
had remembered the custom, which, in a city occupied by
Germans, had not been practised for a long period.

But everything depended still on the castellan. The
knights and people went to the castle where the castellan
lived during the king's absence, and straightway the court
secretary, Father Stanislav, Zavisha, Farurey, Zyndram,
and Povala of Tachev went to him to represent the validity
of the custom, and remind him how he himself had said that
if "law or pretext" were found by them, he would free
Zbyshko. What law could surpass ancient custom, which
had never been broken? The castellan answered, it is true,
that that custom referred more to common people and robbers than to nobles; but he was too well versed in every law
not to recognize the force of it. Meanwhile he covered his
silver beard with his hand and smiled under his fingers, for
he was glad evidently. At last he went out on a low porch;
at his side stood Princess Anna Danuta, with some of the
clergy and knighthood.

Zbyshko, seeing him, raised up Danusia again; the castellan placed his aged hand on her golden hair, held it a while
there, and then nodded his gray head with kindness and dignity.

All understood that sign, and the very walls of the castle
quivered from shouts. "God aid thee! Live long, just
lord! live and judge us!" shouted people from all sides.
New shouts were raised then for Danusia and Zbyshko. A
moment later both ascended the porch and fell at the feet
of the kind princess, Anna Danuta, to whom Zbyshko owed
his life; for with the learned men it was she who had discovered the law and taught Danusia what to do.

"Long live the young couple!" cried Povala, at sight of
them on their knees.

"Long life to them!" repeated others.

But the old castellan turned to the princess and said, —

"Well, gracious lady, the betrothal must take place at
once, for custom demands that."

"The betrothal I will have at once," answered the good
lady, with radiant face; "but I will not permit marriage
without consent of her father, Yurand of Spyhov."

Matsko and Zbyshko consulted with the merchant Amyley
as to what they should do. The old knight looked for his own

speedy death, and because the Franciscan father, Tsybek, skilled in wounds, had foretold it, he wished to go to Bogdanets and be buried with his fathers in the graveyard of Ostrov.

But not all of his "fathers" were lying there, for once the family had been numerous. In time of war they were summoned with the watchword, "Grady" ("Hail"); they had on their shield the Blunt Horseshoe, considering themselves better than other possessors of land, who had not always the right of an escutcheon. In the year 1331, at the battle of Plovtsi, seventy-four warriors from Bogdanets were killed in a swamp by German crossbowmen; only one survived, — Voitek, surnamed Tur (Wild Bull), to whom King Vladislav Lokietek, after crushing the Germans, confirmed in special privilege his shield and the lands of Bogdanets. The bones of the seventy-four relatives lay bleaching thenceforth on the field of Plovtsi; Voitek returned to his domestic hearth, but only to see the utter ruin of his family. For, while the men of Bogdanets were dying beneath the arrows of the Germans, robber knights from adjoining Silesia had attacked their nest, burnt the buildings to the ground, slain the people, or led them captive to be sold in remote German provinces.

Voitek was all alone as the heir of broad but unoccupied lands, which had belonged once to a whole ruling family. Five years later he married and begat two sons, Yasko and Matsko, and while hunting in the forest was killed by a wild bull.

The sons grew up under care of their mother, Kasia of Spalenitsa. who in two expeditions took vengeance on the Silesian Germans for their former injustice. In the third expedition she fell; but already she had built Bogdanets castle with the hands of captives, through which Yasko and Matsko, though from former times they were always called possessors, became considerable people. Yasko, coming to maturity, took in marriage Yagenka of Motsarzev, who gave birth to Zbyshko; but Matsko, remaining unmarried, took care of his nephew's property in so far as military expeditions permitted.

But when, in time of civil war between the Grymaliti and the Nalenchi, the castle in Bogdanets was burned a second time, and the people scattered, the lonely Matsko strove in vain to rebuild it. After he had struggled not a few years, he left the land at last to the abbot of Tulcha, his relative, and went himself with Zbyshko, yet a boy, to Lithuania against the Germans.

But he had never lost sight of Bogdanets. To Lithuania he went with the hope that after he had grown rich from booty he would return in time to redeem the land, settle it with captives, rebuild the castle, and fix in it Zbyshko. Now, after the happy escape of the youth, he was thinking of this and counselling with him concerning it at the house of the merchant, Amyley.

They had something with which to redeem the land. From booty, and ransoms which knights taken captive by them had paid, and from the gifts of Vitold, they had collected supplies which were rather considerable. Especially large was the profit which that battle to the death against the two Frisian knights had brought them. The armor alone which they had taken formed a real fortune in that period; besides armor they took wagons, horses, servants, clothing, money, and a whole rich military outfit. The merchant Amyley purchased much of that booty, and among other things two pieces of wonderful Frisian cloth which the provident and wealthy knights had brought with them in the wagons.

Matsko had sold also the costly armor, thinking that in view of near death it would be of no use to him. The armorer who bought it sold it the next day to Martsin of Vrotsimovitse with considerable profit, since armor of Milan was esteemed above all other armor on earth at that period. Zbyshko regretted the armor with his whole soul.

"If God return health to you," said he to his uncle, "where will you find another such?"

"Where I found that, — on a German," answered Matsko. "But I shall not escape death. The iron broke in my ribs, and the fragment remained in me. By plucking at it, and trying to drag it out with my nails, I pushed it in the more deeply; and now there is no cure for me."

"If you would drink a pot or two of bear's fat!"

"Yes. Father Tsybek also says that that would be well, for perhaps the fragment might slip out in some way. But how can I get it here? In Bogdanets we should only need to take an axe and watch one night under a bee-hive."

"Then we must go to Bogdanets. Only, you must not die on the road."

Old Matsko looked with a certain tenderness on his nephew.

"I know where thou wishest to go, — to the court of Prince Yanush, or to Yurand of Spyhov, to attack Germans of Helmno."

" I do not deny that.   I should go gladly to Warsaw with
the court of the princess, or to Tsehanov, so as to be as long
as possible with Danusia.   I cannot live now without her in
any way; she is not only my lady, but my love.   I am so
glad when I see her that when I think of her a shiver takes
hold of me.   I would go with her even to the end of the
earth, but you are at present my first law.   You did not
leave me, and I will not desert you.   If to Bogdanets, then
to Bogdanets!"

" Thou art a good boy!"

" God would punish me were I not good to you.   See,
they are packing the wagons already, and one I have filled
with hay for you.   Amyley has presented besides a feather
bed, but I know not whether you will be able to stay on it
from heat.   We will drive slowly with the princess and the
court, so that care may not fail you.   Afterward they will
go to Mazovia, and we to our place.   God aid us!"

" Only let me live long enough to rebuild the castle," said
Matsko ; " for I know that after my death thou wilt not think
often of Bogdanets."

" Why should I not think?"

" For in thy head will be love and battles."

" But was there not war in your own head?   I have
marked out exactly what I am to do; the first thing is to
build a castle of strong oak — and we shall have a moat dug
around it in order."

" Is that thy way of thinking?" inquired Matsko, with
roused curiosity.   " But when will the castle be built?   Tell
that!"

" The castle will be built before my visit to Princess
Anna's court in Warsaw or Tsehanov."

" After my death?"

" If you die soon, it will be after your death.   If you die I
will bury you worthily first of all; and if the Lord Jesus give
you health you will stay in Bogdanets.   The princess has
promised that I shall receive a knight's belt from the prince.
Without that, Lichtenstein would not fight with me."

" After that wilt thou go to Malborg?"

" To Malborg, or to the end of the earth, if I can only find
Lichtenstein."

" I will not blame thee in that.   Thy death or his!"

" Ah! I will bring his glove and his belt to Bogdanets,
have no fear."

" But guard against treason.   With them treason is ready."

"I will bow down before Prince Yanush to send to the Grand Master for a safe-conduct. There is peace now. I will go with the safe-conduct to Malborg; at Malborg there is always a throng of foreign knights. Do you know? First, Lichtenstein; and then I will see who have peacock-plumes on their helmets; in turn I will challenge them. May God aid me! Should the Lord Jesus give victory I will perform my vow at once."

Thus speaking Zbyshko smiled at his own thoughts; thereupon his face was like that of a boy who is telling what knightly deeds he will do when he grows up to manhood.

"Hei," said Matsko, nodding his head, "shouldst thou finish three knights of famous stock, not only would thy vow be accomplished, but thou wouldst take some good gear at the same time. O thou dear God!"

"What are three?" cried Zbyshko. "When I was in prison I said to myself that I would not be niggardly with Danusia. As many knights as she has fingers on her hands, — not three!"

Matsko shrugged his shoulders.

"You wonder, but do not believe," said Zbyshko. "I will go from Malborg to Yurand of Spyhov. Why should I not bow down to him, since he is Danusia's father? With him I will go against the Germans of Helmno. You said yourself that he is the greatest wolf-man in Mazovia against Germans."

"But if he will not give thee Danusia?"

"He has no reason not to give her! He is seeking his own revenge, I mine. Whom better can he find? Besides, since the princess has permitted the betrothal, he will not oppose."

"I note one thing," said Matsko, "that thou wilt take all the people from Bogdanets, so as to have a retinue proper for a knight, though the place be left without hands. While I am alive I will not permit this, but when I am dead I see that thou wilt take them."

"The Lord will provide an escort; besides, our relative, the abbot of Tulcha, will not be stingy."

At that moment the doors opened, and, as if in proof that the Lord God was providing an escort for Zbyshko, in walked two men, dark, strong, dressed in yellow kaftans, like Jews. They wore also red skullcaps, and immense, broad trousers. Standing in the door they fell to putting their fingers to their foreheads, their lips, and their breasts, and then to making obeisances down to the floor.

"What sort of renegades are ye?" inquired Matsko. "Who are ye?"

"Your captives," answered the newly arrived, in broken Polish.

"But how is that? Whence are ye? Who sent you here?"

"Pan Zavisha sent us as a present to the young knight, to be his captives."

"Oh, for God's sake, two men more!" cried Matsko, with delight. "And of what people?"

"We are Turks."

"Are ye Turks?" inquired Zbyshko. "I shall have two Turks in my retinue. Uncle, have you ever seen Turks?"

And jumping up to the captives he began to turn the men around and look at them, as he might at strange creatures from beyond the sea.

"As to seeing, I have not seen, but I have heard that the lord of Garbov has Turks in his service, whom he captured when fighting on the Danube with the Roman Cæsar, Sigismond. How is that? Are ye pagans, ye dog brothers?"

"Our lord gave command to christen us," said one of them.

"And ye had not the means to ransom yourselves?"

"We are from afar, from the Asiatic shore; we are from Brussa."

Zbyshko, who listened eagerly to every narrative of war, especially when it concerned deeds of the renowned Zavisha, asked them how they had fallen into captivity. But in the narrative of the captives there was nothing uncommon: Zavisha had attacked some tens of them three years before in a ravine; some he cut down, others he captured; of these he gave away afterward many as gifts. The hearts of Zbyshko and Matsko were filled with delight at sight of such a notable present, especially as it was difficult to get men in that time, and the possession of them was genuine property.

After a while Zavisha himself came, in company with Povala and Pashko. Since all had striven to save Zbyshko and were glad that they had succeeded, each man made him some present in farewell and remembrance. The bountiful lord of Tachev gave him a caparison for his horse, wide, rich, embroidered on the breast with golden fringe; and Pashko, a Hungarian sword worth ten gryvens. Later came Lis, Farurey, Kron, Martsin, and, last of all, Zyndram, each with full hands.

Zbyshko greeted them with overflowing heart, made happy both by the gifts, and by this, that the most renowned knights in the kingdom had shown him friendship. They inquired of him touching his departure, and the health of Matsko, recommending, like experienced people, though young, various ointments and remedies which cured wounds wonderfully.

But Matsko merely recommended Zbyshko to them; as for himself, he was preparing for the other world. It was difficult to live with a piece of iron sticking under the ribs. He complained that he spat blood continually, and had no appetite. A quart of shelled nuts, two spans of sausage, a plate of fried eggs, — that was his whole daily sustenance. Father Tsybek bled him a number of times, thinking to draw the fever from under his heart and restore desire for food; that gave no relief either.

But he was so delighted with gifts for his nephew that he felt better that moment; and when the merchant Amyley commanded to bring a small keg of wine to entertain guests so notable, he sat down to the cup with them. They fell to talking of the rescue of Zbyshko, and of his betrothal. The knights had no thought that Yurand would oppose the will of the princess, especially if Zbyshko would avenge the memory of Danusia's mother and win the peacock-plumes.

"But as to Lichtenstein," said Zavisha, "I am not sure that he will meet thee; he is a monk, and an elder in the Order besides. Nay! the people in his retinue declare that if he waits he will in time be Grand Master."

"Should he refuse combat he will lose his honor," said Lis.

"No," answered Zyndram; "he is not a lay member, hence he is not free to meet in single combat."

"But it happens often that they do."

"Yes, for laws in the Order are corrupted; they make various vows, and are famed for breaking them time after time, — to the scandal of all Christendom. But in a conflict to the death a Knight of the Cross, and especially a comtur, may refuse to appear."

"Ha! then you will meet him only in war."

"They tell us there will be no war, since at present the Knights of the Cross fear our people."

"This peace will not endure long," answered Zyndram. "Agreement with a wolf is impossible, for he must live on others."

" Meanwhile we may have to take Timur the Lame by the shoulders," said Povala. " Prince Vitold has suffered defeat from Edygeï, — that is undoubted."

" And Spytko, the voevoda, has not returned," added Pashko.

" And a multitude of Lithuanian princes remained on the field."

" The late queen foretold this end," said Povala.

" Then we may have to march against Timur."

Here conversation turned to the Lithuanian campaign against the Tartars. There was no longer any doubt that Vitold, a leader more impulsive than skilful, had suffered on the Vorskla a great defeat, in which a multitude of Lithuanian and Russian boyars had fallen, and with them a handful of Polish auxiliaries, and even Knights of the Cross. Those assembled at Amyley's house mourned above all the fate of young Spytko of Melshtyn, the greatest lord in the kingdom; he had gone as a volunteer, and after the battle had disappeared without tidings. They exalted to the sky his real knightly act, which was this: that having received a cap of safety from the leader of the enemy, he would not wear it during battle, preferring a glorious death to life at the favor of a pagan ruler. It was uncertain yet whether he had perished or had been taken captive. From captivity he had, of course, means to ransom himself; because his wealth surpassed reckoning, and besides, King Vladislav had given him all Podolia in vassal possession.

The defeat of the Lithuanians might be terrible for the entire realm of Yagello also; for no one knew well whether the Tartars, encouraged by victory over Vitold, would not hurl themselves on the lands and cities of the Grand Principality. In such case the kingdom too would be involved in the struggle. Many knights, then, who like Zavisha, Farurey, Dobko, and even Povala, were accustomed to seek adventures and battles at foreign courts, remained in Cracow designedly, not knowing what the near future might bring. If Tamerlane, the lord of twenty-seven kingdoms, were to move the whole Mongol world, the danger might become terrible. There were men who thought they foresaw this.

" If the need come, we must measure with the Limper himself. He will not find it so easy to meet our people as all those whom he conquered and destroyed. Besides, other Christian princes will come to assist us."

To this, Zyndram, who was flaming with special hatred against the Order, said with bitterness, —

"As to princes, I know not; but the Knights of the Cross are ready to make friends with the Tartars and strike us on the opposite flank."

"There will be war!" exclaimed Zbyshko. "I will go against the Knights of the Cross!"

But other knights contradicted. "The Knights of the Cross know no fear of God, and seek only profit; still, they will not assist pagans against Christian people. Moreover, Timur is warring somewhere far off in Asia; and the Tartar sovereign, Edygeï, has lost so many warriors in the battle that likely he is terrified at his own victory. Prince Vitold is a man of resources, and surely has supplied his fortresses well; though success has not come to the Lithuanians this time, it is no new thing for them to overcome Tartars."

"Not with Tartars, but with Germans must we fight for life and death," said Zyndram; "from Germans will our ruin come, unless we destroy them. And Mazovia will perish first of all," said he, turning to Zbyshko. "Thou wilt always find work there, have no fear!"

"Ei! if uncle were well, I would go there immediately."

"God strengthen thee!" said Povala, raising his goblet. "To thy health and Danusia's!"

"Destruction to the Germans!" added Zyndram.

And they began to take farewell of him. Meanwhile a courtier from the princess entered with a falcon on his hand, and, bending to the knights present, turned with a certain strange smile to Zbyshko.

"My lady, the princess, commanded me to tell you," said he, "that she will pass this night in Cracow, and take the road to-morrow morning."

"That is well, but why is this? Has any one fallen ill?"

"No. The princess has a guest from Mazovia."

"Has the prince himself come?"

"Not the prince, but Yurand of Spyhov," answered the courtier.

When Zbyshko heard this he was terribly confused, and his heart began to beat as it did when they read the death sentence to him.

CHAPTER V.

PRINCESS Anna did not wonder overmuch at the arrival of Yurand, for it happened often that in the midst of continual pursuits, attacks, and battles with neighboring German knights, he was overcome by a sudden longing to see Danusia. He appeared then unexpectedly either in Warsaw, Tsehanov, or wherever the court of Prince Yanush was living. At sight of the child dreadful grief burst forth in him always; for in the course of years Danusia had grown so much like her mother that when he saw her it seemed to him that he was looking at his dead one, such as he had known her on a time with Princess Anna in Warsaw. More than once people thought that from such grief his heart would break, — that heart given only to vengeance. The princess implored him often to leave his bloody Spyhov and remain at the court near Danusia. Prince Yanush, esteeming Yurand's bravery and value, and wishing also to avoid those vexations to which the continual happenings at the boundary exposed him, offered his favorite the dignity of swordbearer. Always in vain. It was just the sight of Danusia that opened the old wounds in Yurand. After some days he lost desire for food, conversation, and sleep. His heart began evidently to be indignant and to bleed; at last he vanished from the court and returned to the swamps of Spyhov, to drown his grief and anger in bloodshed.

"Woe to the Germans!" said the people then. "They are no sheep, except for Yurand; to the Germans Yurand is a wolf." In fact, after a certain time it was reported that foreign volunteers were seized while passing along the boundary road to the Knights of the Cross; then news came of burnt castles, of captured servants, or of life and death combats, in which the terrible Yurand was always victorious.

With the predatory disposition of the Mazovians and the German knights who by the authority of the Order rented lands and castles in the adjoining Mazovia, even in time of profound peace between the princes of Mazovia and the Order the uproar of battle never ceased on the boundary.

Even while cutting fuel in the forest, or during harvest, citizens went out with spears or crossbows. People lived in uncertainty of the morrow, in continual military preparation, in hardness of heart. No one was satisfied with simple defence, but returned robbery for robbery, fire for fire, attack for attack. And it happened that when Germans were stealing along silently through forest boundaries to surprise some castle, carry off people, or drive away herds, Mazovians at the same time were intent on a similar action. More than once they met and fought to the death, but frequently only the leaders were challenged to a mortal struggle, after which the victor took the retinue of his vanquished opponent. So that when complaints against Yurand were brought to the court in Warsaw, the prince answered with complaints of attacks made by German knights elsewhere. In this way when both sides demanded redress neither side had the wish or the power to give it; all robberies, burnings, attacks went entirely unpunished.

In his swampy Spyhov, which was overgrown with reeds, Yurand, burning with an unappeasable desire of vengeance, became so oppressive to his neighbors beyond the border that at last the fear of him became greater than their stubbornness. The fields adjoining Spyhov lay fallow, the forests were filled with wild hops and hazelnuts, the meadows with weeds. More than one German knight accustomed to fist law in his fatherland tried to settle near Spyhov, but each, after a certain time chose to flee from land, flocks, and servants, rather than live at the side of an implacable enemy. Frequently also knights combined to make a common attack upon Spyhov, but each of these found an end in defeat. They tried various methods. Once they brought in, to challenge Yurand to trampled earth, a knight from the Mien, famed for strength and sternness, a man who in all struggles had won victory. But when they stood within barriers the heart in the German knight fell as if by magic at sight of the terrible Mazovian, and he turned his horse to flee. Yurand, unarmored, shot after the man and pierced him through the back, thus depriving him of the light of day and of honor. Thenceforth the greater alarm seized his neighbors, and if any German, even from afar, saw the smoke of Spyhov he made the sign of the cross on himself and began a prayer to his patron in heaven, for the belief became established that Yurand had sold his soul to unclean powers for the sake of vengeance.

Besides, terrible things were related of Spyhov. It was said that through sticky swamps in the midst of deep quagmires overgrown with duck plant and water snake-weed, a road led to it which was so narrow that two horsemen could not ride abreast there; that on both sides of this road were lying German bones; that in the night-time the heads of drowned people walked along on spider legs, groaning, howling, and dragging down to the depths passers-by with their horses.

It was repeated that at the castle itself stood a picket fence adorned with human skulls. In all this the only truth was that in barred cellars, dug under the house in Spyhov, groaned always some prisoners, or some tens of them, and that the name of Yurand was more terrible than the inventions about skeletons, and ghosts of drowned people.

Zbyshko, when he learned of Yurand's coming, hastened straightway to meet him, but as he was going to Danusia's father there was in his heart a certain fear. He had chosen Danusia as the lady of his thoughts and made a vow to her; no one could forbid that, but later the princess had caused the betrothal. What would Yurand say of that act? Would he consent, or would he not? What would happen were he, as Danusia's father, to shout and say that he would never permit such a thing? These questions pierced Zbyshko's soul with dread, since he cared more for Danusia than for all else on earth. This thought alone gave him solace, that Yurand would consider his attack on Lichtenstein a service, not a drawback, for he had made it to take revenge for Danusia's mother, and had thereby lacked little of losing his own head.

Meanwhile he fell to inquiring of the courtier who had come to Amyley's for him.

"And whither are you taking me? To the castle?"

"To the castle. Yurand has stopped with the court of the princess."

"Tell me, what kind of man is he? — that I may know how to talk with him."

"What shall I tell you? He is a man entirely different from others. They say that once he was gladsome, till the blood boiled in his liver."

"Is he wise?"

"He is cunning, for he plunders others, and does not give himself up. Hei! he has one eye. — the Germans shot out the other with a crossbow, — but with that one he looks right through you. No man can insist on his own with him. But the princess, our lady, he loves, for he took her damsel as wife, and now his daughter is reared with us."

Zbyshko drew a breath of relief.

"Then you say that he does not oppose the will of the princess?"

"I know what you would like to learn, and what I have heard I will tell. The princess spoke with him about your betrothal, for it would not be well to conceal it, but it is unknown what he answered."

Thus conversing they reached the gate. The captain of the royal bowmen, the same who had conducted Zbyshko to death, nodded to him now in a friendly manner; so, passing the guards, they found themselves in the court, and then entered on the right to the part occupied by the princess. The courtier, meeting a page before the door inquired, —

"Where is Yurand of Spyhov?"

"In the Winding Room with his daughter."

"It is over there," said the courtier, indicating the door.

Zbyshko made the sign of the cross on himself, and, raising a curtain in the opened door, entered with beating heart. But he did not see Yurand and Danusia, for the room was not merely "winding," but dark. Only after a while did he see the bright head of the maiden; she was sitting on her father's knees; they did not hear when he entered, so he halted at the curtain, coughed and said at last, —

"May He be praised!"

"For the ages of ages!" answered Yurand, rising.

At that moment Danusia sprang to the young knight, and seizing him by the hand, exclaimed, —

"Zbyshko! Papa has come!"

Zbyshko kissed her hand, and with her approached Yurand.

"I have come to bow down to you," said Zbyshko. "Do you know who I am?"

Then he inclined slightly and made a motion with his hands as if wishing to seize Yurand's feet. But Yurand took his hand, turned him toward the light and examined him silently.

Zbyshko had recovered somewhat, so he raised his eyes full of curiosity to Yurand, and saw before him a man of immense stature, with blond hair and light moustaches, a face pitted with small-pox, and having only one eye, which was of an iron color. It seemed to Zbyshko as if that eye

would bore him through and through; hence confusion again
seized him. Not knowing at last what to say, but wishing
desperately to break the vexatious silence with some speech,
he asked, —

"Are you Yurand of Spyhov, the father of Danusia?"

But the other indicated to him an oaken seat, on which he
himself sat, and without uttering a word he looked at him
longer.

Zbyshko was impatient at last.

"You know," said he, "that it is awkward for me to sit
here as if under judgment."

Only then did Yurand say: "Hadst thou the wish to fight
with Lichtenstein?"

"I had," answered Zbyshko.

In the eye of the lord of Spyhov flashed a kind of wonderful light, and his terrible countenance brightened somewhat. After a while he looked at Danusia and inquired
again, —

"And was it for her?"

"For whom should it be? Uncle must have told you
how I vowed to her to strip peacock-plumes from German
heads! Not three of them, but as many as there are fingers
on both her hands. Therefore I will help you to take revenge; it is for Danusia's mother."

"Woe to them!" said Yurand.

Again silence followed.

Zbyshko noticed that by showing his hatred against the
Germans he was touching Yurand's heart.

"I will not forgive them my own wrongs," said he; "for
they came near cutting my head off." Here he turned to
Danusia and added, "She saved me."

"I know," replied Yurand.

"And you are not angry because of that?"

"Since thou hast promised her, serve her; for such is
knightly custom."

Zbyshko hesitated somewhat, but after a while he began
again with evident alarm, —

"Think of this: she covered my head with a veil; the
whole knighthood heard her say, 'He is mine;' the Franciscan, also, who was at my side with the cross, heard her.
And certain it is that I shall belong to no other till death;
so may God help me!"

Then he knelt again, and wishing to show that he knew
knightly customs, he kissed with great respect the shoes of

Danusia, who was sitting on the arm of the seat; then he turned to Yurand and asked, —

"Have you ever seen another like her?"

Yurand placed his terrible man-killing hands on his own head suddenly, and closing his eyes, said in a deep voice:

"I have, but the Germans killed her."

"Then listen," said Zbyshko, with enthusiasm; "one wrong has met both of us, and one vengeance belongs to us. They, the dog brothers, slew with crossbows a multitude of my relatives from Bogdanets when their horses sank in a quagmire. You will find no one better than me for your labor. It is nothing new to me! Ask uncle. The lance or the axe, the long or the short sword, are all one to me! My uncle has told you of those Frisians? I will slaughter Germans like sheep for you; and as to the maiden, I swear on my knees to fight for her, as God lives, with the very elder of hell; and I will not yield her either for land or for flocks, or for any gear; and though a castle with glass windows were offered me without her, I would reject the castle and wander off to the edge of the world for her."

Yurand sat some time with his head on his hands; but at last he recovered as if from sleep, and said with pity and sadness, —

"Thou hast pleased me, boy; but I will not give her to thee, for she is not fated to thee, poor fellow."

When he heard this, Zbyshko grew dumb and looked at Yurand with round eyes, unable to utter a word. But Danusia hastened to aid him. Zbyshko was very dear to her, and it was pleasant for her to pass, not for a "chit," but a "grown-up young lady." The betrothal pleased her, and the sweet things which the young knight brought in daily; so now, when she understood that they wished to take all this away from her, she dropped as quickly as possible from the arm of the seat, and hiding her face on her father's knee, began to repeat, —

"Tatulo, tatulo (papa dear), I will cry!"

Evidently he loved her above everything, for he placed his hand on her head mildly. His face expressed neither hatred nor anger, only sadness.

Meanwile Zbyshko recovered and asked: "How is that? Then you wish to oppose the will of God?"

"If it be the will of God, you will get her; but I cannot incline my own will. I would be glad to incline it, but that is not possible."

He raised Danusia then, and taking her on his arm, he turned toward the door; when Zbyshko wished to bar the way, he halted for a moment and said, —

" I shall not be angry with thee about knightly service, but ask me not for more; I cannot say another word to thee."

And he passed out.

CHAPTER VI.

THE next day Yurand did not avoid Zbyshko in the least, or hinder him from showing Danusia on the way various services which as a knight it was his duty to show her. On the contrary, Zbyshko, though greatly mortified, noticed that the gloomy lord of Spyhov looked at him in a friendly manner, and, as it were, with sorrow because he had been forced to give such a cruel answer. The young man tried more than once, therefore, to approach him and begin conversation. About an hour's journey from Cracow it was not difficult to find an opportunity, for both accompanied the princess on horseback. Yurand, though usually silent, spoke willingly enough; but when Zbyshko wished to learn something of the secret hindrances separating him from Danusia, conversation stopped on a sudden. Yurand's face became cloudy; he looked unquietly at Zbyshko, as if fearing to betray himself in something. Zbyshko thought that the princess knew facts; so, selecting a favorable moment, he tried to obtain information from her; but neither could she explain much to him.

"There is a secret," said she. "Yurand himself told me this; but he begged me at the same time not to ask him, for he is not only unwilling but unable to tell it. Doubtless he is bound by some oath, as happens among people. God grant, however, that in time all this will explain itself."

"Without Danusia I should be in this world like a dog on a leash, or a bear in a pit. No delight of any kind, no pleasure. Nothing beyond disappointment and sighing. I would go now with Prince Vitold to Tavan, and let the Tartars there kill me. But I must take my uncle home to begin with, and then snatch those peacock-plumes from the heads of the Germans, as I have sworn. Mayhap they will kill me while doing so; I should rather die than see another man taking Danusia."

The princess raised her kindly blue eyes on him, and inquired, with a certain astonishment, —

"And thou wouldst not permit that?"

"That will not be, while there is breath in my nostrils! Unless my hand were to wither, and be without power to hold an axe!"

" Well, thou wilt see."

" But how could I take her in spite of her father? "

To this the princess answered, as if to herself, —

" Mighty God! surely that will not be! Is God's will not stronger than the will of a father?" Then she said to Zbyshko: " And what did Yurand himself say? ' If it be the will of God, he will get her.' "

" He said that to me," replied Zbyshko. ' If it be the will of God,' said he, ' thou wilt get her.' "

" Well, seest thou? "

" Yes, in thy favor, gracious lady, is my only solace."

" Thou hast my favor, and Danusia will adhere to thee. Only yesterday I said to her, ' Danusia, but wilt thou hold to Zbyshko?' and she answered: ' I shall be Zbyshko's, or no one's.' That is a green berry yet, but whatever she says she will hold to, for she is a noble's child, not some wanderer. And her mother was of the same kind."

" May God grant!" replied Zbyshko.

" But remember that thou hold to her; for more than one man is giddy; he promises to love faithfully, and directly he rushes to another, so that thou couldst not hold him on a rope! I tell the truth! And you meet a man sometimes who at every girl he sees neighs like a horse fat on oats."

" May the Lord Jesus punish me first! " cried Zbyshko with energy.

" Well, remember that. And when thou hast taken thy uncle home come to our court. Thou wilt have a chance there to win spurs, and by that time we shall see what God gives. Danusia will have ripened and will feel the will of God, for now she loves thee indeed greatly, — I cannot express it otherwise, — but not yet as mature maidens love. Perhaps too Yurand will incline to thee later, for, as I notice, he would be glad to incline. Thou wilt go to Spyhov too, and with Yurand against the Germans; it may happen that thou wilt serve him in some way and win him completely."

" Gracious lady, I intended to act in just that way, but with permission it will be easier."

This conversation added much courage to Zbyshko. Meanwhile at the first halt old Matsko grew so ill that there was need to stop and wait till he could regain even a little strength for the farther journey. The kind princess, Anna Danuta, left him medicines and remedies from all that she had brought, but she was forced herself to travel on, and the owners of Bogdanets had to part with the Mazovian court.

Zbyshko fell his whole length at the feet of the princess, then once more he vowed true knightly service to Danusia, promised to go soon to Tsehanov, or Warsaw; finally he seized her in his strong arms, and raising her said with a voice of emotion, —

"Think of me, dearest flower; remember me, my golden fish!"

And Danusia, embracing him with her arms, just as a younger sister embraces a dear brother, put her little up-turned nose to his cheek and cried, with tears each as big as a pea, —

"I will not go to Tsehanov without Zbyshko! I will not go to Tsehanov!"

Yurand saw this, but he did not burst out in anger; on the contrary, he took farewell of the youth very kindly, and when he had mounted his horse he turned once again to him, and added, —

"Be with God, and cherish no feeling of offence toward me."

"How should I have a feeling of offence against you, Danusia's father?" said Zbyshko, sincerely. And he inclined before him to the stirrup. Yurand pressed his hand firmly, and said, —

"God give thee luck in all undertakings. Dost understand?"

And he rode away. Zbyshko understood the great good-will in those final words, and turning to the wagon in which Matsko was lying, he said, —

"Do you know, he too would be glad, but something prevents him. You were in Spyhov, and you have quick reason; try to understand what this means."

But Matsko was too ill. The fever which he had in the morning increased toward evening to the degree that he began to lose consciousness; hence, instead of answering Zbyshko, he looked at him as if in astonishment, and asked, —

"But where are the bells ringing here?"

Zbyshko was frightened, for it occurred to him that if the sick man heard bells it was evident that death was approaching. He thought too that the old man might die without a priest, without confession, and thus put himself, if not entirely in hell, at least for long ages in purgatory — hence he resolved to take him farther, so as to bring him to some parish where he might receive the last sacraments.

With this object they moved on during the whole night. Zbyshko sat in the wagon on the hay where the sick man was lying, and watched him till daybreak. From time to time he gave him wine, which the merchant Amyley had furnished for the road, and which the thirsty Matsko drank eagerly, for it brought him evident relief. When he had drunk a second quart he even recovered consciousness; after the third quart he fell asleep, so deeply that Zbyshko bent over him at moments to be sure that he was not dead.

At thought of this, great sorrow seized Zbyshko. Till the time of his imprisonment in Cracow he had not understood how he loved that "uncle," who in life had been to him father and mother. But now he knew well, and also he felt that after the death of that "uncle" he would be terribly alone in the world — without blood relations; save only the abbot who had Bogdanets in pledge, he would be without friends, without aid. At the same time it occurred to him that if Matsko died his death would come through Germans, through whom he himself had lacked little of losing his life, through whom all his family had perished, and Danusia's mother, and many, many blameless people whom he had known, or of whom he had heard from acquaintances; and at last wonder seized hold of him. "Is there," said he to himself, "in this whole kingdom a man who has not suffered injustice from Germans, and who is not thirsting for vengeance?" Here he remembered those with whom he had fought at Vilno, and he thought: "Even Tartars are surely not more cruel in war than the Germans, and of a certainty there is not another such nation on earth."

The dawn interrupted his meditation. The day rose clear, but cool. Matsko was evidently better, for he breathed evenly and quietly. He woke only when the sun had warmed the world well; he opened his eyes and said, —

"I feel better. Where are we?"

"We are entering Olkush. You know — the place where they dig silver, and pay taxes to the treasury."

"Oh, to have what there is in the ground! Then we might build up Bogdanets."

"It is evident that you are better," said Zbyshko, smiling. "Hei! it would be enough to build a walled castle. But let us go to the priest's house, for there they will give us entertainment, and you will be able to confess. All is in God's hands, but it is better to have the conscience in order."

"I am a sinful man; I am glad to be penitent," said Matsko. "I dreamed in the night that devils were pulling the boots from my feet, and were gabbling to one another in German. God was gracious, relief came. But thou didst sleep like a log?"

"How sleep when I was watching you?"

"Then lie down a little. When we arrive I will wake thee."

"What time have I to sleep?"

"But what hinders thee?"

"What unless love?" said Zbyshko, looking at his uncle with the eyes of a child. "Pains have collected in my breast from sighing, but I will sit on horseback a little, and that will relieve me."

He crawled out of the wagon and mounted a horse, which one of the Turks given by Zavisha held carefully. Matsko meanwhile held his side because of pain, but clearly he had something else besides his own sickness in mind, for he shook his head, smacked his lips, and said at last, —

"I wonder, and I cannot stop wondering, how thou hast become so eager for that love, for neither thy father nor I were of that kind."

Zbyshko, instead of answering, straightened himself quickly in the saddle, put his hand on his hips, threw up his head, and thundered with all the power in his breast: —

"I wept all the night, I wept in the morning.
Where hast thou gone, dearest maiden?
Nothing avails me, though I weep my eyes out,
For I never shall see thee, O maiden.
                                        Hei!"

And that "Hei!" rushed through the forest, struck the trees by the roadside, was heard at last in a distant echo, and grew still in the thickets.

But Matsko put his hand again on his side where the German arrow-point had stuck, and said, groaning slightly, —

"Formerly people were wiser — dost understand?" But after a while he grew thoughtful, as if remembering some of the old times, and added: "Though even in old times an odd man was foolish."

Meanwhile they issued from the forest, after which they beheld sheds for miners, and farther on the indented walls of Olkush, reared by King Kazimir, and the tower of the church built by Vladislav Lokietek.

CHAPTER VII.

The canon of the church heard Matsko's confession, and kept the two men all night hospitably, so that they set out again only next morning early. Beyond Olkush they turned towards Silesia, along the boundary of which they were to pass till they reached Great Poland. The road lay for the greater part through a wilderness, in which were heard frequently about sunset the bellowing of wild bulls and bisons, which sounded like underground thunder, in hazelnut thickets at night glittered wolves' eyes. The greatest danger, however, threatening travellers on this road was from Germans or Germanized knights of Silesia, whose castles rose here and there on the border. It is true that, because of war with Opolchyk the naderspan, who was assisted against King Vladislav by his Silesian nephews, Polish hands had destroyed the greater part of these castles, but it was needful at all times to guard one's self, and not let weapons out of one's hands, especially after sunset.

But they advanced slowly, so that the road annoyed Zbyshko, and only when they were one day's wheel-travelling distant from Bogdanets did he on a certain night hear behind them the trampling and snorting of horses.

"Some people are following us," said Zbyshko.

Matsko, who was not sleeping, looked at the stars, and answered, like a man of experience, —

"Dawn is not distant. Robbers would not attack at the end of night, for they must be at home before daylight."

Zbyshko, however, stopped the wagon, arranged his men across the road, faced those who were approaching, pushed forward himself, and waited.

Indeed, after a certain time, he saw in the darkness between ten and twenty horsemen. One rode in front a few yards in advance of the others; evidently he had no intention of hiding, for he was singing. Zbyshko could not hear his words, but to his ears came the joyous : "Hots! hots!" with which the unknown finished each verse of the song.

"Our people!" said he.

But after a while he called, —

"Stop!"

"And do thou sit still!" answered a jesting voice.
"What ones are ye?"
"What others are ye?"
"But why ride onto us?"
"Why do ye stop the road?"
"Answer, for our crossbows are drawn."
"But our bowstrings are stretched — shoot."
"Answer in human fashion, or there will be trouble."
A joyful song answered Zbyshko: —

> "One misery with another is dancing,
> Is dancing at the crossroad —
> Hots! hots! hots![1]
> What good is the dance to them?
> The dance is good, but the miseries —
> Hots! hots! hots!"

Zbyshko was astonished at hearing such an answer; but the song stopped, and the same voice inquired, —
"How is old Matsko? Is he breathing yet?"
Matsko rose up in the wagon, and said, —
"As God lives, that is one of our people!"
Zbyshko moved forward with his horse.
"Who is inquiring about Matsko?"
"A neighbor, Zyh of Zgorzelitse. I am riding a whole week after you, and inquiring of people along the road."
"Oh save us! Uncle! Zyh of Zgorzelitse is here!" cried Zbyshko.
They fell to greeting each other joyfully, for Zyh was their neighbor, and besides a kind man, loved everywhere for his immense joyousness.
"But how are you?" asked he, shaking Matsko's hand. "Is it hots yet, or is it not hots?"
"Hei, no longer hots," said Matsko. "But I am glad to see you. Dear God! this is as if I were already in Bogdanets."
"But how is it with you? I have heard that the Germans shot you."
"They shot me, the dog brothers. The arrow-point remained between my ribs."
"Fear God! Well, what have you done? Have you tried drinking bear's-fat?"
"You see," said Zbyshko, "every bear is full of fat. If

---

[1] The *o* in *hots* is long, like *o* in *note*.

we reach Bogdanets I will go at once in the night with an
axe to a bee's-nest."

"Maybe Yagenka has bear's fat; if not, I will send elsewhere to look for it."

"What Yagenka? But was not yours Malgosia?" inquired
Matsko.

"Oo! what Malgosia? On Saint Michael's it will be the
third autumn that Malgosia is lying in the priest's field. She
was a grand housekeeper — the Lord light her soul! But
Yagenka is like her, only she is young.

"Beyond the valleys shine the mountains;
As the mother, so the daughter —
Hots! hots!"

"But to Malgosia I used to say, 'Do not climb pine trees
when thou art fifty years old.' She would not obey me, she
climbed. A limb broke under her, and flop! she dug a hole
in the ground I tell you; but in three days she gave out her
last breath."

"The Lord light her!" said Matsko. "I remember, I
remember — when she put her hands on her hips and looked
threateningly the boys hid in the hay. But as to housekeeping she was accurate! And to think that she fell from a pine
tree! Do you see people!"

"She flew down like a pine cone in winter. Oi, but there
was grief! Do you know? after the funeral I got so drunk
from sorrow that they could not wake me for three days.
They thought that I too had turned my toes upward. And
how I cried! — you could not have carried out my tears in
a pail! But as to management, Yagenka is accurate. All
is on her head now."

"I hardly remember her. When I went away she was not
taller than an axe-handle. She could walk under a horse
without touching its belly. But that is long ago, and she
must have grown up."

"On Saint Agnes day she finished her fifteenth year; but
I have not seen her either for nearly a twelvemonth."

"What were you doing? Whence are you coming?"

"From the war. It is captivity for me to sit at home when
I have Yagenka."

Matsko, though sick, pricked up his ears eagerly at mention of war, and asked,—

"Were you, perhaps, with Prince Vitold at the Vorskla?"

"I was," said Zyh, joyously. "Well, the Lord God re

fused luck. We suffered a dreadful defeat from Edygeï.
First they killed our horses. The Tartar will not strike
hand to hand, like a Christian, but shoots from a distance
with bows. If thou press him he will flee, and shoot again.
Do thy best, he will have his way. See you, in our army the
knights boasted without bounds, and talked thus : ' We will
not even level a lance, nor draw swords ; we will just dash
that vermin apart with our horse-hoofs.' So they boasted
till shafts groaned around them, till the air was dark with
arrows; and after the battle, what? Barely one out of ten
was alive. Will you believe? More than half the army,
with seventy Lithuanian and Russian princes, remained on
the field; and as to boyars and various courtiers, or whatever
they are called, youths, you could not count them in less
than a fortnight — "

"I have heard," interrupted Matsko. "And of our
auxiliary knights a great many fell also."

"Yes, even nine Knights of the Cross, for these too had
to serve Vitold. And of our people a crowd, for, as you
know, others may look behind, but our people never. The
Grand Prince had most confidence in Polish knights, and
would have no guard but them near his person in battle.
Hi! hi! They lay like a pavement around him, and nothing
touched Vitold! Pan Spytko of Melshtyn fell, and Bernat,
the swordbearer, and Mikolai, the cupbearer, and Prokop,
and Pretslav, and Dobrogost, Yasko of Lazevitse, Pilik
Mazur, Varsh of Mihov, Soha the voevoda, Yasko of Dom-
brova, Pietrko of Miloslavie, Schepetski, and Oderski, and
Tomko Lagoda. Who could count them all? And I have
seen some so filled with arrows that they looked like dead
hedgehogs, till laughter seized me at sight of them."

Then he laughed outright, as if telling the most amusing
thing possible, and began to sing at once, —

> " Oi, thou wilt learn what the Tartar is,
>   When he has rubbed thy skin well ! "

" Well, afterward what? " asked Zbyshko.

" Afterward the Grand Prince fled ; but straightway he
took courage as he does always. The more thou bend him,
the better he springs, like a hazel twig. We rushed then to
defend the Tavan ford. A handful of new knights came
from Poland. All quiet ! Very well ! Edygeï came next day
with a Tartar host, but did nothing. Oh, it was pleasant !
Wherever he tried to pass the ford we gave it in the

snout to him. He could not pass anywhere. We beat
them and seized not a few. I caught five myself, and am
taking them home. You will see in the daylight their dog
snouts."

" In Cracow people said that war may come to our
kingdom."

" But is Edygeï a simpleton? He knows well what a
knighthood we have; and this too, that the greatest knights
stayed at home, for the queen was displeased when Vitold
began the war single-handed. Ei, he is cunning — old
Edygeï! He noticed immediately at Tavan that the prince
grew in strength, and he went back far away beyond the
ninth land!"

" But you returned?"

" I returned. There is nothing there to do now. In
Cracow I learned that you started a little before me."

" How did you know that we were the persons?"

" I knew because I inquired at halting-places everywhere."
Here he turned to Zbyshko. " Ei, my God, I saw thee a
little fellow the last time, but now even in the dark I see
thee as big as a wild bull. And thou art ready at once
to draw the crossbow! It is clear that thou hast been in
war."

" War reared me from childhood. Let uncle tell if I lack
experience."

" Your uncle has no need to say anything. In Cracow
I saw Povala of Tachev — he told me about thee. Likely
that Mazovian does not wish to give thee his daughter, but
I would not be so stubborn, for thou pleasest me. Thou
wilt forget her, only look at my Yagenka. She is a turnip!"

" Not true! I will not forget though I saw ten like your
Yagenka."

" Mochydoly, where the mill is, will go with her; when I
went away there were twelve good mares in the meadows
with their colts. More than one man will bow down to me
for Yagenka — never fear!"

Zbyshko wanted to answer, " But not I!" when Zyh
began to sing again, —

> " I will bow down to your knees,
>   And for that give me Yagna.
>   God grant you! — "

" Gladness and singing are in your head always," remarked Matsko.

"Yes, but what are blessed souls doing in heaven?"

"Singing."

"Well, see then! And the damned weep. I would rather go to the singing than the weeping ones. Saint Peter will say too: 'We must admit him to paradise or the rascal will sing in hell, and that would not be proper.' See, it is dawning already."

And indeed day was coming. After a while they rode out onto a broad plain, where everything was visible. On a lake occupying the greater part of the plain some people were fishing, but at sight of armed men they threw their nets aside, rushed from the water, seized their spears and poles as quickly as might be, and stood in a threatening attitude, ready for battle.

"They have taken us for robbers," said Zbyshko, laughing. "Hei, fishermen! whose are ye?"

They stood some time in silence looking with distrust, but at last the oldest among them recognized the knights, and answered, —

"We belong to the reverend abbot of Tulcha."

"Our relative," said Matsko, "who holds Bogdanets in pledge. This must be his forest, though bought not long since."

"God help you, he buy! He fought for it with Vilk of Brozova, and evidently he won it. A year ago they were to meet on horseback with lances and long swords for all this side of the country here, but I know not how it ended, for I was gone at the time."

"Well, we are relatives, he will not fight with us; he may also remit some of the pledge money."

"He may. If only it accords with his will, he may add something of his own. He is a knightly abbot, for whom it is no novelty to cover his head with a helmet. And he is pious besides, and celebrates mass beautifully. But you must remember — when he thunders out during mass, the swallows under the roofs fly out of their nests. Well, and the glory of God increases."

"Why should I not remember? Why, with his breath he quenches a candle on the altar ten steps away. Has he looked in even once at Bogdanets?"

"Of course he has. He has settled five new men, with their wives, on cleared land. He has been with us too, for, as you know, he baptized for me Yagenka; he has always liked her very much, and he calls her his daughter."

" God grant him to leave me the men," said Matsko.

" Oh, of course! What are five men to such a rich person as he is? Besides, if Yagenka asks him, he will leave them."

Here the conversation ceased for a moment, since above the dark pine wood, and above the ruddy dawn the bright sun rose and lighted up the country. The knights greeted it with the usual " May He be praised!" and then, making the sign of the cross on themselves, they began morning prayers. Zyh finished first and striking his breast repeatedly, said to his companions, —

" Now I will look at you carefully. Hei, you have both changed! You, Matsko, must return to health, the first thing. Yagenka will nurse you, as there is no woman's care in your house. Yes, it is clear that a fragment is sticking between your ribs — and that is not very good." Here he turned to Zbyshko. " Do thou show thyself too — Oh, God of might! I remember thee as a little fellow, how thou wouldst climb over a colt's tail to his back; now, by all the — What a young knight! He has the clean lip of a stripling, but what shoulders! Such a man might close with a bear."

" What is a bear to him?" said Matsko, in answer. " He was younger than he is to-day when that Frisian called him a naked lip, and he, as that name did not please him, plucked out the Frisian's moustache right there."

" I know," said Zyh. " You fought afterward and took their retinue. Povala told me all.

" ' The German went out with great splendor,
But naked his snout when they buried him,
Hots! hots!'"

And he looked at Zbyshko with amusement in his eyes. Zbyshko, too, looked with great curiosity on Zyh's figure as tall as a pole, at his thin face with immense nose, and his round eyes full of laughter.

" Oh," said he, " with such a neighbor, if God would return health to uncle, there would not be any sadness."

" With a joyous neighbor there can be no quarrels," said Zyh. " But listen now to what I will say, in good, Christian fashion. You have not been at home for a long time ; you will find there no order. I will not say in the land management, for the abbot has done well — he has cleared a strip of forest and settled new men on it. But, as he has visited Bogdanets only occasionally, the storehouses will be empty; yes, and in the house itself there is hardly a bench, or a narrow straw-tick to lie down on. A sick man needs comfort. So, do you know what? Come with me. Stay at my house a short month or two; that will be to my heart, and during that time Yagenka will think of Bogdanets. Only depend on her, and let not your head ache about anything. Zbyshko will go to look after the management; I will bring to you the reverend abbot and you can reckon at once with him. The girl will take as much care of you, Matsko, as if you were her own father, and in sickness a woman's care is better than any other. Well, my friends, will you do as I beg you?"

"It is a known fact that you are a kind man, and have always been such," said Matsko, with emotion; "but, see you, if I am to die by this ugly iron in my ribs I prefer to die in my own house. Besides, at home, though a man be sick, he inquires about more than one thing, and arranges more things than one. Should God command me to that world — there is no help for it. Whether the care be greater or less, I shall not twist out. To hardships we are accustomed in war. An armful of pea-straw is pleasant to him who has slept for years on bare earth. But I thank you much for your kindliness, and if I shall not thank you sufficiently, God grant that Zbyshko will."

Zyh, really famous for kindness, and obliging in character, began again to insist and beg, but Matsko had grown stubborn. If he had to die he would die in his own house! He had suffered whole years through his absence from Bogdanets; so now, when the boundary was not distant, he would not renounce it for anything, even were it to be his last camping-place. God had been kind hitherto in even permitting "the old man" to drag himself that far.

Here he pushed away with his fists the tears which had risen under his eyelids, and looked around.

"If these pine woods belong to Vilk of Brozova," said he, "we shall arrive just after mid-day."

"Not Vilk owns them now, but the abbot," said Zyh.

The sick Matsko laughed at this and after a while added, —

"If they are the abbot's they may be ours sometime."

"Oh," cried Zyh, joyously, "a little while since you were talking of death, but now you would like to outlive the abbot."

"Not I would outlive him, but Zbyshko."

Further conversation was interrupted by sounds of horns

in the forest, which were heard far in advance of them. Zyh
reined his horse in at once, and listened.
"Some one is hunting, it would seem," said he. "Wait
a while! It may be the abbot — it would be well if you were
to meet him just now. But be quiet!"
Here he turned to the retinue.
"Halt!"
They halted. The horns sounded nearer, and a little
while later the barking of dogs was heard.
"Halt!" repeated Zyh. "They are coming toward us."
Zbyshko sprang from his horse, and cried, —
"Give me the crossbow! Mayhap a beast will run out
of the forest. Quick! quick!"
And seizing the crossbow from the hands of an attendant,
he pushed it against the ground, pressed it with his stomach,
bent, stretched his back into the form of a bow, and grasping the string in both hands pulled it up in the twinkle of an
eye to an iron notch, then he put in an arrow and sprang
forward into the pine wood.
"He stretched the string without a crank!" whispered
Zyh, astonished at the sight of strength so uncommon.
"Ho! he is a deadly fellow!" whispered Matsko, with
pride.
Meanwhile the horns and the barking of dogs were heard
still nearer, till, all at once, on the right side of the forest
was heard a heavy trampling, the crack of breaking twigs
and branches, and onto the road rushed, like lightning, an
old bearded bison, with gigantic head held low, with bloody
eyes, and tongue hanging out. He was panting terribly.
Coming out at a hole by the roadside he crossed it with a
bound, fell on his forefeet, but rose quickly and was ready
to vanish on the opposite side of the road in a thicket, when
the ominous string of the crossbow whizzed on a sudden,
the whistle of the shaft was heard, the beast reared, squirmed,
bellowed dreadfully, and tumbled to the earth as if struck
by a lightning flash.
Zbyshko stepped out from behind a tree, drew the string of
the crossbow a second time, and, ready to shoot, approached
the prostrate beast, which was still digging the earth with its
hind feet. But after he had looked a while he turned calmly
to the retinue, and cried from a distance, —
"He has so got it that he is dying!"
"But just think," said Zyh, approaching, "from one
arrow!"

"Oh, it was a close shot, and he was running tremendously. Look! not only the point, but the shaft is hidden entirely just behind his foreleg."

"The hunters must be near; surely they will take him."

"I will not give him!" answered Zbyshko; "he was killed on the road, and no one owns the road."

"But if the abbot is hunting?"

"If it is the abbot, let him take the beast."

Meanwhile some tens of dogs rushed from the woods. When they saw the bison they sprang at him with a terrible uproar, fastened to his body in a crowd, and began soon to fight among themselves.

"The hunters will come immediately," said Zyh. "Look, there they are already! but they have come out some distance in front of us and do not see the beast yet. Hop! hop! come this way, come this way! It is lying here! lying here!"

But all at once he was silent, and shaded his eyes with his hand.

"For God's sake, what is this?" called he, after a while. "Am I blind, or am I deceived —"

"There is one in front on a black horse," said Zbyshko.

But Zyh exclaimed quickly, —

"Dear Jesus! As I live, that is Yagenka!"

And he began to shout, —

"Yagna! Yagna!"

Then he rushed forward, but before he could urge his steed to a gallop, Zbyshko saw the most wonderful sight in the world: On a swift pied horse hastened toward them, sitting man fashion, a young girl with a crossbow in her hand and a spear at her shoulder. To her hair, which had dropped down somewhat from the speed of riding, had clung wild hops, her face was as ruddy as the dawn, on her breast was an open shirt, above the shirt a coat with the wool inside. When she had ridden up she reined in her horse suddenly. For a moment incredulity, astonishment, and delight were depicted on her features; but at last, unable to gainsay the testimony of her ears and eyes, she began to cry with a thin voice, which was still somewhat childlike, —

"Tatulo! tatulo!"

In one twinkle she slipped from her horse, and when Zyh had sprung down from his beast to greet her on the ground, she flung herself on his neck. For a long time Zbyshko heard only the sound of kisses and the two words: "Tatulo! (Papa dear!) Yagula! (Aggie dear!)" "Tatulo! Yagula!" repeated with delight.

Both escorts came up; Matsko came also in his wagon, and they were still repeating, "Tatulo! Yagula!" and still had their arms around each other's necks. When at last they had had sufficient exclamations and greetings, Yagenka inquired,—

"Then are you coming from the war? Are you well?"

"From the war. Why should I not be well? And thou? And the younger people? I think they are well — are they not? Otherwise thou wouldst not be flying through the forest. But what is the best that thou art doing here, girl?"

"Thou seest that I am hunting," replied Yagenka, laughing.

"In other people's forests?"

"The abbot gave permission. Besides, he sent me trained men and dogs."

Here she turned to her servants.

"Take off the dogs for me; they will tear the beast's hide!"

Then she addressed Zyh, —

"Oh, but I am glad, glad to be looking at you! All is well at home."

"But am I not glad?" replied Zyh. "Give thy face again, girl!"

And again they began to kiss, and when they had finished Yagenka said,—

"There is a long piece of road from here to the house — so far did we chase after that beast. As many as ten miles, so that the horses are tired. But he is a strong bison — have you seen? He has three of my arrows in him; he must have fallen from the last one."

"He fell from the last one, but not from thine; this young knight here shot him."

Yagenka gathered back her hair, which had dropped to her eyes, and looked quickly at Zbyshko, though not with excess of good-will.

"Dost thou know who he is?" inquired Zyh.

"I do not."

"No wonder that thou dost not know him, for he has grown. But perhaps thou knowest old Matsko of Bogdanets?"

"For God's sake! is that Matsko of Bogdanets?" cried Yagenka.

And approaching the wagon she kissed Matsko's hand.
"Is this you?"

"It is I.   But in a wagon, for the Germans shot me."

"What Germans?   The war surely was with Tartars!   I
know that, for I begged papa not a little to take me with
him."

"There was war with the Tartars, but we were not at
that war, for earlier we were fighting in Lithuania, I and
Zbyshko."

"But where is Zbyshko?"

"Dost thou not know that this is Zbyshko?" asked
Matsko, with a smile.

"Is that Zbyshko?" cried the girl, looking again at the
young knight.

"Of course it is!"

"Give him thy lips for acquaintance!" cried Zyh,
joyously.

Yagenka turned briskly toward Zbyshko, but drew back
on a sudden, and covering her eyes with her hands said,—

"If I am ashamed?"

"But we are acquainted from childhood," said Zbyshko.

"Ah, we know each other well. I remember, I remember! About eight years ago you and Matsko came to us,
and my dead mother brought us nuts and honey. But you,
as soon as the older ones went from the room, put a fist to
my nose, and ate the nuts yourself."

"He would not do that now," said Matsko.   "He has
been with Prince Vitold, and in Cracow at the castle, and
knows courtly customs."

But something else came to Yagenka's head, for turning
to Zbyshko, she asked,—

"Then it was you who killed the bison?"

"I."

"Let us see where the arrow is."

"You will not see, for it is hidden entirely behind the
fore leg."

"Never mind, do not examine," said Zyh.   "We all saw
how he shot him, and we saw something better yet, for he
drew the crossbow in a second without a crank."

Yagenka looked a third time at Zbyshko, but now with
astonishment.

"Did you draw the crossbow without a crank?" asked
she.

Zbyshko felt, as it were, a certain incredulity in her voice,

so he put on the earth the end of the crossbow from which
he had shot before, drew it in a twinkle till the iron hoop
squeaked, then, wishing to show that he knew court customs,
he knelt on one knee and gave it to Yagenka.

The girl, instead of taking it from his hands, blushed suddenly without herself knowing why, and drew up around her
neck the coarse linen shirt which had opened from swift
riding through the forest.

CHAPTER VIII.

The day after their arrival at Bogdanets Matsko and Zbyshko began to look around at their old seat, and soon saw that Zyh spoke correctly when he said that privations not a few would annoy them at first.

In the land management matters moved after a fashion. A few acres were worked by old-time men, or those settled in recently by the abbot. Formerly there had been far more cultivated land in Bogdanets, but from the period when the race of " the Grady " perished to the second last man in the battle of Plovtsi there was a lack of working-hands, and after the attack of the Silesian Germans and the war of the Grymaliti with the Nalenchi, the fields of Bogdanets, formerly fruitful, had grown over for the greater part with forests. Matsko could do nothing unaided. In vain had he tried some years before to attract free cultivators from Kresnia and give them land beyond the meadows, but these preferred to sit on their own " small plots " to working large fields owned by other men. He enticed in, however, some homeless people, and in various wars seized a few prisoners, whom he had married and then settled in cottages ; in this way the village began to increase anew.

But Matsko met difficulty in management ; hence, when a chance to pledge the place offered itself, he mortgaged all Bogdanets quickly, thinking first, that it would be easier for the rich abbot to manage the land, and second, that war would help Zbyshko and him to men and to money.

The abbot had worked indeed actively. He had increased the laboring force in Bogdanets by five families ; he had increased the herds of horses and cattle ; besides, he had built a granary, a brush cow-house, and also a stable of similar material. But, as he was not living in Bogdanets permanently, he had not thought of a house, and Matsko, who had supposed sometimes that when he came back he would find a castle surrounded by a moat and a palisade, found all as he had left it, — with this difference only, that the corners of the house had grown a little crooked and the walls appeared lower, for they had settled and sunk in the earth somewhat.

The house was composed of an enormous front room, two

spacious inner apartments, with chambers and a kitchen.
In the inner rooms were windows with panes of membrane.
In the middle of each room, on a floor made of clay, was a
fireplace from which smoke issued through holes in the ceiling.   This ceiling was blackened completely.   In better
times it had served also as a smoking place, for on hooks
fixed in the beams hung in those days hams of pigs, wild
boars, bears, and elks, hind legs of deer, backs of oxen, and
whole strings of sausage.   In Bogdanets the hooks were
now empty, as well as shelves along the walls, on which in
other " courts " were placed earthen and tin plates.   But
the walls under the shelves did not seem now too naked, for
Zbyshko had commanded his people to hang on them breastplates, helmets, short and long swords, and farther on,
spears, forks, crossbows, and horse-trappings.   The armor
grew black from being hung in the smoke thus, and there
was need to clean it frequently; but, to compensate, everything was at hand; and besides, worms did not gnaw the
wood of lances, crossbows, and axehandles.   Matsko had
commanded to carry carefully to his own sleeping room all
valuable clothing.

In the front chambers, near the windows, were tables of
pine plank, and benches of like material on which the
masters sat down to eat with the servants.   For men unaccustomed during long years of war to comforts, not much
was needed.   But in Bogdanets, bread, flour, and various
other supplies were lacking, and especially utensils.   The
peasants had brought in what they could.   Matsko had
counted mainly on this, that, as happens in such cases,
neighbors would aid him ; and indeed he was not mistaken,
at least not in Zyh.

The second day after his arrival Matsko, wishing to enjoy
the serene autumn weather, was seated on a log before the
house, when Yagenka rode into the yard on the same horse
which she had ridden at the hunt.   The servant, who was
cutting wood near the fence, wished to help her dismount,
but she sprang down in one instant, panting a little from
swift riding, and ruddy as an apple she approached Matsko.

" May He be praised ! I have come to bow down to you
from papa, and to ask about your health."

" It is not worse than on the road," answered Matsko;
" a man has slept in his own house at least."

" But you must feel much discomfort, and a sick man needs
care."

"We are firm fellows. There are no comforts yet, of course, but there is no hunger either. I have commanded to kill an ox and two sheep; there is meat enough. The women have brought in too some flour and eggs, but that is not much with us, the greatest lack is utensils."

"Well, I have had two wagons filled. In one of them are two beds, and cooking utensils ; in the other, food of various kinds. There are cakes and flour, salt meat, dried mushrooms, a small keg of beer, another of mead; there is a little of everything that we have in the house."

Matsko, always pleased with every addition, stretched out his hand and stroked Yagenka's head.

"God repay thee, and thy father. When we begin to manage we will return this."

"God prosper you! But are we Germans, to take back what we give?"

"Well, then God will pay thee and thy father still more. Thy father told what a housekeeper thou art. Thou hast managed all thy father's place for a twelvemonth."

"Yes! And when you want something more send a man, but one who knows what is needed, for at times a dull servant comes who knows not what he was sent for."

Here Yagenka began to-look around somewhat. Matsko, noting this, smiled, and asked, —

"For whom art thou looking ?"

"I am not looking for any one !"

"I will send Zbyshko; let him thank thee and Zyh for me. Has Zbyshko pleased thee ? "

"But I have not looked at him."

"Then look at him now, for he is just coming."

Indeed Zbyshko was coming from watering animals, and seeing Yagenka he hastened his step. He wore an elkskin coat and a round felt cap such as was used under helmets, his hair was without a net, cut evenly above his brows, and at the sides it fell in golden waves to his shoulders. He approached quickly, large, comely, exactly like an armor-bearer of a great house.

Yagenka turned entirely to Matsko to show that she had come only to him, but Zbyshko greeted her joyously, and taking her hand raised it to his lips in spite of the girl's resistance.

"Why kiss me on the hand?" inquired she. "Am I a priest? "

"Resist not! Such is the custom! "

" And should thou kiss her on the other hand for what she has brought," put in Matsko, " it would not be too much."

" What has she brought ? " inquired Zbyshko, looking around in the yard, not seeing anything save the horse tied to a post.

" The wagons have not come yet, but they will come," answered Yagenka.

Matsko began to name what she had brought, not omitting anything. When he mentioned the two beds Zbyshko said :

" I am glad to lie down on an oxskin, but I thank you for having thought of me also."

" It was not I, but papa," said the girl, blushing. " If you prefer a skin you are free to prefer it."

" I prefer what comes to hand. On the field more than once after battle we slept with a dead Knight of the Cross for a pillow."

" But have you ever killed a Knight of the Cross ?   Surely not ! "

Zbyshko, instead of answering, began to laugh.

" Fear God, girl! " cried Matsko; " thou dost not know him! He has done nothing else but kill Germans till it thundered. He is ready for lances, for axes, for everything; and when he sees a German from afar, even hold him on a rope, he will pull to him. In Cracow he wanted to slay Lichtenstein, the envoy, for which they lacked little of cutting his head off. That is the kind of man he is! And I will tell thee of the two Frisians from whom we took their retinue, and a booty so valuable that with one half of it one might buy Bogdanets."

Here Matsko told of the duel with the Frisians, and then of other adventures which had met them, and deeds which they had accomplished. They had fought behind walls, and in the open field with the greatest knights from foreign lands. They had fought with Germans, French, English, and Burgundians. . They had been in raging whirls of battle, when horses, men, arms, Germans, and feathers formed one mass, as it were. And what had they not seen besides! They had seen castles of red brick belonging to Knights of the Cross, Lithuanian wooden fortresses, and churches such as there are not near Bogdanets, and towns, and savage wildernesses, in which Lithuanian divinities, driven out of their sanctuaries, whine in the night-time ; and various marvels. And in all places where it came to battle Zbyshko was in front, so that the greatest knights wondered at him.

Yagenka, who had sat down on the log near Matsko, listened with parted lips to that narrative, turning her head, as if on a pivot, now toward Matsko, now toward Zbyshko, and looking at the young knight with ever increasing wonder. At last, when Matsko had finished, she sighed, and said:

"Would to God that I had been born a man!"

Zbyshko, who during the narrative was looking at her with equal attention, was thinking at that moment of something else evidently, for he said on a sudden, —

"But you are a beautiful maiden!"

"You are more beautiful than I, you see that," said Yagenka, half unwillingly, half in sadness.

Zbyshko might without untruth have replied that he had not seen many maidens like her, for Yagenka was simply radiant with a splendor of health, youth, and strength. It was not without reason that the old abbot declared that she looked half a raspberry, half a pine tree. Everything about her was beautiful, her lithe form, her broad shoulders, her breast as if chiselled from stone, red lips, and blue eyes quickly glancing. She was dressed more carefully than before at the hunt in the forest. She had red beads around her neck, she wore a sheepskin coat open in front and covered with green cloth, a petticoat of strong striped stuff, and new boots. Even old Matsko noted the handsome dress while looking at her, and when he had looked at her a while he inquired, —

"But why art thou arrayed as if for a festival?"

Instead of answering she called out, —

"The wagons are coming! the wagons are coming!"

As they came in she sprang toward them, and after her followed Zbyshko. The unloading continued till sunset, to the great satisfaction of Matsko, who examined every article separately, and praised Yagenka for each one. Twilight had come when the girl was preparing for home. When ready to mount Zbyshko seized her around the waist suddenly, and before she could utter one word he had raised her to the saddle and fixed her there. She blushed like the dawn and turned her face toward him.

"You are a strong lad," said she, in a voice suppressed somewhat.

Zbyshko who because of the darkness took no note of her confusion and blushes, laughed, and inquired, —

" But have you no fear of beasts? Night will come straightway."

" There is a spear in the wagon — give it to me."

Zbyshko went to the wagon, took out a spear, and handed it to her.

" Be well! "

" Be well! "

" God repay you! I will go to-morrow, or the next day to your father's house to bow down to him, and to you for your neighborly kindness."

" Come! We shall be glad! "

And urging forward her horse she vanished in a moment among the thickets by the roadside. Zbyshko turned to his uncle.

" It is time for you to go in."

But Matsko answered without moving from the log, —

" Hei! what a girl! The yard was just bright from her."

" Surely! "

A moment of silence came next. Matsko appeared to be thinking of something while looking at the stars which were coming out; then he continued, as if to himself, —

" And active, and a housekeeper, though not more than fifteen years of age."

" Yes," said Zbyshko, " and old Zyh loves her as the eye in his head."

" They say that Mochydoly will go with her, and there in the meadows is a herd of mares with their colts."

" But in the Mochydoly forests there are terrible swamps, very likely."

" There are beaver dams in them also."

Again followed silence. Matsko looked aslant some time at Zbyshko, and asked at last, —

" What art thou thinking of ? Thou art meditating on some subject."

" Yes, for, see you, Yagenka so reminded me of Danusia that something pained me in the heart."

" Let us go to the house," said the old man. " It is late." And rising with difficulty he leaned on Zbyshko, who conducted him to his room.

Next morning Zbyshko went directly to Zyh's house, for Matsko hurried the visit greatly. He insisted also that for show's sake his nephew should have two attendants, and array himself in his best, so as to show honor in that way and exhibit due gratitude. Zbyshko yielded and went arrayed as if for a wedding, in that same gold-embroidered, golden-clasped, white-satin jacket won by them. Zyh received him with open arms, with delight and with songs. Yagenka, on reaching the threshold of the main room, stopped as if fixed to the spot, and came near dropping the pitcher of wine when she saw Zbyshko, for she thought that some king's son had come to them. She lost her boldness immediately and sat in silence, merely rubbing her eyes from time to time, as if trying to rouse herself from slumber.

Zbyshko, who lacked experience, thought that for reasons which he knew not, she was not glad to see him; so he talked only to Zyh, praising his bounty as a neighbor and admiring his court, which really resembled Bogdanets in nothing.

Abundance and wealth were there visible on all sides. In the rooms were windows with panes of horn scraped so smooth and thin that they were almost as transparent as glass. There were no fires in the middle of rooms, but great chimneys with niches in the corners. The floor was of larch plank well washed, on the walls were arms and a multitude of plates, shining like the sun, a beautifully cut-out spoon-rack with rows of spoons, two of which were silver. In one place and another hung carpets plundered in wars, or obtained from travelling merchants. Under the tables lay gigantic tawny skins of wild bulls, also skins of wild boars and bisons.

Zyh showed his wealth with willingness, saying from moment to moment that that was Yagenka's housekeeping. He conducted Zbyshko also to a room, odorous of pitch and mint, from the ceiling of which hung wolf, fox, beaver, and marten skins in whole bundles. He showed him the cheese house, he showed stores of wax and honey, barrels of flour and rusks, hemp, and dried mushrooms. Then he took him to the granaries, the cowhouses, the stables and pens, to sheds in which were wagons, implements for hunting, with nets for fishing, and so dazzled his eyes with abundance that when the young man came back to supper he could not refrain from expressions of wonder.

"One should live here and never die," said Zbyshko.

"In Mochydoly there is almost the same order," said Zyh. "Thou dost remember Mochydoly? That is toward Bogdanets. Formerly our fathers quarrelled about the boundary, and sent challenges to each other to fight, but I will not quarrel."

Here he touched his tankard of mead with Zbyshko's, and asked, —

" But, perhaps, thou hast the wish to sing something? "

" No," replied Zbyshko, " I listen to you with curiosity."

" The young bears, seest thou, will get this place. If only they do not fight about it some time! "

" How, the young bears? "

" Yes, the boys, Yagenka's brothers."

" Hei! they will not need to suck their paws in winter."

" Oh no. But neither will Yagenka's mouth in Mochydoly lack a bit of cheese."

" Surely not! "

" But why not eat and drink? Yagenka, pour out to him and to me! "

" I am eating and drinking as much as I am able."

" If thou art not able to eat more, ungirdle — That is a beautiful belt! Ye must have taken brave booty in Lithuania? "

" We make no complaint," answered Zbyshko, who used the occasion to show that the heirs of Bogdanets were not poor little possessors. " We sold a part of the booty in Cracow and received forty gryvens of silver — "

" Fear God! One might buy a village for that much."

" Yes, for there was one suit of Milan armor which uncle sold when expecting to die, and that, you know — "

" I know! That is worth going to Lithuania for. In my time I wanted to go, but I was afraid."

" Of what? The Knights of the Cross? Ei, who is afraid of the Germans? Why fear till they attack? — and when they attack there is no time for fear. I was afraid of those pagan gods or devils. In the forest there are as many of them as of ants, very likely."

" But where are they to live, since their temples are burnt? In old times they had plenty, but now they live only on ants and mushrooms."

" But hast thou seen them? "

" I have not seen them myself, but I have heard that people do see them. One of those devils will thrust out his hairy paw from behind a tree, and shake it, asking to give him something."

" Matsko said the same thing." remarked Yagenka.

" Yes, on the road he said the same thing to me," added Zyh. " Well, it is no wonder! For that matter, with us here, though the country is Christian this long time, some-

thing laughs in the swamps, and even in houses; though the
priests scold, it is better always to put out a plate of food
for the imps, or they will scrape on the wall so that thou
wilt not close an eye — Yagenka! put out a plate on the
threshold, daughter."

Yagenka took an earthen plate full of paste with cheese
and put it on the threshold.

"The priests blame and punish!" said Zyh. "But the
glory of the Lord Jesus will not be decreased by some paste;
and when satisfied and well-wishing, the imps will guard a
man from fire, and from evil-doers."

"Thou mightst ungirdle and sing something," said he,
turning to Zbyshko.

"Sing you, for I see that you have the wish this long
time; but perhaps Panna Yagenka would sing?"

"We will sing in turn," cried Zyh, rejoiced. "There is
a lad in the house too who plays on a wooden flute and
accompanies us. Call him!"

They called the lad, who took his seat on a block, put the
flute to his mouth, spread his fingers over it, and looked at
those present, waiting to see whom he was to accompany.

They began to dispute then, for none wished to be first.
Finally Zyh commanded Yagenka to set an example; Yagenka, though greatly abashed before Zbyshko, rose from the
bench, put her hands under her apron, and began, —

"Oh, had I wings like a wild goose,
   I would fly after Yasek, I would fly after him to Silesia!"

Zbyshko opened his eyes widely to begin with, then sprang
to his feet and cried in a loud voice, —

"Whence do you know that?"

Yagenka looked at him with astonishment.

"But all sing it here. What wonder to you?"

Zyh, who thought that Zbyshko had drunk a little too
much, turned to him with delighted face, and said, —

"Ungirdle thyself! It will be easier right away."

Zbyshko stood for a while with changing face, then mas-
tering his emotion he said to Yagenka, —

"Pardon me. I remembered something unexpectedly.
Sing on."

"Maybe it makes you sad to listen?"

"Ei, why?" asked he, with a quivering voice. "I could
listen all night to that song."

Then he sat down, covered his brows with his hand, and was silent, not wishing to lose a word. Yagenka sang the second verse, but when she had finished it she saw a great tear passing over Zbyshko's fingers; then she pushed up to him quickly, and touching him with her elbow inquired, —

"Well, what is the matter? I do not wish you to weep. Tell what the matter is."

"Nothing! nothing!" replied Zbyshko, with a sigh. "It would take long to tell. What happened has passed. I am more cheerful now."

"Perhaps you might drink some sweet wine."

"Honest girl!" cried Zyh. "Why say 'you' to each other? Say 'Zbyshko' to him, and say thou 'Yagenka' to her. Ye knew each other from childhood." Then he turned to his daughter. "That he beat thee in the old time is nothing! He will not do so now."

"I will not," said Zbyshko, joyously. "Let her beat me if she chooses."

At this Yagenka, wishing to amuse him perfectly, closed her hand, and while laughing pretended to beat him.

"Here is for my broken nose! and here! and here!"

"Wine!" cried the jollified Zyh.

Yagenka ran to the cellar and soon brought out a stone jug full of wine, two beautiful tankards ornamented with silver flowers, wrought by silversmiths of Vrotslav, and two cakes of cheese, odorous from afar.

This sight made Zyh, who had something in his head, altogether tender; so gathering the stone jug to himself he pressed it to his bosom, feigning to think it Yagenka, and repeated, —

"Oi, my dear daughter! Oi, poor orphan! What shall I, lone unfortunate, do here when thou art taken from me? What shall I do?"

"You will have to give her away before long!" cried out Zbyshko.

In the twinkle of an eye Zyh passed from tenderness to laughter.

"Hi! hi! The girl is fifteen years of age, but she is drawn toward those two boys already! When she sees one from afar her knees smite each other."

"Papa, I will go away!" said Yagenka.

"Go not! It is pleasant in thy company."

Then he blinked mysteriously at Zbyshko.

"The two will come here: one, young Vilk, son of old Vilk of Brozova; the other, Stan of Rogov. If they should find thee here they would grit their teeth at thee as they do at each other."

"Oh!" exclaimed Zbyshko.

Then he turned to Yagenka, and saying "thou" to her according to Zyh's command, he inquired,—

"Which one dost thou prefer?"

"Neither."

"But Vilk is strong!" remarked Zyh.

"Let him howl in some other direction!" retorted Yagenka.

"And Stan?"

Yagenka laughed.

"Stan," said she, turning to Zbyshko, "has as much hair on his face as a goat, his eyes are covered; and there is as much fat on him as on a bear."

Zbyshko struck his head as if remembering something on a sudden, and said,—

"But if ye would be so kind I should beg of you; have ye not bear's fat in the house? My uncle needs it for medicine, and in our house I have not been able to find any."

"We had some," said Yagenka, "but the men took it to rub on their bows, and the dogs ate what was left."

"Was none left?"

"They licked it up clean."

"There is no way but to look for fat in the woods."

"Call a hunt; there is no lack of bears, and shouldst thou need hunter's gear we will give it."

"How can I wait? I will go for a night to the bee nests."

"Take about five assistants. There are good fellows among them."

"I will not go with a crowd; they would frighten the beast away."

"How then? Wilt thou go with a crossbow?"

"What should I do with a crossbow in the dark in a forest. Besides, the moon does not shine at present. I will take a barbed fork, with a good axe, and go alone to-morrow."

Yagenka was silent for a while, then alarm was evident on her face.

"Last year," said she, "Bezduh, a hunter, went from here, and a bear tore him to pieces. It is always most dangerous, for when the bear sees a lone man in the night, and moreover at bee nests, he stands on his hind legs immediately."

"Should he run away, thou wouldst never get him," answered Zbyshko.

Zyh, who had been dozing, woke up on a sudden, and began to sing,—

> "But thou, Kuba, art coming from labor,
> And I, Matsek, am coming from sport!
> Go early with plow to the clear land,
> But I 'd rather visit with Kasia the wheat,
> Hots! hots!"

Then he said to Zbyshko, —

"Thou knowest there are two of them: Vilk of Brozova, and Stan of Rogov — and thou — "

But Yagenka, fearing lest Zyh might say too much, approached Zbyshko quickly, and inquired,—

"And when wilt thou go? To-morrow?"

"To-morrow after sunset."

"To what bee nests?"

"To ours in Bogdanets, not far from your hillocks, at the side of the Radzikov swamp. People tell me that there bears are found easily."

CHAPTER IX.

ZBYSHKO set out as he had said, for Matsko felt worse, considerably. In the beginning delight and the first occupations at home enlivened him, but his fever returned on the third day, and the pain in his side made itself felt so acutely that he was forced to lie down. Zbyshko made a first visit to the forest in the daytime, examined the bee nests, and saw that near them was an immense trail to the swamp. He spoke with the bee keeper, Vavrek, who slept near by at night in a hut, with a couple of fierce shepherd dogs of Podhale; but Vavrek was just about moving to the village because of severe autumn frosts.

The two men pulled the hut apart, took the dogs in hand, and smeared a little honey here and there on the trees to lure the bear on by its odor. Zbyshko went home then and prepared for the trial. For warmth's sake he put on a sleeveless short coat of elkskin, and also an iron helmet with wire cape, lest the bear might tear his scalp off; he took then a well-tempered fork with two barbed tines, and a broad steel axe on an oak handle, which was not so short as those used by carpenters. In his place at the time of evening milking, he selected a convenient spot, made the sign of the cross on himself, sat down, and waited.

The rays of the setting sun shone among the evergreen branches. Crows had assembled on the pine tops, cawing and clapping their wings; here and there hares were springing swiftly toward the water, making a rustle among berry bushes which were growing yellow, and among fallen leaves; at times the swift marten sped past. In the thickets was heard yet the twittering of birds, which ceased gradually.

At the moment of sunset there was no rest in the forest. A herd of wild boars, with great uproar and grunting, soon passed by near Zbyshko, then elks in a long row, each holding its head near the tail of another. The dry branches cracked beneath their hoofs, and the forest resounded, shining red in the sunrays; they were hastening to the swamp, where at night they felt safe and happy. At last the evening light shone in the sky; from this the tops of the pines seemed as if in fire, burning, and gradually all became quiet.

The forest went to sleep. Gloom rose from the earth and lifted itself toward the bright light of evening, which at last began to fail, to grow sombre, to be black, and to perish. "Now it will be silent till the wolves begin," thought Zbyshko.

He regretted, however, that he had not taken a crossbow, for he could have brought down an elk or a wild boar with ease. Meanwhile from the side of the swamp came for some time yet stifled voices, like painful groaning and whistling.

Zbyshko looked toward that swamp with a certain timidity, for the man Radzik, who on a time had lived in a mud hut there, had vanished with his family, as if he had dropped through the earth. Some said that robbers had borne them away, but there were persons who saw later along the side of the hut certain strange tracks, neither human nor animal, and they racked their heads over this greatly; they were even thinking whether or not to bring the priest from Kresnia to bless that place. It did not come to this, it is true, for no man was found willing to live there, and the hut, or rather the clay on the brush walls of it, dropped down during rain, but thenceforth the place enjoyed no good repute. Vavrek, the bee man, did not indeed care for that; he spent his nights there in summer, but there were various reports about Vavrek also.

Zbyshko, having a fork and an axe, had no fear of wild beasts, but he thought of unclean powers with a certain alarm, and was glad when these noises ceased finally.

The last gleams of light had vanished, and perfect night had come. The wind ceased; there was not even the usual sigh in the tops of the pine trees. Now and then here and there a pine cone fell, giving out on the background of the general stillness a far-reaching, sharp sound; except this, the silence was such that Zbyshko heard his own breathing.

He sat a long time in this manner, thinking first of the bear that might come, and then of Danusia, who was moving with the Mazovian court into distant regions. He remembered how he had caught her in his arms at the moment of parting with the princess, how her tears had flowed down his cheeks; he remembered her bright face, her blond head, her garland of star thistles, her singing, her red shoes with long tips, which he had kissed at the moment of parting, — finally, everything that had happened since they had become acquainted; and such sorrow seized him because she was not near, and such longing for her, that he was sunk in it thoroughly; he forgot that he was in the forest, that he was hunting a wild beast, and he said in his soul, —

"I will go to thee, for I cannot live without thee."

And he felt that this was true, that he must go to Mazovia; if not, he would perish in Bogdanets. Yurand came to his mind, and his wonderful resistance; hence he thought it all the more needful to go, and to learn what the secret was, what the obstacles were, and if some challenge to a mortal struggle might not remove them. Finally it seemed to him that Danusia was stretching her hands to him, and crying: "Come, Zbyshko, come!" How was he to avoid going to her?

He did not sleep — he saw her as clearly as in a vision or a dream. Behold, Danusia was riding near the princess, thrumming on her lute and singing. She was thinking to see him soon, and perhaps she was looking around to see if he were not galloping up behind them; meanwhile he was in the dark forest.

Here Zbyshko came to himself — and he came to himself, not merely because he saw the dark forest, but for the reason that from afar behind him was heard a certain rustling. He grasped the fork in his hands more firmly, held his ear forward, and listened.

The rustling approached and after a time became perfectly clear. Dry limbs crackled under cautious footsteps, the fallen leaves and the berry bushes gave out their sounds. Something was advancing.

At times the rustling ceased, as if the beast halted at trees, and then such silence set in that there was noise in Zbyshko's ears; then again were heard slow and careful footsteps. In general there was something so cautious in that approach that amazement seized Zbyshko.

"It must be that the 'Old Fellow' fears the dogs which have been at the hut here," said he to himself; "but perhaps a wolf sniffs me."

Meanwhile the steps ceased. Zbyshko heard clearly that something had halted, perhaps twenty or thirty steps behind him, and had sat down, as it seemed. He looked around once and a second time, but, though the trees were outlined clearly enough in the darkness, he could not see anything. There was no other way but to wait.

And he waited so long that astonishment seized him a second time.

" A bear would not come here to sleep under the bee nest, and a wolf would have smelt me and would not wait here till morning."

Suddenly shivers passed from head to foot through him.

" Had something 'foul' crawled from the swamps and come up from behind toward him? Would the slippery arms of some drowned one grasp hold of him unexpectedly, or the green eyes of a vampire leer into his face, or something laugh dreadfully there at his back, or some blue head on spider legs creep out from beyond a pine tree? "

And he felt that the hair was rising under his iron helmet.

But after a while rustling was heard in front, this time more distinctly than ever. Zbyshko drew a breath of relief. He admitted, it is true, that the same " wonder " had gone around him, and was approaching now from the front; but he preferred this. He grasped the fork well, rose in silence, and waited.

At that moment he heard the sound of the pine trees above his head, on his face he felt a strong breeze from the swamp, and the same instant there flew to his nostrils the odor of a bear.

There was not the least doubt now, the bear was approaching!

In a moment Zbyshko ceased to fear, and, inclining his head, he exerted his sight and his hearing. The steps came up, heavy, distinct, the odor grew sharper; soon panting and growling were heard.

" If only two are not coming! " thought Zbyshko.

But at that moment he saw before him the great and dark form of a beast which advancing with the wind could not smell him till the last moment, especially as the beast was occupied with the odor of honey rubbed on the tree trunks.

" Come on, grandfather! " cried Zbyshko, pushing out from behind the pine.

The bear gave a short roar, as if frightened by the unexpected vision, but was too near to save itself by flight, so in one instant it rose on its hind legs, opening its forelegs, as if to embrace. This was just what Zbyshko was waiting for; so, collecting himself, he sprang like lightning, and with all the power of his strong arms, together with his own weight, drove the fork into the bosom of the beast.

The whole forest trembled then from a penetrating roar. The bear seized the fork with his paws wishing to tear it away, but the barbs at the points held it in; so, feeling pain, he thundered all the more terribly. Trying to reach Zbyshko he pressed onto the fork and drove it into himself the more effectually. Zbyshko, not knowing whether the points had sunk deeply enough, did not let go the handle. The man and the beast pulled and struggled. The pine wood trembled unceasingly from the roar, in which rage and despair were united.

Zbyshko could not use the axe till he had first planted the other sharp end of the fork in the earth, and the bear, grasping the handle with his paws, shook both it and Zbyshko, as if understanding what the struggle meant, and, despite the pain caused by every movement of the deeply buried barbs, he did not let himself be " planted." In this way the terrible struggle continued, and Zbyshko understood that his strength would be worn out at last. He might fall, too, and in that case be lost; so he collected himself, stretched his arms, planted his feet apart, bent forward, like a bow, so as not to be thrown on his back, and in his excitement repeated through set teeth, —

" My death, or thine ! "

Finally such rage possessed him, and such resolution, that really he would have preferred at the moment to die, rather than let that bear go. At last his foot struck a root of the pine; he tottered and would have fallen had it not been that a dark figure stood by him; another fork " propped " the beast, and a voice right at his ear cried, —

" With the axe ! "

Zbyshko in the ardor of battle did not stop for the twinkle of an eye to learn whence the unexpected aid had come, but grasped his axe and struck terribly. The fork handle cracked, then broke from the weight and the last convulsions of the bear, which, as if struck by a lightning flash tumbled to the earth, and groaned there. But the groaning stopped immediately. Silence followed, broken only by the loud panting of Zbyshko, who leaned against the tree, for the legs were tottering under him. He raised his head only after a while, looked at the figure standing by his side, and was frightened, thinking that, perhaps, it was not a person.

" Who art thou ? " asked he, in alarm.

" Yagenka ! " answered a thin female voice.

Zbyshko was dumb from amazement, not believing his own ears.

But his doubt did not last long, for Yagenka's voice was heard again.

"I will strike a fire," said she.

At once the steel sounded against the flint, sparks flew, and with their twinkling light Zbyshko saw the white forehead and dark brows of the maiden, her lips pushed forward in blowing the lighted punk. Only then did he think that she had come to that forest to help him, that without her fork it might have gone ill with him, and he felt such immense gratitude that, without thinking long, he grasped her by the waist and kissed both her cheeks.

Her punk and steel fell to the ground.

"Let me go! What is this?" said she, in a smothered voice; still she did not push his face away; on the contrary, her lips even touched his, as if by accident.

He let her go, and said, —

"God reward! I know not what might have happened without thee."

Yagenka, feeling around in the darkness to find the punk and steel, began to explain, —

"I feared that something might harm thee. Bezduh went out also with a fork and an axe, but the bear tore him. God guard from that! Matsko would suffer; as it is, he is barely breathing. Well, I took the fork and came."

"So that was thou behind the pines there?"

"I."

"And I thought it was the ' evil one.' "

"No small fear seized me too, for here around the Radzikov swamp it is not well in the night without fire."

"Why didst thou not call?"

"I was afraid that thou mightst drive me away."

Then she struck fire again, and placed dry hemp-stalks on the punk; these shot up a bright flame immediately.

"I have two handfuls, but do thou collect dry limbs in a hurry; there will be a fire."

After a time a really cheerful fire burst forth, the flames of which shone on the enormous ruddy carcass of the bear, which was lying in a pool of blood.

"Ei! a savage creature!" said Zbyshko, with a certain boastfulness.

"But the head is almost cut in two! O Jesus!"

When she said this she bent down and buried her hand in the bear's fur to learn if he had much fat; then she raised it with a gladsome face.

"There will be fat for a couple of years!"

"But the fork is broken. Look!"

"That is a pity; what can I say at home?"

"What dost thou need to say?"

"Something, for papa would not have let me come to the forest, so I had to wait till all were in bed."

After a while she added, —

"Say not that I was here, so that they may not wonder at me."

"But I will conduct thee home, for the wolves might attack thee, and thou hast no fork."

"Well, do so!"

And they conversed thus for some time by the cheerful light of the fire, near the body of the bear, both like some young creatures of the forest.

Zbyshko looked at Yagenka's charming face, lighted by the gleam of the flame, and said in involuntary astonishment:

"Another girl like thee there is not in the whole world, I think. Thou shouldst go to the war!"

She looked into his eyes for a moment, then answered almost sadly, —

"I know — but do not laugh at me."

CHAPTER X.

YAGENKA herself melted out a large pot of bear's fat, the first quart of which Matsko drank with pleasure, for it was fresh, not burnt, and had the odor of angelica, which the girl, skilled in plants, had added to the pot in measure. Matsko was strengthened in spirit at once, and received hope of recovery.

"That was needed," said he. "When everything inside is oiled properly, that dog mother of an arrow-point may slip out of me somewhere."

The succeeding quarts did not taste so well to him as the first, but he drank because of good sense. Yagenka comforted him too, saying, —

"You will recover. Zbilud of Ostrog had a link of armor driven deeply into his shoulder, and it came out from bear's fat. But when the wound opens one must stop it with beaver fat."

"Hast thou that fat?"

"We have. If fresh fat is needed we can go with Zbyshko to the beaver dam. It is not hard to get beavers. But it would be no harm either, if you would make a vow to some saint who is a patron of the wounded."

"That came to my head also, but I know not well to what saint. Saint George is the patron of knights. He guards a warrior from accidents, and in need gives him valor; they say that often in his own person he stands on the just side and helps to conquer those who are hateful to God. But a saint who fights gladly is rarely willing to cure, and there is perhaps another with whom he would interfere if he did so. Every saint has his own work in heaven, his own management — that we understand. One of them never meddles with another, for disagreements might spring up, and in heaven it would not befit saints to dispute or to quarrel. There are Cosmo and Damian, great saints too; to these doctors pray, so that disease may not vanish from the earth; if it did doctors would have no subsistence. There is also Saint Appolonia for teeth, and Saint Liborious for the gravel — but all this is not to the point! The abbot will come and tell me to whom I should turn, for not every common priest knows all God's secrets, and not every one knows such things though he have a shaven head."

"But might you not make a vow to the Lord Jesus himself?"

"Certainly, because He is above all. But that would be as if, for example, thy father killed a peasant of mine and I should go with a complaint to the king at Cracow. What would the king say? He would say this to me: 'I am master over the whole kingdom, and thou comest to me with thy peasant! Are there not officials? Canst thou not go to the town, to my castellan, and my intermediary?' The Lord Jesus is master over the whole world — dost understand? but for small affairs He has saints."

"Then I will tell you what," said Zbyshko, who came in at the end of the conversation, "make a vow to our late queen that, if she acts for you, you will make a pilgrimage to her tomb in Cracow; are the miracles few that were performed in our presence there? Why seek foreign saints when we have our own lady, who is better than others?"

"True! If I knew that she was for wounds."

"And if she is not for wounds! No common saint will dare refuse her, and should he refuse she will get what she asks from the Lord God, for she is no ordinary weaver woman, but the Queen of Poland."

"Who brought the last pagan land to the Christian faith. Thou hast spoken wisely," said Matsko. "She must stand high in God's counsels, and it is certain that no common person will contradict her. So, to gain health, I will do as thou sayest."

This advice pleased also Yagenka, who could not refrain from admiring Zbyshko's good sense; and Matsko made a solemn vow that same evening, and thenceforth drank bear's fat with still greater confidence, waiting from day to day for unfailing recovery. But in a week he began to lose hope. He said that the fat was "storming," in his stomach, and on his skin near the last rib something was rising which looked like a knob. After ten days he was still worse; the lump increased and grew red; Matsko was very weak, and when a fever came he began to prepare again for death. On a certain night he roused Zbyshko on a sudden.

"Light the torch quickly," said he, "for something is happening me, — whether good or bad, I know not."

Zbyshko sprang to his feet, and, without striking a flint, blew a fire in the next room, lighted a pine torch and returned.

" What is the matter? "

" What is the matter with me? Something has pricked through the knob! Surely an arrow-head! I hold it! I cannot pull it out, but I feel it clink and move."

" The point! nothing else. Catch it firmly and pull."

Matsko squirmed and hissed from pain, but he thrust his fingers deeper and deeper till he held the hard object firmly; then he dragged and pulled.

" O Jesus ! "

" You have it? " asked Zbyshko.

" I have. Cold sweat has come out on me. But here it is! Look ! "

He showed Zbyshko a long, sharp splinter which had broken from the badly bound arrow and had stuck for some months in his body.

" Glory to God and Queen Yadviga! You will get well now."

" Perhaps; I am relieved, but I feel terrible pain," answered Matsko. squeezing the sore, from which blood mixed with matter flowed abundantly. " The less of this vileness there is in a man, the more must sickness leave him. Yagenka said that now we must apply beaver's fat."

" We will go for a beaver to-morrow."

Next day Matsko grew notably better. He slept till late, and on waking called for food. He could not look at bear's fat, but they broke up twenty eggs to be fried for him, as through caution Yagenka would not permit more. He ate these with relish, together with half a loaf of bread, and drank a pot of beer. He asked to bring Zyh then, for he felt joyous.

Zbyshko sent one of his Turks for Zyh, who mounted a horse and came before mid-day, just when the young people were preparing to go to Odstayani Lake for a beaver. At first there was laughing. joking, and singing over mead beyond measure. but later the old men talked of the children, and each praised his own.

" What a man that Zbyshko is," said Matsko; " in the world there is not another such. He is brave, he is as nimble as a wild cat, and skilful. And, do you know, when they were leading him to death in Cracow the girls in the windows were squealing as if some one behind were sticking awls into them; and what girls! — the daughters of knights and castellans, not to mention various wonderful daughters of citizens."

" Let them be daughters of castellans, and wonderful, but they are not better than my Yagenka," said Zyh.

" Do I tell you that they are better? A nicer girl to people than Yagenka could not be found, I think."

" Neither do I say anything against Zbyshko; he can draw a crossbow without a crank."

" And will prop up a bear himself alone. Have you seen how he cut him? Split off his head and one paw."

" He knocked off his head, but he did not prop him alone. Yagenka helped him."

" Did she help him? He did not tell me that."

" For he promised her — because the girl was ashamed to go at night to the forest. She told me right away how it was. Others would be glad to invent, but she will not hide the truth. Speaking sincerely I was not pleased, for who knows — I wanted to shout at her, but she said: 'If I cannot guard myself, you, papa, will not guard me;' but never fear, Zbyshko knows also what knightly honor is."

" That is true."

" They have gone alone to-day."

" But they will come back in the evening. The devil is worse at night; girls need not be ashamed then, for it is dark."

Matsko thought a while, then said, as if to himself, —

" But in every case they are glad to see each other."

" Oh, if he had not made a vow to that other one ! "

"That, as you know, is a knightly custom. Whoso among young men has not his lady is looked on by others as a simpleton. He has vowed peacock-plumes, and he must get them, for he has sworn on his knightly honor; he must also get Lichtenstein, but the abbot may free him from other vows."

" The abbot will come any day."

" Do you think so?" inquired Matsko. " But what is such a vow when Yurand told him directly that he would not give the girl. Whether he had promised her to another, or devoted her to the service of God, I know not, but he said directly that he would not give her."

"I have told you," said Zyh, "that the abbot loves Yagenka as if she were his own. The last time he spoke thus to her: 'I have relatives only by the distaff,[1] but by that distaff there will be more threads for thee than for them.'"

At this Matsko looked with alarm, and even suspiciously, at Zyh, and answered only after a while, —

[1] This means on the female side of the family.

" Still you wish no injustice to us."

" Mochydoly will go with Yagenka," said Zyh, evasively.

" Right away? "

" Right away. I would not give it to another, but I will to her."

" As things stand, half Bogdanets is Zbyshko's, and if God grant health I will work for him, as is proper. Do you like Zbyshko? "

At this Zyh began to blink, and said, —

" The worst is that, when Zbyshko is mentioned, Yagenka turns to the wall that moment."

" And when you mention others? "

" When I mention another she just flies up, and says: ' What?' "

" Well now, do you see? God grant that with such a girl Zbyshko will forget the other. I am old, and I too would forget. Will you drink some mead? "

" I will drink some."

" Well, the abbot — there is a wise man for you! Among abbots there are, as you know, laymen; but this abbot, though he does not live among monks, is a priest, and a priest always gives better counsel than a common man, for he understands reading, and he is near the Holy Ghost. But you will give the girl Mochydoly immediately — that is right. And I, if the Lord Jesus give me health, will entice his people away from Vilk of Brozova as far as I am able. I will give good land by lot to each man, for in Bogdanets there is no lack of land. Let them bow down to Vilk on Christmas and then come to me. Are they not free to do so? In time I will build a castle, a nice castle, oak with a moat around it. Let Zbyshko and Yagenka go hunting together now — I think that we shall not wait long for snow. Let them grow accustomed to each other, and the boy will forget that first one. Let them go together. Why talk long over this? Would you give him Yagenka, or would you not? "

" I would give her. Besides, we have long ago arranged that one was for the other, and that Mochydoly and Bogdanets would be for our grandchildren."

" Hail! " cried Matsko, with delight. " God grant them to come like hail ! The abbot will christen them."

" If he would come ! " cried Zyh, joyously. " But it is long since I have seen you so delighted."

" I am pleased at heart. The splinter has come out; but

as to Zbyshko, have no fear of him.   Yesterday, when Yagenka was mounting her horse — you know — the wind was blowing.   I asked Zbyshko then, 'Didst thou see?' and right away a shiver took him.   And I noted too that at first they talked little, but now whenever they walk together they are always turning their heads toward each other, and talking and talking.   Drink some more."

"I will drink."

"To the health of Zbyshko and Yagenka!"

CHAPTER XI.

THE old man was not mistaken when he said that Zbyshko
and Yagenka were glad to be together, and even that they
yearned for each other. Yagenka, under pretext of visiting
the sick Matsko, came frequently to Bogdanets, with her
father or alone. Zbyshko, through simple gratitude, looked in
from time to time at Zyh's, so that soon in the course of days
close intimacy and friendship grew up between them. They
began to like each other and to consult together willingly,
which meant " to talk" about everything which could concern
them. There was also a little mutual admiration in this friendship. For the young, stately Zbyshko, who had distinguished
himself in war, taken part in tournaments, and been in kings'
chambers, seemed to the girl a real courtly knight, almost a
king's son in comparison with Stan or Vilk; and he at times
was astonished at the beauty of Yagenka. He remembered
his Danusia faithfully, but more than once when he looked
at Yagenka on a sudden, whether in the house or the forest, he said to himself involuntarily, " Ei! that's a deer!"
but when he caught her by the waist, placed her on horseback, and felt under his hands her body firm as if cut from
stone, disquiet took hold of him, and as Matsko said,
" shivers" seized the youth, and something passed through
his bones and deadened him like a dream.

Yagenka, haughty by nature, quick to laugh, and even to
attack, grew more obedient to him gradually, altogether like
a servant who only looks into the eyes to learn how to
serve and to please. He understood this great inclination of
hers, he was grateful, and it was more and more agreeable
for him to be with her. At last, especially since Matsko
had begun to drink bear's fat, they saw each other almost
daily, and after the arrow splinter came out they went together for a beaver to get fresh fat, greatly needed to heal
the wound.

They took crossbows, mounted their horses, and rode on,
first to Mochydoly, which was to be Yagenka's dower, then
toward the forest, where they left the horses with a servant, and went farther on foot, since it was difficult to ride
through swamps and thickets. On the road Yagenka pointed

out broad meadows covered with weeds, as well as a blue line of forests.

"Those forests belong to Stan of Rogov," said she.

"To him who would be glad to take thee."

"He would take if I would only give myself," said she, laughing.

"Thou canst defend thyself easily, having Vilk as assistant, who, as I hear, grits his teeth at the other. It is a wonder to me that a challenge to the death has not passed between them already."

"It has not because papa, when he was going to the war, said: 'If ye fight I shall not set eyes on either of you.' What were they to do? When at our house they fume at each other, but drink at the inn afterward in Kresnia together till they fall under the table."

"Stupid fellows!"

"Why?"

"Because when Zyh was not at home, one or the other ought to have made an attack and taken thee forcibly. What could Zyh have done, if on his return he had found thee with a child in thy arms?"

Yagenka's blue eyes flashed at once.

"Dost thou think that I would have yielded? — or that we have not people, or that I cannot handle a spear, or a crossbow? If they had tried! I should have hunted each man of them home; besides, I should myself have attacked Brozova or Rogov. Papa knows that he can go to the war very safely."

Thus speaking she wrinkled her beautiful brows, and shook the crossbows so threateningly that Zbyshko laughed and said, —

"Well, thou shouldst be a knight, not a maiden."

But she grew calm and said, —

"Stan guarded me from Vilk, and Vilk from Stan. I was under the care of the abbot, moreover, and it is better for every man not to dispute with the abbot."

"Oh, indeed!" answered Zbyshko; "every one here fears the abbot. But I, so help me Saint George as I speak the truth, should have feared neither the abbot nor Zyh, nor the hunters at thy father's house, nor thee, but I would have taken thee — "

At this Yagenka stopped on the spot, and raising her eyes to Zbyshko, inquired with a certain strange, mild, halting voice, —

"Wouldst thou have taken me?"

Then her lips parted, and she waited for the answer, blushing like the dawn. But clearly he was thinking only of what he would have done in the place of Vilk or Stan, for after a while he shook his golden head, and said, —

" Why should a maiden fight with men, when she has to marry? If a third one does not come, thou must choose one of them, for how — "

" Do not say that to me," answered she, sadly.

" Why not? I have not been here long, hence I know not whether there is any one near by who would please thee more."

" Ah! " exclaimed Yagenka. " Give me peace! "

They went on in silence, pushing forward through the thicket, which was all the denser because the brush and trees were covered with wild hops. Zbyshko went ahead, tearing apart the green ropes, breaking branches here and there. Yagenka pushed after him, with crossbow on her shoulders, resembling some hunting goddess.

" Beyond this thicket," said she, " is a deep stream, but I know a ford."

" I have leggings to the knees, we shall pass over dry," answered Zbyshko.

After a time they reached the water. Yagenka, knowing the Mochydoly forest well, found the ford easily. It turned out, however, that the little stream had risen from rain somewhat, and was rather deep. Then Zbyshko, without a question, caught the girl up in his arms.

" I could go on foot," said Yagenka.

" Hold to my neck! " said Zbyshko.

He went through the swollen water slowly, trying with his foot at every step whether there was not a deep place, she nestled up to him according to command; at last, when they were not far from the other shore, she said, —

" Zbyshko! "

" Well? "

" I will not have either Stan or Vilk."

Meanwhile he carried her over, put her down carefully on the gravel, and said with some agitation, —

"May God give thee the best one! He will not suffer."

It was not far to the lake now. Yagenka, going in advance this time, turned at moments and, putting her finger to her lips, enjoined silence on Zbyshko. They advanced through a clump of gray weeping-willows, over wet and low ground. From the right hand the uproar of birds flew to them.

Zbyshko wondered at this; for at that season birds had already departed.

"This is a swamp that never freezes," said Yagenka; "ducks winter here, but even in the lake water freezes only at the shore in time of great frost. .See how it steams!"

Zbyshko looked through the willows and saw before him, as it were, a cloud of mist; that was Odstayani Lake.

Yagenka put her finger to her lips again, and after a while they arrived. First the girl climbed in silence a large old weeping-willow bent over the water completely. Zbyshko climbed another, and for a long time they lay in silence without seeing anything in front of them because of the mist, hearing only the complaining call of mews above their heads. At last the wind shook the willows with their yellow leaves, and disclosed the sunken surface of the lake, wrinkled somewhat by the breeze, and unoccupied.

"Is there nothing to be seen?" whispered Zbyshko.

"Nothing to be seen. Be quiet!"

After a while the breeze fell and perfect silence followed. On the surface of the water appeared a dark head, then a second; but at last, and much nearer, a bulky beaver let himself down from the bank to the water, with a freshly cut limb in his mouth, and began to swim through the duckweed and cane, keeping his jaws in the air, and pushing the limb before him. Zbyshko, lying on a tree somewhat lower than Yagenka, saw all at once how her elbow moved silently, and how her head bent forward; evidently she was aiming at the animal, which suspected no danger, and was swimming not farther than half a shot distant, toward the open surface of the lake.

At last the string of the crossbow groaned, and at the same moment Yagenka cried, —

"Struck! struck!"

Zbyshko climbed higher in a twinkle of an eye, and looked through the branches at the water. The beaver was diving, and coming to the surface, plunging, and showing at moments his belly more than his back.

"He has got it well! He will be quiet soon!" said Yagenka.

She had told the truth, for the movements of the animal grew fainter and fainter, and at the end of one Hail Mary he came to the surface belly upward.

"I will go to bring him," said Zbyshko.

"Go not. Here at this shore is an ooze as deep as the height of many men. Whoever does not know how to manage will be drowned surely."

"But how shall we get him?"

"He will be in Bogdanets this evening. Let not thy head ache over that; but for us it is time to go."

"But thou hast shot him well!"

"Oh, he is not my first beaver."

"Other girls are afraid to look at a crossbow, but with such as thou one might hunt through the forests for a lifetime."

Yagenka, on hearing this praise, smiled with pleasure, but said nothing, and they returned by the same road through the willows. Zbyshko inquired about the beaver dam, and she told him how many beavers there were in Mochydoly, how many in Zgorzelitse, and how they waded along the paths and mounds.

On a sudden she struck her hip with her hand.

"Oh," cried she, "I have forgotten my arrows on the willow! Wait here."

And before he could answer that he would go himself for them, she had sprung away like a deer, and vanished from his sight in a moment.

Zbyshko waited and waited; at last he began to wonder why she was gone so long.

"She must have lost her arrows, and is looking for them," said he to himself; "I will go to see if anything has happened."

He had gone barely a few steps when the girl stood before him with the crossbow in her hand, the beaver on her shoulder, her face ruddy and smiling.

"For God's sake!" cried Zbyshko, "but how didst thou get him?"

"How? I went into the water! It is not the first time for me; I would not let you go, for if a man does not know how to swim there the ooze will swallow him."

"But I have been waiting here, like an idiot! Thou art a cunning girl!"

"Well, and what? Was I to undress before thee, or how?"

"So thou hadst not forgotten the arrows?"

"No, I only wanted to lead thee away from the water."

"Well! but if I had followed thee, I should have seen a wonder. There would have been something to wonder at! Would there not?"

" Be quiet ! "

" As God is dear to me, I should have gone ! "

" Stop ! "

After a while, wishing evidently to change the conversation, she said, —

" Squeeze out my hair, for it wets my shoulders."

Zbyshko grasped her tresses near her head with one hand, with the other he twisted them, saying, —

" Better unbraid them, the wind will dry thy hair immediately."

But she would not because of the thicket through which she had to push. Zbyshko took the beaver on his shoulder.

" Matsko will recover now quickly," said Yagenka, walking ahead; " there is no better remedy than bear's fat to drink, and beaver's fat to rub outside. He will be on horseback in a fortnight."

" God grant ! " said Zbyshko. " I await that as salvation, for I cannot in any way leave him sick, but for me it is a punishment to stay here."

" Punishment for thee to stay here?" inquired Yagenka. " How so?"

" Has Zyh told thee nothing of Danusia?"

" He told me something — I know — that she covered thee with a veil — I know — he told me also that every knight makes some vow, that he will serve his lady — But he said that such a service was nothing — for some men, though married, serve a lady; and that Danusia — Zbyshko, what is she? Tell me? Who is Danusia?"

And, pushing up nearer, she raised her eyes and began to look with great alarm at his face. Without paying the least heed to her voice of alarm and her gaze, he said, —

" She is my lady, but also my dearest love. I do not say that to any one, but I will say it to thee as my beloved sister, for we know each other from the time that we were little. I would follow her beyond the ninth river, and beyond the ninth sea, to the Germans, and to the Tartars, for in the whole world there is not such another. Let uncle stay here in Bogdanets, but I will go straight to Danusia. For what is Bogdanets to me without her, what are utensils and herds, and the wealth of the abbot ! I will mount a horse and go against the Germans, so help me God ! What I have vowed to her I will accomplish, unless I fall first."

" I did not know this," said Yagenka, in a dull voice.

Zbyshko then told how he had become acquainted with Danusia in Tynets, how he had made a vow to her immediately, and all that had. happened afterward, hence his imprisonment, and how Danusia had rescued him, Yurand's refusal, their farewell, his longing, and finally his delight that after Matsko's recovery he would be able to go to the beloved maiden, and do what he had promised. The narrative was only interrupted at sight of the man waiting with horses at the edge of the forest.

Yagenka mounted her horse at once, and began to take leave of Zbyshko.

"Let the man take the beaver with thee, but I will go home."

"But wilt thou not go to Bogdanets? Zyh is there."

"No, papa was to return, and he told me to go home."

"Well, God reward thee for the beaver."

"With God!"

And after a while Yagenka was alone. While riding homeward through the heather, she looked some time after Zbyshko, and when at last he had vanished behind the trees, she covered her eyes with one hand, as if guarding them from sunrays. But soon from beneath her hand great tears flowed along her cheeks and fell one after the other, like peas, on the mane of the horse and the saddle.

CHAPTER XII.

AFTER the conversation with Zbyshko, Yagenka did not show herself for three days in Bogdanets. Only on the third day did she drop in with the news that the abbot had come to her father's.

Matsko received the news with a certain emotion. He had, it is true, something with which to pay the amount of the mortgage, and even had calculated that enough would remain to increase the number of settlers, and introduce herds and other things needful in management; still in the whole affair much depended on the good-will of the wealthy relative who could, for example, take away the men settled by him in the clearings, or leave them, and by that act decrease or heighten the value of the property.

Matsko, therefore, made very minute inquiries of Yagenka touching the abbot. In what mood had he come? Was he gladsome, or gloomy? What had he said of them, and when would he visit Bogdanets?

Yagenka answered his questions wisely, trying to strengthen and calm him on every point. She said that the abbot had arrived in good health and spirits, with a considerable retinue, in which, besides armed attendants, were some wandering clerics and choristers; that he was singing with Zyh, and was glad to lend his ear not only to hymns, but to worldly melodies. She remarked also, that he had inquired with great attention about Matsko, and had listened eagerly to Zyh's narratives of Zbyshko's adventures in Cracow.

"Ye yourselves know better what to do," said the shrewd girl, at last; "but I think that it would be well for Zbyshko to go at once and greet the elder relative, without waiting for him to come first to Bogdanets."

This advice struck Matsko, and convinced him; hence he commanded to call Zbyshko, and said, —

"Array thyself nicely, and go to embrace the feet of the abbot, show him honor, so that he also may be gracious to thee."

Then he turned to Yagenka: "Even wert thou simple, I should not wonder, for thou art a woman, but because thou hast wit I admire thee. Tell me how to entertain the abbot best, and how to please him when he comes hither."

"As to eating, he will tell himself what he relishes. He likes to eat well, but if there is plenty of saffron it will not hurt!"

When he heard this Matsko seized his head.

" Where shall I find saffron for him? "

" I have brought some," said Yagenka.

" God grant that such girls be born on stones! " cried Matsko, delighted. " And to the eye they are dear, and good housekeepers, and wise, and pleasant to people. Oh, if I were young, I would take thee this minute! "

Yagenka glanced now an instant at Zbyshko, and, sighing in silence, said, —

" I have brought also dice and a cup and a cloth, for after every meal he likes to amuse himself with dice."

" He had this custom before, but therewith he was very quick-tempered."

" He is quick-tempered now; often he throws the cup to the ground, and rushes out through the door to the field. But afterward he comes back smiling, and is the first to blame his own anger — besides you know him; only do not oppose, and there is no better man in the world."

" But who would oppose him, since he has more mind than others? "

They were conversing in this way while Zbyshko was dressing in his room. He came out at last so fine-looking that Yagenka was dazzled, just as she had been when first he came in his " white jacket " to her father's house. But now deep sorrow possessed her at the thought that that beauty of his was not for her, and that he loved another.

Matsko was glad, for he believed that the abbot would be pleased with Zbyshko, and would raise no difficulty in bargaining. He was even pleased so much at this thought that he decided to go himself.

" Command to get the wagon ready," said he to Zbyshko. " I was able to ride hither from Cracow with iron between my ribs, I can go now without iron to Zyh's house."

" Unless you faint on the road," said Yagenka.

" Ei, nothing will happen me, for I feel strength in myself. And even if I should faint a little, the abbot will know how I hurried to him, and will show himself the more bountiful."

"Your health is dearer to me than his bounty," said Zbyshko.

But Matsko was determined and insisted on his own way. He groaned on the road somewhat, but did not cease to tell Zbyshko how he must bear himself; especially did he enjoin on him obedience and humility in presence of the rich relative, who never endured the least opposition.

On reaching Zyh's "court" they found him and the abbot on the porch looking out at God's serene universe and drinking wine. Behind, on a bench near the wall, sat six attendants in a row, among them two choristers and one pilgrim, whom it was easy to distinguish by his curved staff, by the bag at his girdle, and by the shells worked on his dark mantle. The others looked like clerics, for they had shaven crowns, but they wore the dress of laymen, they were girded with oxhide, and had swords at their sides.

At sight of Matsko in the wagon, Zyh went out quickly; but the abbot, mindful as it seemed of his spiritual dignity, remained in his seat, only he began to speak to his clerics, some more of whom came out through the open door of the front room. Zbyshko and Zyh brought in the feeble Matsko, holding him by the arms.

"I am a little weak yet," said Matsko, kissing the abbot's hand; "but I have come to bow down to you, my benefactor, to thank you for your management, and beg your blessing, which is needed most of all by a sinful man."

"I have heard that you are better," said the abbot, pressing his head, "and that you have made a vow to the tomb of our late queen."

"Not knowing to which saint I should turn, I betook myself to her."

"You have done well!" cried the abbot, passionately; "she is better than others, and let any one dare to envy her!"

And anger came to his face in one moment, his cheeks filled with blood, his eyes began to flash.

Those present knew his irritability, so Zyh laughed, and cried, —

"Strike, whoso believes in God!"

The abbot panted loudly, turned his eyes on all present, then laughed as suddenly as he had burst out before, and looking at Zbyshko inquired, —

"This is your nephew, and my relative?"

Zbyshko inclined, and kissed his hand.

" I saw him when he was little; I should not have known him now.   But show thyself ! "

He examined Zbyshko from head to foot, with quick eyes. " Too good-looking!   A maiden, not a knight ! " said he, at last.

" The Germans took that maiden to dance," said Matsko; " but whoever took her fell, not to rise again,"

" And he bent a bow without a crank ! " cried Yagenka, suddenly.

" But what art thou doing here? " asked the abbot, turning to her.

She blushed till her neck and ears were rosy, and said in great confusion, —

" I saw him."

" Have a care that he should not shoot thee perchance; thou wouldst need three-quarters to recover."

At this the choristers, the pilgrim, and the " wandering clerics " burst into one immense laugh, from which Yagenka lost herself completely, so that the abbot took compassion on her, and, raising his arm, showed her the enormous sleeve of his robe.

" Hide here, girl," said he, " for the blood will spurt from thy cheeks."

Meanwhile Zyh seated Matsko on the bench, and commanded to bring wine, for which Yagenka hurried.   The abbot turned his eyes to Zbyshko.

" Enough of joking! " said he, " I compared thee to a girl, not to blame thee, but from pleasure at thy good looks, which more than one maiden might envy.   I know that thou art a splendid fellow!   I have heard of thy deeds at Vilno; I have heard of the Frisians, and of Cracow.   Zyh has told me everything — dost understand ! "

Here he looked sharply into Zbyshko's eyes, and after a while said again, —

" If thou hast vowed three peacock-plumes, find them, it is praiseworthy and pleasing to God to hunt down the enemies of our race; but if thou hast vowed something else in addition, know that while thou art waiting here I can absolve thee from those vows, for I have the power."

" When a man has promised something in his soul to the Lord Jesus, what power can absolve him? " said Zbyshko.

On hearing this, Matsko looked with a certain dread at the abbot; but evidently the abbot was in excellent humor, for, instead of bursting into anger, he threatened Zbyshko joyously with his finger, and said, —

"Ah, thou art a witling! See that that does not happen thee which happened the German, Beyhard."

"And what happened him?" inquired Zyh.

"They burned him at the stake."

"Why?"

"Because he said that a layman is just as well able to understand the secrets of God as a spiritual person."

"They punished him severely!"

"But justly!" thundered the abbot, "for he blasphemed against the Holy Ghost. What do ye think? Can a layman make any decisions as to God's secrets?"

"He cannot in any way!" called the wandering clerics, in an agreeing chorus.

"But ye 'playmen' sit quietly," said the abbot; "for ye are no clerics, though ye have shaven crowns."

"We are not thy playmen nor indigents, but the attendants of your grace," answered one of them, looking that moment at a great pitcher from which at a distance came the odor of hops and malt.

"See! he talks as if from a barrel!" cried the abbot. "Hei, thou bearded! Why look at the pitcher? Thou wilt not find Latin at the bottom of it."

"I am not looking for Latin, but beer which I cannot find."

The abbot turned then to Zbyshko, who was gazing at those attendants with wonder, and said, —

"All these are 'clerici scholares,' though each one would prefer to fling his book away, seize a lute and wander through the world with it. I have taken them all in and feed them, for what can I do? They are good-for-nothings, inveterate vagrants; but they know how to sing, and have picked up the divine liturgy a little, so in the church I find use for them, and defence in them when need comes, for some are resolute fellows. This pilgrim here says that he has been in the holy land; but it would be vain to ask him about any sea or land, for he does not know the name of the Greek emperor, or in what city he has his residence."

"I knew," said the pilgrim, in a hoarse voice, "but when the fever shook me on the Danube, it shook everything out of me."

"I wonder most at their swords," said Zbyshko; "for I have never seen such at any time with wandering clerics."

" They are free to carry swords," replied the abbot; "for they are not consecrated, and that I bear a sword too at my side is no wonder. A year ago I challenged Vilk to trampled earth, for those forests through which you passed before reaching Bogdanets. He did not appear."

" How was he to meet a spiritual person?" interrupted Zyh.

At this the abbot grew excited, and, striking the table with his fist, he cried, —

" When in armor I am not a priest, but a noble! And he did not appear, because he preferred to attack me at night with his attendants in Tulcha. That is why I carry a sword at my side! *Omnes leges, omniaque iura vim vi repellere cunctisque sese defensare permittunt.* (All laws, all rights, permit us all to defend ourselves with force against force.) That is why I have given them swords."

When they heard the Latin, Zyh and Matsko and Zbyshko grew silent and bent their heads before the wisdom of the abbot, for not a man understood one word of it; he looked around a while longer with angry eyes, and said at last, —

" Who knows that he will not attack me here?"

" Oh, just let him come!" said the wandering clerics, grasping their sword hilts.

" Let him attack! It is dreary for me too without a battle."

" He will not attack," said Zyh; " he will come with obeisance and peace rather. He has renounced the forest; he is thinking now of his son — you understand. But there is no use in his waiting."

Meanwhile the abbot was pacified, and said, —

" I saw young Vilk drinking with Stan in the inn at Kresnia. They did not know us at first, for it was dark; besides they were talking of Yagenka." Here he turned to Zbyshko, " And of thee."

" What did they want of me?"

" They did not want anything; but it was not to their liking to find a third man in the neighborhood. This is how Stan spoke to Vilk: ' When I tan his skin he will not be pretty;' and Stan said: ' Maybe he will fear us; if not, I will break his bones in a twinkle!' Then both declared that thou wouldst be afraid."

When Matsko heard this, he looked at Zyh, Zyh at him, and their faces took on a cunning and delighted expression.

Neither felt sure as to whether the abbot had really heard such conversation, or had invented it only to prick Zbyshko. Both understood, but especially Matsko, who knew Zbyshko well, that there was no better way in the world to push him to Yagenka.

"And indeed they are deadly fellows!" added the abbot, as if purposely.

Zbyshko did not betray anything on his face, but he asked Zyh, with a kind of strange voice, —

"Will to-morrow be Sunday?"

"Sunday."

"Shall you go to holy mass?"

"Yes."

"Whither — to Kresnia?"

"Yes, for it is nearer.   Where should we go?"

"Very well, we shall go!"

THE KNIGHTS OF THE CROSS.

178

CHAPTER XIII.

ZBYSHKO, when he had overtaken Zyh and Yagenka, who were riding in company with the abbot and his clerics, joined them, and they rode together to the church; for with him the question was to show the abbot that he had no fear of Vilk or Stan, and did not think of hiding before them. From the first moment he was astonished again at the beauty of Yagenka, for though he had seen her more than once at her father's house, and in Bogdanets dressed beautifully to appear among guests, he had never seen her arrayed for church as at present. She wore a robe of red cloth, lined with ermine, red gloves, and a gold-trimmed ermine hood, from under which two braids of hair dropped on her shoulders. She was not sitting on the horse man-fashion, but on a lofty saddle with a handle, and with a bench beneath her feet, which were barely visible under the long petticoat plated in even folds. For Zyh, who permitted the girl to wear at home a skin coat and boots of cowhide, was anxious that in front of the church every one should know that not the daughter of some gray-coated landowner, or patented noble had come, but a young lady of a rich, knightly house. With this object, her horse was led by two youths whose lower garments were close-fitting, and the upper ones wide, as was usual with pages. Four house attendants rode behind, and near them the abbot's clerics, with swords and lutes at their girdles.

Zbyshko admired the whole company greatly, above all Yagenka, who looked like an image, and the abbot, who, in red and with immense sleeves to his robe, seemed to him like some prince on a journey. Attired most plainly of all was Zyh, who desired ostentation in others, but for himself only gladness and singing.

When Zbyshko came up, they rode on in a line, the abbot, Yagenka, Zbyshko, and Zyh. The abbot at first commanded his "playmen" to sing pious hymns, only later, when he had listened sufficiently, did he begin to talk with Zbyshko, who looked with a smile at his mighty sword, which was not smaller than the two-handed blades of the Germans.

"I see," said he, with seriousness, "that thou art wondering at my sword.   Know then that the synods permit swords to the clergy and even balistas and catapults, on a journey, and we are on a journey.   Moreover, when the Holy Father forbade swords and red garments to priests, he surely had men of low station in mind.   God created the noble for arms, and whoso should wish to disarm him, would resist God's eternal decrees."

"I have seen Henryk, Prince of Mazovia, who took part in tournaments," answered Zbyshko.

"He is not to be blamed because he took part in tournaments," replied the abbot, raising his finger; "but because he married, and moreover unhappily, for he married a *fornicariam et bibulam mulierem*, who from youth, as they say, worshipped Bacchus and was moreover *adulteram*, from whom nothing good could come."

Here he stopped his horse and exhorted with still greater seriousness, —

"Whoso wishes to choose a wife, and to marry, must see that she is God-fearing, of good habits, a housekeeper, and neat, — all of which is enjoined not only through the fathers of the church, but through a certain pagan sage by name Seneca.   And how wilt thou know that thou hast hit well if thou know not the nest from which thy comrade for a lifetime is chosen ?   For another sage of the Lord says, *Pomus nam cadit absque arbore* (The apple falls from its tree).   As the ox, so the skin, as the mother, so the daughter, — from which take this lesson, sinful man, seek a wife not in the distance, but near by; for if thou find a malicious and gallant one, thou wilt weep for her more than once, as wept that philosopher whose quarrelsome mate used to throw out always on his head in her anger *aquam sordidam* (dirty water)."

"*In secula seculorum* (For the ages of ages), amen !" thundered in unison the wandering clerics, who, always answering the abbot in that way, were not very careful whether they answered according to meaning.

All listened to the abbot's words with deep attention, wondering at his eloquence and skill in the Scriptures.   He did not direct this conversation straight at Zbyshko, but rather turned to Zyh and Yagenka, as if to edify them in particular.   Yagenka understood evidently what the point was, for she looked carefully from beneath her long eyelashes at the youth, who wrinkled his brows and dropped his head, as if in deep meditation over what he had heard.

After a time the company moved on, but in silence; only when Kresnia was in sight did the abbot feel at his girdle and turn the side toward the front so that he might seize his swordhilt easily.

"Old Vilk of Brozova will come, and surely with a large retinue," said he.

"Surely," confirmed Zyh, "but the servants said something about his being sick."

"One of my clerics heard that he was to attack us before the inn after mass."

"He would not do that without announcement, and especially after holy mass."

"May God send him thoughtfulness; I seek war with no man, and endure injustice patiently."

Here he looked around on his "playmen," and said, —

"Do not draw your swords, and remember that ye are clerical servants; but if the others draw theirs first, go at them!"

Zbyshko, riding at Yagenka's side, inquired of her touching that which concerned him principally.

"We shall find young Vilk and Stan in Kresnia, surely. Show the men to me at a distance, so that I may know them."

"Very well. Zbyshko," answered Yagenka.

"Before church and after church they meet thee, of course. What do they do then?"

"They serve me as they know how."

"They will not serve thee to-day, dost understand?"

She answered again, almost with humility, "Very well, Zbyshko."

Further conversation was interrupted by the sound of wooden knockers, because there were no bells then in Kresnia. After a while they arrived. From the crowds, waiting for mass before the church, came forth at once young Vilk and Stan; but Zbyshko was quicker, he sprang from his horse before they could come, seizing Yagenka by the side he helped her from the saddle, took her arm, looked at them challengingly, and led her to the church.

At the entrance a new disappointment was awaiting them. Both hastened to the holy water font, and dipping their hands in it, extended them to the maiden. But Zbyshko did the same: she touched his fingers, made the sign of the cross on herself, and entered the church with him. Not only young Vilk, but Stan of Rogov, though he had a small mind, divined that all was done purposely; and such savage anger seized both that the hair rose beneath their head nets. They preserved presence of mind enough to refrain in their anger from entering the church, through fear of God's punishment. Vilk rushed out and flew like a mad man among trees through the graveyard, not knowing himself the direction in which he was going. Stan flew behind him, not knowing with what intent he was acting.

They stopped in the corner of the fence where large stones lay prepared for the foundation of a bell tower to be built in Kresnia. Then Vilk, to get rid of the anger which was raging in his breast to the throat, seized a stone and began to shake it with all his strength; seeing this, Stan grasped it also, and after a while both rolled it with rage through the graveyard as far as the church gate.

People looked at them with wonder, thinking that they were performing some vow, and that they wished in this way to aid in building the bell tower. But the effort relieved them considerably, so that both regained composure, only they had become pale from exertion, and panted, looking at each other with uncertain glance. Stan was the first to break silence.

"Well, and what?" asked he.

"But what?" answered Vilk.

"Shall we attack him right off?"

"How! attack him in the church?"

"Not in the church, but after mass."

"He is with Zyh — and with the abbot. Dost remember what Zyh said: 'Let there be a fight, and I will drive both from Zgorzelitse.' Had it not been for that I should have broken thy ribs for thee long since."

"Or I thine for thee!" replied Stan, as he clinched his strong fists.

And their eyes began to flash ominously; but both soon moderated, for they had greater need of concord than ever. More than once had they fought, but they had always grown reconciled afterward, for though love for Yagenka divided them, they could not live without each other, and yearned for each other always. At present they had a common enemy, and both felt him to be terribly dangerous. So after a time Stan inquired, —

"What is to be done? Send a declaration to Bogdanets."

Vilk was wiser, but he did not know what to do at the moment. Fortunately the knockers came to their aid,

and sounded a second time, in sign that mass was about to
begin.

" What shall we do ? " repeated Vilk.   " Go to mass;
what God gives will come."

Stan was pleased with this wise answer.

" Maybe the Lord Jesus will inspire us," said he.

" And bless us," added Vilk.

" According to justice."

They went to the church, and after they had heard mass
piously they received consolation.   They did not lose their
heads even when Yagenka, after mass, took holy water
again from Zbyshko's hand at the entrance.   In the graveyard at the gate they fell at the feet of Zyh and Yagenka,
though the abbot was old Vilk's enemy, they fell also at his
feet.   They looked at Zbyshko with a frown, it is true; but
neither one grumbled, though the hearts in their breasts
were whining from anger, from pain, and from jealousy, for
never had Yagenka seemed to them so queenlike, so wonderful.   Only when the brilliant company moved homeward,
and when from afar the gladsome song of the wandering
clerics came to them, did Stan wipe the sweat from his face
with young beard on it, and snort as a horse might.   But Vilk
gnashed his teeth and said, —

" To the inn ! to the inn ! Woe to me ! "

Remembering then what had eased them before, they
seized the stone a second time, and rolled it to its former
place, passionately.

Zbyshko rode at Yagenka's side listening to the songs of
the abbot's playmen ; but when they had gone about the third
of a mile, he reined in his horse suddenly, —

" Oh, I was to have a mass said for my uncle's health,"
cried he ; " but forgot it, I am going back."

" Do not go ! " said Yagenka, " we can send from
Zgorzelitse."

" I will return ; do not wait for me.   Farewell ! "

" Farewell ! " said the abbot.   " Go back ! "

And his face became gladsome.   When Zbyshko had vanished from their sight, he punched Zyh in the side slightly,
and added, —

" Dost understand ? "

" What am I to understand ? "

" He will fight Vilk and Stan in Kresnia, as sure as there
is amen in Our Father; that is what I wanted, and that is
what I have brought about."

"They are deadly fellows! They will wound him; but what of that?"

"How, what of that? If he fights for Yagenka, how can he think of Yurand's daughter? Yagenka will be his lady — not that one; this is what I want, for he is my relative, and pleases me."

"But the vow?"

"While he is waiting, I will absolve him. Have you not heard me promise already?"

"Your head is equal to anything," answered Zyh.

The abbot was pleased with the praise; he pushed up to Yagenka, and inquired, —

"Why art thou so serious?"

She bent in the saddle, and, seizing the abbot's hand, raised it to her lips. "Godfather, but maybe you would send a couple of 'playmen' to Kresnia?"

"What for? They would get drunk in the inn, nothing more."

"But they might prevent some quarrel."

The abbot looked her quickly in the eyes, and said, with some harshness, —

"Even should they kill him!"

"Then let them kill me," cried Yagenka.

And the bitterness which had collected with sorrow in her breast from the time of talking with Zbyshko flowed down now in a sudden flood of tears. Seeing this, the abbot embraced the girl with one arm, so that he covered her almost with his immense sleeve.

"Fear not, my daughter," said he. "A quarrel may happen; but still those two are nobles, they will not attack him together, but will challenge him to the field according to knightly custom; and there he will help himself, even had he to fight with both at one time. And as to Yurand's daughter of whom thou hast heard, there are no trees growing in any forest for that bed."

"Since she is dearer to him, I do not care for him," answered Yagenka, through her tears.

"Then why art thou sniffling?"

"I am afraid that some one will harm him."

"There is woman's wit!" said the abbot, laughing. Then, bending down to Yagenka's ear, he said, —

"Moderate thyself, girl, though he should marry thee, it will happen him to fight more than once; a noble is for that work." Here he bent still lower, and added, —

" But he will marry thee, and that before long, as God is in heaven ! "

" Well, we shall see ! " answered Yagenka.

And at the same time she began to laugh through her tears, and look at the abbot as if wishing to ask how he knew that.

Meanwhile Zbyshko returned to Kresnia, and went straight to the priest, for he wished a mass said for his uncle's recovery; then he went directly to the inn in which he expected to find young Vilk and Stan of Rogov.

In fact he found both, and also a crowd of people, — nobles by birth and patent, landworkers, and some jugglers showing various German tricks.

At the first moment he could not distinguish any one, for the inn windows, with oxbladder panes, let in little light; and only when a boy of the place threw pine sticks on the fire did he see in one corner Stan's hairy snout, and Vilk's angry, passionate visage behind tankards of beer.

Then he went toward them slowly, pushing people aside on the way; and at last coming up, he struck the table with his fist till he made everything thunder through the inn.

They rose at once, and pulled up their leather girdles before grasping their sword hilts. Zbyshko threw his glove on the table, and, speaking through his nose as was the custom of knights when they challenged, he uttered the following unexpected words, —

" If either of you two, or other knightly men in this room deny that the most wonderful and most virtuous maiden in the world is Panna Danusia, the daughter of Yurand of Spyhov, I challenge him to a combat on foot, or on horseback, to his first kneeling, or his last breath."

Stan and Vilk were astonished, as the abbot would have been had he heard anything similar; and for a time they could utter no word. What lady is that? Moreover for them the question was of Yagenka, not of her, and if that wildcat did not care about Yagenka, what did he want of them? Why had he made them angry before the church? Why had he come there? Why was he seeking a quarrel? From these queries such confusion rose in their heads that their mouths opened widely. Stan stared as if he had before him, not a man, but some kind of German wonder.

Vilk, being quicker-witted, knew something of knightly customs, and knew that knights often vow service to some women and marry others; he thought that in this case it

might be so, and that if there was such a chance of taking
Yagenka's part, he ought to seize it on the wing. So he
pushed from behind the table, and approached Zbyshko
with a hostile face.

"How is that, dog brother?" asked he. "Is not Yagenka,
the daughter of Zyh, the most wonderful?"

After him came Stan, and people began to crowd around
them; for it was known to all present that this would not
end in anything common.

CHAPTER XIV.

On reaching home Yagenka sent a servant straightway to Kresnia to learn if a fight had taken place at the inn, or if any man had challenged another. But he, receiving coin on the road, began to drink with the priest's men, and had no thought of returning. Another, sent to Bogdanets to inform Matsko of a visit from the abbot, returned after he had done his errand, and declared that he had seen Zbyshko playing dice with his uncle.

This calmed Yagenka somewhat, for, knowing Zbyshko's skill and experience, she had not such fear of a challenge as of some harsh, severe accident in the inn. She desired to go with the abbot to Bogdanets, but he opposed, for he wished to talk with Matsko about the mortgage, and about another affair, of still greater importance, in which he did not wish to have Yagenka as witness.

Moreover he was preparing to spend the night there. When he heard of Zbyshko's happy return, he fell into excellent humor, and commanded his wandering clerics to sing and to shout till the pine woods should quiver, so in Bogdanets itself all the cottagers looked out of their cottages to see if there were not a fire, or if some foe were not attacking. But the pilgrim with curved staff rode ahead and quieted them, declaring that a spiritual person of high dignity was travelling. So they bowed down, and some even made the sign of the cross on their breasts; the abbot, seeing how they respected him, rode on in joyous pride, delighted with the world and full of good-will to men.

Matsko and Zbyshko, on hearing the shouts and songs, went to the gate to give greeting. Some of the clerics had been with the abbot in Bogdanets earlier, but some had joined the company recently, and saw the place for the first time. The hearts of these fell at sight of the poor house, which could not be compared with the broad court in which Zyh lived. They were strengthened, however, at sight of smoke making its way through the straw thatch of the roof, and were comforted perfectly when on entering the first room they caught the odor of saffron and various meats, and saw also two tables full of pewter dishes, empty as yet, it is true, but so large that all eyes must be gladdened at sight of them. On the smaller table shone a plate of pure silver, prepared for the abbot, and also a tankard carved wonderfully; both of these had been won with other wealth from the Frisians.

Matsko and Zbyshko invited at once to the table; but the abbot, who had eaten heartily before leaving Zyh's house, refused, all the more since something else held him occupied. From the first moment of his coming, he had looked carefully and also unquietly at Zbyshko, as if wishing to find on him traces of fighting; seeing the calm face of the young man, he was evidently impatient, till at last he could restrain his curiosity no longer.

" Let us go to the small room," said he, " and talk of the mortgage. Resist not, or I shall be angry! "

. Then he turned to the clerics and thundered, —

" But sit ye here quietly, and let me have no listening at the doorway! " Then he opened the door to the room, in which he could hardly find place, and after him entered Matsko and Zbyshko. There, when they had seated themselves on boxes, the abbot turned to his youthful relative, —

" Didst thou go back to Kresnia? "

" I did."

" Well, and what ? "

" I gave money to celebrate mass for my uncle's recovery, and returned."

The abbot moved impatiently on the box. " Ha !" thought he, " he did not meet Stan or Vilk; maybe they were not there, maybe he did not look for them. I was mistaken ! "

But he was angry because he thought that he had been mistaken, and because his calculation had failed, so his face grew red at once, and he panted, —

" Let us talk of the mortgage," said he, after a while. "Have ye money ? — if ye have not, the land is mine."

At this Matsko, who knew how to act with him, rose in silence, opened the box on which he was sitting, took out a bag of gryvens already prepared, as it seemed, and said:

" We are poor people, but we have money, and we will pay what is proper, as it stands on the ' paper' and as I have promised with the sign of the Holy Cross. If you wish increased pay for the management and the cattle, we will not oppose, we will pay your demand, and embrace your feet, benefactor."

Saying this he bowed down to the abbot's knees, and after him Zbyshko did the same. The abbot, who expected disputes and bargaining, was greatly astonished by such action, and even was not at all glad, for in bargaining he wanted to bring forward various conditions, meanwhile the opportunity had vanished. So in delivering the "paper," on which Matsko had drawn the sign of the cross, he said, —

"What is this about paying in addition ?"

"We do not wish to take for nothing," answered Matsko, cunningly, knowing that the more he opposed in this case the more he should win.

In fact the abbot grew red in the twinkle of an eye.

"Look at them!" said he. "They will not take any-thing for nothing from a relative! Bread troubles people! I did not receive wildernesses, and I do not return them. If it please me to throw this bag away I will throw it!"

"You will not do that!" cried out Matsko.

"I will not do it? Here is your mortgage! And here is your money! I gave the money because of good-will; and if I wish I will leave it on the road, that is no concern of yours. This is what I will do!"

So saying, he caught the bag by the mouth, and hurled it to the floor, so that coin rolled out through the torn linen.

"God reward you! God reward you, father and bene-factor!" cried Matsko, who was only waiting for that moment. "From another I would not take it, but I will from a priest and a relative."

The abbot looked threateningly for some time, first at Matsko, then at Zbyshko, at last he said, —

"I know what I am doing, though I am angry, so keep what you have; for I tell you this, you will not see another grosh from me."

"We did not expect the present gift."

"But know ye that Yagenka will have what remains after me."

"And the land too?" inquired Matsko, innocently.

"The land too!" roared the abbot.

At this Matsko's face lengthened, but he mastered him-self, and said, —

"Ei! to think of death! May the Lord Jesus give you a hundred years, or more, but before that a good bishopric."

"And even if He should! Am I worse than others?" asked the abbot.

"Not worse, but better."

These words acted soothingly on the abbot, for in general his anger was short lived.

"Yes," said he, "ye are my relatives, while she is only a goddaughter, but I like her and Zyh these many years. A better man than Zyh there is not on earth, nor a better girl than Yagenka. Who will say aught against them?"

And he looked around with challenging glance; but Matsko not only made no contradiction, he asserted quickly that it would be useless to search the whole kingdom to find a better neighbor.

"And as to the girl," said he, "I could not love my own daughter more. She was the cause of my recovery, and till death I shall never forget it."

"Ye will be damned both the one and the other, if ye forget her," said the abbot; "and I shall be the first man to curse you. I wish you no harm, for ye are my blood relatives, hence I have thought out a method by which everything left by me will be yours and Yagenka's. Do ye understand?"

"God grant that to happen!" said Matsko. "Dear Jesus! I would walk from the queen's grave in Cracow to Bald Mountain to bow down before the wood of the Holy Cross."

The abbot was delighted at the sincerity with which Matsko spoke, so he laughed and continued, —

"The girl has the right to be choice; she is beautiful, she has a good dowry, she is of good stock. What is Stan or Vilk to her when a voevoda's son would not be too much? But if I, without alluding to any one, propose a bridegroom, she will marry him; for she loves me, and knows that I would not give bad advice to her."

"It will be well for the man whom you find for Yagenka," said Matsko.

"And what sayst thou?" asked the abbot, turning to Zbyshko.

"I think as uncle does."

The honest face of the abbot grew still brighter; he struck Zbyshko with his hand on the shoulder, so that the sound filled the room, and asked, —

"Why didst thou not let Stan or Vilk come near Yagenka at church? Why?"

"Lest they might think that I feared them, and lest you also might think so."

"But thou gavest her holy water."

"I did."

The abbot struck him a second time.

" Then — take her ! "

" Take her ! " exclaimed Matsko, like an echo.

At this Zbyshko gathered his hair under the net, and answered calmly, —

" How am I to take her when I made a vow in Tynets before the altar to Danusia, the daughter of Yurand ? "

" Thou didst promise peacock-plumes, find them, but take Yagenka now."

" No," answered Zbyshko, " when she threw a veil over me I promised to marry her."

The abbot's face was filling with blood, his ears became blue, and his eyes were swelling out ; he approached Zbyshko, and said in a voice choking with anger, —

" Thy vows are chaff, and I am wind, dost understand? Here ! "

And he blew at his head with such force that his hair net flew off, and the hair was scattered in disorder over his arms and shoulders. Then Zbyshko wrinkled his brows, and, looking straight into the abbot's eyes, answered, —

" In my vow is my honor, and I am guardian myself of that honor."

When he heard this the abbot, unaccustomed to resistance, lost breath to the degree that speech was taken for a time from him. Next came an ominous silence, which Matsko broke finally, —

" Zbyshko ! " cried he, " remember thyself. What is the matter with thee ? "

The abbot now raised his arm, and, pointing at the young man, he shouted, —

" What is the matter with him? I know what the matter is. The soul in him is not knightly, and not noble, it is the soul of a hare ! This is the matter with him, he is afraid of Vilk and Stan."

But Zbyshko, who had not lost his cool blood for an instant, shrugged his shoulders, and said, —

" Oh, pshaw ! I smashed their heads in Kresnia."

" Fear God ! " cried Matsko.

The abbot looked at Zbyshko for some time with staring eyes, anger struggled in him with admiration ; and at the same time his native quick wit began to remind him that from that beating of Vilk and Stan he might gain for his plans some advantage. So, recovering somewhat, he shouted at Zbyshko, —

" Why didst thou not mention that?"

" I was ashamed. I thought that they would challenge me, as became knights, to battle on foot, or on horseback; but they are robbers, not knights. First, Vilk took a plank from the table, Stan took another, and at me! What was I to do? I caught up a bench, well — you know what! "

" But didst thou leave them alive? " asked Matsko.

" Alive, though they fainted. But they regained breath before I left the inn."

The abbot listened, rubbed his forehead, then sprang up suddenly from the box on which he had been sitting for better thought, and cried, —

" Wait! I will tell thee something now."

" And what will you tell? " inquired Zbyshko.

" I will tell thee this, that if thou hast fought for Yagenka, and broken men's heads for her, thou art her knight, not the knight of another, and thou must take her."

Saying this, he put his hands on his sides, and looked triumphantly at Zbyshko.

But Zbyshko only smiled and said, " Hei, I knew well why you wished to set me at them; but it has failed you completely."

" How failed me? — Tell! "

" I told them to acknowledge that the most beautiful and most virtuous maiden in the world was Danusia, the daughter of Yurand; and they took the part of Yagenka exactly, and that was the cause of the battle."

When he heard this, the abbot stood in one place for a while, as if petrified, and only by the blinking of his eyes was it possible to know that he was alive yet. All at once he turned in his place, pushed the door open with his foot, rushed into the front room, seized the hooked staff from the hands of the pilgrim, and began to belabor his " playmen," bellowing meanwhile like a wounded bison, —

" To horse, ye buffoons! to horse, dog-faiths! A foot of mine will never be in this house again. To horse, whoso believes in God! to horse! — "

And opening another door he went out, the terrified, wondering clerics followed after. So moving with an uproar to the sheds, they fell to saddling the horses in haste. Matsko ran out after the abbot in vain, in vain did he beg him, implore him, declare in God's name that no fault attached to him — nothing availed! The abbot cursed the house, the people, the fields; and when they gave him his horse, he sprang on without putting his foot in the stirrup, and went at a gallop from the place, and with his great sleeves blown apart by the wind he looked like a red giant bird. The clerics flew after him in fear, like a herd hastening after its leader.

Matsko looked at the party till it vanished in the pine wood; then he turned slowly to the house, and, nodding his head gloomily, said to Zbyshko, —

"Thou hast done a fine thing!"

"This would not have happened had I gone away earlier; I did not go because of you."

"How, because of me?"

"Yes; for I would not go leaving you in sickness."

"But now how will it be?"

"Now I will go."

"Whither?"

"To Mazovia, to Danusia, — and to seek peacock-plumes among the Germans."

Matsko was silent a while, then he said, —

"He has given back the 'paper,' but the pledge is recorded in the court book. The abbot will not forgive us a grosh now."

"Let him not forgive. You have money, and I need none for the road. People will receive me everywhere, and give food to my horses; while I have armor on my back, and a sword in my grasp, I have no care for anything."

Matsko fell to thinking, and began to weigh everything that had happened. Nothing had gone according to his wish, or his heart. He had desired Yagenka for Zbyshko with all his soul; but he understood that there could be no bread from that flour, and that, considering the abbot's anger, considering Zyh and Yagenka, considering finally the battle with Vilk and Stan, it was better that Zbyshko should go than be the cause of more disputes and quarrels.

"Ah!" said he, at last, "thou must seek heads of the Knights of the Cross anyhow; so go, since there is no other way out. Let it happen according to the will of the Lord Jesus; but I must go to Zgorzelitse at once, mayhap I can talk over Zyh and the abbot — I am sorry, especially for Zyh."

Here he looked into Zbyshko's eyes, and asked quickly:

"But art thou not sorry for Yagenka?"

"May God give her health, and all that is best!" replied Zbyshko.

CHAPTER XV.

MATSKO waited a number of days patiently. Would some news come from Zyh's house? Would the abbot be pacified? At last he was wearied from waiting in uncertainty, and resolved to visit Zyh. Everything that had happened had happened without fault of his, but he wished to know whether Zyh felt offended; as to the abbot, Matsko was convinced that his anger would continue to weigh on him and his nephew.

He wished, however, to do all in his power to soften that anger; hence, on the road he was thinking and fixing in his mind what to say to diminish the feeling of offence and maintain old neighborly friendship. Somehow the thoughts in his head did not cleave to one another; hence, he was glad to find Yagenka alone. She received him in former fashion, with an obeisance, a kissing of the hand, — in a word, with friendliness, though with some sadness.

"Is your father at home?" inquired Matsko.

"At home, but he has gone to hunt with the abbot — short waiting till they come."

She conducted him to the chief room, where, when they had sat down, both were silent for some time.

"Is it dull for you alone in Bogdanets?" asked she, breaking the silence.

"Dull," answered Matsko. "Dost thou know that Zbyshko is gone?"

"I know," answered Yagenka, sighing silently. "I knew the same day, and thought that he would come here to say even a kind word; but he came not."

"How was he to come? The abbot would have torn him; and thy father would not have been glad to see him."

"Ei! I would not have let any one harm him," said Yagenka, shaking her head.

At this Matsko, though he had a tempered heart, was moved; he drew the girl toward him, and said, —

"God reward thee, girl! For thee there is sadness; but for me also. I will only tell thee that neither the abbot nor thy own father loves thee more than I. Better I had died

from this wound of which thou hast cured me, if he had only
taken thee, and not another."

Hereupon came to Yagenka one of those moments of
grief and sorrow in which one can make no concealment.

"I shall never see him again, or if I see him it will be
with Yurand's daughter, and I would rather cry my eyes out
than see them," said she, raising a corner of her apron, and
covering her tearful eyes with it.

"Be quiet!" said Matsko. "He has gone; but with
God's favor he will not bring Yurand's daughter back with
him."

"Why should he not?" asked Yagenka, from under her
apron.

"Because Yurand will not give her to him."

Yagenka uncovered her face suddenly, and, turning to
Matsko, inquired with vivacity, —

"He told me that, but is it true?"

"True, as God is in heaven."

"But why?"

"Who knows. Some vow, and for a vow there is no
remedy! Zbyshko pleased him in so far as he promised to
aid him in seeking revenge, but even that did not help. The
intercession of Princess Anna was useless. Yurand would
not listen to prayer, persuasion, or command. He said that
he could not. Well, it is clear that the cause is such that
he cannot; and he is a firm man, who does not change what
he says. Do not lose courage, girl, and be strong. In
truth, the boy had to go, for he swore in the church to get
peacock-plumes; the girl, too, covered him with a veil,
in sign that she wanted him for husband, without which they
would have cut off his head, — for this he is indebted to
her; there is nothing to be said on that point. She will
not be his, God grant, but according to law he is hers. Zyh
is angry with him; the abbot will be sure to take revenge on
him till his skin smarts; I am sorry for this affair, too: still,
when we look over everything, what was Zbyshko to do?
Since he was indebted to that girl, he had to go to her.
Besides, he is a noble. I will tell thee this though, that
unless the Germans in those parts maim him, he will return
as he went, — and will return not only to me, old man, not
only to Bogdanets, but to thee, for he is wonderfully glad to
see thee."

"Glad to see me?" Then she pushed up to Matsko, and
touching him with her elbow, asked, —

"How do you know? How? Surely it is not true."

"How do I know? I saw how pained he was to go. And besides, when it was decided that he must, I asked him: 'Art thou not sorry for Yagenka?' and he answered: 'May God give her health, and all that is best.' He began to sigh then, as if he had the bellows of a blacksmith in his breast."

"Surely not true!" repeated Yagenka, in a low voice; "but tell on."

"As God is dear to me it is true! That other one will not be so pleasant to him after thee, for thou knowest thyself that a firmer and a fairer maiden than thou is not to be found in all the world. He felt the will of God for thee, never fear — perhaps more than thou for him."

"Fear God!" cried Yagenka.

And noting that she had said something impulsively, she covered her face, which was as ruddy again as an apple. Matsko smiled, drew his hand along his moustaches, and said, —

"Ei, if I were young! But be patient, for I see how it will end. He will go, he will get his spurs at the Mazovian court; the boundary is near, and it is easy to find Knights of the Cross. I know that among Germans there are strong men, and that iron does not rebound from his skin, but I think that no common man will be able to meet him, for in battle the rogue is tremendously skilful. See how he knocked down Vilk and Stan in one flash, though people call them strong as bears, and grand fellows. He will bring his plumes, but he will not bring them to Yurand's daughter; for I too have talked with Yurand, and I know how matters are. Well, and what will be afterward? Afterward he will come hither, for whither should he go?"

"When will he come?"

"Well, if thou wait not there will be no feeling against thee. But now repeat to Zyh and the abbot what I tell thee. Let them soften their anger against Zbyshko even a little."

"How am I to explain? Papa is vexed rather than angry, but it is dangerous to speak of Zbyshko in presence of the abbot. He gave it to me, and to papa, because of the man whom I sent to Zbyshko."

"What man?"

"We had a Cheh here, you know, whom papa captured at Boleslavets, a good man and faithful. His name is Hlava.

Papa gave him to me as attendant, for the man said that he was a noble in his own country. I gave Hlava good armor, and sent him to attend Zbyshko, to guard him in danger, and, which God forefend! — to inform us (should anything happen). I gave him a purse for the road, and he swore to me by his soul's salvation that till his death he would serve Zbyshko faithfully."

"Oh, thou my girl! May God reward thee! But did Zyh not oppose?"

"Of course he opposed. At first he would not permit this for anything; only when I seized his feet was the victory on my side. There is no trouble with papa, but when the abbot heard of the matter from his buffoons he cursed the whole room-full in one moment, and there was such a day of judgment that papa ran out to the barns. Only in the evening did the abbot take pity on my tears, and give me besides a rosary. But I was willing to suffer, if only Zbyshko had. a larger retinue."

"As God is dear to me, I know not which one I love more, Zbyshko or thee, but in every case he had a good retinue — and I gave him money too, though he did not wish to take it. Moreover, Mazovia is not beyond the sea."

Further conversation was interrupted by the barking of dogs, shouts, and the sound of brass trumpets in front of the house. When they heard these Yagenka said, —

"Papa and the abbot are coming from the hunt. Let us go to the porch, for it is better that the abbot should see you first from a distance, and not in the house on a sudden."

Then she conducted Matsko to the porch, from which they saw on the snow in the yard a crowd of men, horses, dogs; also elks and wolves pierced with spears, or with bolts shot from crossbows. The abbot, seeing Matsko before dismounting, hurled a spear toward him, — not to strike, it is true, but to show in that way more definitely his resentment against the people of Bogdanets. But Matsko bowed to him from afar, cap in hand, as if he had noticed nothing. Yagenka had not observed this, for she was astonished first of all at the presence of her two suitors in the retinue.

"Stan and Vilk are there!" cried she, "they must have met papa in the forest."

And with Matsko it went so far that something seemed to prick his old wound at sight of them. It passed through his head in a flash that one of the two might get Yagenka, and with her Mochydoly, the lands of the abbot, his forests

and his money. Sorrow and rage seized his heart, especially
a moment later when he saw something new. Vilk, though
the abbot had wished not long before to fight with his
father, sprang to the abbot's stirrup to assist him from the
horse, and he in dismounting leaned in a friendly manner on
the young noble's shoulder.

"The abbot will be reconciled with old Vilk in this way,"
thought Matsko, "that he will give the forests and the land
with the girl." But these bitter thoughts of his were interrupted by Yagenka, who said at that moment, —

"The beating they got from Zbyshko is healed, but
though they were to come here every day, nothing will be
waiting for them!"

Matsko looked; the girl's face was as ruddy from anger as
it was cold, and her blue eyes flashed with rage, though she
knew well that Vilk and Stan had stood up for her in the
inn, and were beaten because of her.

"But you will do what the abbot commands," said
Matsko.

"The abbot will do what I want," said she from where
she stood.

"Dear God," thought Matsko, "and that foolish Zbyshko
ran away from such a girl!"

CHAPTER XVI.

THE " foolish Zbyshko " had ridden out of Bogdanets with a heavy heart, really. First, he felt strange somehow and awkward without his uncle, from whom during many years he had not parted, and to whom he was so accustomed that he did not know well how to live without him either on the road or in war. Second, he regretted Yagenka; for, though he said to himself that he was going to Danusia, whom he loved with all his soul, it had been so pleasant for him near Yagenka that he felt now for the first time what delight there had been in her company, and what sadness there might be without her. And he wondered at his regret, and was even disturbed by it. Had he been longing for Yagenka as a brother for a sister it would be nothing; but he saw that he wanted to grasp her by the waist and seat her on the horse, or take her from the saddle, to carry her through streams, squeeze water from her hair, go with her through the forests, look at her, and take " counsel " with her. So accustomed had he grown to this, and so pleasant was it to him that now, when he began to think of it, he forgot straightway and entirely that he was journeying on a long road to Mazovia, and immediately that moment was present to his eyes when Yagenka gave him aid in the forest while he was struggling with the bear. And it seemed to him that that was yesterday, as also it was yesterday when they were going to find the beaver in Odstayani Lake. He had not seen her when she swam in after the beaver, but now it seemed to him that he saw her, and at once those same shivers seized him which had seized him a couple of weeks earlier, when the wind played too freely with Yagenka's clothing. Then he remembered how she had gone to church in Kresnia dressed splendidly, and he had wondered that a simple maiden seemed to him like some lady of high lineage on a journey with her court.

All this was the cause that around his heart something began to make a disturbance, at once sweet and sad and full of desire, and if he thought besides that he might have done what he wished with her, that she was drawn to him also, if he remembered how she gazed into his eyes, how she nestled

up to him, he was hardly able to sit on his horse. "If I
had met her somewhere and said farewell and embraced her
on the road," said he to himself, " she might have let me ; "
then he felt that that was untrue, and that she would not have
let him, for at the very thought of such a parting sparks
passed along his body, though there was frost in the world at
that moment.

At last he was frightened at those recollections, too much
resembling desires, and he shook them from his soul as he
would dry snow from an overcoat.

"I am going to Danusia, to my dearest," said he to himself. And he remarked at once that that was another
love, as it were, — more pious, and passing less through the
bones. Gradually, too, in proportion as his feet became
chilled in the stirrups, and the cold wind cooled his blood,
all his thoughts flew to Danusia. To her in truth he owed
them. Had it not been for her, his head would have fallen
long before on the square of Cracow. For when she said,
in presence of knights and citizens, "He is mine," she took
him by those words from the hands of the executioner, and
thenceforth he belonged to her as much as a slave to his
master. It was not he who had taken her, it was she who
had taken him ; no opposition from Yurand could avail
against that fact. She alone could release him, as a lady
might release a servant, though he in that case would not go
far, for he was bound by his vow. But he thought that she
would not release, that she would rather go with him even
from the Mazovian court to the end of the world ; and thinking thus he began in his soul to praise her to the prejudice
of Yagenka, as if it were Yagenka's fault exclusively that
temptations had attacked him, and that his heart had been
divided. It did not occur to him now that Yagenka had
cured old Matsko, and besides, without her aid, perhaps the
bear that night would have taken the skin from his head ;
and he was deliberately indignant at Yagenka, thinking that
he was serving Danusia in that way, and justifying himself
in his own eyes.

But now appeared the Cheh, Hlava, who had been sent
by Yagenka, and who brought with him a pack-horse.

"Let Him be praised!" said he, bowing low.

Zbyshko had seen the man once or twice at Zyh's house,
but did not recognize him ; so he said, —

"Praised for the ages of ages! But who art thou?"

"Your attendant, renowned lord."

"How my attendant? Here are my attendants," said he, pointing to the two Turks given him by Zavisha, and two sturdy youths who sitting on two stumpy horses were leading the knight's stallions. "These are mine — but who sent thee?"

"Panna Yagenka."

"Panna Yagenka?"

Zbyshko, who had been full of indignation, and whose heart was full yet of ill-will, said, —

"Go home and thank Panna Yagenka for her kindness. I do not need thee."

The Cheh shook his head.

"I will not go, lord. I have been given to you; and besides, I have sworn to serve you till death."

"If thou hast been given me, then thou art my servant."

"Yours, lord."

"Then I command thee to return."

"I have sworn, and though I am a prisoner and a poor man, I am a noble."

Zbyshko was angry.

"Be off! How is this? Wilt thou serve me against my will, or what? Be off, or I shall command to draw a crossbow on thee."

Hlava unstrapped quietly a cloth mantle lined with wolf-skin, and gave it to Zbyshko, saying, —

"Panna Yagenka sent you this, lord."

"Dost wish that I should break thy bones?" inquired Zbyshko, taking a spear from the hands of an attendant.

"And here is a purse at your command."

Zbyshko aimed the spear, but remembering that the man, though a prisoner, was a noble by blood, who had remained with Zyh only because he had not the means to redeem himself, lowered the spear point. The Cheh bowed to his stirrup, and said, —

"Be not angry, lord. If you do not command me to go with you, I will go behind you one or two furlongs; but I will go, for I have sworn on my soul's salvation to do so."

"But if I give command to kill, or to bind thee?"

"If you command to kill me it will not be my sin; if you command to bind me I will remain bound till good people unbind me, or till wolves devour me."

Zbyshko did not answer, he merely urged his horse forward, and his people moved after him. Hlava, with a cross-

bow at his shoulder and an axe in his hand, dragged on
behind, taking shelter in the shaggy skin of a bison; for
a sharp wind began to blow, bringing snow-flakes.

The storm increased with every moment. The Turks,
though in skin coats, were stiff from cold. Zbyshko's
attendants began to swing their arms, to beat themselves
with their hands, and he also, not clothed sufficiently, cast
his eyes once and a second time on the wolf-skin mantle
brought by Hlava, and after a while told one of the Turks
to bring it to him.

Wrapping himself closely in the mantle he soon felt
warmth passing over his whole body; especially convenient
was the hood, which sheltered his eyes and a considerable
part of his face, so that the storm almost ceased to annoy
him. Then he thought, in spite of himself, that Yagenka
was an honest maiden to the bones, and he reined in his
horse somewhat, for the desire seized him to ask Hlava
about her, and everything that had happened at Zyh's
house. So beckoning to the man he asked, —

"Does old Zyh know that Panna Yagenka sent thee
to me?"

"He knows."

"And he did not oppose?"

"He opposed."

"Tell how it was."

"Pan Zyh was walking through the room, and Panna
Yagenka after him. He screamed, but she not a word;
when he turned toward her she dropped to her knees. And
not a word. Pan Zyh said at last: 'Art thou deaf, that
thou sayst nothing in answer to me? Speak, for at last I
shall permit, and when I permit the abbot will take off my
head.' Then the young lady saw that she would get what
she wanted, and began to thank him with tears. The old
man reproached her for tormenting him, and complained
that everything had to be as she wished, but at last he
said: 'Promise me that thou wilt not run out in secret
to take farewell of him; if thou promise I will permit,
otherwise I will not.' Panna Yagenka was vexed, but she
promised; and he was glad, for he and the abbot were
terribly afraid that the wish might come to her to see your
grace. But that was not the end, for later the lady wished
that there should be two horses, and he refused; she wanted
a wolf-skin and a purse; he refused. But what value in
those refusals? If she had thought to burn down the house

her father would have consented. For this reason you have
the second horse, the wolf-skin, and the purse."

"An honest girl!" thought Zbyshko in his soul. After
a time he asked, —

"But was there no trouble with the abbot?"

Hlava laughed like a shrewd man, who takes note of
everything passing around him, and answered, —

"They both kept secrets from the abbot, and I know not
what would have happened if he had known this, for I went
away earlier. The abbot, as an abbot, thunders sometimes
at the young lady, but then he casts his eyes at her, and
looks to see if he has not done her too much injustice. I
have seen myself how he scolded her once, and then hurried
to a casket and brought a chain such that a better could
not be found in Cracow, and he said, 'Here.' She can
get on with the abbot too, for her own father does not love
her more than he does."

"That is true certainly."

"As God is in heaven."

Here they were silent, and went on farther through the
wind and the snow-flakes; but suddenly Zbyshko reined in
his horse, for from one side of the forest was heard a certain complaining voice, half smothered by the sound of the
trees.

"Christian, save a servant of God from misfortune!"

At the same moment a person dressed half like a cleric,
half like a layman, ran out to the road, where he stood before
Zbyshko and said, —

"Whoever thou be, O lord, give aid to a man and a neighbor in dire distress!"

"What has happened, and who art thou?" asked the
young knight.

"I am a servant of God, though without ordination, and
it has happened this morning that my horse broke away, having on his back a casket with sacred objects. I was left
alone, without arms; evening is coming, and it is short waiting till savage beasts will be heard in the forest. I shall
perish unless you save me."

"If thou perish because of me must I answer for thy sins?
How am I to know that thou speakest truth, and that thou
art not a cutpurse, or a vagabond, many of whom are
dragging along the roads these days?"

"You will know by my caskets. More than one man
would give a purse filled with ducats to possess what is in

them, but I will share their contents with you if you take me and them."

"Thou callest thyself God's servant and knowest not that a man is to be rescued for heavenly, not for earthly rewards. But how hast thou kept the caskets, since the horse ran away?"

"Before I found the horse the wolves had devoured him in an opening of the forest, and the caskets were left. I brought them to the road so as to wait for the favor and help of good people."

Thus speaking, and wishing to show that he had told truth, he pointed at two bark caskets lying under a pine tree. Zbyshko looked at the man rather suspiciously, for to him this stranger did not seem over honest; and besides, his speech, though pure, betrayed an origin in distant regions. Zbyshko, however, was loath to refuse assistance, and permitted the man to sit, with his caskets, which proved to be very light, on that detached horse led by Hlava.

"May God increase your victory, valiant knight!" said the unknown. Then, seeing the youthful face of Zbyshko, he added in an undertone, "and also the hairs in your beard."

A moment later he was riding by the side of the Cheh. For some time they could not talk, as a strong wind was blowing and the noise of the forest was tremendous, but when it had calmed somewhat Zbyshko heard the following conversation behind, —

"I do not deny thy visit to Rome, but thou hast the look of a beer guzzler."

"Guard thyself against eternal damnation," answered the unknown, "for thou art talking with a man who last Easter ate hard-boiled eggs with the Holy Father. Talk not on such a cold day to me of beer, even though it were heated; but if thou hast on thy person a flask of wine, give me two or three gulps of it, and I will give a month's indulgence from purgatory."

"Thou art not ordained, for I heard thee say so thyself; how couldst thou, then, give me indulgence for a month of purgatory?"

"I am not ordained, but I have a shaven head, for which I received a dispensation; besides, I bear with me indulgences and relics."

"In those caskets?"

"In these caskets. And if thou wert to see what I have,

thou wouldst fall on thy face, — not only thou, but all the
pines in the forests, and all the wild beasts."

The Cheh, who was clever and experienced, looked suspiciously at the dealer in indulgences, and added, —

" But the wolves ate thy horse."

"They did, for they are the devil's relatives; but they
burst. I saw one of them burst with my own eyes. If thou
hast wine give it, for though the wind has stopped, I am
chilled from sitting at the roadside."

Hlava did not give the wine, and again they rode on in
silence, till the dealer in relics inquired,—

" Whither are ye going? "

" Far. But at present to Sieradz. Wilt thou go with us? "

" I must. I will sleep in the stable, and to-morrow mayhap that pious knight will give me a horse, and I shall go
farther."

" Whence comest thou? "

" From the land of the Prussian lords, from near Malborg."

Hearing this, Zbyshko turned his head, and beckoned the
unknown to him.

" Thou art from near Malborg? Whence comest thou
now? "

" From near Malborg."

" But thou art not a German, thou speakest our language
so well. What is thy name? "

" I am a German, and they call me Sanderus; I know
your language, for I was born in Torun, where all people
speak it. Later I lived in Malborg, but it is the same there.
Nay! even brothers of the Order understand your language."

" And art thou long from Malborg? "

" I have been in the Holy Land, in Constantinople, and
in Rome, whence I returned through France to Malborg;
from Malborg I went to Mazovia, carrying holy relics, which
pious Christians buy gladly to save their souls."

" Wert thou in Plotsk, and also in Warsaw? "

" I was in both places. May God give health to both
princesses! Not without cause do the Prussian lords themselves love Princess Alexandra; she is a saintly lady, though
Princess Anna, the wife of Prince Yanush, is not inferior."

" Hast thou seen the court in Warsaw? "

" I have not met it in Warsaw, but in Tsehanov, where the
prince and the princess received me hospitably as a servant
of God, and gave me rich gifts for the road. But I left
relics which must bring them God's blessing."

Zbyshko wished to inquire about Danusia, but at once a certain indecision possessed him, and a certain shame; for he understood that that would be the same as to confess his love to an unknown man of low origin, who, besides, had a suspicious look, and might be some common deceiver. So after a moment's silence, he asked, —

"What relics art thou bearing through the world?"

"I bear indulgences and relics; the indulgences are various. I have plenary indulgences, indulgences for five hundred years, for three hundred, for two hundred years, and less, cheaper, so that even poor people acquire them, and thus shorten the torments of purgatory for themselves. I have indulgences for past sins, and for future; but do not think, lord, that I put away the money which people pay for them. A morsel of black bread and a gulp of water suffices me; the rest of what I collect I take to Rome, so that in time I may make a new journey. There are many money grabbers who go through the world, it is true, but have only false things, indulgences, relics, testimonials, and seals; such persons as these the Holy Father pursues justly with his letters, but on me the prior of Sieradz has wrought injustice and wrong, for my seals are genuine. Look, lord, at the wax and you will know yourself."

"But what did the prior of Sieradz do?"

"Oh, as God lives, I thought unjustly that he was tainted with the heretical teaching of Wyclif. And if, as your attendant has told me, you are going to Sieradz, I prefer not to show myself to him, so as not to bring him to sin and blaspheme against holy things."

"That means, without saying much, that he took thee for a cheat and a cutpurse."

"May I forgive him, lord, through love for my neighbor, as indeed I have done already; but he has blasphemed against my sacred wares, for which I fear greatly that he will be damned beyond rescue."

"What sacred wares hast thou?"

"Such that it is not proper to speak of them with covered head; but since I have indulgences with me, I give you, O lord, permission not to take off your cowl, since the wind is now blowing afresh. Buy of me, therefore, a little indulgence to have in supply, and the sin will not be accounted to you. What is it that I have not? I have a hoof of the ass on which the flight to Egypt took place; it was found near the pyramids. The King of Aragon offered me indeed fifty ducats for it. I have a feather from a wing of the Archangel Gabriel, who dropped it during the Annunciation; I have two heads of quails sent to the Israelites in the wilderness; I have oil in which pagans wished to boil Saint John, and a round from the ladder which Jacob saw in his vision. I have tears dropped by Mary of Egypt, and some rust from the keys of Saint Peter. I cannot mention all, because I am chilled, and your attendant, O lord, would not give me wine; and moreover I could not name them all between this time and evening."

"Those relics are great if they are genuine," said Zbyshko.

"If they are genuine? Take the lance from the hand of that attendant and plant it before you, for the devil is near who gives you such ideas. Keep him, O lord, at the length of the lance. And if you will not bring misfortune on yourself buy of me an indulgence for that sin; unless you do, the one whom you love most on earth will die in three weeks."

Zbyshko was terrified at the threat, for Danusia came to his mind, and he said, —

"It is not I who doubt, but the prior of Dominicans in Sieradz."

"Look yourself at the wax of the seals; as to the prior, God knows if he is alive yet, for Divine justice is swift."

But when they arrived at Sieradz it appeared that the prior was alive. Zbyshko even betook himself to him to give for two masses, one of which was to be offered for the benefit of Matsko, the other on account of those peacock-plumes for which Zbyshko was going. The prior, like many in Poland at that time, was a foreigner, from Tsylia by origin, but during fourteen years' residence in Sieradz he had learned Polish well, and was a great enemy of the Knights of the Cross. When he heard, therefore, of Zbyshko's undertaking, he said: "A greater punishment of the Lord will meet them yet, but I will not dissuade thee from what thou hast intended; first, because thou hast taken an oath, and, second, because a Polish hand can never squeeze them sufficiently for what they did here in Sieradz."

"What did they do?" inquired Zbyshko, who was glad to hear of every injustice committed by the Knights of the Cross.

Here the old prior spread apart his hands and began to repeat audibly "Eternal rest;" then he sat on a bench, and kept his eyes closed for a while, as if to summon old memories.

"Vincent of Shamotur brought them here," said he at last. "I was twenty years old then, and had just come from Tsylia, whence my uncle, Petzoldt, the custodian, brought me. The Knights of the Cross attacked this town in the night, and burned it immediately. From the walls we saw them put men, women, and children to the sword on the market square, and hurl infants into the fire; I saw them kill even priests, for in their rage they spared no man. And it happened that the prior Mikolai, from Elblang by origin, knew Hermann, the comtur, the leader of the Germans. The prior went out with the older monks to that savage knight, and kneeling down, implored him in German to spare Christian blood. 'I understand not,' replied Hermann the comtur, and gave command to go on with the slaughter. Then they slew the monks, and with them my uncle, Petzoldt; next they bound Mikolai the prior to the tail of a horse. Toward morning there was not a living man in the town, save the Knights of the Cross, — and save me; I was hidden on a beam in the belfry. God punished them for that at Plovtsi, but they are rising up continually to the destruction of this Christian kingdom, and they will rise up till the arm of God crushes them utterly."

"At Plovtsi too," answered Zbyshko, "nearly all the men of my family perished; but I feel no regret for them, since God gave King Lokietek such a victory, and destroyed twenty thousand Germans."

"Thou wilt see a still greater war, and greater victories," said the prior.

"Amen!" replied Zbyshko. And they spoke then of something else.

The young knight asked a little about the dealer in relics whom he had found on the road, and learned that many such cheats were wandering about on the highways, deceiving the credulous. The prior told him also that there were papal bulls commanding bishops to punish such dealers, and, in case a man had not genuine letters and seals, to condemn him immediately. Since the testimonies of this wanderer had seemed suspicious to the prior, he wished to send him at once to the jurisdiction of the bishop. If it appeared that he was a genuine bearer of indulgences no wrong would be done him. But this man preferred flight. Perhaps he feared delay on his journey, but through this flight he subjected himself to still greater suspicion.

Toward the end of Zbyshko's visit the prior invited the

young man to rest and pass the night in the cloister; but he could not accept, since he wished to hang up a card before the inn with a challenge to battle "on foot or on horseback" to all knights who should deny that Panna Danusia was the most beautiful and virtuous maiden in the kingdom. It was not proper in any way to attach such a challenge to the gate of the cloister. Neither the prior nor other priests would even write a card for him. In consequence of this the young knight grew greatly vexed and knew not at all how to help himself. It occurred to him only on his return to the inn to ask aid of the dealer in indulgences.

"The prior does not know whether thou art a rascal or not, for he says: 'If he has genuine testimony why did he fear the bishop's court?'"

"I fear not the bishop, but monks who have no knowledge of seals. I wished to go to Cracow, but as I have no horse I must wait till some man gives me one. Meanwhile I will send a letter, to which I shall put my own seal."

"I too thought to myself that if thou wouldst show that thou knowest letters it would be a sign that thou art not a simple fellow. But how wilt thou send the letter?"

"Through some pilgrim or wandering monk. Are the people few in number who go to the queen's grave in Cracow?"

"But couldst thou write a letter for me?"

"I will write anything that you command, smoothly and to the point, even on a board."

"Better on a board," said Zbyshko, delighted, "for it will not drop off, and will be good for another time."

So when Zbyshko's attendants had found and brought in a new board, Sanderus sat down to write. Zbyshko could not read what he wrote, but he commanded straightway to fasten the challenge on the gate, and to hang beneath it his shield, which the Turks guarded one after the other. Whoso should strike the challenge with his spear would indicate that he accepted it. But in Sieradz there was evidently a lack of volunteers for such matters, for neither on that day nor the day following till noon did the shield resound from a blow; at noon the young man, somewhat vexed, continued his journey. But first Sanderus came to him and said, —

"If you had hung up your shield in the land of the Prussian lords surely your attendant would have to strap on your armor."

"How is that? Knights of the Cross, being monks, cannot have ladies whom they love, for it is not permitted them."

"I know not whether it is permitted, but I know that they have them. It is true that a Knight of the Cross cannot engage without sin in single combat, for he takes an oath that he will fight with others only for the faith, but there is a multitude of lay knights from distant lands who come to aid the Order. These men are looking only to find some one with whom to fight, especially the French knights."

"Oh, indeed! I have seen them at Vilno, and God grant me to see them also at Malborg. I need peacock-plumes from helmets, for I have vowed to get them — dost understand?"

"Buy, O lord, two or three drops of the sweat which fell from Saint George when he fought the dragon. No relic is of more service to a knight. Give for them that horse on which you commanded me to sit. I will give besides an indulgence for the Christian blood which you will shed in the struggle."

"Say no more, or I shall be angry. I will not take thy wares till I know that they are genuine."

"You are going, lord, as you said, to the Mazovian court, to Prince Yanush. Inquire there how many relics they took of me, — the princess herself and knights and damsels at weddings where I was present."

"What weddings?"

"As usual before Advent. The knights marry one with more haste than another, because people say that there will be war between the King of Poland and the Prussian knights for the land of Dobryn. A man says to himself: 'God knows whether I shall return alive;' and he wishes, before the war comes, to experience happiness with a woman."

The news of the war occupied Zbyshko greatly, but still more that which Sanderus had said about weddings; so he inquired, —

"What damsels were married?"

"Oh, Princess Anna's damsels. I know not whether one remained, for I heard her say that she would have to seek new ladies-in-waiting."

When he heard this Zbyshko was silent for a time; after that he asked with a somewhat changed voice, —

"But Panna Danuta, the daughter of Yurand, whose name stands on the board, — was she married also?"

Sanderus hesitated in answering, first, because he knew nothing clearly, and second, because he thought that by keeping the knight in suspense he would win a preponderance over him and be able to exploit him the better. He had considered already in his mind that he ought to hold fast to that knight, who had a good retinue and sufficient supplies. Sanderus knew men and things. Zbyshko's great youth permitted him to suppose that the knight would be bountiful and not provident, casting around money easily. He had observed also that costly Milan armor, and the immense stallions for battle, which not every man could own; so he said to himself that with a young lord like him he would find secure hospitality at courts, and more than one chance to sell indulgences with profit; he would have safety on the road, and, finally, abundance of food and drink, which for him was supremely important. So when he heard Zbyshko's question he wrinkled his forehead, raised his eyes as if straining his memory, and answered, —

"Panna Danuta, — but whence is she?"

"Danuta, the daughter of Yurand of Spyhov."

"I saw them all, but what their names were I do not remember clearly."

"She is young yet, plays on the lute, and rejoices the princess with singing."

"Ah! — young — plays on the lute — young maidens also got married. Is she not dark as an agate?"

Zbyshko was relieved.

"That is not she! She is white as snow, but there is a blush on her cheeks, she is blond."

"One as black as an agate," said Sanderus, "remained with the princess, almost all the others got married."

"Thou sayst 'almost all;' that means not to the last one. By the dear God! if thou wish of me anything then bring it to mind."

"In three or four days I could recall everything; but most precious to me would be a horse on which I could carry my sacred objects."

"If thou tell truth, thou wilt get one."

"The truth will be known at the Mazovian court," said Hlava, who had been listening to the conversation from the first and was laughing in his fist.

Sanderus looked at him awhile and asked; "Dost thou think that I fear the Mazovian court?"

"I do not say that thou hast fear of the Mazovian court, but if it shall appear that thou hast lied thou wilt not go away on thy own legs, for his grace will give command to break both."

"As true as life!" said Zbyshko.

In view of such an announcement Sanderus thought it better to be cautious, and answered, —

"If I had wished to lie I should have answered at once that she was married, or was not married, but I said that I did not remember. If thou hadst wit thou wouldst have noted my virtue at once by this answer."

"My wit is not a brother to thy virtue, for thy virtue may be a dog's sister."

"My virtue does not bark like thy wit, and whoso barks during life may easily howl after death."

"And in truth thy virtue will not howl after death, but gnash, unless during life it loses its teeth in the service of Satan."

And they began a war of words, for the Cheh had a nimble tongue, and for every word from the German he found two. Meanwhile Zbyshko gave command to start, and they pushed on, having inquired first carefully of experienced people about the road to Lenchytsa. A little beyond Sieradz they entered deep pine forests with which the greater part of the country was covered. But through them in parts was a road, ditched at the sides, in low places even paved with round stones, a remnant of King Kazimir's management. It is true that after his death, amid disorders of the war roused by the Nalenchi and the Grymaliti, roads had been neglected somewhat, but during Yadviga's time, after the pacification of the kingdom, spades appeared again in the hands of dexterous people along swamps and in forests appeared axes. Toward the end of her life the merchant might conduct his laden wagons between the most important towns without fear of seeing them broken in ruts or stuck fast in mud holes. Wild beasts or robbers might meet one on the road, but against beasts there were torches at night, and crossbows during daylight; as to robbers and rascals, there were fewer of them than in neighboring countries. Moreover, the man who went with an escort and armed might advance without fear.

So Zbyshko feared neither robbers nor armed knights; he did not even think of them, for great alarm had fallen on him, and his whole soul was at the Mazovian court. Would he find his Danusia a damsel of the princess, or the wife of some knight of Mazovia? He knew not himself, and from daylight till darkness he wrestled with his thoughts on this question. Sometimes it seemed to him impossible that she should forget him, but at other times it came to his head that perhaps

Yurand had come to the court from Spyhov and given her in marriage to some friend or neighbor. He had told him while in Cracow that Danusia was not fated for him, Zbyshko, and that he could not give her; so, evidently, he had promised her to another; evidently he was bound by an oath, and now he was keeping it. It seemed certain to Zbyshko that he would not see her again as a maiden. Then he called Sanderus and inquired a second time, but he merely made the affair still more doubtful. More than once he recollected the damsel, the daughter of Yurand, and her wedding, and then suddenly he put his finger to his lips, thought a moment, and answered, " It must be that it was not that one." In wine, which was to create clearness in his head, the German did not regain memory, and he kept the young knight continually between hope and mortal fear.

So Zbyshko travelled on in anxiety, suffering, and uncertainty. On the way he had no thought of his own or of Zyh's house, he was thinking only of what it behooved him to do. First of all was the need to go and learn the truth at the Mazovian court; hence he rode on hurriedly, halting only for short night rests at courts, inns, and towns, so as not to wear out his horses. In Lenchytsa he commanded to hang up his board again with the challenge before the gate, understanding in his soul that, whether Danusia remained in a maiden condition or was married, she was always the lady of his heart, and he was obliged to do battle for her. But in Lenchytsa there were not many who knew how to read the challenge; those of the knights to whom clerics skilled in letters explained it, shrugged their shoulders, not knowing foreign customs, and said : " Some fool is travelling ; how can any man agree with him, or contradict him. unless he has seen the girl with his own eyes ? "

And Zbyshko went on with increasing vexation and increasing haste. Never had he ceased to love his Danusia ; when at home and while " advising " almost daily with Yagenka, and looking at her beauty, he had not thought so often of the other, but now she did not leave his eyes, his memory, or his thoughts day or night. In sleep even he saw her before him, blond-haired, with a lute in her hand. with red shoes, and with a garland on her head. She stretched forth her hands to him, but Yurand drew her away. In the morning, when dreams fled, greater longing than ever came straightway in place of them, and never had Zbyshko loved that maiden when in Bogdanets as he loved

her then, when he was not sure but they had taken her away
from him.

It came also to his head that surely she had been married
in spite of her; hence at heart, he did not blame Danusia,
especially since, being a child, she could not have her own
will yet.   But in soul he was angry at Yurand and Princess
Anna, and when he thought of Danusia's husband his heart
rose to his throat, and he looked around threateningly on
his attendants who carried his armor under a covering.   He
settled too, with himself, that he would not cease to serve
her, and that though he might find her the wife of another
he would lay the peacock-plumes down at her feet.   But
there was more grief in that thought than solace, for he
knew not what he could begin to do afterward.   Nothing
consoled him save the thought of a great war.   Though he
had no wish to live without Danusia, he did not promise
to perish surely, but he felt that somehow his spirit and
his memory would be so diverted during war that he would
be free of all other cares and vexations.   And a great war
was hanging in the air, as it were.   It was unknown whence
news of it had come, for peace reigned between the king
and the Order; still in all places whithersoever Zbyshko
went, men spoke on no other subject.   People had, as it
were, a foreboding that it must come, and some men said
openly: " Why did we unite with Lithuania, unless against
those wolves, the Knights of the Cross?   We must finish
with them once and forever, so that they may be rending
our entrails no longer."   But others said: " Mad monks!
Plovtse did not suffice them ! death is hanging over them,
and still they seized Dobryn, which they must vomit up with
their blood."   And throughout all territories of the kingdom
people without boasting prepared seriously, as is usual in
a life-and-death struggle, with the deep determination of
strong men who had endured injustice too long and were
making ready at last to mete out dreadful punishment.   In
all houses Zbyshko met men who were convinced that the
need might come any day to sit on horseback; and he was
astonished, for though thinking, as well as others, that war
must come, he had not heard that it would begin so soon.
It had not occurred to him that the desire of people had
anticipated events that time.   He believed others, not himself, and was rejoiced in heart at sight of that hurry pre-
ceding conflict which he met everywhere.   In all places
all other anxieties gave way to anxiety about a horse and

armor; everywhere men were testing with great care lances,
swords, axes, spears, helmets, mail, straps for breastplates,
horse trappings. Smiths were beating night and day on
iron plates with their hammers, forging rude heavy armor
which elegant knights of the West could hardly move, but
which the sturdy "heirs" of Great and Little Poland carried
easily. Old men drew forth from caskets in their closets
faded bags with coin in them, to procure military outfits for
their sons. Once Zbyshko passed the night with a rich
noble, Bartosh of Belav, who having twenty-two stalwart
sons mortgaged broad lands to the cloister in Lovich so as
to buy twenty-two suits of armor, as many helmets, and
other arms for the conflict. So Zbyshko, though he had not
heard of this in Bogdanets, thought, also, that he would have
to go to Prussia directly, and thanked God that he was
equipped for the expedition so splendidly.

Indeed his armor roused admiration everywhere. People
esteemed him the son of a voevoda, but when he said that
he was only the son of a simple noble, and that such armor
might be bought among the Germans if one would pay
with an axe properly, hearts gained warlike desire. But
more than one man unable to stifle greed at sight of this
armor caught up with Zbyshko on the road, and asked,
"Well, wilt thou fight for it?" But being in a hurry he
would not fight; besides, the Cheh drew his crossbow.
Zbyshko ceased even to hang out the board with the challenge at inns, for he noticed that the farther he advanced
from the boundary the less people understood it, and the
more they considered him foolish.

In Mazovia men spoke less of the war. They believed
even there that it was coming, but they knew not the time.
In Warsaw there was peace, the more since the court was at
Tsehanov, which Prince Yanush had built over after the old
attack of the Lithuanians, or rather he had built it entirely
new, for of the earlier place there remained only the castle.
In the town of Warsaw Yasko Soha, the starosta of the
castle, son of the voevoda Abraham, who fell at the Vorskla,
received Zbyshko. Yasko knew the young knight, for he
had been with Princess Anna in Cracow; hence he was glad
to entertain him. But before sitting down to food and drink
Zbyshko inquired about Danusia. "Had she not been given
in marriage at the same time with other damsels?"

Yasko could not answer that question. The prince and
princess had lived in the castle of Tsehanov since early

autumn. In Warsaw only he and a handful of bowmen had remained as a guard. He heard that in Tsehanov there had been various amusements and weddings, as happens usually before Advent, but who of the damsels had married and who had remained single he, as a married man, had not inquired.

"I think, however," said he, "that Yurand's daughter is not married. How could the marriage take place without Yurand? and I have not heard of his arrival. Two brothers of the Order are visiting at the court, — one is from Yansbork, the other from Schytno, — and with them are some foreign guests, it is likely ; at such times Yurand never comes, for the sight of a white mantle rouses him to madness. Unless Yurand was there, there was no wedding. But if it is thy wish I will send a messenger to inquire, and will order him to return quickly, though, as I live, I think that thou wilt find Yurand's daughter yet in the maiden state."

"I shall go myself to-morrow, but God reward thee for the comfort. Only let my horses rest, and I shall go, for I cannot rest till I know the truth. But God repay thee; thou hast relieved me at once."

Soha did not stop here; he inquired of one and another among the nobles, who were stopping by chance in the castle, and the soldiers, if any had heard of the marriage of Yurand's daughter. No one had heard, though there were men who had been in Tsehanov, and had even been at weddings. "Unless some one had taken her during recent weeks or recent days." It might have happened, indeed, for in those days people did not lose time in reflection. But Zbyshko went to sleep greatly strengthened. While there in bed he thought whether or not to dismiss Sanderus on the morrow; but he considered that the man might be useful, because of his knowledge of German, when the time came to go against Lichtenstein. He thought, too, that Sanderus had not deceived him; and though at inns he was very expensive, since he ate and drank as much as four persons, still he was serviceable, and showed his new lord a certain attachment. Besides, he had the art of writing, thus surpassing the Cheh and Zbyshko himself.

All these considerations caused the young knight to let Sanderus go to Tsehanov; at which the man rejoiced, not only because of the food, but because he thought that in honorable company he would rouse more confidence and find purchasers more easily for his relics. After another night

spent at Naselsk, and travelling neither too briskly nor too
slowly, they saw toward evening of the next day the walls
of Tsehanov Castle. Zbyshko halted at the inn to put on
his armor and enter the castle, according to knightly custom,
in a helmet, and lance in hand. So he mounted his gigantic
stallion and advanced, after he had made a sign of the cross
in the air.

But he had not gone ten steps when the Cheh riding.
behind caught up with him, and said, —

" Your grace, certain knights are riding up after us, —
Knights of the Cross, I think."

Zbyshko turned his horse and saw a showy retinue not
farther than fifty rods distant; at the head of it on strong
Pomeranian horses rode two knights, both in full armor, each
in a white mantle with a black cross, and in a helmet with
lofty peacock-plumes.

" Knights of the Cross, by the dear God! " said Zbyshko.

And involuntarily he inclined in the saddle, and placed his
lance half-way down to the horse's ears; seeing which, the
Cheh spat on his palm so that the axe might not slip from it.

Zbyshko's attendants, men of experience, knowing the
custom of war, stood ready also, — not for battle, it is true,
for in knightly conflicts servants took no part, but to measure
out a space for the struggle on horseback, or to trample the
snowy earth for a combat on foot.

Being a noble, the Cheh was to take part; but he too
hoped that Zbyshko would speak before he struck, and in
his soul he was wonderfully astonished even that the young
lord lowered his lance before challenging.

But Zbyshko recollected himself in season. He recalled
that mad act of his near Cracow when he wished without
foresight to do battle with Lichtenstein, and remembered all
the misfortunes which had come of it; so he raised his lance,
which he gave to the Cheh, and without drawing his sword
moved on horseback toward the Knights of the Cross. When
he had ridden up he saw that besides them there was still a
third knight. also with plumes upon his helmet, and a fourth,
long haired, without armor; to him this last man seemed a-
Mazovian. When he saw them he said to himself, —

" I vowed in prison to my lady, not three plumes, but as
many as she has fingers on her hands; but three, if they are
not envoys, might be found at once." He thought, however,
that they must surely be envoys to the Prince of Mazovia;
so he called aloud, —

"Praised be Jesus Christ."

"For the ages of ages," answered the long-haired, un-armored horseman.

"God give you fortune!"

"And to you, lord."

"Glory to Saint George!"

"He is our patron. Lord, be greeted on the road."

Here they bowed to each other; and then Zbyshko announced his name, his escutcheon, his watchword, and the place whence he was going to the court of Mazovia. The long-haired knight declared that he was Yendrek of Kropivnitse, and that he was conducting guests of the prince, Brother Gottfried and Brother Rotgier, with Foulk de Lorche of Lorraine, who, while visiting the Knights of the Cross, wished to see with his own eyes the Prince of Mazovia, and especially the princess, daughter of the famous "Kynstut." [1]

While their names were in course of mention, the foreign knights, sitting erect on their horses, bent their heads covered with iron helmets, and bowed repeatedly; for they thought, judging from Zbyshko's brilliant armor, that the prince had sent out some distinguished person, perhaps a son or relative, to meet them.

"The comtur," continued Yendrek, "or, as you would say in our language, the starosta, of Yansbork is stopping as a guest with the prince, to whom he mentioned these three knights. 'They have a lively desire to come,' said he, 'but do not dare, especially the Knight of Lorraine, because, journeying from afar, he thinks that immediately beyond the boundary of the Order dwell Saracens, with whom war never ceases.' The prince, as a hospitable lord, sent me at once to the boundary to conduct them in safety among the castles."

"Could they not have passed without your aid?"

"Our people are terribly enraged at the Knights of the Cross, and not so much for their attacks, since we look in at them also, as for their great treachery. If a Knight of the Cross embrace thee to thy face and kiss thee, he is ready to plunge a knife into thy back at that very moment, — a custom quite swinish and hateful to us Mazovians. Yes! that is it! Every one will receive a German under his roof and do no harm to his guest, but on the road he is glad to attack him. And there are some who do nothing else

[1] Keistut.

through revenge, or for the glory which may God grant to every one."

" Who is the most famous among you? "

" There is one, and it would be better for a German to look at death than see him; they call him Yurand of Spyhov."

The young knight's heart quivered when he heard this name; he determined at once to draw Yendrek by the tongue.

" I know," said he; " I have heard of him; he is the man whose daughter Danusia was Princess Anna's damsel till she was married."

As he said this he looked carefully at the eyes of the Mazovian, stopping the breath in his breast almost; but the other answered with great astonishment: " Who told you that? She is a damsel. True it happens that damsels marry, but Yurand's daughter is not married. Six days ago, when I rode away from Tsehanov, I saw her with the princess. How could she marry in Advent? "

Zbyshko, while hearing this, used all his strength of will to avoid seizing the Mazovian by the neck and shouting, " God reward thee for the news! " but he restrained himself, and said, —

" I heard that Yurand gave her to some one."

" The princess, not Yurand, wanted to give her in marriage, but she could not go against Yurand's will. She wanted to give her to a knight in Cracow, who made a vow to the girl, and who is loved by her."

" Is he? " cried Zbyshko.

At this Yendrek looked at him quickly, smiled, and said, —

" Do you know, somehow you are terribly curious about that girl? "

" I am curious about acquaintances to whom I am going."

Little of Zbyshko's face could be seen under the helmet, — barely his eyes, his nose, and a small part of his cheeks, — but his nose and his cheeks were so red that the crafty Mazovian, who was given to jesting, said, —

" It is sure that your face has grown as red from cold as an Easter egg."

The young man was still more confused and answered, " Sure."

They moved on, and rode some time in silence; only the horses snorted, throwing out columns of steam from their nostrils, and the foreign knights began to jabber among themselves. After a while, however, Yendrek asked, —

" What is your name, for I did not hear well? "

" Zbyshko of Bogdanets."

" Oh, indeed! he who made the vow to Yurand's daughter had the same name."

" Do you think that I shall contradict? " answered Zbyshko, quickly and with pride.

" No, for there is no reason.   Dear God, then you are that Zbyshko whose head the girl covered with a veil!   After the return from Cracow the damsels talked of no one but you, and, while listening, tears flowed down the cheeks of more than one of them.   So this is you!   Hei!   there will be joy at the court, for the princess also is fond of you."

" God bless her, and bless you for the good news — for when people told me that she was married I suffered."

" What, marry!   A girl like that is a dainty bit, for all of Spyhov stands behind her; but though there are many shapely fellows at the court, no one has looked into her eyes, for each respects her deed and your vow.   Neither would the princess permit such conduct.   Hei! there will be joy. It is true that sometimes the damsels jested with her; one would say, ' Your knight will not come,' then she would stamp with her feet and cry, ' He will! he will!'   Though more than once, when some one told her that you had taken another, it came to tears."

These words touched Zbyshko, but anger at peoples' talk seized him straightway; so he said, —

" I will challenge any one who barked such things of me ! "

" Women said them," answered Yendrek, beginning to laugh.   " Will you challenge women?   What can you do with a sword against a distaff?"

Zbyshko, glad that God had sent him so kind and cheerful a companion, fell to inquiring about Danusia, then about the habits of the Mazovian court, and again about Danusia; then about Prince Yanush and the princess, and again about Danusia.   But at last, remembering his vows, he told Yendrek what he had heard on the way about war, how people were preparing, how they were waiting day by day for it, and at last he inquired if they had the same thoughts in Mazovia.

Yendrek did not think war so near.   People said that it must be near, but he had heard the prince say to Pan Mikolai once that the knights had drawn in their horns, and, since they feared the power of King Yagello, were he to insist, they would withdraw from the lands of Dobryn which they had seized, or at least they would put off the war till they were well prepared.

"Moreover," said he, "the prince went to Malborg, where, during the absence of the Master, the Grand Marshal entertained him and had tournaments for him, and at present comturs are visiting the prince, and now fresh guests are on the way to him."

Here he stopped and added after a while, —

"People say that the knights are visiting us, and Prince Ziemovit in Plotsk. They would like, of course, that in case of war our princes should help them and not the King of Poland; and if they are unable to bring the princes to act thus to induce them to remain aside quietly — But this will not happen."

"God grant that it will not! How could you stay at home? Your princes are connected with the Polish kingdom. They would not sit quietly, I think."

"They would not."

Zbyshko looked again at the foreign knights and at their peacock-plumes.

"Then are these going for that purpose?" asked he.

"The brothers of the Order, perhaps, for that purpose. Who knows?"

"And that third man?"

"The third is going because he is curious."

"He must be some considerable person."

"Yes! three wagons follow him with rich utensils, and he has nine attendants. God grant to close with such a man! It brings water to one's mouth."

"But can you not do it?"

"How! The prince commanded me to guard him. A hair will not fall from his head till he reaches Tsehanov."

"But if I should challenge them? They might like to do battle with me."

"You would have to do battle with me first, for while I live nothing of that sort will happen."

When Zbyshko heard this he looked in a friendly manner at the young noble, and said, —

"You understand what knightly honor is. I will not fight with you, for I am your friend; but in Tsehanov I shall find a cause against the Germans, God grant."

"In Tsehanov do what may please you. It will not pass there without tournaments; then it may go to the sharp edge, should the prince and the comturs give permission."

"I have a board on which is a challenge to every man who will not admit that Panna Danusia, the daughter of Yurand, is the most beautiful and virtuous maiden on earth. But, do you know, people everywhere shrugged their shoulders, and laughed — "

"Yes, for that is a foreign custom, and, to tell the truth, stupid, which people among us do not know unless somewhere on the borders. So this man of Lorraine too attacked a noble on the road, commanding him to glorify some lady of his above others. But nobody understood him, and I would not let them do battle."

"How is that? He commanded to glorify his lady? Fear God! It must be that he has no shame in his eyes."

Here he glanced at the foreign knight, as if he wished to be sure how a man looked who had no shame in his eyes; but in his soul he had to confess that Foulk de Lorche did not seem at all like a common rascal. On the contrary, from beneath his raised visor gazed mild eyes; his face was youthful, but full of a certain pensiveness. Zbyshko saw with astonishment, also, that the knight's neck was thrice surrounded by a rope of hair which passed along his armor to one ankle, and ended by being wound around it three times.

"What kind of rope is he wearing?" inquired Zbyshko.

"I could not learn accurately myself, for they do not understand our language, except Brother Rotgier, who is able to say a couple of words, but not very well. I think, however, that that young knight has made a vow not to remove the rope till he has performed some great knightly deed. In the day he wears it over his armor, in the night on his bare body."

"Sanderus!" called Zbyshko, suddenly.

"At your service!" answered the German, approaching.

"Ask that knight who is the most virtuous and most wonderful maiden in the world."

"Who is the most wonderful and most virtuous maiden in the world?" asked Sanderus.

"Ulrica de Elner!" answered De Lorche. And raising his eyes he sighed repeatedly.

Indignation stopped the breath in Zbyshko's breast when he heard blasphemy like that; great anger seized him and he reined in his stallion on the spot; but before he was able to speak Yendrek interposed his own horse between him and the foreigner, and said, —

" You will not quarrel here!"

Zbyshko turned again to the dealer in relics, and commanded, —

" Tell him from me that he loves an owl."

" My lord declares, noble knight, that you love an owl," repeated Sanderus, as an echo.

At this De Lorche dropped his reins, and with his right hand began to straighten and then to draw off his iron glove ; next he threw it in the snow before Zbyshko, who beckoned to his Cheh to raise it with the point of his lance.

Hereupon Yendrek turned to Zbyshko with a face now threatening, and said, —

" You will not meet, I say, while my guard lasts. I will not permit you or him."

" But I did not challenge him, he challenged me."

" Yes, but for the owl. This is enough for me, but if any one opposes — hei! I know how to twist a girdle."

" I do not wish to do battle with you."

" But you will have to meet me, for I have sworn to defend this man."

" How will it be? " asked the stubborn Zbyshko.

" It is not far to Tsehanov."

" But what will the German think? "

" Let your man tell him that there cannot be a meeting here, and that first there must be permission from the prince for you, and from the comturs for him."

" But if they will not give permission? "

" Then manage as you like. Enough has been said."

Zbyshko, seeing that there was no way out, and understanding that Yendrek could not permit a battle, called Sanderus again to explain to the Knight of Lorraine that they would give battle only when in the place for it. De Lorche, on hearing the German's words, nodded in sign that he understood, and then extending his hand held Zbyshko's palm for a moment, and pressed it three times firmly, which, according to knightly custom, signified that they would do battle with each other wherever and whenever they could find opportunity. They moved then in apparent concord toward Tsehanov Castle, whose broad-topped towers were now visible on the background of the ruddy sky.

They entered during daylight; but before they had announced themselves at the castle gate and the bridge had been lowered, deep night had come.

They were received and entertained by Zbyshko's acquaintance, Pan Mikolai, who commanded the garrison made up of a handful of knights and three hundred unerring Kurpie bowmen.

Immediately after entering Zbyshko learned to his great vexation that the court was not present. The prince, wishing to entertain the comturs of Schytno and Yansbork, had arranged a great hunt in the Kurpie wilderness, to which the princess also and the ladies of her court had gone so as to lend greater brilliancy to the spectacle. Of ladies whom he knew Zbyshko found only Pani Ofka, the widow of Kryh of Yarzambek, who was housekeeper in the castle. She was very glad to see him, for from the time of their return from Cracow she had told every one who was willing or unwilling to listen, of his love for Danusia and his adventure with Lichtenstein. These narrations had won for her high esteem among the younger courtiers, and the damsels; hence she was grateful to Zbyshko, and tried now to console the young man in the sadness with which the absence of Danusia filled him.

"Thou wilt not know her," said she. "The maiden's years advance, the seams of her robe are splitting at the neck, for everything in her is growing. She is not a chit as before, and she loves thee differently now from what she did the first time. Let any one cry 'Zbyshko!' in her ear, it is as if some one pricked her with an awl. Such is the lot of us women, against which no help avails. Since it is at God's command — But thy uncle, thou say'st, is well? Why did he not come? — That is our fate. It is dreary for a woman alone in the world. It is a mercy from God that the girl has not broken her legs, for she climbs the tower daily and looks down the road. Every woman of us needs friendship —"

"I will only feed my horses, and go to her, even if I go in the night," answered Zbyshko.

"Do so, but take a guide from the castle, or thou wilt go astray in the wilderness."

Indeed at the supper, which Mikolai made ready for the guests, Zbyshko declared that he would follow the prince straightway, and begged for a guide. The road-weary brothers of the Order pushed up, after the feast, to the immense fireplaces in which whole logs of pine wood were burning, and decided to go only on the morrow, after they had rested. But De Lorche, when he had inquired what the question was, declared his wish to go with Zbyshko, saying that otherwise they might be late for the hunt, which he wished to see absolutely.

Then he approached Zbyshko, and extending his hand to him pressed his palm thrice again.

CHAPTER XVII.

But it was not to come this time either to a battle, for
Pan Mikolai, learning from Yendrek of the question between
them, took his word from each that he would not do battle
without knowledge of the prince and the comturs; in case of
opposition he threatened to close the gates. Zbyshko desired to see Danusia at the earliest, hence he dared not
oppose; and De Lorche, who fought willingly when there was
need, was not bloodthirsty, and took an oath readily on his
knightly honor, that he would wait for permission from the
prince, all the more that acting otherwise he might fear to
offend him. The Knight of Lorraine, who had heard many
songs about tournaments, liked brilliant assemblies and
showy solemnities; he wished to combat in presence of court
dignitaries and ladies, for he thought that his victory would
thus obtain greater fame, and that thus he would win golden
spurs the more easily. Moreover, the country and the
people roused his curiosity; hence delay pleased him, especially as Mikolai, who had passed whole years in captivity
among Germans and was able to talk easily with foreigners,
told wonders of the prince's hunts, and of various beasts
unknown in western regions. So De Lorche started with
Zbyshko about midnight for Prasnysh, having his own
numerous retinue and people, with torches as a defence
against wolves, which during winter collected in countless
numbers, and might show themselves terrible, even for more
than ten horsemen, though armed in the best manner possible.
At the south side of Tsehanov there was no lack of forests,
either, which not far beyond Prasnysh were lost in the giant
Kurpie wilderness, which joined on the east with the impenetrable forests of Podlasie and Farther Lithuania. Somewhat previous to that time the wild Lithuanians, avoiding,
however, the terrible Kurpie, came out by those forests, usually to Mazovia. In 1337 they came to Tsehanov and
destroyed it. De Lorche listened with the utmost curiosity
to narratives of this event told by the old guide, Matsko of
Turoboy, for he was burning in soul with desire to measure himself with Lithuanians, whom he, like other knights
of the West, considered Saracens. He had come to those

regions for an expedition with the Knights of the Cross, wishing to win glory, and also salvation for his soul. While on the road he thought that war, even with the Mazovians, as a people half pagan, would secure him a plenary indulgence. He hardly believed his eyes, therefore, when on his arrival in Mazovia he saw churches in the towns, crosses on the towers, priests, knights with sacred emblems on their armor, and a people turbulent, it is true, passionate, ready for quarrel and battle, but Christian, and in no way more given to robbery than the Germans through whose country the young knight had passed. When they told him, therefore, that those people had confessed Christ for generations, he knew not what to think of the Knights of the Cross; when he learned that Lithuania too had been baptized by the late queen, his astonishment, and at the same time his sorrow, had no bounds.

He asked Matsko then if in those forests to which they were going there were not dragons to which people were forced to offer maidens, and with which it was possible to fight. But Matsko's reply in this regard too caused complete disappointment.

" In the forests live various good beasts, such as wolves, bisons, wild bulls, and bears; against these there is plenty of work," answered the Mazovian. " It may be too that foul spirits dwell in the swamps, but I have not heard of dragons; even if there were some, surely we should not give them maidens, but should go in a crowd against them. And even had there been dragons here long ago, the Kurpie would be wearing girdles of their skin now."

" What kind of people are the Kurpie, and cannot one fight with them? "

" Yes, that is possible, but it is not healthy," answered Matsko; " and finally it does not become a knight, since the Kurpie are peasants."

" The Swiss also are peasants. Do they recognize Christ? "

" There are none in Mazovia who do not, and they are our people, subject to the prince. But you have seen the bowmen at the castle. Those are Kurpie; there are no better bowmen on earth."

" The English and Scotch whom I saw at the Burgundian court — "

" I saw them also in Malborg," interrupted the Mazovian. " Sturdy fellows, but may God never let them stand against

the Kurpie! Among the Kurpie a boy of seven years gets
nothing to eat till he shoots down his food from the top of a
pine-tree."

" Of what are ye talking?" asked on a sudden Zbyshko,
whose ears had been struck frequently by the word "Kurpie."

" We are talking of the Kurpie and the English bowmen.
This knight says that the English, and therefore the Scotch,
surpass all."

" I, too, saw them at Vilno. Oh, pshaw! I heard their
arrows around my ears. There, too, from all countries were
knights who declared that they would eat us without salt;
but when they had tried us once and a second time they lost
desire for the food."

Matsko laughed, and repeated Zbyshko's words to De
Lorche.

" That was mentioned at various courts," replied the Knight
of Lorraine ; " the bravery of your knights was praised, but
they were blamed because they defend pagans against the
cross."

" We defended against invasion and injustice a people
who wanted baptism. The Germans wished to hide them
behind paganism, so as to have an excuse for war."

" God will judge them," said De Lorche.

" And He may judge them soon," replied Matsko.

But the Knight of Lorraine, hearing that Zbyshko had
fought at Vilno made inquiries of Matsko, because tidings of
knightly battles and duels fought there had gone about the
world widely. The imagination of Western warriors was
roused, especially by that duel in which four French and four
Polish knights had engaged. So De Lorche began now to
look with more esteem on Zbyshko as a man who had taken
part in such famous battles; and he rejoiced in heart that
he would have to meet no common person.

They went on in apparent concord, showing politeness to
each other at halting-places and entertaining each other with
wine, of which De Lorche had considerable supplies in his
wagons. When, from conversation between him and Matsko,
it turned out that Ulrica de Elner was not a maiden, but a
matron forty years old, with six children, Zbyshko's pride was
the more indignant that that strange foreigner not only dared
to compare an " old woman " to Danusia, but to exact superiority. He thought, however, that perhaps the man was
not in full mind, that he was one for whom a dark chamber
and whips would be better than a journey through the world,

and this thought restrained in him an outburst of immediate anger.

"Think you not," said he to Matsko, "that the evil spirit has disturbed his reason? The devil may be sitting in his head, like a worm in a nut kernel, and may be ready in the night to jump out of him and into one of us. We ought to be careful."

Matsko opposed this, it is true, but still began to look with a certain dread at the Knight of Lorraine.

"Sometimes it happens," said he at last, "that a hundred and more of them are sitting in a possessed man, and if crowded they are glad to seek residence in another. The worst devil also is one sent in by a woman." Then he turned to the knight on a sudden. "Praised be Jesus Christ!" said he.

"I, too, praise Him," answered De Lorche, with astonishment.

Matsko was set at rest perfectly.

"Well, you see," said he, "if the evil one had been in him he would have foamed at the mouth-right away, or the devil would have thrown him to the earth, for I broke out to him on a sudden. We may travel on."

So they moved forward without fear. From Tsehanov to Prasnysh was not very far; in summer a courier on a good horse might in two hours pass over the road between the two places. But they went much more slowly because of the night, the halts, and the snowdrifts in the forest; and since they had set out considerably after midnight, they arrived about daybreak at the prince's hunting house, which was beyond Prasnysh, on the brink of the forest. The house stood almost resting on the wilderness, strong, low, built of wood, but having glass panes in its windows. Before the house were two sheds for horses, and a well-sweep; around the house was a crowd of huts, made hastily from pine branches, and tents formed of skins. In the gray of dawn fires glittered brightly; in front of the tents, and around them, were huntsmen in sheepskin coats, the wool outside, in fox, wolf, and bear skin mantles. To De Lorche it seemed as if he were looking at savage beasts on two legs before the fire, for the greater number of those people wore caps made of skins from the heads of wild animals. Some were leaning on spears, others on crossbows; some were occupied in making enormous rope nets, others were turning over the coals immense quarters of bisons and elks, intended evidently for the morning meal. The glitter of the flame fell on the snow, lighting up also those wild forms, veiled somewhat by the smoke of the fires, the cloud of breaths, and the steam which rose from roasting meat. Beyond them were visible the ruddy-colored trunks of giant pines, and new crowds of people, the number of which astonished the Knight of Lorraine, unaccustomed to the sight of such hunting multitudes.

"Your princes go to a hunt as to a war," said he.

"As you see," answered Matsko of Turoboy, "they lack neither hunting gear nor people. These are the prince's beaters, but there are others also who come from the depth of the wilderness to trade."

"What shall we do?" interrupted Zbyshko; "they are asleep in the house yet."

"Wait till they wake," answered Matsko. "We will not strike the doors and wake our lord the prince."

So saying, he conducted them to a fire near which the Kurpie threw down bison and bear skins, and then began promptly to entertain them with steaming meat. Hearing foreign speech, they crowded to look at the German. Soon it was spread about by Zbyshko's retinue that the stranger was a knight "from beyond the sea," and then they so crowded about that Matsko had to use his authority to save the foreigner from overmuch curiosity. In the crowd De Lorche noticed women dressed in skins also, but ruddy as apples and uncommonly good-looking; so he inquired if they took part in hunts also.

Matsko explained that they did not belong to the hunts, but that they came with the beaters through female curiosity, or as to a fair to buy local products and sell the wealth of the forest. Such was the case in reality. That house of the prince was a centre around which, even during his absence, two elements met, — those of the town and the forest. The Kurpie did not like to go forth from their wilderness, for they felt strange without the sound of trees above their heads; so the people of Prasnysh took to that edge of the forest their renowned beer; flour ground in local windmills or in watermills on the Vengerka; salt, rare in the forest and sought for with eagerness; iron implements, straps, and similar products of industry. In return they received skins, costly furs, dried mushrooms, nuts, healing herbs, or pieces of amber found without too much trouble among the Kurpie. So a continual market was active around the house of Prince Yanush. The activity was intensified during the prince's hunts, when duty and curiosity brought out people who dwelt in the depths of the forests.

De Lorche listened to Matsko's narrations, looking with interest at the forms of the beaters, who, living in wholesome air and nourished mainly on flesh, as were most peasants for that matter in those days, astonished foreign travellers more than once by their strength and great stature. But Zbyshko, sitting near the fire, looked unceasingly at the doors and windows of the house, barely able to stay in one place. One window was lighted, evidently that of the kitchen, for smoke came out through cracks between panes not sufficiently fastened. Other windows were dark, gleaming only from daylight, which grew whiter every instant, and silvered with growing intensity the snowy wilderness behind the hunting-house. In small doors, cut in the side walls of the building, appeared in time servants in the prince's colors, who with pails or pots on their shoulders ran to the wells for water. When inquiry was made of these servants if all were sleeping yet, they answered that the court, wearied by yesterday's hunt, was still resting, but that food for the early meal to be eaten before they started was cooking.

In fact, through the kitchen windows the odor of meat and saffron began to issue and spread far about among the fires. At last the main door squeaked and opened, discovering the interior of a hall brightly lighted, and out to the porch came a man in whom at first glance Zbyshko recognized a chorister whom he had seen among Princess Anna's servants in Cracow. At that sight, without waiting for De Lorche or Matsko, he sprang toward the house with such impetus that the Knight of Lorraine was astounded.

" What has happened to that youthful knight?" inquired he.

" Nothing," answered Matsko; " but he loves a damsel of the princess and would like to see her at the earliest."

" Ah!" answered De Lorche, putting both hands to his heart. And raising his eyes he sighed time after time, so sadly that Matsko shrugged his shoulders and said inwardly, —

" Is he sighing in that way to his old woman? Is he not really unsound in mind?"

Meanwhile he conducted him to the house, and both found themselves in a spacious hall adorned with great horns of bisons, elks, wild bulls and deer, and illuminated by dry logs blazing on an immense fireplace. In the centre stood a table covered with matting and plates ready for food.

Barely a few courtiers were present, with whom Zbyshko was talking. Matsko made them acquainted immediately with De Lorche, but as they had no knowledge of German, he had himself to entertain the knight further. But every moment new courtiers came, — for the greater part splendid fellows, untrained yet, but large, broad-shouldered, yellow-haired, dressed as if for the wilderness.

Those who were acquainted with Zbyshko and knew of his Cracow adventure greeted him as an old friend, and it was evident that he enjoyed consideration among them. Some looked on him with that wonder with which people look on a man over whose neck the axe of the executioner has been lifted. Round about were heard voices: " Yes, the princess is here! Yurand's daughter is here, thou wilt see her at once, my dear fellow." " And thou wilt go to the hunt with us?" With that entered two guests, Knights of the Cross, — Brother Hugo von Danveld, starosta in Ortelsburg, or in Schytno, whose relative had in his time been Marshal; and Siegfried von Löwe, whose family had rendered service in the Order, — he was bailiff of Yansbork. The first was rather young yet, but fat, — he had the face of a crafty beer-guzzler, with moist and thick lips; the other was tall, with stern though noble features.

It seemed to Zbyshko that he had seen Danveld somewhere with Prince Vitold, — that Henry, Bishop of Plotsk, had unhorsed him in a tournament; but this recollection was disturbed by the entrance of Prince Yanush, to whom courtiers and Knights of the Cross made obeisance. De Lorche and the comturs and Zbyshko approached him; he greeted them affably, but with dignity on his beardless, rustic face, surrounded with hair cut evenly on the forehead, but hanging to the shoulders on both sides.

Soon trumpets thundered outside in sign that the prince was ready to take his seat at the table: they thundered once, twice, thrice. The third time the heavy door on the right of the dining-hall opened, and in it appeared Princess Anna, having at her side a marvellous golden-haired maiden with a lute hanging from her shoulder.

Seeing her, Zbyshko pushed forward, and putting his joined hands to his lips, dropped on both knees in a posture full of respect and homage.

At this sight a murmur rose in the hall, for Zbyshko's act had astonished the Mazovians, and some of them were even offended.

" By my faith," said some of the older men, " he has learned that custom surely from knights beyond the sea, and perhaps from real pagans, for it does not exist even among Germans." " That is not strange," thought the younger ones, " for he owes his life to the maiden." The princess and Danusia did not recognize Zbyshko immediately, for he had knelt with his back toward the fire and his face was shaded. Princess Anna thought at the first moment that he was a courtier who had failed in duty to the prince and was begging her intercession ; but Danusia, who had a quicker glance, pushed forth a step, and inclining her bright head, cried suddenly in a voice thin and piercing, —

" Zbyshko ! "

Then, without thinking that the whole court and the foreign guests were looking at her, she sprang like a deer toward the young knight, and seizing him with her arms fell to kissing his eyes, his lips, his cheeks, nestling up to him and piping meanwhile with great delight, till the Mazovians thundered forth in one great burst of laughter, and the princess drew her to herself by the collar. Danusia looked then at the people, and, confused terribly, hid behind the princess with equal swiftness, covering herself with the folds of her robe so that barely the tip of her head remained visible.

Zbyshko embraced Princess Anna's feet; she raised him, greeted him, and at the same time inquired about Matsko, — was he dead, or was he alive yet; if alive, had he come to Mazovia ? Zbyshko answered those questions with no very great presence of mind, for, bending to one side and the other, he tried to see behind the princess Danusia, who thrust her head out from that lady's robe and then dived into its folds again. The Mazovians seized their sides at sight of this, even the prince himself laughed, till at last the hot dishes were brought and the delighted lady turned to Zbyshko with these words, —

" Serve us, dear attendant, and God grant not only at this table, but forever."

Then she said, —

" But thou, tortured fly, crawl out from behind my robe, or thou wilt tear it to pieces."

Danusia came out flushed, confused, raising from moment to moment on Zbyshko eyes that were frightened, put to shame, and curious, and so marvellous that the heart was not only melting in him but in other men. Hugo von Danveld

put his hand to his thick moist lips repeatedly; De Lorche
was astonished, raised both hands, and inquired, —

"By Saint Iago of Compostello, who is that maiden?"

To this Danveld, who with his fatness was of low stature,
rose a finger's length, and said in the ear of the Knight of
Lorraine, —

"The devil's daughter."

De Lorche looked at him, blinked, then frowned, and said
with nasal accent, —

"He is not a true knight who calumniates beauty."

"I wear golden spurs, and I am a monk," replied Hugo,
with haughtiness.

So great was the respect for belted knights that De Lorche
dropped his head; but after a while he replied, —

"I am a blood relative of the princes of Brabant."

"Pax! Pax! (Peace! Peace!)," said the Knight of the
Cross. "Honor to the powerful princes and friends of the
Order, from whose hands you will receive golden spurs
shortly. I do not deny beauty to that maiden, but hear who
her father is."

He was not able, however, to tell, for at that moment
Prince Yanush took his seat, and learning previously from
the Starosta of Yansbork of the great connections of De
Lorche, he gave a sign to him to sit near. Opposite Prince
Yanush sat the princess with Danusia. Zbyshko took his
place, as in Cracow, behind their chairs, at their service.
Danusia held her head over the dish as low as possible, for
she felt shame in the presence of people, but a little to one
side, so that Zbyshko might see her face. He looked eagerly
and with rapture at her small bright head, at her rosy
cheeks, at her shoulders dressed in a closely fitting garment,
— shoulders which had ceased to be those of a child, — and
he felt rising in him, as it were, a river of new love which
would inundate his whole being. He felt also on his eyes,
on his lips, on his face her recent kisses. She had given
them before as a sister to a brother, and he had received
them as from a dear child. Now at the fresh remembrance
of them this happened which happened when he was with
Yagenka, — shivers seized him, and a faintness possessed
him beneath which was hidden a warmth, like a fire covered
with ashes. Danusia seemed to him an entirely grown lady,
for she had bloomed in reality and matured. Besides, so
much had been said in her presence of love, and so frequently,
that as a bunch of flowers warmed with sun rays grows

beautiful and opens more and more, so her eyes were opened
to love, and in consequence there was something in her then
which had not been there previously, — a certain beauty no
longer a child's beauty, a certain mighty attraction, intoxi-
cating, issuing from her as heat from a flame or as odor
from a rose.

Zbyshko felt this, but did not give himself account of it,
for he forgot himself. He forgot even that he had to serve
at the table. He did not see that the courtiers were looking
at him, nudging each other with their elbows, showing
Danusia and him to one another, and laughing; neither did
he notice De Lorche's face, as it were petrified by amazement, nor the staring eyes of Danveld, which were fixed on
Danusia, and reflecting the flame of the chimney seemed as
red and as flashing as the eyes of a wolf. He recovered
only when the trumpet sounded again in sign that it was
time for the wilderness, and when Princess Anna turned to
him and said, —

"Thou wilt go with us, so as to be able to have pleasure,
and speak to the maiden of love; to this I shall be glad to
listen."

She left the table then with Danusia, so as to be ready
to mount. Zbyshko sprang to the yard where men were
holding horses covered with hoar frost, and snorting. These
were for the prince and princess, guests, and courtiers. In
the yard there were not so many people as before, for the
beaters had gone out in advance with snares, and had vanished in the wilderness. The fires had died down; day had
appeared, bright, frosty, the snow squeaked under foot; and
the trees, moved by a light breeze, scattered dry, glittering
frost flakes.

The prince came out promptly and mounted; he was followed by an attendant with a crossbow, and a spear so heavy
and long that few men could wield it. Prince Yanush
wielded it, however, with ease, for he, like other Mazovian
Piasts, possessed uncommon strength. There were even
women of that stock, who in marrying foreign princes
wound around on their fingers at the wedding feast broad
plates of iron. Near the prince were two other attendants
ready to aid in emergency; these were chosen from all heirs
in the lands of Tschanov and Warsaw, and they were tremendous to look at, with shoulders like forest trees. De
Lorche, who had come from afar, looked on these men with
amazement.

Now the princess and Danusia came out, both wearing hoods of white weasel-skin. The undegenerate daughter of Keistut knew better how to "sew" with an arrow than a needle. So behind her was borne a crossbow a little lighter than others, and adorned. Zbyshko, kneeling on the snow, held out his hand, on which the lady rested her foot when mounting; Danusia he raised to the saddle as he had Yagenka in Bogdanets; and they rode on.

The retinue stretched out like a long snake, turned to the right from the house, varied and shining on the border of the wilderness, like a colored selvage on the edge of black cloth, and then began to sink into it slowly.

They were rather deep in the forest when the princess said, turning to Zbyshko, —

"Why dost thou not talk? Now talk to her."

Zbyshko, though thus encouraged, was silent awhile yet, since a certain irresolution had mastered him; and only after the length of one or two Hail Marys did he say, —

"Danusia!"

"What, Zbyshko?"

"I love thee so."

Here he stopped to seek words which were difficult to find, for though he had knelt like a foreign knight before Danusia, though he showed her honor in every way, and strove to avoid common expressions, he strove in vain for courtliness, since his soul being full he could only speak simply. Hence he said, after a while, —

"I love thee so that my breath stops!"

She raised on him from beneath her weasel hood blue eyes, and a face which the cold forest breeze had made rosy.

"And I, Zbyshko!" said she, as if in haste. And she covered her eyes with their lids, for she knew then what love was.

"Hei, thou my little one! hei, thou my maiden!" said Zbyshko.

And again he was silent from emotion and happiness; but the kind and also curious princess came to aid him a second time.

"Tell her," said she, "how dreary it was for thee without her, and when there is a thicket, thou mightst even kiss her on the lips. I shall not be angry, for that is the best way to give witness of thy love."

So he began to tell her how dreary his life had been without her in Bogdanets while he was caring for Matsko, and while he was among the "neighbors." Of Yagenka the cunning avoider uttered no word. As to the rest he spoke truly, for at that moment he so loved the fair Danusia that he would have seized her, taken her over on to his horse, kept her before him, and held her at his breast.

He did not dare to do this; but when the next thicket separated them from the courtiers and the guests riding behind, he bent toward her, put his arm around her waist, and hid his face in the weasel-skin hood, testifying to his love by that act.

But as in winter there are no leaves on hazelnut bushes, Danveld and De Lorche saw him; courtiers saw him also, and began to talk among themselves.

"He kissed her in presence of the princess! I believe that the lady will soon have the wedding."

"He is a gallant fellow, but Yurand's blood is sulphurous."

"Flint and steel, though the girl seems like a dove. Sparks will fly from them, never fear! He has fastened a claw to the quick in her."

So they conversed, laughing; but Hugo turned to De Lorche his goatish, malignant, lustful face.

"Could you wish that some Merlin would change you by magic into that young knight?" asked he.

"And you?" inquired De Lorche.

At this the Knight of the Cross, in whom evidently envy and desire were now boiling, jerked his horse with impatient hand, and answered, —

"On my soul! — "

In that moment, however, he recollected himself, and inclining added —

"I am a monk who has vowed chastity."

And he looked quickly at De Lorche, fearing lest he might see a smile on his face; for the Order had an evil fame in the world on that point, and Danveld among monks had the worst. Some years before, when assistant starosta in Sambria, complaints had become so loud against him that in spite of every condescension with which such things were regarded in Malborg they had to transfer him to the post of commander in Schytno. Having arrived some days before with a secret commission to the court of Prince Yanush, and seeing the charming daughter of Yurand, he was inflamed with desire for her, against which Danusia's age was no curb, for in those days girls younger than she were given in marriage. But since at the same time Hugo knew of what stock she was, and since in his mind the name of Yurand connected her with dreadful reminiscences, his desire rose on the basis of savage hatred.

De Lorche fell to inquiring about those events.

"You have called this beautiful maiden 'devil's daughter;' why have you called her thus?"

Hugo narrated then the history of Zlotoria, — how at the building of the castle they had seized the prince and his court, how in that affair the girl's mother had perished, and how Yurand had avenged her since that time on all Knights of the Cross in a fearful manner. During the narrative Hugo's hatred burst forth like a flame, since for this feeling he had personal reasons also. He had met Yurand two years before, but at sight of the terrible "Wild boar of Spyhov" the heart fell in him, for the first time in life, so contemptibly that he deserted two relatives, deserted his attendants, left his plunder, and fled a whole day like a madman, till he reached Schytno, where he was sick a long time from fright. When he returned to health the Grand Marshal of the Order brought him to trial. The sentence of the knightly court released him, it is true, for Hugo swore, on the cross and his honor, that an enraged horse had borne him away from the field of battle; but it closed his path to higher dignities in the Order. In presence of De Lorche the Knight of the Cross was silent about these events; but he made so many complaints against the cruelty of Yurand and the insolence of the whole Polish nation, that what he said could hardly find place in the head of the Knight of Lorraine.

"But," said De Lorche, after a while, "we are with Mazovians, not Poles."

"The principality is separate, but the people are the same," answered Hugo; "their vileness and hatred of the Order are equal. God grant the German sword to destroy the whole race!"

"You speak truly, lord; for, just think, this prince, apparently honorable, dared to build a hostile castle on your land; I have never heard of such lawlessness, even among pagans."

"The castle was hostile, but Zlotoria is on his land, not ours."

"Then, glory to Christ who gave you the victory. How did that war end?"

"There was no war at the time."

"And did you gain a victory at Zlotoria?"

" Just in this did God bless us, that the prince was without an army; he had only a court and women."

"How was that?" asked De Lorche, looking at the knight with astonishment. "Then you fell upon women in time of peace, and upon the prince who was building a castle on his own land?"

"When the glory of the Order and Christianity are in question no deeds are dishonorable."

"And that terrible knight is only avenging his young wife killed in time of peace by you?"

"Whoso raises a hand against a Knight of the Cross is a son of darkness."

De Lorche was amazed when he heard this, but he had no time to answer Danveld, for they had ridden out onto a broad, snowy, weed-covered plain, on which the prince had alighted from his horse, and after him others began to dismount.

Skilled foresters under the lead of the chief huntsman disposed guests and the court in a long row at the edge of the plain, so that being in concealment themselves they had in front of them an empty space which facilitated shooting from crossbows and bows. The two shorter sides of the plain were beset with snares, behind which were woodmen, whose duty it was to turn a beast toward the hunters, or if it would not be frightened it became entangled in the snares and they killed it with spears.

Innumerable crowds of Kurpie, disposed skilfully in a so-called circle, were to drive out every living creature to the plain from the depth of the forest.

Beyond the hunters was a net, so that any beast which succeeded in passing the line might be caught in its meshes, and killed.

The prince stood in the centre of the line, in a slight depression which passed through the whole width of the plain. The chief huntsman, Mrokota of Motsarzev, chose this position for him, knowing that just there the largest beasts would seek escape from the circle. The prince had a crossbow in his hand, near his side stood against a tree a heavy spear, and a little behind him were two "defenders" with axes on their shoulders, immense fellows, as bulky as trees of the forest, who besides axes had drawn crossbows, to be given to the prince should he need them.

The princess and Danusia did not dismount; the prince never permitted that, because of danger from wild bulls and bisons, before whose rage it was harder in case of attack to escape on foot than on horseback. De Lorche, though invited by the prince to take a place at his right, begged permission to remain on horseback to defend the ladies, and took his position at some distance from the princess, looking like a long bar with a knight's spear, at which the Mazovians smiled jeeringly in silence, as at a weapon of small value in hunting.

Zbyshko planted his spear in the snow, put his crossbow on his shoulder, and standing near Danusia's horse, raised his head and whispered to her; at moments he embraced her feet and kissed her knees, for he did not hide his love now at all from people. He ceased only when Mrokota, who in the wilderness made bold to reprimand the prince even, enjoined silence severely.

Meanwhile far, far away in the depth of the wilderness, were heard the horns of the Kurpie, which were answered briefly from the plain by the shrill sound of winding trumpets; then followed perfect silence. Only, at long intervals, did a grossbeak cry in the top of a pine tree. Sometimes men in the circle croaked like ravens. The hunters strained their eyes over the empty space, on which a breeze moved the frost-covered weeds and the leafless clumps of brush, — each waiting with impatience to see what beast would be first to appear on the snow. In general a rich and splendid hunt was predicted, for the wilderness was swarming with bisons, wild bulls, and wild boars.

The Kurpie had smoked out from their dens a certain number of bears, which thus roused went through the thickets, mad, alert, and hungry, feeling that they would soon have to struggle, not for a quiet winter's sleep, but for life.

There was still a long time of waiting, since the men who were urging the beasts to the clasps of the circle, and to the plain, occupied an enormous extent of forest, and were coming from such a distance that the ears of hunters were not touched even by the barking of dogs, which immediately after the sounding of trumpets were freed from their leashes. One of these dogs, freed evidently too early, or wandering apart after men, appeared on the plain, and having run over all of it with his nose to the ground, passed between the hunters. Again the place was empty and silent; only the woodmen cawed continually like ravens, announcing in this way that work would begin soon.

In fact, after an interval long enough to repeat a few Our

Fathers, at the edge appeared wolves, which, as the most wary, tried first to escape from the circle. Of these there were few. After they had come out on the plain and caught the odor of people, they plunged into the forest anew, seeking evidently another escape. Wild boars sprang out next and ran in a long black chain over the snowy expanse, seeming in the distance like a drove of tame pigs, which at the call of a woman hurry homeward with shaking ears. But that chain halted, listened, scented, turned and listened again, bore to one side toward the snares, sniffed the woodmen, moved again toward the hunters, grunting, approaching more and more cautiously, but still nearer, till at last the sound of iron was heard on the crossbows, then the whiz of arrows, and the first blood stained the white, snowy surface.

A piercing squeal was heard and the drove scattered, as if struck by lightning; some went at random straightforward, some rushed toward the snares, some ran either singly or in small groups, mixing among other beasts with which the plain was now swarming. At this time was heard clearly the sound of horns, the barking of dogs, and the distant noise of men advancing along the main line from the depth of the forest. The beasts of the wilderness, driven from both sides by the extended wings of the circle, filled the forest plain more and more densely. No sight like that could be seen in foreign parts, or even in other Polish lands, where there were no such wild forests as in Mazovia. The Knights of the Cross, though they had been in Lithuania, where at times bisons by striking an army produced confusion in it, wondered not a little at the immense number of beasts, but especially did De Lorche wonder. Standing near the princess and the damsels, like a stork on the watch, and unable to speak with any one, he had begun to be annoyed, while freezing in his armor, and thinking that the hunt was a failure. At last he saw before him whole herds of fleet-footed deer, yellow stags, and elks with weighty-horned heads, mingled together, storming over the plain, blinded with fear and seeking in vain for an exit.

The princess, in whom at sight of this the blood of her father Keistut began to play, sent shaft after shaft into that many-colored throng, and screamed with delight when a stricken deer or an elk rose in its career, then fell heavily and dug the snow with its feet. Damsels bent their faces often toward the crossbows, for the ardor of hunting had seized every person.

Zbyshko alone had no thought for hunting, but leaning his elbow on Danusia's knees, and his head on his palm, he gazed into her eyes; and she, half smiling, half abashed, tried to close his eyelids with her fingers, as if unable to endure such a glance.

De Lorche's attention was occupied by a bear, enormous, with gray legs and shoulders, which had come out of the weeds unexpectedly near the hunters. The prince sent a bolt from his crossbow, and then attacked the beast with a spear. When the bear, roaring awfully, rose on his hind legs the prince pierced him before the eyes of the whole court, so quickly and surely that neither of the two " defenders " had need of an axe.

The young Knight of Lorraine thought then that there were not many lords in the castles at which he had stopped on his journey who would have had courage for amusement like that, and that with such princes and such people the Order might have a difficult adventure, and pass through grievous hours sometime. But farther on he saw pierced in that same way by other men terrible, immense, white-tusked boars, far larger and more savage than any in Lower Lorraine or the forests of Germany. Never had he seen such trained hunters, nor any so confident in the strength of their hands, nor such spear-thrusts. As a man of experience, he concluded that all those people living in boundless forests were accustomed from years of childhood to the crossbow and spear, hence they attained greater skill in the use of them than others.

At last the plain was strewn thickly with bodies of all kinds of beasts, but it was far to the end of the hunt yet. The most interesting and also the most dangerous moment was coming, for the circle had just pressed to the open space a number of tens of wild bulls and bisons. Though in the forest these lived apart usually, they went now mixed together, but not at all headlong from fear; they were rather threatening than terrified. They advanced not very quickly, as if confident, in the feeling of immense power, that they would break every obstacle and pass; the earth resounded beneath the weight of them. Bearded bulls, going in crowds with their heads close to the ground, halted at moments as if considering in what direction to strike. From their monstrous lungs went forth deep roars which were like underground thunder. From their nostrils issued steam, and digging the snow with their fore feet they seemed to be looking with bloody eyes from beneath their shaggy manes for a hidden enemy.

Meanwhile the woodmen raised a mighty shout, to which answer was given from the main line and from the wings of the circle by hundreds of loud voices; horns and whistles made an uproar; the wilderness quivered to its remotest depths, and at the same moment the dogs of the Kurpie rushed out to the plain with a fearful tumult, and chased along on the trail. The sight of them roused rage in the twinkle of an eye among female beasts which had their young with them. The herd of animals, going hitherto slowly, scattered over the whole plain in mad haste. A wild bull, tawny, gigantic, almost monstrous, surpassing bisons in size, rushed with great springs toward the line of hunters; he turned toward the right side of the plain, then, seeing horses some tens of yards distant, among the trees, he halted, and roaring, began to plough the earth with his horns, as if rousing himself to spring forward and fight.

At this sight the woodmen raised a still greater shout. In the line of hunters were heard piercing voices, —

" The princess! the princess! Save the princess! "

Zbyshko grasped his spear planted in the snow and sprang to the edge of the forest; after him went a number of Lithuanians ready to die in defence of the daughter of Keistut; meanwhile a crossbow sounded in the hands of the lady, a shaft whistled, and, flying over the inclined head of the bull, it fastened in his neck.

" He has got it! " cried the princess; " he will come no nearer! "

But a roar so dreadful that horses rose on their haunches drowned further words of hers. The bull hurled himself like a storm straight against the princess. But suddenly, and with no less impetus, the manful De Lorche rushed forth from among the trees; bent forward on his horse, with lance lowered as in a knightly tournament, he bore straight on the animal. In one twinkle of an eye those present saw buried in the neck of the bull a lance which bent like a reed and broke into small splinters, then the immense horned head disappeared altogether under the belly of De Lorche's horse, and before any one present could utter a cry, the steed and the rider flew through the air as if sent from a sling.

The horse, falling on his side, began in mortal agony to struggle with his feet, entangling them in his own intestines, which had dropped from the body. De Lorche lay near by motionless, looking like an iron wedge on the snow. The wild bull seemed for an instant to hesitate whether to pass them and strike other horses; but having his first victims there before him, he turned again and began to gloat over the hapless steed, crushing him with his head, and tearing in rage the open belly with his horns.

People rushed out from the forest, however, to save the foreign knight. Zbyshko, concerned for the safety of the princess and Danusia, came first, and thrust in his sharp spear behind the foreleg of the beast. But he struck with such force that the handle, when the bull turned suddenly, broke in his hand, and he himself fell face forward on the snow.

"He is lost! he is lost!" cried Mazovians, rushing to aid him.

Meanwhile the bull's head had covered Zbyshko and was pressing him to the earth. From the prince's side two powerful "defenders" rushed up; but help would have been late had not Hlava, the man given by Yagenka, preceded them luckily. He ran ahead, and raising a broad-axe with both hands cut the bent neck of the bull right behind his horns.

The blow was so terrible that the beast dropped as if struck by lightning, his backbone was severed and his head half chopped away; but in falling he pressed Zbyshko. Both "defenders" pulled off the monstrous body in a twinkle, but meanwhile the princess and Danusia sprang from their horses, and dumb with fright, ran to Zbyshko. Pale, covered with his own blood and the blood of the bull, he raised himself somewhat, tried to stand, but staggered, fell on his knees, and leaning on his hand could utter only one word:

"Danusia!"

Then he threw out blood through his mouth, and darkness embraced his head. Danusia, standing at his back, seized his arms, but unable to hold him, cried for assistance. People surrounded him from all sides, rubbed him with snow, poured wine into his mouth; finally the chief hunter, Mrokota, gave command to put him on a cloak, and stay the blood-flow with soft pine punk.

"He will live if only a rib and not his spine is broken," said he, turning to the princess.

Meanwhile other damsels, assisted by hunters, were saving De Lorche. They turned him on every side, seeking on his armor for dints or holes made by the horns of the bull; but beyond traces of snow, packed in between joints of the armor, they could find nothing. The bull had taken revenge mainly on the horse, now dead, with all his entrails out under him; De Lorche had not been struck. He had only fainted from the fall, and, as appeared later, his right arm was disjointed. When they removed his helmet and poured wine into his mouth, he opened his eyes straightway and regained consciousness. Seeing the anxious faces of young and comely damsels bent over him, he said in German, —

"Surely I am in paradise, and angels are above me."

The damsels did not understand what he said, it is true, but glad that he had recovered and spoken, they smiled at him, and, with the help of hunters, raised him from the snow. Feeling pain in his right arm he groaned; with his left he leaned on the arm of one of the "angels;" for a while he stood motionless, fearing to move a step, for he did not feel firm on his feet. Then he cast a glance, which was dull yet, over the field of struggle. He saw the yellow carcass of the bull, which near by seemed enormous. He saw Danusia wringing her hands over Zbyshko, and Zbyshko himself on a cloak.

"Did that knight come to aid me?" inquired he. "Is he alive?"

"He is hurt seriously," answered one of the courtiers, who knew German.

"From this day forth I shall fight not against him, but for him," said the man of Lorraine.

At that moment Prince Yanush, who had been standing over Zbyshko, approached De Lorche and praised him, saying that by his daring deed he had guarded the princess and other ladies from great peril, and had even saved their lives, perhaps, for which, in addition to knightly rewards, he would be surrounded by fame among people then living, and among their descendants.

"In these effeminate times," said he, "fewer and fewer real knights pass through the world; be my guest, therefore, as long as is possible, or stay in Mazovia altogether, for you have won my favor, and you will win as easily the favor of people by your worthy deeds."

De Lorche's heart, eager for glory, was melted by these words; for when he considered that he had accomplished such a preponderant deed of knighthood, and won such praise in those distant Polish lands of which in the West such marvellous things were related, his delight was such that he hardly felt any pain in his disjointed arm. He understood that a knight who at the court of Brabant or Burgundy could say that he had saved at a hunt the life of Princess Anna of Mazovia, would walk in glory as in sunlight. Under the influence of these thoughts, he wanted even to go directly to the princess and vow, on his knees, faithful service to her; but the lady herself and Danusia were busied with Zbyshko.

Zbyshko had regained consciousness again for a moment; but he only smiled at Danusia, raised his hand to his forehead, now covered with cold sweat, and fainted a second time. Experienced hunters, seeing his closed hands and open mouth, said that he would not recover; but the still more experienced Kurpie, many of whom carried on their persons marks of bears' claws, wild boars' tusks, or wild bulls' horns, gave better hope, asserting that the bull's horn had slipped along the knight's ribs; that one or two ribs might be broken, but that his spine was safe; otherwise he could not have raised himself up for a moment. They showed also a snow-drift on the place where Zbyshko had fallen, that had saved him; for the beast, pressing him between his horns, was unable to crush either his breast or his back.

Unfortunately Father Vyshonek, Princess Anna's doctor, though usually at hunts, was not present; he was occupied at the house in baking wafers. The Cheh, learning this, hurried after him, but meanwhile the Kurpie carried Zbyshko on a cloak to the prince's house. Danusia wished to go on foot with him, but Princess Anna opposed, for the road was long, and in the forest depths was much snow; haste, therefore, was needed.

Danveld helped the girl to mount, and then riding near her, just behind the men who were carrying Zbyshko, spoke in Polish, in a suppressed voice, so that he could be heard by her only : —

"I have in Schytno a wonderful healing balsam, which I got from a hermit in the Hercynian forest, and which I could bring in three days."

"God will reward you," answered Danusia.

"God rewards every deed of mercy, but can I hope for pay from you also?"

"What could I pay you?"

The Knight of the Cross pushed up near her with his horse;

246 THE KNIGHTS OF THE CROSS.

evidently he wished to tell something, but hesitated, and only after a while did he say, —

"In the Order, besides brothers, there are sisters; one of them will bring the healing balsam, and then I will mention pay."

CHAPTER XVIII.

FATHER VYSHONEK dressed Zbyshko's wound. He found only one rib broken, but the first day he could not answer for recovery, since he could not tell "whether the heart in the sick man was wrenched, or his liver torn." Toward evening so great a faintness seized De Lorche that he had to lie down. On the following day he could move neither hand nor foot without great pain in all his bones.

The princess and Danusia, with other damsels, attended the sick men, and prepared for them, according to directions of the priest, various ointments and herbs. Zbyshko was seriously wounded, and from time to time vomited blood, which alarmed the priest greatly. Still, he was conscious, and the next day, though very much weakened, when he learned from Danusia who it was to whom he was indebted for life, he called his Cheh, to thank and reward him. But he had to remember that Hlava had come from Yagenka, and that had it not been for her well-wishing heart he would have perished. This thought was to him even burdensome, for he felt that he never could repay the honest girl with good for good, and that he would be for her only the cause of suffering and terrible sadness. He said to himself, it is true, immediately after, "I cannot indeed hew myself in two," but at the bottom of his soul there remained, as it were, a reproach of conscience. The Cheh inflamed still more this internal disquiet.

"I swore to my lady," said he, "on my honor as a noble, to guard you, and I will do so without any reward. Not to me, but to her, are you indebted for rescue."

Zbyshko gave no answer, but began to breathe heavily. Hlava was silent for a while, then he said, —

"If you command me to hurry to Bogdanets, I will hurry. You might wish to see the old lord, for God knows what will happen you."

"What does the priest say?" inquired Zbyshko.

"The priest says that he will know at the new moon, and there are four days to the new moon."

"Ei! there is no need to go to Bogdanets. Either I shall die before my uncle could come, or I shall recover."

"You might send even a letter to Bogdanets. Sanderus will write it all clearly. They would know about you, at least, and perhaps have a mass said."

"Leave me at present, for I am weak. If I die, thou wilt return to Zyh's house, and tell how it was; they will give money then for a mass there. And people will bury me here, or in Tsehanov."

"In Tsehanov, or in Prasnysh, for only Kurpie are buried in the forest, where wolves howl over them. I have heard from the servants, also, that the prince will go with the court in two days to Tsehanov, and thence to Warsaw."

"They will not desert me here," said Zbyshko.

In fact he had divined rightly, for the princess had gone that very day to the prince with the request to let her stay in the forest house with Danusia, the damsels, and the priest, who was opposed to the early removal of Zbyshko to Prasnysh.

De Lorche was considerably better in two days, and was on his feet. But learning that the "ladies" would remain, he remained also to accompany them on their return, and in case of a "Saracen" attack, to defend them from evil accident. Whence these "Saracens" were to come was a question which the gallant knight of Lorraine had not given himself. In the distant west, it is true, Lithuanians were called thus; from them, however, no danger could threaten the daughter of Keistut; she was the full sister of Vitold, and the cousin of Yagello, the "mighty king at Cracow."

But in spite of what he had heard in Mazovia of the christening of Lithuania, and the union of two crowns on the head of one sovereign, De Lorche had lived too long among Knights of the Cross not to believe that every evil might be expected from Lithuanians at all times. The Knights of the Cross had told him this, and he had not entirely lost faith in the Order.

Meanwhile an event happened which fell as a shadow between the Knights of the Cross and Prince Yanush. On the day before the departure of the court, brothers Gottfried and Rotgier arrived; they had been in Tsehanov before; and with them came a certain De Fourcy as the herald of news unfavorable for Knights of the Cross. Behold, it had happened that foreign guests visiting with the starosta of Lubov, namely, he, De Fourcy, De Bregov, and Meinegger, all from families of previous merit in the Order, when they had heard of Yurand of Spyhov, not only were they not frightened, but they decided to entice the renowned warrior to the field and convince themselves whether he was really as terrible as people declared him.

The starosta, it is true, opposed, referring to the peace between the Order and the princes of Mazovia; but at last, in the hope, perhaps, of freeing himself from a terrible neighbor, he determined not only to look at the affair through his fingers, but to let men at arms go also.

The knights sent a challenge to Yurand, who accepted it eagerly on condition that they would send away their men, and they three fight with him and two comrades on the very boundary of Prussia and Spyhov. When they were unwilling to dismiss their men at arms and withdraw from the lands of Spyhov, he fell upon them, slew their men at arms, thrust a spear through Meinegger, took Bregov prisoner and threw him into the dungeon of Spyhov. De Fourcy alone was unhurt, and after wandering three days through Mazovian forests, he learned from a tar-boiler that Knights of the Cross were tarrying in Tsehanov; he made his way to these knights so as to complain with them to the majesty of the prince, pray for punishment, and a command to free Bregov.

These tidings obscured at once the good relations between Prince Yanush and the guests, for not only did the two brothers who arrived then, but also Danveld and Siegfried von Löwe demand of the prince insistently to do justice to the Order, free the boundary of a robber, and mete out punishment with usury for all his offences. Danveld, especially, having with Yurand his own old accounts, the remembrance of which burnt him with pain and with shame, demanded vengeance almost threateningly.

"A complaint will go to the Grand Master," said he, "and if we obtain no justice from your Princely Grace, he will be able to find it, even should all Mazovia take the part of that murderer."

The prince, though mild by nature, grew angry, and said:

"What justice are ye asking for? If Yurand had been the first to attack you, if he had burnt villages, driven away herds, and killed people, I should summon him to judgment, and measure out punishment. But it was ye who attacked him. Your starosta let armed men go on the expedition; but what did Yurand do? He accepted your challenge, and only asked you to send off your serving men. How am I to punish him for that, or to summon him to judgment? Ye attacked a dreadful man, feared by all, and of your own choice brought down on your own heads disaster. What do ye want, then? Am I to command him not to defend himself whenever ye are pleased to attack him?"

"It was not the Order who attacked him, but guests, foreign knights," replied Danveld.

"The Order answers for guests, and besides, with them were men at arms from the Lubov garrison."

"Was the starosta to yield up guests, as for slaughter?"

At this the prince turned to Siegfried, and said, —

"See what justice becomes in your mouths, and see if your evasions are not offensive to God."

"De Bregov must be freed from captivity," answered the stern Siegfried; "for men of his family were chiefs in the Order, and have rendered great service to the Cross."

"And the death of Meinegger must be avenged," added Hugo.

The prince gathered the hair on both sides of his head, and rising from his seat, approached the Germans with an ominous face; but after a moment he remembered evidently that they were his guests; so he restrained himself once more, placed his hand on Siegfried's arm, and said, —

"Listen, starosta, you wear the cross on your mantle, so answer on that cross according to conscience. Was Yurand right or not?"

"De Bregov must be freed from captivity," answered Siegfried.

"God grant me patience," said the prince, after a moment of silence.

"The injustice which has met us in the persons of our guests is merely an additional cause of complaint," continued Siegfried, in a voice as sharp as a sword-edge. "Since the Order is an order, never in Palestine, or in Transylvania, or in pagan Lithuania up to this time, has one common man done us so much evil as that bandit of Spyhov. Your Princely Grace, we desire redress and punishment, not for one injustice, but a thousand; not for one battle, but for five hundred; not for one blood spilling, but for whole years of deeds for the like of which the fire of heaven should burn that godless nest of cruelty and wickedness. Whose groans are calling to God there for vengeance? Ours! Whose tears? Ours! In vain have we brought complaints, in vain have we called for judgment. Never has satisfaction been rendered us."

When he heard this Prince Yanush nodded his head. "In former years," said he, "Knights of the Cross were guests often in Spyhov, and Yurand was not your enemy till his beloved wife died in your bonds. How many times have you attacked him yourselves, as now, because he challenged and conquered your knights? How many times have you set murderers on him, or sent bolts at him from crossbows in the pine woods? He has attacked you, it is true, for vengeance was burning him; but have not you, or knights living on your lands, attacked peaceful people in Mazovia? Have you not driven away herds, burnt villages, slaughtered men, women, and children? And when I made complaint to your Master he answered from Malborg: 'An ordinary brawl on the boundary!' Give me peace! It does not become you to complain, you who seized me when I was unarmed, in time of peace, on my own land; and had it not been for terror before the anger of the king at Cracow, I might have been groaning to this hour in your underground dungeons. That is how you paid me, who came from the family of your benefactors. Leave me in peace; it is not for you to speak of justice!"

When they heard this the Knights of the Cross looked at one another with impatience, for it was bitter to them and a shame that the prince mentioned that event in Zlotoria in presence of De Fourcy; so Danveld, wishing to put an end to further conversation on that subject, said, —

"In the case of your Princely Grace there was a mistake, which we corrected, not out of fear of the king at Cracow, but for the sake of justice. As to brawls on the boundary, our Master cannot answer for them, since in all kingdoms of the world everywhere there are turbulent spirits on the boundaries."

"Thou sayst that, but art calling for justice against Yurand. What do ye wish?"

"Justice and punishment."

The prince balled his bony fists and repeated, —

"God give me patience!"

"Let your Princely Grace remember this, too," continued Danveld, "that our turbulent men harm only lay persons not of the German race; but yours raise their hands against the German Order, by which they offend the Saviour himself. And what tortures and punishments can suffice those who offend the Cross?"

"Hear me!" said the prince. "Do not carry on war by means of God, for Him thou wilt not deceive!" And placing his hands on the shoulders of the Knight of the Cross, he

shook him violently. The German was alarmed at once, and
began in a milder voice,—

"If it be true that the guests attacked Yurand first, and
they did not dismiss their men at arms, I do not applaud
them. But did Yurand really accept the challenge?"

Then he looked at De Fourcy, blinking stealthily the while,
as if to inform him that he was to deny; but De Fourcy, unable, or unwilling to do so, replied,—

"He wished in company with two other men to do battle
against us, after we had sent away the men at arms."

"Are you certain?"

"On my honor! De Bregov and I agreed, but Meinegger
would not join us."

"Starosta of Schytno!" interrupted the prince, "you know
better than other men that Yurand does not avoid a challenge." Here he turned to all, and said: "Whoever of you
would like to challenge Yurand to a battle on foot or on horseback, to him I give permission. Should Yurand be killed, or
taken captive, Bregov will be freed without ransom. Ask no
more of me, for you will not receive it."

After these words deep silence followed. Danveld and
Siegfried, and Brother Rotgier, and Brother Gottfried, though
brave, were too well acquainted with the terrible heir of Spyhov for any man of them to undertake a life-and-death battle
against him; only a stranger might do that,—a man from
distant parts, like De Lorche, or De Fourcy; but De Lorche
was not present at the conversation, and De Fourcy was still
too much influenced by heartfelt fear.

"I have seen him once," muttered he, "and have no wish
to look at him a second time."

"A monk is not permitted to engage in single combat,"
said Siegfried, "unless with special permission of the Master
and the Grand Marshal; but we do not demand permission
for battle, only that De Bregov be liberated from captivity,
and Yurand put to death."

"You are not the law in this land."

"We have endured patiently, so far, a grievous neighborhood. But our Master will be able to measure out justice."

"Therefore there will be justice to the Master and to you
from Mazovia!"

"Behind the Master are the Germans and the Roman
emperor."

"And behind me is the Polish king, to whom more lands
and nations are subject."

"Does your Princely Grace wish war with the Order?"

"If I wished war, I should not wait for you in Mazovia, I should go to you; but do not threaten me, for I am not afraid."

"What am I to report to the Master?"

"Your Master has made no inquiry of me. Report what you like to him."

"Then we will measure out punishment and revenge ourselves."

The prince stretched out his arms and began to move his finger threateningly in the very face of the Knight of the Cross.

"Have a care!" said he, in a voice of suppressed anger. "Have a care; I have permitted you to challenge Yurand, but if you break into my country with troops of the Order, I will strike you — and you will sit here, not as a guest, but a captive."

Evidently his patience was exhausted, for he threw his cap against the table with all his strength, went out of the room, and slammed the door behind him. The Knights of the Cross were pale from rage, and De Fourcy looked at them as if bewildered.

"What will happen now?" inquired Brother Rotgier.

But Danveld sprang almost with closed fists at De Fourcy.

"Why didst thou say that ye attacked Yurand first?"

"Because it is true!"

"There was need of a lie."

"I came here to fight, not to lie."

"Thou hast fought fiercely — there is no word on that score!"

"And hast thou not run away before Yurand to Schytno?"

"Pax, pax!" exclaimed Siegfried. "This knight is a guest of the Order."

"It is all one what he said," put in Brother Gottfried. "They would not have punished Yurand without trial, and at a trial the affair would have been explained."

"What will happen now?" repeated Brother Rotgier.

A moment of silence followed.

"We must finish finally with that bloody cur!" said Siegfried, in a stern and resolute voice. "De Bregov must be freed from confinement. Let us assemble the garrisons from Schytno, Insburg, and Lubov. Let us summon the nobles of Helmno, and attack Yurand. It is time to put an end to him!"

But the adroit Danveld, who knew how to weigh everything on both sides, put his hands on his head, frowned,
and said, after thinking, —

"Impossible, without permission of the Master."

"If it succeeds, the Master will praise," said Gottfried.

"But if not? If the prince moves his spearmen, and
falls on us?"

"There is peace between him and the Order; he will not
strike."

"Yes, there is peace, but we shall be the first to break it.
Our garrisons are not enough against the Mazovians."

"Then the Master will take our side, and there will be
war."

Danveld frowned again, and was thoughtful.

"No, no," said he, after a while. "If it succeeds, the
Master will be glad at heart. Envoys will go to the prince,
there will be discussions, and we shall get off without punishment. But in case of defeat, the Order will not take our
part, and will not declare war against the prince. For that
another Master would be needed. Behind Prince Yanush
stands the Polish king, and the Grand Master will not
quarrel with him."

"Still, we took the land of Dobryn; it is evident that
Cracow is not a terror to us."

"There were pretexts, — Opolchyk. We took, as it were,
a mortgage, and even that —" Here he looked around, and
added in a low voice, "I have heard in Malborg that if we
were threatened with war, we should give up the mortgage,
if the money were returned."

"Ach!" said Rotgier, "if Markward of Salzbach were
among us, or if Schaumberg, who smothered Vitold's whelps,
— they would manage Yurand. Who is Vitold? Yagello's
viceroy! — Grand Prince; still Schaumberg cared nothing,
— he smothered Vitold's children — made nothing of it.
Indeed, there is a lack among us of men who can find
means to do anything."

Hearing this, Hugo von Danveld put his elbows on the table
and his head on his hands, and sank for a long time in thought.
Suddenly his eyes grew bright, he wiped his thick moist lips
with the back of his hand as his wont was, and said, —

"Blessed be the moment in which you recalled, pious
brother, the name of the valiant Schaumberg."

"Why so? Have you thought of something?" inquired
Siegfried.

"Speak quickly!" cried Rotgier and Gottfried.

"Listen: Yurand has a daughter here, his only child, whom he loves as the sight of his eye."

"He has; I know her. Princess Anna Danuta loves her also."

"She does. Now listen: If you were to carry off that maiden, Yurand would give for her not only Bregov, but all the prisoners, with himself and Spyhov in addition."

"By the blood of Saint Boniface shed in Dohum!" cried Brother Gottfried, "it would be as you say."

Then they were silent, as if frightened by the boldness and the difficulties of the undertaking. Only after a while did Brother Rotgier turn to Siegfried.

"Your wit and experience," said he, "are equal to your valor; what do you think of this?"

"I think it a question which deserves consideration."

"For," continued Rotgier, "the maiden is a companion of the princess; more, she is almost a beloved daughter. Think, pious brothers, what an uproar would rise."

"You have said yourself," said Hugo, laughing, "that Schaumberg smothered Vitold's whelps, — and what was done to him for doing so? They will raise an outcry for any cause; but if we should send Yurand in chains to the Master, reward would await us more certainly than punishment."

"True," said Siegfried, "there is a chance for attack. The prince will go away, Anna Danuta will remain here with only her damsels. But an attack on the prince's court in time of peace is no common matter. The prince's court is not Spyhov. Then it will be again as in Zlotoria. Again complaints will be sent to all kingdoms, and to the Pope, against the violence of the Order; again the cursed Yagello will be heard with a threat, and the Master — you know him, moreover — he is glad to take what he can, but he does not want war with Yagello. Yes! a shout would rise in all the lands of Mazovia and Poland."

"Meanwhile Yurand's bones would be bleaching on a hook," said Danveld. "Besides who tells you to snatch her away here from the court, from the side of the princess?"

"Not from Tsehanov, I hope, where in addition to nobles there are three hundred bowmen."

"No. But may not Yurand get sick, and send people for his daughter? The princess would not forbid her to go in that case, and should the girl be lost on the road, who will say to you or to me, 'Thou didst snatch her away?'"

"Pshaw!" said Siegfried, impatiently; "then make Yurand get sick and send for the maiden."

At this Hugo smiled in triumph, and answered, —

"I have a goldsmith at home, who was driven out of Malborg for crime, and who settled in Schytno. This man can imitate any seal; I have men too, who, though our subjects, are descended from Mazovians. Dost not understand me yet?"

"I understand!" exclaimed Gottfried excitedly.

Brother Rotgier raised his hands aloft, and said, —

"God give thee happiness, pious brother, for neither Markward of Salzbach, nor Schaumberg would have found a better method."

Then he blinked as if trying to see something in the distance. "I see," said he, "Yurand standing with a rope around his neck at the Dantzig Gate in Malborg, and our men at arms kicking him."

"And his daughter will be a servant of the Order," added Hugo.

Hearing this, Siegfried turned severe eyes at Danveld, who drew the back of his hand ⌐ ross his lips again, and said, —

"But now to Schytno as quickly as possible."

CHAPTER XIX.

But before starting for Schytno, the four brethren and De Fourcy had to take farewell of the prince and the princess. That was a farewell not over friendly, but the prince, in accord with ancient Polish custom, unwilling to let guests depart empty handed, gave each man a fine bundle of fur, and a gryven of silver; they received these with delight giving assurance that, as brethren of the Cross, who had vowed poverty, they never kept money, but gave it to the poor, whom they recommended at the same time to pray for the health, glory, and future salvation of Prince Yanush.

The Mazovians smiled under their moustaches at these statements, for the greed of the Order was well known to them, and still better known were the lies of the Knights of the Order. In Mazovia the saying was, "A Knight of the Cross lies as a skunk gives out odor." The prince waved his hand and said after they had gone that a man might go to heaven on their prayers, perhaps crab fashion.

But still earlier, at parting with the princess, when Siegfried kissed her hand, Danveld approached Danusia, placed his hand on her head, and while stroking it said, —

"It is commanded us to return good for evil, and love even our enemies; so a sister of the Order will bring to you, young lady, the healing balsam."

"How am I to thank you?" answered Danusia.

"Be a friend of the Order, and the Knights of the Cross."

De Fourcy had noted this conversation, and because the beauty of the maiden had struck him, he asked after they had moved toward Schytno, —

"What beautiful damsel is that with whom you were talking?"

"She is the daughter of Yurand."

"The one whom you are going to seize?" asked De Fourcy, in wonder.

"The same. And if we have her, Yurand is ours."

"It is clear that not everything coming from Yurand is evil. It is worth while to be the keeper of such a prisoner."

"Do you think that it would be easier to war with her, than with Yurand?"

"That means that I think the same as you do. Her father is an enemy of the Order, but with the daughter you have spoken words rubbed with honey, and have promised her a balsam, besides."

Apparently Hugo von Danveld felt the need of justifying himself in some words before Siegfried, who, though not better than others, still observed strict rules of morality, and therefore had criticised certain brothers more than once.

"I have promised her a balsam," said he, "for that young knight who was crushed by the bull, and to whom she is betrothed, as you know. Should there be an outcry after we have seized the girl, we shall say that not only have we wished no harm, but we have sent them a cure according to Christian charity."

"Very well," replied Siegfried. "But we must send some safe person."

"I will send a pious woman completely devoted to the Order. I will command her to observe, and to listen. When our people go, as if sent by Yurand, they will find everything ready."

"It will be difficult to bring such people together."

"No. We have men who speak the same language that they do. We have them even among servants and the garrison, — men who are outlawed from Mazovia, fugitives, murderers, criminals, it is true, but fearless, and ready for anything. I shall promise them every reward if they do the work ; if they fail, the halter."

"Very well! But in case of treason?"

"There will be no treason, for every man of them has earned impalement on the stake, and upon each one a sentence is hanging. We only need to give them proper clothing and they will pass for real servants of Yurand, but the main thing is a letter with Yurand's seal."

"We must foresee everything," said Rotgier. "After the last battle Yurand will wish to see the prince, perhaps, so as to complain of us, and justify himself. Being in Tsehanov he will go to his daughter in the forest. It may happen that our men appearing on Yurand's business will meet Yurand himself."

"The men whom I shall select are cunning ruffians. They know that if they strike Yurand they will go to the hook. Their lives will depend on not meeting him."

"Still, should it happen them to be captured?"

"We shall get rid of them, and the message. Who will say that we sent them? Finally if the girl is not carried away, there will be no outcry, and if a few gallows'-birds of Mazovia are quartered, no harm will happen from that to the Order."

"I understand neither your politeness nor your fear lest it be known that the girl was carried away by our command," said Brother Gottfried, the youngest among the Knights. "Having her once in hand we must, of course, send some person to Yurand to say to him: 'Thy daughter is with us; dost thou wish that she should receive freedom, give for her Bregov and thyself.' How else is it to be? But then it will be known that we seized the girl."

"True," said De Fourcy, whom the whole affair did not please overmuch. "Why hide that which must be discovered?"

But Danveld laughed, and turning to Brother Gottfried asked,—

"How long do you wear the white mantle?"

"The sixth year will be finished the first week after Trinity Sunday."

"When you have worn it another six years you will understand the Order more intimately. Yurand knows us better than you do at present. This will be told him: 'Brother Schaumberg has charge of thy daughter, and if thou squeak a word, remember the children of Vitold.'"

"But later?"

"Later Bregov will be free, and the Order will be rid of Yurand."

"Well!" exclaimed Brother Rotgier, "everything is so wisely thought out that God must bless our undertaking."

"God will bless all undertakings that have for object the good of the Order," replied the gloomy Siegfried.

They went on in silence, and before them, two or three arrow-shots distant, went their escort to clear the road, which was drifted, for abundant snow had fallen in the night. On the trees was deposited much frost; the day was cloudy, but warm, so that steam rose from the horses. From the forest, toward human dwellings, flew flocks of crows, filling the air with foreboding caws.

De Fourcy fell back behind the knights a little, and rode on in deep thought. He had been for some years a guest of the Order; he had taken part in expeditions to Lithuania, where he had shown great valor and had been received everywhere as only Knights of the Cross knew how to receive guests from distant regions. He had grown strangely attached to them, and, not having a fortune, intended to enter their ranks. Meanwhile he had lived in Malborg; he had visited known localities, seeking in journeys amusement and adventures. Having come shortly before to Lubov with the wealthy Bregov, and hearing of Yurand, he had become excited with the desire to measure himself with a man who roused universal terror. The arrival of Meinegger, who had come out victorious from every encounter, hastened the adventure. The comtur of Lubov had given them men, but had told the three knights not only of the fierceness, but the stratagems and perfidy of Yurand, so that when the latter had asked them to send away their men they would not agree, fearing that should they do so he would surround and destroy them, or throw them into the dungeons of Spyhov. Yurand, thinking that they had in mind not only a knightly struggle, but robbery, attacked them offensively and inflicted a dreadful defeat.

De Fourcy saw Bregov overturned with his horse, he saw Meinegger with a broken lance in his bowels, he saw men simply begging for pity. He had been barely able himself to break away, and had wandered for days over roads and through forests where he might have died of hunger, or fallen a prey to wild beasts had he not come by chance to Tsehanov, where he found Gottfried and Rotgier. From the whole expedition he brought away a feeling of humiliation and hatred together with sorrow for Bregov, who was a near friend of his. He joined, therefore, heartily in the complaint of the Knights of the Cross when they demanded punishment for Yurand and liberation for their unfortunate comrade, and when that complaint found no attention, he was ready at the first moment to use every means of vengeance against Yurand. But now sudden scruples were roused in him. More than once while listening to conversations of the knights, and especially to Hugo's words, he could not avoid astonishment. Having become acquainted more intimately in the course of years with the Knights of the Cross, he saw really that they were not what in Germany and in the West they claimed to be. In Malborg he had known a few just and strict knights, those same who had often made charges against the corruption of the Brotherhood, against their profligacy and want of discipline, and De Fourcy felt that these charges were true; but being himself profligate

and undisciplined, he did not take those faults into account
too much, especially as Knights of the Cross atoned for them
with valor.   He had seen them at Vilno, meeting breast to
breast with Polish knights, at the taking of castles defended with superhuman resolve by Polish garrisons; he had
seen them dying under blows of swords and axes, in general
storms or in single combat.   They were unsparing and cruel
to Lithuania, but they were lion-like, and walked in glory as
in sunlight.   Now, however, it seemed to De Fourcy that
Hugo von Danveld was saying things and proposing methods
which ought to shock the soul in every knight; and the other
brothers not only did not rise against him, but confirmed
every word of his.   Hence astonishment possessed him more
and more, and at last he began to think deeply as to whether
he could put his hands to such deeds.

Had it been simply a question of snatching a girl away, or
exchanging her for Bregov later on, perhaps he might consent, though the beauty of Danusia had touched him and
captivated his heart.   If it had come to him to be her guardian he might perhaps have had nothing against the task, or
even would not have been sure that she would go from his
hands in the same state in which she had come to them.
But with the Knights of the Cross the question was clearly
something else.   Through her they wished to get, with Bregov,
also Yurand himself, by promising him that they would release her if he would give himself for her; then they would
kill him, and with him, to conceal the deceit and the crime
beyond any doubt, kill the girl herself also.   In every case
the same fate threatened her that came on the children of
Vitold in case Yurand dared to complain.   "They will not
observe anything; they will deceive both and kill both,"
thought De Fourcy; "still they carry the cross and ought
to hold honor higher than others."

And the soul stormed up in him more and more mightily
every moment because of such shamelessness; but he determined to satisfy himself as to how far his suspicions were
just, so he rode up to Hugo again and inquired, —

"If Yurand gives himself to you, will you liberate the
girl?"

"If we should liberate her the whole world would know at
once that we took both of them."

"But what will you do with her?"

Hugo inclined toward the speaker, and exhibiting by his
smile the decayed teeth under his thick lips, asked, —

"Of what are you inquiring?   Of what we shall do with her *before* or *after?*"

De Fourcy, knowing now what he wanted, was silent; for a while he seemed to struggle with himself, then rising in his stirrups somewhat, he said so loudly that all four Knights of the Cross heard him, —

"The pious Brother Ulrich of Jungingen, a model and ornament of chivalry, said once to me: ' Among the old men in Malborg thou wilt still find worthy brothers of the Cross; but those in the boundary districts bring naught save reproach to the Order.'"

"We are all sinners; but we serve the Saviour," said Danveld.

"Where is your knightly honor?   The Saviour is not served by infamous actions.   Know, then, that not only will I take no part in this action, but I will not permit you to do so."

"Why will you not permit?"

"To permit deceitful attack, treason, infamy?"

"But how are you going to prevent?   In the battle with Yurand you lost your escort and your wagons.   You must live by the favor of the Order; you would die of hunger should we be unwilling to throw a piece of bread to you. Besides, are we not four here while you are one?   How will you prevent?"

"How will I prevent?" repeated De Fourcy.   "I can return to the house and forewarn the prince; I can announce your intention before the whole world."

At this the Knights of the Cross looked at one another, and their faces changed in the twinkle of an eye.   Especially did Danveld look for a time with an inquiring glance into the eyes of Siegfried; then he turned to De Fourcy.

"Your ancestors," said he, "served in the Order, and you wish to enter it; but we will not receive traitors."

"In answer to that I say that I will not serve traitors."

"Ho! you will not carry out your threat.   Understand this, that the Order knows how to punish not merely brothers of the Cross."

De Fourcy, roused by these words, drew his sword; he seized its edge with his left hand, his right hand he placed on the hilt, and said. —

"On this hilt, which has the form of a cross, on the head of Saint Dionysins, my patron, and on my knightly honor, I shall warn the Prince of Mazovia and the Grand Master."

Danveld looked again with an inquiring glance at Siegfried, and the latter closed his eyes, as if in sign that he agreed to something. Then Danveld spoke with a strangely changed and dull voice, —

"Saint Dionysius might have carried his severed head under his arm," said he, " but if yours once falls — "

"Are you threatening me?" interrupted De Fourcy.

"No, but I shall kill you!" answered Danveld.

And he plunged a knife into his side with such force that the blade was hidden to the handle. De Fourcy shrieked with a terrible voice; for a moment he tried to seize with his right hand the sword which before he had held in his left, but he dropped it to the ground; that same moment the other three brothers fell to stabbing him without mercy in the breast and the bowels, till he dropped from the horse.

Then came silence. De Fourcy, bleeding terribly from a number of wounds, quivered on the snow, and tore it with fingers twisted by convulsions. From beneath a leaden sky came only the croaking of crows as they flew from empty deserts to human habitations.

And then a hurried conversation began among the murderers.

"The attendants have seen nothing!" said Danveld, in a panting voice.

"Nothing. The attendants are in advance, they are out of sight," answered Siegfried. "Listen: there will be occasion for a new complaint. We shall spread the report that Mazovian knights attacked us, and killed our comrade. We will make a noise, — until Malborg hears that the prince sets murderers on guests even. Do you hear? We must say that the prince not only was unwilling to listen to our complaints against Yurand, but that he gave command to kill the man who made the complaint."

De Fourcy meanwhile turned on his back during his last convulsion, and lay motionless with bloody foam on his lips, and terror in his eyes now opened widely. Brother Rotgier looked at him, and said, —

"Consider, pious brothers, how God punishes even the intention of treason."

"What we have done has been done for the good of the Order," said Gottfried. "Praise to him who did the deed — "

But he stopped, for in that instant from behind them, at the turn of the snowy road, appeared a horseman who raced with the speed of his horse. Seeing him, Hugo called quickly, —

"Whoever that man be, he must die."

"I recognize him," said Siegfried, who, though the oldest among the brothers, had an uncommonly quick eye. "He is the attendant who killed the wild bull with an axe. True, that is he!"

"Hide your knives, lest he be frightened," said Danveld. "I will strike first again; you support me."

Meanwhile the Cheh rode up, and about ten or eight steps away checked his horse in the snow. He saw a corpse in a pool of blood, a horse without a rider, and astonishment was depicted on his face; it remained, however, but the twinkle of an eye. Next moment he turned to the brethren as though he had seen nothing, and said, —

"I salute you, brave knights!"

"We recognized thee," answered Hugo, approaching him slowly. "Hast thou any question with us?"

"The knight Zbyshko of Bogdanets, whose spear I carry, has sent me, — he who was wounded by the wild bull at the hunt: he was not able himself to come."

"What does your master want of us?"

"Because you complained of Yurand of Spyhov unjustly, to the detriment of his knightly honor, my master gives command to declare to you that you have not acted as true knights, but that you have barked as dogs; and that he summons the man who used the words to a combat on foot or on horseback to the last breath, in which struggle he will meet you when you indicate the place, and when, with God's favor and mercy, his present sickness permits him."

"Tell your master that Knights of the Cross endure insults patiently, for the sake of the Saviour; as to a struggle without personal permission from the Master or the Grand Marshal. they cannot answer, but for this permission, however, we will write to Malborg."

Again the Cheh looked at the body of De Fourcy, for it was to him that he had been sent specially. Zbyshko knew that the Knights of the Cross did not accept challenges; but hearing that among the five was a lay knight, he wished to challenge that one, thinking thus to influence and win Yurand. Now the man was lying there slaughtered like an ox in the presence of four Knights of the Cross.

Hlava, it is true, did not know what had happened; but, inured from childhood to danger of all kinds, he sniffed

peril of some sort. He was astonished also that Danveld,
while talking, drew up more and more to him, and the others
began to surround him from the sides, as if wishing to encircle
him without being noticed. For these reasons he began to
have a care of himself, especially since he had no weapons
on his person; for in his haste he had not succeeded in taking
them.

Meanwhile Danveld was there before him, and continued :
"I have promised thy master a healing balsam, so then he
repays kindness with evil. Among Poles this is common;
but since he is grievously wounded, and may soon appear
before God, tell him — "

Here he placed his left palm on the Cheh's shoulder.
"Tell him then that just this is what I answer."

That moment a knife gleamed near Hlava's throat; but
before Danveld could stab, the Cheh, who had noted his movements, seized with his two iron hands the right arm, which
he twisted till joints and bones cracked in it, and only
when he heard a terrified roar of pain did he put spurs to his
horse and shoot off like an arrow, before the others were able
to stop him.

Brothers Rotgier and Gottfried started to chase, but returned soon, frightened by the terrible cry of Danveld.
Siegfried held him by the shoulder; but he, with pale and
blue face, cried so that the attendants, who had advanced
with the wagons considerably, stopped their horses.

"What is the matter?" inquired the brothers.

But Siegfried ordered them to ride on with all speed and
bring a wagon, for evidently Danveld could not hold himself
in the saddle. After a while cold sweat covered his forehead,
and he fainted.

When the wagon was brought he was placed on straw, and
they moved toward the boundary. Siegfried hurried, for he
understood, after what had happened, that they had no time
to lose, even in nursing Danveld. Sitting with him on the
wagon, he rubbed his face with snow from time to time,
but was unable to bring him to consciousness. Only when
near the boundary did Danveld open his eyes and look
around, as if in astonishment.

"How is it with you?" asked Siegfried.

"I feel no pain, but neither do I feel my hand."

"It is benumbed, so feeling has vanished. In a warm
room pain will return to you. Meanwhile thank God, even
for a moment of relief."

Then Rotgier and Gottfried approached the wagon.

"An accident has happened," said the first; "what are we to do now?"

"We will say," answered Danveld, with a weak voice, "that the attendant killed De Fourcy."

"Their new crime, and the author of it, is known!" added Rotgier.

CHAPTER XX.

MEANWHILE the Cheh flew with all speed straightway to the hunting-house, and finding the prince there, told him first of all what had happened. Fortunately there were courtiers who had seen that the Cheh had ridden out without weapons. One of them had even called on the road to him, half jestingly, to take some kind of iron, or the Germans would beat him. He, fearing lest the Germans might pass the boundary, had sprung to his horse in his jacket, and rushed after them. These testimonies scattered all doubts of the prince as to who could have murdered De Fourcy; but it filled him with alarm and such anger that in the first moment he wished to send pursuit after the Germans, so as to convey them in chains to the Grand Master for punishment. After a while, however, he saw himself that pursuit could not reach the knights before the boundary, and he said, —

"Still, I will send a letter to the Master and inform him what they are doing here. Evil has begun in the Order; formerly obedience was absolute, now any comtur does what he pleases. God grant that after offence will come punishment."

He thought a while and then said to the courtiers, —

"I cannot understand why they killed a guest, and were it not that the young man went without weapons, I should suspect him."

"You might," said the priest; "but what wish could he have to kill a man whom he had never seen before, and then, if he had weapons, how was he, one man, to attack five, and their armed escort in addition?"

"You speak truth," said the prince. "It must be that that guest opposed them in something, or that he would not lie as they wished; even here I noticed that they winked at him to say that Yurand was the first to begin."

"The Cheh is a gallant fellow," said Mrokota, "if he has crushed the paw of that dog of a Danveld."

"He says that he heard the bones break in the German," answered the prince; "and noticing how he fought in the forest that may well be. It is clear that both servant and master are doughty fellows. Had it not been for Zbyshko

the wild bull would have hurled himself at the princess'
horse.   Both he and the Knight of Lorraine did much to save
her."
   "Indeed he is a resolute man," said Father Vyshonek;
"even now when barely breathing he takes Yurand's part
and has challenged those Germans.   The master of Spyhov
needs just such a son-in-law."
   "Yurand talked rather differently in Cracow?—but he
will not object now, I think," said Prince Yanush.
   "The Lord Jesus will bring it about," said the princess,
who entering that moment heard the last words of the
conversation.   "Yurand cannot refuse now, if God return
health to Zbyshko.   But there must be a reward from us
also."
   "The best reward for him is Danusia, and I think that
he will get her, for this reason, that when women undertake
something even a Yurand is helpless."
   "But have I not undertaken a good work?" inquired the
princess.   "That Zbyshko is impulsive I will not deny;
but there is not a truer man on earth than he.   And the girl
is as true as he is.   She does not go one step from him, she
thinks of him only, and he smiles at her in his pain so that
tears fall from my eyes at moments.   I tell thee the truth.
Love like that is worth helping, for God's own mother de-
lights in seeing human happiness."
   "If only the will of God be there," said the prince,
"happiness will come.   But to tell the truth, they came
near cutting his head off because of that maiden, and now
the wild bull has crushed him."
   "Do not say because of her!" exclaimed the princess;
"no other but Danusia saved him in Cracow."
   "That is true; but had it not been for her he would never
have struck against Lichtenstein to wrest the plume from his
helmet, and he would not have exposed himself for the man
of Lorraine with such readiness.   As to the reward, I have
said that that belongs to both, and in Tsehanov I will provide it."
   "Nothing would Zbyshko like to see so well as the belt of
a knight and golden spurs."
   The prince smiled good-naturedly, and added, —
   "Let the girl take them to him, and when his wound is.
healed we shall see that all is finished in proper fashion.
And let her take them quickly, for sudden pleasure is
best."

The princess, hearing this, embraced her husband in presence of the courtiers; then she kissed his hands repeatedly. He smiled meanwhile, and said, —

"Well, you see, a good affair is settled! The Holy Ghost has not withheld wit even from women! Call the girl in."

"Danusia! Danusia!" cried the princess.

After a while, in the doorway of the side chamber appeared Danusia, her eyes red from watching, in her hands a two-handled basin, full of steaming kasha with which Father Vyshonek was to poultice Zbyshko's bruised bones, and which an old court lady had just given her.

"Come, little orphan," said the prince. "Put down the vessel and come hither."

She approached him somewhat timidly, for the "Pan" roused a certain dread in her; he drew her toward him kindly, and stroked her face, saying, —

"Well, child, grief has come to thee, has it not?"

"It has indeed!" replied Danusia. And having sorrow in her heart, and tears ready, she burst into weeping at once, but quietly, so as not to offend Prince Yanush.

"Why art thou crying?" inquired he.

"Because Zbyshko is sick," replied she, putting her fists in her eyes.

"Have no fear; nothing will harm him. Is not that true, Father Vyshonek?"

"By God's will he is nearer marriage than death," said the kind priest.

"Wait," said the prince; "I will give a medicine that will help, or cure him altogether."

"The balsam which the Knights of the Cross sent?" cried Danusia, vivaciously, taking her hands from her eyes.

"Better rub a dog with what the Knights of the Cross sent than thy dear young knight whom thou lovest. I will give thee something else." Then he turned to the courtiers and called: "Will some one go to the store chamber for spurs and a belt?"

When they were brought, he said to Danusia: "Take these to Zbyshko, and say that henceforth he is belted. If he dies he will stand before God a belted warrior; if he lives I will finish the rest in Tsehanov or Warsaw."

When Danusia heard this she embraced the prince's feet; then she grasped with one hand the insignia of knighthood, with the other the basin, and sprang to the room in which

Zbyshko was lying. The princess followed, not wishing to lose sight of their pleasure.

Zbyshko was very sick, but seeing Danusia, he turned to her with face pale from pain, and asked, —

"But the Cheh, my berry, has he returned?"

"What matter about him? I bring better news. Our lord has belted thee as a knight, and here are the things which he has sent by me," said she, placing the belt and golden spurs at his side.

Zbyshko's pale cheeks flushed with delight and astonishment; he looked at Danusia, next at the insignia; then he closed his eyes, and asked, —

"How could he belt me as a knight?"

But when at that moment the princess came in, he raised himself on his arms somewhat and thanked her, asking pardon of the gracious lady because he could not fall at her feet, for he divined at once that through her intercession it was that such fortune had befallen him. She commanded quiet, however, and with her own hands helped Danusia to lower his head to the pillow.

Meanwhile the prince entered, and with him Father Vyshonek, Mrokota, and a number of others. From a distance Prince Yanush gave a sign with his hand that Zbyshko was not to move, and then, sitting down by the bedside, spoke as follows : —

"It is no wonder to people, as you know, that there is reward for noble and valiant deeds ; were there not, honor would go unconsidered, and injustice would move through the world without punishment. Since thou hast not spared thy life, and with loss of health hast defended us from terrible sorrow, we permit thee to gird thyself with the belt of a knight, and to be henceforth in renown and in honor."

"Gracious lord," answered Zbyshko, "I should not grieve for ten lives —"

He was unable to continue, both from emotion and because the princess placed her hand on his lips, when Father Vyshonek forbade him to speak. But the prince continued, —

"I think that thou knowest the duties of a knight, and wilt wear these ornaments worthily. Thou art to serve our Redeemer, as is befitting, and war against the elder of Hell. Thou art to be loyal to the Lord's anointed on earth, avoid unjust wars. defend oppressed innocence, in which may God and His Holy Passion assist thee!"

'Amen!" responded the priest.

Then the prince rose, took farewell of Zbyshko, and in going away, added, —

"When thou art well, come directly to Tsehanov; whither I will bring Yurand also!"

CHAPTER XXI.

THREE days later came the promised woman with the Hercynian balsam, and with her a captain of bowmen from Schytno bearing a letter signed by the brothers, and furnished with Danveld's seal. In this letter the Knights of the Cross called heaven and earth to witness the wrongs which had met them in Mazovia; and under threat of God's vengeance demanded punishment for the murder of their "guest and dear comrade." Danveld had added to the letter a complaint of his own, demanding, in words both humble and menacing, payment for the grievous maiming of himself, and a sentence of death against Hlava.

The prince tore the letter before the eyes of the captain, threw it under his feet, and said, —

"The Master sent them, oh, their crusading mothers, to gain my good-will, but they have brought me to anger. Tell them from me that they slew the guest themselves, and tried to slay the Cheh; of this I shall write to the Master, and I shall add also that he is to choose other envoys if he wishes me to be neutral when war comes between the Order and the king at Cracow."

"Gracious lord," replied the captain, "is that the only answer that I am to take to the pious and mighty brotherhood?"

"If that is not enough, say that I look on them as dog brothers, and not as real knights."

This ended the audience. The captain rode away, for the prince went that day to Tsehanov. But the "sister" remained with the balsam, which the suspicious Father Vyshonek would not use, especially as the sick man had slept soundly the night before, and woke in the morning weakened greatly, it is true, but without fever. After the prince's departure the sister sent back one of her servants immediately, as if for a new remedy, a "basilisk's egg," which, as she declared, had power to restore strength even to the dying. She went herself along the court submissively, and without the use of one hand, in a lay dress, — but one resembling that of a religious, — with a rosary, and a small pilgrim gourd at her girdle. Speaking Polish well, she inquired of the servants with great care about Zbyshko and Danusia; when the occasion offered, she made Danusia a present of a rose of Jericho; and the following day, when the maiden was sitting in the dining-hall, she pushed up to her and said, —

"God bless you, young lady. Last night, after prayer, I dreamed that two knights came through the snow to you; one arrived first, and wound you in a white mantle, but the other said, 'I see only snow, she is not here;' and he went back again."

Danusia, who wished to sleep, opened her blue eyes at once, and inquired, —

"But what does that signify?"

"This, that the one who loves you most will get you."

"That is Zbyshko!"

"I cannot tell, for I saw not his face; I saw only a white mantle, and I woke then immediately, for every night the Lord Jesus sends me pain in my feet; and one arm He has taken from me altogether."

"But has the balsam not helped you?"

"Even the balsam will not help me, young lady, because of my sin, which is too great; if you wish to know what it is, I will tell you."

Danusia nodded, in token that she was willing to know; so the sister continued, —

"There are in the Order women also who serve, though they make no vows, for they can marry, still, with respect to the Order they are bound to serve the Brotherhood; and whoever of them is met by such a favor and honor receives a pious kiss from a brother knight in sign that henceforth in deed and speech she is to serve the Order. Oh, young lady, such a great favor was to visit me; but I, in my sinful stubbornness, instead of receiving it gratefully, committed much sin, and drew down on myself punishment."

"What did you do?"

"Brother Danveld came and gave me the kiss of the Order. I thought it given through frivolousness, and raised my godless hand on him."

Then she beat her breast, and repeated a number of times, —

"O God, be merciful to me a sinner!"

"And what happened?" inquired Danusia.

"My hand was taken at once from me, and from that hour I have been maimed. I was young and foolish; I was ignorant! Still, I was punished. For though it might seem to a woman that a brother of the Order wished to do something evil, she must leave judgment to God; she is not to oppose, for should she oppose a Knight of the Cross, or a Brother, God's anger would blast her."

Danusia listened to those words with disgust and with fear; the sister, however, sighed, and continued, —

" I am not old even to-day, barely thirty ; but God, when He took the use of my hand from me, took my youth also and beauty."

"If your hand had not been taken," said Danusia, " you might live without complaint."

After that, followed silence.   Then the sister, as if calling something to mind, said, —

" But I dreamt that some knight wrapped you in a white mantle on the snow ; he was a Knight of the Cross, perhaps, they wear white mantles."

" I want neither the Knights of the Cross nor their mantles," answered the maiden.

Further conversation was stopped by the priest, who entered the hall, nodded at Danusia, and said, —

" Praise God, and go to Zbyshko.   He is awake, and wishes to eat.   He is much better."

Such was the case in reality.   Zbyshko's health had improved, and Father Vyshonek felt almost certain that he would recover, when all at once an unexpected event disturbed all combinations and hopes.   Messengers from Yurand came to the princess with a letter which contained the worst and most terrible tidings.   A part of Yurand's castle in Spyhov had caught fire.   He himself, while trying to save the building, had been crushed by a burning beam. Father Kaleb, who had written the letter in Yurand's name, declared, it is true, that Yurand might recover, but that the sparks and coals had so burnt his sound eye, that not much sight was left in it, and inevitable blindness threatened him.

For this reason Yurand summoned his daughter to come quickly to Spyhov; he wished to see her once more before blindness seized him.   He said, too, that she would remain thenceforth with him; for if even blind men who go out to beg bread have each of them a child to lead him and show the way, why should he be deprived of this last consolation, and die among strangers?   The letter contained also profound thanks to the princess, who had reared the girl as if she had been her mother, and at the end Yurand promised that, though blind, he would visit Warsaw again to fall at the feet of the lady, and implore her favor for Danusia in the future.

When Father Vyshonek read this letter to her, the princess was hardly able to utter a word for some time. She had hoped that when Yurand, who visited his child five or six times every year, came at the approaching holidays, she would, by her authority and that of Prince Yanush, win him over to Zbyshko, and gain his consent to an early wedding. This letter not only destroyed all her plans, but deprived her of Danusia, whom she loved as if she had been her own daughter. It occurred to her also that Yurand might give the girl immediately to one of his neighbors, so as to pass the rest of his days among his own kindred. A visit by Zbyshko to Spyhov was out of the question, for his ribs had only just begun to knit, and besides, who could tell how Yurand would receive him? The princess knew that Yurand had refused him outright, and told her that for mysterious reasons he would never permit the marriage. In her grievous vexation, Princess Anna gave command to summon the elder among the messengers so as to inquire of him touching the misfortune at Spyhov, and learn something of Yurand's plans also.

She was astonished when a man entirely unknown answered her summons, not old Tolima, Yurand's shield-bearer, who came with him usually. The stranger explained that Tolima had been terribly wounded in the last battle with the Germans; that he was wrestling with death in Spyhov; that Yurand, brought down with great pain, begged for the speedy return of his daughter, for he saw less and less, and in a couple of days might be blind altogether. The messenger begged, therefore, earnestly for permission to take the girl the moment his horses had rested, but as it was evening the princess opposed decisively. She would not break the hearts of Zbyshko and Danusia and herself utterly by such a sudden parting.

Zbyshko knew of everything already, and was lying in his room as if struck on the head with the poll of a hatchet; and when the princess entered, wringing her hands and saying at the threshold, "There is no help, for this is a father," he repeated after her, like an echo, "There is no help," and closed his eyes like a man who thinks that death will come to him straightway.

But death did not come, though increasing grief rose in

his breast, and through his head darker and darker thoughts flew, like clouds which, driven by a storm one after another, hide the light of day and extinguish all earthly pleasure. Zbyshko understood, as well as the princess, that if Danusia went to Spyhov she would be the same as lost to him. "Here," thought he, "all wish me well; there Yurand may not even receive me, or listen to me, especially if a vow or some unknown reason binds him. Besides, how can I go to Spyhov when I am sick and barely able to move on this bed." A few days before, by the favor of the prince, golden spurs with the belt of a knight had been given him. He thought on receiving them that joy would overcome sickness, and he prayed with his whole soul to rise quickly and measure himself with the Knights of the Order, but now he lost every hope, for he felt that if Danusia were absent from his bedside, desire to live would be absent and the strength to struggle with death would be absent also. To-morrow would come, and the day after, and the eves of festivals, and the festivals themselves; his bones would pain him in just the same way, and in just the same way would faintness seize him, and that brightness would not be near him, which spread through the whole room from Danusia, nor would that delight for the eyes which looked at her. What a consolation, what a solace to ask a number of times every day, "Am I dear to thee?" and to see her as, laughing and confused, she covered her eyes with her hands, or bent down and answered, "Who could be dear if not Zbyshko?" Sickness will stay behind, and pain and grief, happiness will go, and not return to him.

Tears gleamed in Zbyshko's eyes and flowed over his cheeks slowly; then he turned to the princess and said, —

"Gracious lady, I think that I shall never see Danusia in this life again."

"Wert thou to die from grief it would not be a wonder," answered the princess, herself full of sorrow. "But the Lord Jesus is merciful."

After a while, wishing to strengthen him even a little, she added, —

"Though if Yurand were to die before thee, without giving this as an example, guardianship would come to the prince and to me, and we should give thee the maiden immediately."

"If he dies!" answered Zbyshko.

But all at once some new thought flashed through his head,

for he raised himself, sat up in the bed, and said in changed accents, —

"Gracious lady — "

At that point he was interrupted by Danusia, who ran in weeping and began to call from the threshold, —

"Thou knowest already, Zbyshko! Oi, I am sorry for papa, but I am sorry for thee, poor boy!"

Zbyshko, when she came near him, gathered in with his sound arm his darling, and said, —

"How am I to live without thee? It was not to lose thee that I made vows and served thee. It was not to lose thee that I have ridden hither through forests and rivers. Hei! grief will not relieve me, tears will not relieve me, death itself will not relieve ; for though the green grass were to grow over me, my soul would not forget thee even in the court of the Lord Jesus, and in the chambers of God the Father Himself. I say there is no help, but help must be found; without help there is no escape anyhow! I feel torture in my bones and great pain, but do thou, Danusia, fall at the feet of our lady, for I am not able to do so, and do thou beg a favor for both of us."

When Danusia heard this she sprang to the feet of the princess, and embracing them hid her bright face in the folds of her heavy robe ; the lady turned her eyes, which were filled with pity but also with astonishment, at Zbyshko.

"How can I show favor? If I do not let the child go to her father I shall bring down the anger of God on my head."

Zbyshko, who had raised himself previously, dropped again to the pillow, and for a time made no answer because breath was lacking him. But gradually he moved one hand up to the other on his breast till at last he joined both as if in prayer.

"Rest," said the princess, "then tell what thy wish is, but do thou, Danusia, rise from my knees."

"Do not rise, but join in my prayer," said Zbyshko. Then he began in a weak and broken voice, —

"Gracious lady — Yurand was opposed to me in Cracow — he will be opposed to me now, but if Father Vyshonek marries me to Danusia — she may go to Spyhov, for then no human power can take her from me."

These words were so unexpected for Princess Anna that she sprang up from the bench, then sat down again, and said, as if not understanding well what the question was, —

" God's wounds!— Father Vyshonek?"

" Gracious lady! gracious lady!" begged Zbyshko.

" Gracious lady!" repeated Danusia after him, embracing the knees of the princess a second time.

" How could that be without parental permission?"

"The law of God is superior," answered Zbyshko.

" But fear God!"

"Who is a father, if not the prince? who a mother, if not you, gracious lady?"

" Gracious beloved mother!" said Danusia.

" True! I have been, and am a mother to her," said the princess, " and besides it was from my hand that Yurand received his wife. True! The moment the marriage takes place all is finished. Yurand may be angry, still he is bound to the prince, as his lord. Moreover we need not tell him immediately unless he wants to give her to another, or make her a nun. — And if he has taken some vow it will not be his fault (that she is married). Against the will of God no man can do anything. — By the living God! maybe this is Heaven's will."

" It must be!" cried Zbyshko.

"Wait," said the princess, filled with emotion, "let me think a little! If the prince were here I should go to him now and ask, ' Are we to give Danusia, or not?' But without him I am afraid to act. — My breath just stops, and there is no time for waiting in this case, since the girl must go in the morning. — O dear Jesus! let her go married, if only there is peace. But I cannot come to my mind, and somehow I am afraid. Art thou not afraid, Danusia? Speak!"

" If this is not done I shall die!" exclaimed Zbyshko.

Danusia rose from the knees of the princess, and because she was really admitted by the kind lady not only to intimacy, but to fondling, she seized her around the neck, and pressed her with all her strength.

" Without Father Vyshonek I will say nothing to thee," answered the princess. " Run for him as quickly as possible."

Danusia ran for Father Vyshonek; Zbyshko turned his pallid face to the princess, and said, —

" What the Lord Jesus has predestined will happen, but for this comfort may God reward you, gracious lady."

" Do not bless me yet," said the princess, " for it is unknown what will happen. And thou must swear to me on thy honor that if the marriage takes place thou wilt not prevent Danusia from going at once to her father, so as not to draw his curse on thyself and on her; against that may God guard thee."

"I swear on my honor," answered Zbyshko.

"Well, remember thy oath. But there is no need for the girl to say anything to Yurand at present. Better keep back the news lest it burn him like fire. We will send for him from Tsehanov, to come with Danusia, and then I will tell him myself; I will beg the prince even to do so. When he sees that there is no help for it he will consent. For that matter, Yurand has not disliked thee."

"No, he has not disliked me, so he may even be glad in soul that Danusia will be mine. For if he has made a vow he will not be in fault if I get her."

The coming of Father Vyshonek and Danusia interrupted further conversation. The princess called him to counsel that instant, and told him with great excitement of Zbyshko's wish, but he, after barely hearing what the question was, made the sign of the cross on himself, and said, —

"In the name of the Father, Son, and Holy Ghost! — how can I do this? Why, it is Advent!"

"As God lives, that is true!" cried the princess.

Silence followed. The anxious faces showed what a blow Father Vyshonek's words were to all of them.

After a while he added, —

"Were there a dispensation I would not oppose, since I sympathize with you. I should not ask absolutely for Yurand's permission; if you permit, gracious lady, and guarantee the consent of the prince, our lord, of course he and you are father and mother of all Mazovia. But without a dispensation from the bishop — I cannot. If Bishop Yakob of Kurdvanov were among us, perhaps he would not refuse a dispensation, though severe, — not like his predecessor, Bishop Mamphiolus, who answered every question with ' Bene! bene!'" (Granted! granted!)

"Bishop Yakob loves the prince and me greatly," put in the lady.

"Then I say that he would not refuse a dispensation, if there are reasons for it.— The girl must go, and this young man is sick, and will die, perhaps — Hm! *in articulo mortis.* But without a dispensation it is impossible."

"I could get a dispensation of Bishop Yakob later, — and though I know how severe he is, he will not refuse me this favor. — Oh, I guarantee that he will not refuse."

To this Father Vyshonek, who was a good and mild man, replied, —

"The word of an anointed of God like you is great. I am afraid of the bishop, but your word has power. The young man too might promise something to the cathedral in Plotsk — I know not. — Seest thou this is always a sin till dispensation comes, and the sin of no one but me? — Hm! the Lord Jesus is indeed merciful; if any man sins not to his own profit, but out of compassion for the suffering of others He forgives the more readily. — But this is a sin, and should the bishop be stubborn, who would absolve me?"

"The bishop will not be stubborn!" cried Princess Anna.

"That Sanderus, who came with me has indulgences for everything," said Zbyshko.

Father Vyshonek did not believe altogether, perhaps, in Sanderus's indulgences, but he was glad to seize at a pretext even, if only it favored Zbyshko and Danusia, for he had great love for the maiden, whom he had known from her childhood. At last he considered that church penance was the worst that might befall him, so he turned to the princess and said, —

"I am a priest, it is true, but also I am the prince's servant. What do you command, gracious lady?"

"I do not command, I request," replied she. "But if that Sanderus has indulgences —"

"He has. But it is a question of the bishop. He deals strictly with rules there in Plotsk."

"Have no fear of the bishop. He has forbidden to priests bows and swords, as I hear, as well as various acts of license, but he has not forbidden good deeds."

"Then let it be according to your will," said Father Vyshonek, raising his eyes and his hands.

At these words delight possessed their hearts. Zbyshko dropped again to his pillow, but the princess, Danusia, and Father Vyshonek sat around the bed and "counselled" how the affair was to be accomplished. They determined to preserve the secret, so that not a living soul in the house should know of it; they determined also that neither ought Yurand to know till the princess herself should inform him in Tsehanov of everything. The priest was to write a letter immediately from the princess to Yurand, asking him to come at once to Tsehanov, where they could find better cures for his wounds, and he would not be so troubled by loneliness. Finally it was arranged that Zbyshko and Danusia should prepare for confession. The marriage would take place in the night, when all had lain down to sleep.

For a moment Zbyshko had thought to take the Cheh as a witness of the marriage, but he rejected the plan when he remembered that Hlava had come from Yagenka. For a while Yagenka stood before him in memory, as if living. She stood in such a way that it seemed to him that he was looking at her ruddy face, and her eyes that had been weeping, and he heard her imploring voice, which said: "Do not do that! do not pay me with evil for good, with misfortune for love!" All at once great compassion for her seized him, because he felt that grievous pain would be inflicted on her, after which she would not find solace either under her father's roof or in the depth of the forest, or in the field, or in the gifts of the abbot, or in the love-making of Stan and Vilk. So he said to her in spirit: "God grant thee, O maiden, everything that is best, but, though I should be glad to bend down the heavens for thee, I cannot." And, in fact, the conviction that that was not in his power brought relief at once and restored peace to him, so that he thought then only of Danusia and the marriage.

But he could not dispense with the aid of the Cheh, so, though he had determined to say nothing in his presence of what was to happen, he asked to have him called.

"I am going to confession," said he to Hlava, "and to the Table of the Lord; so array me in the best manner possible, as if I were going to royal chambers."

The Cheh was alarmed somewhat, and looked at his face. Zbyshko understood what this meant, and said, —

"Have no fear; people confess before other events as well as death; but this time is all the more fitting since the holidays are near, when the princess and Father Vyshonek are going to Tsehanov, and there will be no priest nearer than Prasnysh."

"But will your Grace not go?" asked the attendant.

"I shall go if I recover; but my recovery is in God's hands."

Hlava was pacified, and hurrying to the box brought that white, gold-embroidered jacket in which the knight arrayed himself for great solemnities, and also a beautiful rug to cover his feet in the bed. Then, when he had raised Zbyshko, with the aid of the two Turks, he washed him, combed his long hair, around which he put a scarlet head-band. Finally he

propped him, thus arrayed, against red pillows, and, pleased
with his own work, he added, —

"If your Grace were able to dance now, you might go to a
wedding."

"They would have to do without our dancing," answered
Zbyshko, with a smile.

Meanwhile, the princess in her chamber was thinking how
to array Danusia, since for her womanly nature it was a
question of great importance, and she was unwilling that the
dear maiden reared by her should stand up to be married in an every-day garment. The maidens to whom information was given that Danusia had arrayed herself in the
color of innocence for confession, found white robes easily in
the boxes. For the dressing of her head there was trouble.
At the thought of this wonderful sadness possessed the
princess, so that she fell to complaining, —

"O thou my orphan, where shall I find a garland of rue
for thee? In this forest there is no little flower of any sort,
nor a leaf, unless mosses flourish under the snow."

Danusia, standing there with flowing hair, was troubled
also, for she, too, wished a garland; but after a while she
pointed to strings of immortelles hanging on the walls of the
chamber, and said, —

"Use those, for I shall find nothing else, and Zbyshko will
take me even in such a garland."

The princess would not consent at first, fearing a bad
omen, but since there were no flowers in that house, to which
they came only for hunting, they settled on what they had.
Father Vyshonek, who had heard Zbyshko's confession,
came, and took Danusia now to confess; after that dark night
appeared. When supper was over, the servants went to
bed at command of the princess. Yurand's messengers lay
down, some in the servants' rooms, others with the horses in
the stables. Fires in the servants' rooms were covered with
ashes and went down, till at last it was perfectly silent in the
hunting-lodge, save that from time to time dogs barked
toward the forest at wolves.

But in the chambers of the princess, of Father Vyshonek,
and of Zbyshko the windows did not cease to give light;
they cast ruddy gleams on the snow which covered the courtyard. In these chambers they were watching in silence,
listening to the beating of their own hearts, disquieted and
filled with the solemnity of that moment which was to come
very soon. After midnight the princess took Danusia's

hand and conducted her to Zbyshko's chamber, where Father Vyshonek was waiting for them with the Lord God (the Holy Sacrament).

In that chamber a great fire was burning in the chimney, and by its abundant but uneven light, Zbyshko beheld Danusia, somewhat pale from lack of sleep, in white, with a garland of immortelles on her temples, dressed in a stiff robe which reached the floor. Her eyelids were closed from emotion, her arms were dropped at her sides, and she looked like a painting on window-panes. There was something church-like about her, so that Zbyshko wondered at the sight; for it seemed to him that that was not an earthly maiden, but some heavenly soul which he was to take in marriage. And he thought so still more when she knelt with folded hands for communion, and with head thrown back closed her eyes altogether. She seemed to him as if dead, so that terror even seized his heart. But this did not last long, for hearing the voice of the priest saying, *Ecce Agnus Dei*,[1] he became collected in spirit, and his thoughts flew toward God straightway. In the chamber no noise was heard now save the solemn voice of the priest: *Domine, non sum dignus*,[2] and the crackling of the sparks in the fire, and the crickets singing persistently, and, as it were, with sadness in a cranny of the chimney. Outside the house the wind rose and sounded through the snow-covered forest, but it fell again.

Zbyshko and Danusia remained some time in silence. Father Vyshonek took the chalice to the chapel, and returned soon, not alone, however, but with De Lorche, and, noticing astonishment on the faces of those present, he put his finger on his lips as if to prevent an exclamation.

"I understood," said he, "that it would be better to have two witnesses of the marriage; hence, I have just instructed this knight, who has sworn to me on his honor and on relics that he will keep the secret as long as may be needed."

De Lorche knelt first before the princess then before Danusia. After that he rose and stood in silence, arrayed in ceremonial armor, along the joints of which bright reflections shone from the fire. Tall, motionless, sunk as it were in ecstasy; for to him also that white maiden with a garland of immortelles on her head seemed an angel on the window-panes of a Gothic cathedral.

---

[1] Behold the Lamb of God.   [2] Lord, I am not worthy.

The priest brought her to Zbyshko's bedside, and, putting his stole over their arms, began the usual ceremony. Tears one after another flowed down the honest face of the princess, but in her soul there was no fear at that moment; for she felt that she was doing good by uniting those two wonderful and innocent children.

De Lorche knelt a second time, and, leaning with both hands on the hilt of his sword, he looked exactly like a knight who has a vision.

The couple repeated the words of the priest in turn: " I — take thee — to myself — " and in accompaniment to these low and pleasant words the crickets chirped again in the crevices of the chimney, and the fire crackled in the billets of hornbeam.

When the ceremony was over, Danusia fell at the feet of the princess, who blessed both, and who said as she gave them into the guardianship of the heavenly powers, —

" Rejoice now, for she is thine, and thou art hers."

Then Zbyshko stretched out his sound arm to Danusia, and she encircled his neck with her arms, and for a while the others heard how they repeated to each other, —

" Thou art mine, Danusia ! "

" Thou art mine, Zbyshko ! "

But immediately after Zbyshko grew weak, for the emotion was too great for his strength, and dropping on the pillow he breathed heavily. He did not faint, however, and did not cease to smile at Danusia, who wiped his face, bedewed with cold sweat, and he did not cease to repeat even yet, " Thou art mine, Danusia ! " at which she bent her blond head each time toward him. This spectacle moved to the utmost De Lorche, who declared that in no land had it happened him to see such tender hearts, wherewith he made a solemn vow to meet on foot or on horseback any knight, magician, or dragon who might dare to stand in the way of their happiness. And, in fact, he took that vow immediately on the cross-formed hilt of a misericordia, or small sword, which served knights in despatching the wounded. The princess and Father Vyshonek were called as witnesses of that vow.

The princess, not understanding a marriage without some rejoicement, brought wine, and they drank of it. The hours passed one after another. Zbyshko, overcoming his weak-ness, drew Danusia toward him a second time, and said, —

" Since the Lord Jesus has given thee to me, no one will take thee from me now, dearest berry."

"Papa and I will come to Tsehanov," answered Danusia.

"If only sickness or something else does not attack thee. God guard thee from evil event. Thou must go to Spyhov, I know. Hei! thanks to the highest God, and the gracious lady that thou art mine, for the power of man cannot unmake a marriage."

But since that marriage had taken place in the night and mysteriously, and since immediately afterward a separation was to follow, a certain strange melancholy seized at moments, not only Zbyshko, but all. Conversation was interrupted. From time to time the fire ceased to blaze in the chimney, and peoples' heads sank in obscurity. Father Vyshonek threw new sticks on the coals then, and when a stick crackled with a plaintive sound, as it does sometimes when the wood is fresh, he said, —

"What dost thou wish for, O soul doing penance?"

The crickets answered him, and the increasing flame, which brought out from the shadow watching faces, was reflected in the armor of De Lorche, illuminating at the same time Danusia's white robe and the garland on her head.

The dogs in the yard barked again toward the forest as if at wolves.

And as the night passed silence fell more and more on them, till at last the princess said, —

"Dear Jesus! is it to be thus after a marriage? Better go to sleep; but since we must wait till morning, play to us on the lute, little flower, play, for the last time before thy going, to me and to Zbyshko."

Danusia, who was weary and drowsy, was glad to rouse herself with anything; so she sprang for the lute, and returning after a while with it sat by Zbyshko's bed.

"What am I to play?" asked she.

"What shouldst thou play," asked the princess, "if not that song which thou didst sing in Tynets, when Zbyshko saw thee the first time?"

"Hei! I remember — and till death I shall not forget," said Zbyshko. "After that always the tears came to my eyes when I heard it."

"I will sing it in that case," said Danusia.

And straightway she began to finger the lute; then throwing her head back as usual she began: —

"Oh, had I wings like a wild goose,
  I would fly after Yasek;

I would fly after him to Silesia!
I would sit on a fence in Silesia.
Look at me, Yasek dear,
Look at the poor little orphan."

But all at once her voice broke, her lips quivered, and
from beneath her closed lids tears came out on her cheeks in
spite of her. For a time she tried not to let them come, but
she had not power to restrain them, and at last she wept
heartily, just as she had when, the time before, she sang that
same song to Zbyshko in the prison at Cracow.

"Danusia !   What is thy grief, Danusia?" asked
Zbyshko.

"Why art thou weeping? What kind of wedding is
this?" cried the princess. "Why dost thou weep?"

" I know not," answered Danusia, sobbing. "I feel so
much sadness. I grieve so for Zbyshko and the lady."

Therefore all were sad, and fell to comforting her, explain-
ing that her absence would not be lasting; that surely she
would go with her father at Christmas to Tsehanov. Zbyshko
embraced her again with his arm, drew her to his bosom, and
kissed the tears from her eyes; but the weight remained on
all hearts, and under this weight the remaining hours of the
night passed.

At last a noise was heard in the yard, so sudden and
sharp that all quivered. The princess, springing up from
her seat, cried, —

" Oh, as God lives ! The well-sweeps ! They are watering
the horses!"

Father Vyshonek looked through the window, in which the
glass panes were taking on a gray color, and said, —

" Night is growing pale, and day is coming. *Ave Maria,
gratias plena!*" (Hail, Mary, full of grace !)

Then he went out of the chamber, and returning after a
while, said, —

" Day is dawning, though the day will be gloomy.
Yurand's people are watering the horses. It is time for
thee to take the road."

At these words the princess and Danusia broke into loud
weeping, and they and Zbyshko lamented, as do simple
people when they part; that is, in their lament there was
something ceremonial, a complaint, half spoken, half chanted,
which comes forth from full souls as naturally as tears from
the eyes, —

" Hei, weeping will help us no longer.
  We give thee farewell, dearest love;
Weeping will help us no longer,
  We give thee farewell.
God aid thee, we give thee farewell! "

Zbyshko drew Danusia to his bosom for the last time, and held her there long, as long as his breath lasted, and until the princess tore her away from him to dress her for the road.

Day had dawned now completely. All in the house were awake and moving.

Hlava came to Zbyshko to learn about his health and ask for orders.

" Draw the bed to the window," said the knight.

The Cheh drew the bed easily to the window, but he wondered when Zbyshko commanded him to open it; but he obeyed, covering, however, the lord with his own fur, for it was cold out of doors, though cloudy, and abundant soft snow was falling.

Zbyshko looked through the snow-flakes flying from the clouds. In the yard a sleigh was visible; around it, on steaming horses which had hoar frost on them, were Yurand's people. All were armed, and over their sheepskins some wore armor, on which the pale and uncertain light of day was reflected. The forest was covered entirely with snow; the fences and the gate were hardly visible.

Danusia rushed into Zbyshko's room once more, wrapped now in her shuba and fur cloak; once more she put her arms around his neck, and once more she said to him in parting :

"Though I go, I am thine."

He kissed her hands, her cheeks, and her eyes, which he could hardly see under the foxskin hood, and said, —

" God guard thee! God go with thee! Thou art mine, mine till death! "

And when they drew her away from him again, he raised himself as much as he was able, rested his head against the window, and looked. Through the snow-flakes, as through a kind of veil, he saw Danusia take her place in the sleigh; he saw the princess hold her long in her embrace, and the court damsels kiss her, and Father Vyshonek make the sign of the cross on her for the road. She turned toward him once more at the very parting, and stretched out her arms.

" Be with God, Zbyshko! "

"God grant me to see thee in Tschanov —"

But the snow fell as thickly as if it wished to benumb and cover everything, hence those last words were so dulled when they reached them that it seemed to both as if they were calling from afar to each other.

CHAPTER XXII.

AFTER abundant snow, followed severe frosts, with bright, dry weather. In the daytime the frosts sparkled in the rays of the sun, ice bound the rivers and stiffened the swamps. Clear nights came, during which frost increased so much that trees in the forest burst with explosions; birds approached houses; the roads became dangerous because of wolves, which collected in great numbers and attacked, not only single people, but even villages. Men, however, rejoiced in their smoky cottages at their firesides, predicting a fruitful season after the frosty winter, and awaited the near holidays joyfully. The princess, with her court and Father Vyshonek, had left the hunting-lodge and gone to Tsehanov.

Zbyshko, notably stronger, but not strong enough yet to travel on horseback, had remained with his men, Sanderus and the Cheh, with the servants of the place, over whom a steady woman exercised the authority of housekeeper.

But the soul in the knight was rushing to his young wife. The idea that now Danusia was his, and that no human power could take her away, was to him an immense solace, indeed, but, on the other hand, that very same idea intensified his yearning. For whole days he had sighed for the moment in which he could leave the lodge, and he was meditating what to do then, whither to go and how to win over Yurand. He had moments of oppressive alarm, it is true, but, on the whole, the future seemed to him delightful. To love Danusia and split helmets with peacock-plumes on them was to be his life employment. Many a time the desire seized him to talk about this with the Cheh, whom he had taken now into his affection, but he remembered that Hlava, devoted with whole soul to Yagenka, would not be glad to talk about Danusia; bound moreover by a secret, he could not tell him all that had happened.

His health improved daily. A week before Christmas he mounted a horse for the first time, and, though he felt that he could not work yet in armor, he was comforted. He did not think that the need would come suddenly of putting on a breast-plate and a helmet, but he hoped in the worst event to have strength enough soon to do that were it needed. In his room he tried to use his sword for pastime, and his success was not bad; the axe proved too heavy, still he thought that by using both hands he could wield it effectively.

At last, two days before Christmas eve, he gave command to make the sleighs ready and saddle the horses, informing the Cheh at the same time that they would go to Tsehanov. The trusty attendant was concerned somewhat, especially as there was a splitting frost, but Zbyshko said to him, —

" Not thy head commands here. There is nothing for us to do in this hunting-lodge, and even should I fall ill, there will be no lack of nursing in Tsehanov. Moreover, I shall not go on horseback, but on runners, up to my neck in hay, and under furs; only at the edge of Tsehanov itself shall I be on horseback."

Thus was it managed. The Cheh had learned already to know his young master, and understood that it would be ill for him to oppose, and still worse not to carry out a command quickly; so they started one hour later. At the moment of parting Zbyshko, seeing Sanderus enter a sleigh with his caskets, said to him, —

" But thou, why fasten to me like some burr to a sheep's fleece? Hast thou not said that thou wert going to Prussia? "

" I said that I wished to go to Prussia, but how could I go there alone in such snow? The wolves would devour me before the first stars came out, and here I have nothing to work at. For me it is more agreeable to edify people in a town by my piety, offer sacred wares, and save men from Satan's snares, as I swore in Rome to the father ·of all Christendom that I would do. Besides, I have conceived a wonderful affection for your Grace, and will not leave you till I set out for Rome, since it may happen me to render you a service."

" He is always ready, lord, to eat and drink for your sake," said Hlava, " and is most delighted to render such service. But if a great cloud of wolves fall on us in Prasnysh forest, we will throw him out to them at parting, for never will he be better fitted for another thing."

" But look to it that a sinful word does not freeze to your lips," retorted Sanderus; " for such icicles could be thawed only in hell."

" Oh. pshaw ! " answered Hlava, reaching with his gloved hand to his mustaches, which had hardly begun to be frosty.

"I shall see first to heating some beer for the journey, but I shall not give thee any."

"The commandment is to give drink to the thirsty. A new sin on your side!"

"Then I will give thee a measure of water, but for the moment, this is what I have ready—"

Thus speaking, he gathered as much snow as he could take in his gloved hands, and threw it at Sanderus' beard; who dodged, and said,—

"You have nothing to show in Tsehanov, for there is a tame bear in that place which shovels snow."

Thus they abused and chaffed each other mutually. Zbyshko did not prevent Sanderus from going with him, for this strange man amused him, and seemed also to be attached to his person. They left the hunting-lodge on a bright morning in a frost so great that it was necessary to blanket the horses. The entire country was covered with deep snow. The tops of the houses were barely indicated under it; in places the smoke seemed to come straight up from white drifts and go to the sky arrow-like, rosy from the morning sunlight, and spread at the top in the form of a bush, like plumes on a knight's helmet.

Zbyshko rode in a sleigh, first to spare his strength, and second because of the great cold, against which he could defend himself more easily in an equipage filled with hay and fur. He commanded the Cheh to sit with him and to have the crossbows at hand for defence against wolves: meanwhile he chatted with him pleasantly.

"In Prasnysh," said he, "we shall only feed our horses, warm ourselves, and move on then immediately."

"To Tsehanov?"

"First to Tsehanov, to salute the prince and princess and go to church."

"And then?"

Zbyshko smiled and answered,—

"Then who knows that we may not go to Bogdanets?"

The Cheh looked at him with astonishment. The idea flashed into his head that the young man might have given up Yurand's daughter, and it seemed to him the more likely since she had left the princess, and the report had come to his ears in the hunting-lodge that the lord of Spyhov was opposed to Zbyshko. Hence the honest fellow was rejoiced, though he loved Yagenka; still he looked at her as a star in the sky, and would have been delighted to purchase for her happiness, even with his own blood. He loved Zbyshko, too, and desired from his whole soul to serve both to the death.

"Then your Grace will live at home," said he, with delight.

"How am I to live at home, when I have challenged those Knights of the Cross, and still earlier Lichtenstein? De Lorche said that very likely the Grand Master would invite the king to Torun. I may attach myself to the royal retinue, and I think that Zavisha of Garbov or Povala of Tachev will obtain from our lord permission for me to meet those monks of the Order. Surely they will fight in company with their attendants; so thou wilt have to fight also."

"I would do so even if I had to become a monk," answered Hlava.

Zbyshko looked at him with satisfaction.

"Well, it will not be pleasant for the man who comes under thy metal. The Lord Jesus has given thee tremendous strength, but thou wouldst do badly wert thou to plume thyself over-much on it, for modesty is the ornament of a genuine attendant."

The Cheh nodded in sign that he would not boast of his strength, but also that he would not spare it on the Germans. Zbyshko smiled, not at the attendant, but at his own thoughts.

"The old man will be glad when we return," said Hlava after a moment, "and there will be gladness at Zyh's house."

Zbyshko saw Yagenka as clearly as if she had been at his side in the sleigh. It happened always that when he chanced to think of Yagenka he saw her with wonderful definiteness.

"No!" said he to himself, "she will not be glad, for if I go to Bogdanets, it will be with Danusia — and let her take another." Then Vilk and young Stan flashed before his eyes, and the thought was bitter to him that the girl might go into the hands of one of those two. "Better far the first man she meets," thought he; "they are beer guzzlers and dice throwers, while the girl is honest." He thought also that in every case it would be disagreeable for his uncle to learn what had happened, but he comforted himself with this, that Matsko's first thought had always been turned to wealth and descent, so as to raise the distinction of his family. Yagenka, it is true, was nearer, for she was at the boundary of their land, but as a recompense Ynrand was a greater heir than Zyh; hence it was easy to foresee that Matsko would not be angry very long over such a connection, all the more since he knew of his nephew's love, and knew how much that nephew was under obligations to Danusia. He would scold, and then be glad and love Danusia as if she were his own child.

And suddenly Zbyshko's heart moved with affection and yearning for that uncle, who was a firm man, and who, moreover, loved him as the sight of his eyes. In battles that uncle had guarded him more than his own life; he had taken booty for him; he had worked to gain property for him. There were two lone men of them in the world. They had no relatives even, unless distant ones, like the Abbot of Tulcha; hence, when it came to parting, neither knew what to do without the other, especially the old man, who had no desires for himself any longer.

"Hei! he will be glad; he will be glad!" thought Zbyshko, "and I could only wish Yurand to receive me as he will."

And he tried to imagine what Yurand would say and do when he learned of the marriage. In this thought there was some dread, but not over-much, especially since the latch had fallen. It was not fitting that Yurand should challenge him to battle, for were he to oppose too much, Zbyshko might answer: "Consent while I beg you, for your right to Danusia is human, while mine is a divine one; she is not yours now, but mine." He had heard in his time from a cleric wise in Scriptures that a woman must leave father and mother and follow her husband; hence he felt that on his side was greater authority. Moreover, he hoped that between him and Yurand it would not come to stubborn disagreement and anger, for he considered that the prayers of Danusia would effect much, and also much, if not more, the mediation of the prince, of whom Yurand was a subject, and the princess, whom Yurand loved as the foster-mother of his daughter.

People advised them to pass the night in Prasnysh, and warned them against wolves, which, because of the cold, had gathered in such packs that they fell upon wayfarers even in large parties. But Zbyshko would not consider this; for it happened that in the inn he met a number of Mazovian knights, with their escorts, who were going to the prince at Tsehanov, and a number of armed merchants from Tsehanov itself, who were bringing laden sleighs from Prussia. In such large companies there was no danger; hence they set out for an all-night journey, though toward evening a sudden wind rose which brought clouds, and a fog set in. They

travelled on, keeping closely together, but so slowly that
Zbyshko began to think that they would not reach Tsehanov
even on Christmas eve.

In some places it was necessary to clear the drifts, for
horses could not wade through them. Fortunately, the forest
road was definite. Still it was dusk in the world when they
saw Tsehanov.

It may be even that they would have gone around the
place in the snow-storm and the whistling of the wind without knowing that they were right there, had it not been for
fires which were burning on the height where the new castle
was standing. No one knew certainly whether those fires
had been lighted on that eve of the Divine Birth to serve
guests, or because of some ancient custom, but neither did
any one of those accompanying Zbyshko care at that moment,
for all wished to find a refuge at the earliest.

The tempest increased every instant. The cutting and
freezing wind swept along immense clouds of snow. It broke
trees, roared, went mad, tore away entire drifts, carried
them into the air, twisted them, shot them apart, covered
horses and wagons with them, cut the faces of travellers with
them as if with sharpened sand, stopped with them the breath
and speech of people. The sound of bells fastened to sleigh
tongues was not heard in the least, but in the howling and
the whistling of the whirlwind sounded complaining voices,
as if voices of wolves, as if distant neighing of horses, and
sometimes as if the cries of people filled with fear and calling
for assistance. Exhausted horses, leaning each with its side
against the other, advanced more and more slowly.

"Hei! this is a snow tempest, indeed it is!" said the
Cheh, with a panting voice. "It is lucky enough that we
are near the town, and that those fires are burning, otherwise
it would go hard with us."

"It is death to be out now," said Zbyshko; "but I do
not see even the blaze there."

"Because there is such a mist that the light of the fire
cannot pass through it. Besides that, the fire and the wood
may have been blown away."

On other sleighs merchants and knights were also saying
that whoever was caught by the storm at a distance from
human dwellings would hear no church bell on the morrow.
But Zbyshko was disquieted all on a sudden, and said, —

"May God not grant that Yurand be out on the road
somewhere!"

The Cheh, though occupied altogether with looking toward the fires, turned his head on hearing Zbyshko's words, and asked, —

"Then was the master of Spyhov to come?"

"He was."

"With the young lady?"

"But really the fire is hidden," remarked Zbyshko.

The flame had died out, in fact, but on the road right there near the sleighs appeared a number of horsemen.

"Why ride onto us?" cried the watchful Cheh, grasping his crossbow. "Who are ye?"

"People of the prince, sent to help wayfarers."

"Jesus Christ be praised!"

"For the ages of ages."

"Conduct us to the town!" called out Zbyshko.

"Has none of you dropped behind?"

"None."

"Whence come ye?"

"From Prasnysh."

"And saw ye no other travellers on the way?"

"We did not. But perhaps there are others on other roads."

"Men are looking for them on all the roads. Come with us. Ye have lost the road! Turn to the right!"

They turned their horses. For some time nothing was heard save the roar of the tempest.

"Are there many guests in the old castle?" asked Zbyshko, after a while.

The nearest horseman, who had not heard distinctly, bent toward him and asked, —

"What did you say?"

"I asked if there were many guests with the prince and princess."

"As usual, a good number of them!"

"But the lord of Spyhov, is he there?"

"He is not, but they expect him. People have gone out to meet him also."

"With torches?"

"How go with torches in this wind?"

They were unable to converse longer, for the noise of the snow-tempest increased.

"A real devil's wedding!" said the Cheh.

Zbyshko commanded him to be silent, and not mention foul names.

" Dost thou know," said he, " that on such holidays hellish
power grows benumbed and devils hide themselves in holes?
Fishermen found one of those devils once in a pond near
Sandomir the day before Christmas eve. He had a pike in
his snout, but when the sound of church bells reached him,
he lost strength right away, and they beat him with sticks
until evening. This storm is a stiff one, but it is by permission of the Lord Jesus, who wishes the morrow to be filled
all the more with rejoicing."

" True enough! If we were only at the castle; but had it
not been for these men, we might have ridden till midnight,
for we had got off the road," answered Hlava.

He said this, for the fire had gone down.

They had now really entered the town. Drifts of still
deeper snow were lying on the streets there; so great were
these drifts that in many places they almost hid the windows. For this reason people passing outside the town could
not see lights. But the storm seemed less violent. On
the streets none were celebrating the Christmas festival;
citizens were sitting already at supper. Before some houses
boys, with a crib and a goat, were singing in spite of the snow-
storm. On the square were men wrapped in pea-straw, and
acting as bears, but in general the place was empty. The
merchants who accompanied Zbyshko, and other nobles on
the road, remained in the town. Zbyshko and the nobles
went to the old castle, in which the prince dwelt, and which
had, even at that time, glass windows, which, in spite of
the storm, shone brightly in front of the wayfarers when
they drew near.

The drawbridge on the moat had been let down, for the
old time of Lithuanian attacks had passed, and the Knights
of the Cross, foreseeing war with the King of Poland, sought
the friendship of the Prince of Mazovia. One of the prince's
men blew a horn, and the gate was open directly. There
were between ten and twenty bowmen there, but on the walls
not a living soul, for the prince had given leave to go
down. Old Mrokota, who had arrived two days earlier, met
the guests, greeted them in the prince's name, and conducted
them to rooms in which they could array themselves properly
for the table.

Zbyshko fell at once to asking him about Yurand of
Spyhov, and he answered that Yurand was not there, but
that they expected him, since he had promised to come, and
if his health had grown worse he would have informed them.

Still they had sent out a number of horsemen to meet him, because the oldest men could not remember such a storm.

"Then perhaps he will be here soon."

"Surely before long. The princess has commanded to set plates for them on her table."

Zbyshko, though he had always feared Yurand, rejoiced in heart, and said to himself: "Though I know not what he has done, he cannot undo this, that it is my wife who will come, my dearest Danusia!" And when he repeated that to himself, he was hardly able to believe his own happiness. Then he thought that perhaps she had told Yurand all; that perhaps she had won him over, and persuaded him to give her at once. "In truth, what better has he to do? Yurand is a wise man, and knows that though he might forbid me, though he might refuse her to me, I would take her in every case, for my right is the strongest."

While dressing, Zbyshko talked with Mrokota; asked him about the health of the prince, and especially the princess, whom from the time of his visit in Cracow he had loved as a mother. He was glad also when he learned that all in the castle were well and gladsome, though the princess grieved much at the absence of her dear little singer.

"Now Yagenka, whom the princess likes well, plays on the lute to her, but not in any way as the other."

"What Yagenka?" asked Zbyshko, with wonder.

"Yagenka of Velgolas, the granddaughter of an old man from Velgolas, — a nice girl, with whom that man from Lorraine has fallen in love."

"Then is Pan de Lorche here?"

"Where should he be? He came from the hunting-lodge, and he remains here because it is pleasant for him. There is never a lack of guests in our prince's castle."

"I shall look on the Knight of Lorraine with pleasure; he is a man whom no one can reproach in any way."

"He, too, esteems you. But let us go; for the prince and princess will take their places at table directly."

They went out. In two chimneys of the dining hall great fires were burning, which were cared for by youths, and there was a multitude of guests and courtiers. The prince entered first in the company of a voevoda and a number of attendants. Zbyshko bent down to his knees, and then kissed his hand.

In return, the prince pressed his head, and, going a little aside with him, said, —

"I know of everything. I was angry at first that you did that without my permission, but in truth there was no time, for I was then in Warsaw, where I intended to pass the holidays. Finally, it is known that if a woman undertakes a thing, better not oppose her; for thou wilt effect nothing. The princess wishes as well to you as if she were your mother, and I prefer always to please rather than oppose her; for I wish to spare her tears and sadness."

Zbyshko bent a second time to the knees of the prince.

"God grant me to serve your princely Grace sufficiently."

"Praise to His name that thou art well. Tell the princess how kindly I have received thee. She will be gladdened. As God lives, her pleasure is my pleasure! And to Yurand I will say a good word in thy favor, and I think that he will give his permission; for he too loves the princess."

"Even should he be unwilling to give it, my right is the first."

"Thy right is the first, and he must agree; but he may withhold his blessing. No man can wrest that by force from him; and without a parent's blessing there is no blessing from God."

Zbyshko grew sad when he heard these words; for up to that time he had not thought of this. At that moment, however, the princess came in with Yagenka of Velgolas and other damsels; so he sprang forward to pay homage to the lady. She greeted him still more graciously than had the prince, and began at once to tell him of the expected arrival of Yurand. "Here are plates set for them, and men are sent to bring them out of the storm. It is not according to decorum to delay the Christmas eve supper, for 'the lord' does not like that; but they will come surely before the end of supper."

"As to Yurand," said the princess, "it will be as God inspires. Either I shall tell him everything to-day or to-morrow after mass, and the prince has promised to add his word also. Yurand is self-willed, but not toward those whom he loves, and to whom he is under obligation."

Then she told Zbyshko how he was to bear himself toward his father-in-law, not to offend him — God forbid that! — and not to lead him to stubbornness. In general, she was of good hope; but a person knowing the world better and looking at it more quickly than Zbyshko, would have noted a certain alarm in her speech. Perhaps it was there because the lord of Spyhov was in general not an easy man, and perhaps, too, the princess began to be alarmed somewhat because they were so long in appearing. The storm was becoming more cruel out of doors, and all said that the man found in the open field by it might remain there. Another supposition also occurred to the princess, namely, that Danusia had confessed to her father that she had been married to Zbyshko, and Yurand, being offended, had resolved not to come to Tsehanov at all. She did not wish, however, to confide these thoughts to Zbyshko, and there was not even time for it, since the young men in waiting had begun to bring in the food and place it on the table. But Zbyshko hastened to fall at her feet again, and ask, —

"But if they come, gracious lady, how will it be? Pan Mrokota has told me that there is a separate division for Yurand, where there will be hay beds for the attendants. But how will it be?"

The princess laughed, and striking him lightly on the face with her gloves, said, —

"Be quiet! Wait till you see him!"

And she went to the prince, for whom the armor-bearers had already arrayed his chair, so that he might take his seat. Before doing that, however, one of them gave him a flat dish filled with thin strips of cake and bits of meat to be divided by the prince among guests, courtiers, and servants. Another similar one was held for the princess by a beautiful youth, the son of the Castellan of Sohachev. At the opposite side of the table stood Father Vyshonek, who was to bless the supper set out upon sweetly smelling hay.

In the door at this moment appeared a man covered with snow, who called aloud, —

"Gracious lord!"

"What?" asked the prince, not glad that the ceremony was interrupted.

"On the Radzanov road are travellers covered up in the snow. We must send more people to dig them out."

All were frightened when they heard this. The prince was alarmed, and turning to the Castellan, cried, —

"Horsemen with shovels, quickly!"

Then he turned to the man who had brought the news.

"Are many snowed in?"

"We could not discover. There is a terrible darkness in the air. There are sleighs and horses, a considerable escort."

"Do ye not know whose they are?"

"People say that it is the heir of Spyhov."

CHAPTER XXIII.

WHEN Zbyshko heard the unfortunate tidings, without even asking permission of the prince, he rushed to the stables, and commanded to saddle his horse. The Cheh, who, as a nobly born attendant, was with him in the supper hall, had barely time to go to their room and bring a warm fur robe; but he did not try to detain his young master; for having by nature strong sense, he knew that any endeavor to restrain him was useless, and that delay might be fatal. Mounting a second horse, he seized at the gate, from the keeper, a number of torches, and directly they were moving with the prince's people, whom the old Castellan led forward hastily. Beyond the gate darkness impenetrable surrounded them, but the storm seemed to have weakened. They might, perhaps, have gone astray immediately outside the town, had it not been for the man who had brought information, and who was leading them the more quickly and surely that he had with him a dog which knew the road.

On the open field the storm began to strike sharply in their faces, partly because they were going speedily. The highway was drifted in; in places there was so much snow that they were forced to go slowly; for the horses were in snow to their bellies. The prince's men lighted torches and lamps, and rode on amid the smoke and flame of torches which the wind blew as fiercely as if it wished to sweep those flames away from the pitchy sticks and carry them off into the fields and forests.

The road was a long one. They passed the villages nearer to Tsehanov and Nedzborz, then they turned toward Radzanov. Beyond Nedzborz, however, the storm subsided sensibly and grew weaker; the gusts of wind became fainter, and no longer carried whole clouds of snow with them. The sky became clearer. Some snow fell yet, but soon that stopped. Next a star glittered in a rift of the clouds. The horses snorted; the riders breathed more freely. The stars increased in number each moment, and the frost bit. After the expiration of a few " Our Fathers," the storm had ceased altogether.

De Lorche, who rode near Zbyshko, comforted him, saying that surely Yurand, in the moment of danger, had thought first of all of his daughter, and, though they should dig out all the others dead, they would find her alive surely, and sleeping under furs, perhaps. But Zbyshko understood little of what he said, and at last had not even time to listen; for after a while the guide going in advance turned from the road.

The young knight pushed forward and asked, —

" Why do we turn aside? "

" Because they were not snowed in on the highway, but off there! Do you see the alder grove? "

He pointed to a grove, which looked dark in the distance, and which could be seen on the white plain of snow when the clouds uncovered the shield of the moon and things became visible.

It was evident that they had left the highway.

" The travellers lost the highway, and rode in a curved line along a river. In time of storm and snow fog it is easy to do so. They went on and on until their horses failed."

" How did you find them? "

" The dog led us."

" Are there no houses near by? "

" There are, but on the other side of the river. The Vkra is right here."

" Hurry on! " cried Zbyshko.

But it was easier to give a command than to execute it; for although the frost was sharp, there lay on the field snow yet unfrozen, drifts freshly collected and deep, in which the horses waded above their knees; so they were forced to push forward slowly. All at once the barking of a dog reached them. Straight in front appeared the large and bent trunk of a willow, on which, in the light of the moon, gleamed a crown of leafless branches.

" They are farther on," said the leader, " near the alder grove; but here too must be something."

" There is a drift under the willow. Light up for us! "

A number of the prince's men dismounted and lighted the place with their torches; then some one cried on a sudden, —

" Here is a man under the snow! We can see his head right here! "

" There is a horse too! " cried another immediately.

" Dig him out! "

Shovels began to sink in the snow and throw it on both sides.

After a while they saw sitting under the tree a man with head inclined on his breast and his cap pulled deeply over his face. With one hand he was holding the reins of a horse lying at his side with nostrils buried in the snow. Evidently the man had ridden away from the company, perhaps to reach human dwellings more quickly and obtain help, but when his horse fell he took refuge under the willow on the side opposite the wind, and there he was chilled.

" Bring a light!" called Zbyshko.

An attendant pushed up a torch to the face of the frozen man ; it was difficult to recognize him at once. But when another attendant turned the face upward, one cry was wrested from the breasts of all present, —

" The Lord of Spyhov!"

Zbyshko commanded two men to carry him to the nearest cottage and care for him; he himself, without losing time, galloped on with the rest of the servants and the guide to rescue the remainder of the party. On the way he thought that he should find Danusia there, his wife, perhaps not alive, and he urged the last breath out of his horse which struggled breast-deep in snow. Fortunately it was not very far, at the most a few furlongs. In the darkness voices were heard, " Come this way! " — voices from the prince's men who had remained near the people snowed in. Zbyshko rushed up and sprang from his horse.

" To the shovels!"

Two sleighs had been dug out already by those left on guard. The horses and the men in the sleigh were frozen beyond recovery. Where the others were might be known by hills of snow, though not all sleighs were entirely covered. At some were visible horses with their bellies pressed against drifts, as if while exerting themselves in running they had grown stiff in a supreme effort. In front of one pair stood a man sunk to his waist, and as immovable as a column ; at more distant sleighs the men had died near the horses while holding their bridles. Evidently death had caught them while trying to free the beasts from snow-drifts. One sleigh at the very end of the line was free altogether. The driver was on the seat with his hands over his ears ; behind lay two people ; the long lines of snow blown across their breasts were united with a bank at the side and covered them like a blanket, so that they seemed sleeping calmly and peacefully. Others, however, had perished while struggling to the last with the storm, for they were frozen in postures full of effort. Some sleighs were overturned; in some the tongues were broken. Time after time the shovels uncovered backs of horses bent like bows, or heads with teeth driven into the snow; men were in the sleighs and around the sleighs, but they found no women. At moments Zbyshko worked with the shovel till the sweat flowed from his forehead; at moments he looked with throbbing heart into the eyes of corpses, thinking whether he would see among them a beloved face — all in vain! The light shone only on the stern moustached visages of warriors from Spyhov; neither Danusia nor any other woman was present.

"How is this?" asked the young knight of himself, with astonishment.

And he called to those who were working farther away, asking if they had not found anything; but they found only men. At last the work was done. The attendants attached their own horses to the sleighs, and sitting on the seats moved with the bodies toward Nedzborz, to see if they could not in the heat there restore to life any of the bodies. Zbyshko remained with the Cheh and two others. It came to his mind that Danusia's sleigh might have separated from the party if drawn, as was proper to suppose, by the best horses. Yurand might have ordered to drive it ahead or might have left it somewhere on the roadside at a cottage. Zbyshko knew not what to do; in every case he wanted to search the near drifts, the alder grove, and then turn back and search along the highway.

In the drifts they found nothing. In the alder grove wolf eyes gleamed at them repeatedly, but they found no trace of people or horses. The plain between the alder grove and the highway was glittering then in moon rays, and on the white sad expanse were seen here and there at a distance, a number of dark spots, but those too were wolves which at the approach of men vanished speedily.

"Your Grace," said Hlava at last, "we are riding and searching here uselessly, for the young lady of Spyhov was not in the retinue."

"On the highway!" answered Zbyshko.

"We shall not find her on the highway; I looked with care to discover if there were not boxes in the sleighs, and things pertaining to women. There was nothing. The young lady has remained in Spyhov."

The correctness of this remark struck Zbyshko, so he answered: —

"God grant it to be as thou sayest."

The Cheh went deeper still into his own head for wisdom.

"If she had been in a sleigh the old lord would not have left it, or if he left the sleigh he would have taken her on the horse in front of him, and we should have found them together."

"Let us go there once more," said Zbyshko, in a voice of alarm, for it occurred to him that it might be as Hlava had said. In that case they had not searched with sufficient diligence. Yurand, then, had taken Danusia before him on the horse, and when the beast fell Danusia went away from her father to find some assistance. In that event she might be near by somewhere under the snow.

But Hlava, as if divining these thoughts, said, —

"In that case we should have found her things in the sleigh, for she would not go to the court with only the dress that she was wearing."

In spite of this just conclusion they went again to the willow, but neither under it nor for a furlong around the tree did they find anything. The prince's men had taken Yurand to Nedzborz, and round about all was deserted. Hlava made the remark, still, that the dog which had run with the guide and which had found Yurand, would have found the young lady also. Thereupon Zbyshko was relieved, for he became almost certain that Danusia had remained at Spyhov. He was able even to explain how it had happened. Evidently Danusia had confessed all to her father; he, not agreeing to the marriage, had left her at home purposely, and was coming himself to lay the affair before the prince and ask his intervention with the bishop. At this thought Zbyshko could not resist the feeling of a certain solace, and even delight, for he understood that with the death of Yurand all obstacles had vanished.

"Yurand did not wish, but the Lord Jesus has wished," said the young knight to himself, "and the will of God is always the stronger."

Now he needed only to go to Spyhov, take Danusia as his own, and then accomplish his vow, which was easier on the boundary than in distant Bogdanets. "God's will! God's will!" repeated he in his soul. But he was ashamed of his hurried delight the next moment, and said, turning to Hlava, —

"I am sorry for him, and I will say so to every one."

"People declare," answered the attendant, "that the Germans feared him as death." Then after a moment he asked: "Shall we return to the castle now?"

"By way of Nedzborz," answered Zbyshko.

So they went to Nedzborz, and stopped before a residence in which an old noble, named Jeleh, received them. Yurand they did not find, but the old man gave good news.

"We rubbed him with snow to the bones almost," said he, "and poured wine into his mouth; then we steamed him in a bath, where he regained breathing."

"Is he alive?" inquired Zbyshko, with delight; for at this news he forgot his own affairs.

"He is alive, but God knows if he will recover; for the soul is not glad to turn back when it has made half the journey."

"Why was he taken from here?"

"He was taken because men from the prince came. We covered him with all the feather beds in the house, and they took him."

"Did he not mention his daughter?"

"He had barely begun to breathe; he had not recovered speech."

"But the others?"

"Are now behind God's stove. Poor people; they will not be at mass unless at that one which the Lord Jesus Himself will celebrate in heaven."

"Did none revive?"

"None. Enter, instead of talking at the porch. If you wish to see them, they are lying near the fire in the servants' hall. Come in."

But they did not go, though the old man pressed them; for he was glad to detain people and "chat" with them. They had a long piece of road yet from Nedzborz to Tsehanov; besides, Zbyshko was burning to see Yurand at the earliest, and learn something.

They rode, therefore, as rapidly as possible along the drifted highway. When they arrived it was past midnight, and the mass was just finishing in the castle chapel. To Zbyshko's ears came the lowing of cattle and the bleating of goats, which pious voices imitated according to ancient custom, in memory of the Lord's birth in a stable. After mass the princess came to Zbyshko with a face full of fear and anxiety.

"But where is Danusia?" asked she.

"She has not come. Has not Yurand told?—for I hear that he is alive."

"Merciful Jesus! This is a punishment from God, and woe to us! Yurand has not spoken, and he is lying like a block of wood."

"Have no fear, gracious lady. Danusia remained in Spyhov."

"How dost thou know?"

"I know, because in no sleigh was there a trace of a change of clothing for her. She would not have come in one cloak."

"True, as God is dear to me!"

And quickly her eyes began to sparkle with pleasure.

"Hei, dear Jesus, Thou who wert born this night, it is evident that not Thy anger, but Thy blessing is upon us."

Still the arrival of Yurand without Danusia surprised her; so she inquired further, —

"What could have kept her at home?"

Zbyshko explained his surmises. They seemed correct, but did not cause her excessive alarm.

"Yurand will owe his life to us now," said she; "and to tell the truth, it is to thee that he owes it; for thou didst go to dig him out of the snow. He would, indeed, have a stone in his breast were he to resist any longer! There is in this a warning of God, for him not to resist the holy Sacrament. The moment that he recovers and speaks, I will tell him so."

"He must recover first; for it is unknown why Danusia has not come. But if she is ill?"

"Do not talk foolishness. As it is, I am sorry that she is not here. If she had been ill he would not have left her."

"True!"

And they went to Yurand. It was as hot in the room as in a bath, and perfectly lighted; for immense logs of pine were burning in the chimney. Father Vyshonek was watching the sick man, who was lying on a couch under bearskins; his face was pale, his hair damp from perspiration, his eyes closed. His mouth was open, and his breast moved with labor, but so violently that the skins with which he was covered rose and fell from the breathing.

"How is he?" asked the princess.

"We have poured a mug of heated wine into his mouth," answered the priest. "and he is perspiring."

"Is he sleeping?"

"It may be that he is not sleeping; for his breast moves tremendously."

"Have you tried to speak with him?"

"I have tried, but he gives no answer, and I think that he will not speak before daylight."

"We will wait for daylight," said the princess.

The priest insisted that she should go to rest, but she would not listen to him. It was with her a question always and in everything to equal in Christian virtues, and, therefore, in nursing the sick, the late queen, Yadviga, and redeem her father's soul by her merits; hence, in a country which had been Christian for centuries she missed no opportunity to show herself more zealous than others, and thus efface the remembrance that she had been born in pagan error. Moreover, the wish was burning her to learn something from Yurand touching Danusia; for she was not altogether at rest concerning her. So, sitting down at the side of his couch, she began to repeat the rosary, and then to doze. Zbyshko, who was not entirely well yet, and who in addition had labored immensely in the riding of the night, soon followed her example, and after an hour they had both fallen asleep so soundly that they would have slept till a late hour, perhaps, had not the bell of the castle chapel roused them at daybreak.

It roused Yurand also, who opened his eyes, sat erect on the couch quickly, and looked around with blinking eyes.

"Praised be Jesus Christ! How is it with you?" asked the princess.

But apparently he had not regained consciousness; for he looked at the princess as though he knew her not.

"Come this way! come this way to dig the drift!" called he after a moment.

"In God's name! You are in Tschanov!" cried the lady.

Yurand wrinkled his forehead like a man who is collecting his thoughts with difficulty, and answered, —

"In Tschanov? My child is waiting for me — and the prince and princess — Danusia! Danusia!"

Then closing his eyes, he dropped again to the pillow. Zbyshko and the princess were terrified lest he had died; but at that very instant his breast moved with deep breath, as in the case of a man seized by heavy sleep.

Father Vyshonek placed a finger on his own lips and made a sign not to rouse the man; then he whispered, —

"He may sleep all day in this manner."

"True; but what did he say?" asked the princess.

"He said that his child was waiting for him in Tsehanov," answered Zbyshko.

"He said that because he has not regained consciousness," explained the priest.

CHAPTER XXIV.

THE priest even feared that at a second awakening dizziness might seize the sick man and deprive him of his mind for a long time. But he promised the princess and Zbyshko that when Yurand spoke he would inform them. They left the chamber, and he went to sleep himself.

Yurand woke on the second day just before noon, but this time in perfect consciousness. The princess and Zbyshko were with him. He sat up on the couch, looked at the princess, recognized her, and said, —

"Gracious lady — as God lives, am I in Tsehanov, then?"

"Yes, and you have slept over Christmas."

"The snow covered me. Who saved me?"

"This knight, Zbyshko of Bogdanets. You remember, you saw him in Cracow."

Yurand looked a while with his sound eye at the young man, then said, —

"I remember. But where is Danusia?"

"Did she come with you?" asked the princess, with alarm.

"How could she come with me when I was going to her?"

Zbyshko and the princess looked at each other, thinking that fever was speaking through Yurand's mouth yet.

"Come to thyself," said the lady, "by the dear God! Was not the girl with you?"

"The girl! With me?" asked Yurand, with amazement.

"All your attendants perished, but she was not found among them. Why did you leave her in Spyhov?"

Yurand repeated once more, but now with alarm in his voice, —

"In Spyhov? Why, gracious lady, she is living with you, not with me."

"But you sent people and a letter for her to the hunting-lodge."

"In the name of the Father and the Son!" answered Yurand. "I have not sent for her at all."

That moment the princess grew pale.

"What is this?" asked she. "Are you sure that you are in your right mind?"

" By the mercy of God ! where is my child?" cried Yurand, springing up.

" Listen. An armed escort came for Danusia to the hunting-lodge, bringing a letter from you. In the letter it was written that during a fire beams had crushed you; that you were half blind, and wished to see your daughter. Then they took Danusia and drove away."

" Woe!" cried Yurand. " As God is in heaven, there was no fire in Spyhov, and I did not send for her."

Now the priest returned with a letter, which he gave to Yurand, and asked, —

" Is this the writing of your priest?"

" I do not know."

" But the seal?"

" The seal is mine. What is in the letter?"

Father Vyshonek read the letter; Yurand listened, grasping his own hair.

" The letter is false," said he; " the seal imitated! Woe to my soul! They have seized my child, and will destroy her."

" Who?"

" The Knights of the Cross!"

" God's wounds! We must inform the prince. Let him send messengers to the Grand Master!" cried the lady. " Merciful Jesus, rescue her, aid her!"

Saying this, she hurried out of the room with a cry. Yurand sprang from his bed, and began feverishly to draw the clothing onto his immense back. Zbyshko sat as if petrified, but after a while his set teeth gritted ominously.

" How do you know that the Knights of the Cross took her?" asked the priest.

" I will swear on the Passion of Christ!"

" Wait! It is possible. They went to the hunting-lodge to complain against you. They wanted vengeance."

" They carried her away!" cried Zbyshko on a sudden.

He rushed out of the room, and running to the stables commanded to make sleighs and saddle horses ready, without knowing clearly himself why he did so. He understood only this, that they must rescue Danusia, and go at once, — even to Prussia, — and there snatch her from enemies' hands or perish.

He returned then to tell Yurand that arms and horses would be ready immediately. He was sure that Yurand also would go with him. In his heart anger was boiling, and pain and sorrow, but he did not lose hope; for it seemed to him that he and the terrible Knight could do anything, and that they might attack even all the power of the Order.

In the room, besides Yurand, the priest, and the princess, he found Prince Yanush, De Lorche, and Pan Mikolai, whom the prince, when he had learned of the affair, summoned-also to counsel; and he did so because of the old man's sound sense and perfect knowledge of the Knights, among whom he had passed long years in captivity.

"We should begin prudently; avoid mistakes caused through anger, and not ruin the girl," said Pan Mikolai. "We should complain at once to the Grand Master, and if your Princely Grace gives me a letter, I will deliver it."

"I will give the letter, and you will go with it," answered the prince. "We will not let the girl perish, so help me God and the holy cross! The Grand Master fears war with the King of Poland, and for him it is important to win over my brother and me. You may be sure that she was not carried off at his command — and he will order that she be delivered to us."

"But if it was at his command?" asked the priest.

"Though he is a Knight of the Cross, there is more honor in him than in others," answered the prince, "and as I have said to you, he would prefer at present to please rather than anger me. Oh, they put tallow into our skins as long as they were able, but now they understand that if we Mazovians help Yagello, it will go ill with them."

"True," said Pan Mikolai. "The Knights of the Cross do nothing without a reason; so I conclude that if they have carried off the girl, they have done so only to knock the sword from Yurand's hand, or get a ransom, or exchange her."

Here he turned to the lord of Spyhov.

"Whom have you among prisoners?"

"De Bergov," answered Yurand.

"Is he a considerable person?"

"Evidently a man of distinction."

De Lorche hearing the question inquired about him, and when he learned what the question was, said, —

"He is a relative of the Count of Guelders, a great benefactor of the Order, and of a family which has served it."

"That is true," said Pan Mikolai, after he had interpreted

De Lorche's words to those present. "Men of his family have held high office in the Order."

"Danveld and De Löwe mentioned him very emphatically," said the prince. "Whenever one of them opened his mouth he said that De Bergov must be liberated. As God is in heaven, they carried off the girl beyond doubt to liberate him."

"Then they will yield her up," said the priest.

"But it is better to learn where she is," said Pan Mikolai. "For suppose that the Grand Master asks, 'Whom shall I command to yield her up?' what answer shall we give?"

"Where is she!" asked Yurand, in a dull voice. "They are not keeping her surely on the boundary, out of fear that I might capture her, but they have taken her somewhere to a distant island of the sea, or the Vistula."

"We will find her and rescue her,' said Zbyshko.

But the prince broke out suddenly with suppressed anger:

"The dog brothers! they have seized her from my house, and insulted me; while I live I shall not forgive them. I have had enough of their treasons! enough of their attacks! Better for any one to have wolf men for neighbors! But now the Grand Master must punish those comturs, return the girl, and send envoys to me with excuses. Otherwise I will summon a levy!"

Here he struck the table with his fist, and added, —

"Oh, indeed! My brother of Plotsk will go with me, and Vitold, and the power of Yagello the king. There is an end of moderation! A saint would snort patience out of himself through the nostrils. I have had enough of it!"

All grew silent, waiting with their counsel till the prince's anger should be calmed. The princess rejoiced that he took the affair of Danusia to heart so much, for she knew that he was patient, but resolute, and that once he had undertaken a thing he would not leave it until he had won victory.

Then Father Vyshonek began, —

"Once there was obedience in the Order, and no comtur dared begin anything without permission of the Chapter and the Grand Master. For this reason God gave into their hands countries so considerable that He raised them almost above every other temporal power. But now there is among them neither obedience, justice, faith, nor honesty. Nothing but greed and such rage as if they were wolves and not men. How are they to obey the commands of the Grand Master or the Chapter when they do not obey those of God? Each in his own castle is like a ruling prince, and each helps the other in wickedness. If we complain to the Master they will deny. The Master will command them to yield up the girl, but they will not do so, or they will even say: ' She is not with us; we did not carry her away.' If he commands them to take an oath, they will take one. What are we to do then?"

" What are we to do?" said Pan Mikolai. " Let Yurand go to Spyhov; if they carried her away, either they will give her for a ransom or exchange her for De Bergov; they must inform some one, and they will inform no one else but Yurand."

" The men who came to the hunting-lodge took her," said Father Vyshonek.

" Then the Grand Master will summon them to account, or command them to meet Yurand in the field."

" They must meet me!" exclaimed Zbyshko, " for I sent the first challenge."

Yurand took his hands from his face, and inquired, —

" Who were at the hunting-lodge?"

" Danveld, old De Löwe, and the two brothers, Gottfried and Rotgier," answered the priest. " They complained and wished the prince to command you to free De Bergov from captivity. But the prince, learning from De Fourcy that the Germans attacked first, reproached them and sent them away unsatisfied."

" Go to Spyhov," said Prince Yanush, " for they will make announcement there. They have not done so yet, because the armor-bearer of this young knight here crushed Danveld's arm when he carried the challenge. Go to Spyhov, and when they make announcement let me know. They will send you your child in place of De Bergov, but still I shall not omit revenge, for they have offended me by taking her from my house."

Here anger seized him anew, for really the Knights of the Cross had exhausted his patience, and after a while he added, —

" Hei! they have blown and blown the fire, but at last they will burn their own snouts in it."

" They will deny!" repeated the priest.

" As soon as they notify Yurand that they have the girl, they will not be able to deny," answered Pan Mikolai, somewhat impatiently. " I believe that they are not keeping her on the boundary, and that, as Yurand has justly remarked, either they took her to some distant castle or to some island near the coast, but when there is proof that they did it they will not deny before the Master."

But Yurand began to repeat in a kind of strange and terrible voice, —

"Danveld, De Löwe, Gottfried, Rotgier!"

Pan Mikolai recommended besides to send experienced and very adroit men to Prussia to inquire in Schytno and Insbork about Danusia, — was she there, and if not whither had they taken her. The prince seized his staff and went out to give needful orders; the princess turned to Yurand, wishing to strengthen him with a kind word.

"How do you feel?," asked she.

He made no answer for a while, just as if he had not heard the question, but later he said on a sudden, —

"As if some one had struck me in an old wound."

"Have faith in God's mercy, — Danusia will return; only give them De Bergov."

"I would not begrudge them even blood."

The princess hesitated whether or not to mention the marriage to him, but when she had thought a little she did not like to add a new pain to Yurand's misfortunes, which were already grievous, and moreover a certain fear seized her. "He and Zbyshko together will search for her; let Zbyshko tell him at an opportunity," thought she; "but now it might disturb his brain altogether." So she preferred to talk of something else.

"Do not blame us," said she. "Men came in your colors with a letter bearing your seal, and announcing that you were sick; that sight was leaving you; that you wished to see your child once more. How could we oppose, and fail to carry out the order of a father?"

Yurand fell at her feet.

"I blame no one, gracious lady."

"And know this, that God will restore her to you; for His eye is above her. He will send her rescue, as he sent it at the last hunt when the wild bull attacked us, and the Lord Jesus inspired Zbyshko to defend Danusia and me, for which reason the prince gave him spurs and a belt. You see! the hand of God is above her. Of course you grieve for your daughter, and I myself am filled with sorrow. I thought that she would come with you; that I should see my dearest, but meanwhile —"

Her voice trembled and tears came to her eyes, but in

Yurand despair, which up to that moment had been restrained, burst forth; for a while it was as sudden and terrible as a whirlwind. He seized his long hair with his hands and fell to beating the timbers of the wall with his head, groaning and repeating in a hoarse voice, —

"O Jesus! O Jesus! O Jesus!"

Zbyshko sprang to him, and shaking him by the arms with all his might, cried, —

"To the road with us! To Spyhov!"

CHAPTER XXV.

"Whose escort is this?" asked Yurand beyond Radzanov, starting up from meditation as if from a dream.

"Mine," answered Zbyshko.

"But did all my men perish?"

"I saw them dead in Nedzborz."

"The old warriors are gone!"

Zbyshko made no answer, and they rode on in silence, but quickly; for they wished to be in Spyhov at the earliest, hoping to find there messengers from the Knights of the Cross. Fortunately for them, frosts had come, and the roads were beaten, hence they could hurry. Toward evening Yurand spoke again, and inquired about those monks of the Order who had been at the hunting-lodge. Zbyshko explained everything, and told also of their complaints and their departure; of the death of De Fourcy, and the action of his own armor-bearer, who had crushed Danveld's arm in such terrible fashion. During this narrative one circumstance struck him, the presence at the lodge of that woman who had brought the healing balsam from Danveld. At the stopping-place he fell to inquiring of Hlava and Sanderus touching this person, but neither of them knew exactly what had become of her. It seemed to them that she had gone away either with the men who had come for Danusia or soon after. It occurred then to Zbyshko that she might have been sent to warn those men in case Yurand had been present at the hunting-lodge. In that event, they would not have presented themselves as people from Spyhov; they could have some other letter prepared to give the princess, instead of the false one attributed to Yurand. All this was planned with hellish acuteness, and Zbyshko, who till then had known the Knights of the Cross in the open field only, thought for the first time that hands were not sufficient to oppose them, but that a man had to conquer them with his head also. To him this thought was bitter; for his immense pain and sorrow turned first of all to desire for blood and struggle. To him even the rescue of Danusia presented itself as a series of battles, either alone or in company; meanwhile he saw that it might be needful to chain down desire of revenge and head-breaking as he would a bear, and seek new ways entirely of finding and saving Danusia. While thinking of this, he regretted that Matsko was not with him. Matsko was as adroit as he was valiant. Still he resolved to send Sanderus from Spyhov to Schytno to find that woman, and endeavor to learn from her what had become of Danusia. He said to himself that though Sanderus might wish to betray him, he could not injure the cause much, and if he were true he might render considerable service; for his occupation gave him access to all places.

Wishing to take counsel first with Yurand, he deferred this matter till they reached Spyhov, all the more as night had fallen, and it seemed to him that Yurand, as he sat on his lofty saddle of a knight, had fallen asleep from his toils, his suffering, and grievous sorrow. But Yurand was riding with hanging head only for the reason that misfortune had bent him. And it was evident that he was thinking of it continually; for his heart was full of cruel fears, since he said at last, —

" Would that I had frozen to death at Nedzborz. Was it thou who dug me out of the snow? "

" I, with others."

" And at that hunt it was thou who saved my child? "

" What was it my duty to do? "

" And now wilt thou help me? "

But in Zbyshko love for Danusia burst forth, and hatred against the Knights of the Cross so great that he rose in his saddle and spoke through his set teeth as if with difficulty, —

" Listen to what I say: Though I had to gnaw Prussian castles with my teeth, I would gnaw them down and get her."

A moment of silence followed. The vengeful and unrestrained nature of Yurand responded evidently with all its force under the influence of these words; for he gritted his teeth in the darkness, and after a while repeated the names, —

" Danveld, Löwe, Rotgier, Gottfried."

In his soul he thought that if they wished him to release De Bergov he would release him; if they demanded pay in addition, he would pay, though he were to add all Spyhov. But woe later on to those who had raised hands on his only child.

All that night sleep did not close the eyes of those two

men for one moment. Toward morning they could hardly
recognize each other, so much had their faces changed in
that single night. At last Zbyshko's suffering and resolve
astonished Yurand ; so he said, —

"She covered thee with a veil and wrested thee from
death — I know that. But dost thou love her besides?"

Zbyshko looked him straight in the eyes with a face almost
insolent, and answered, —

"She is my wife."

At this Yurand stopped his horse, and gazed at Zbyshko,
blinking from amazement.

"What hast thou said?" inquired he.

"I say that she is my wife, and that I am her husband."

The Knight of Spyhov covered his eyes with his glove, as
if his sight had been dazzled by a lightning flash, but he said
nothing. After a while he rode on, and pushing to the head
of the escort advanced in silence.

CHAPTER XXVI.

ZBYSHKO, riding behind, was unable to restrain himself
long, and said in his soul, "I would rather see him burst
out in anger than become stubborn."

So he rode up and said, touching Yurand's stirrup with
his own, —

"Listen and hear how it was. You know what Danusia
did for me in Cracow, but you do not know that in Bogdanets
they wished me to marry Yagenka, the daughter of Zyh of
Zgorzelitse. My uncle, Matsko, and her father wished the
marriage, and the Abbot of Tulcha, our relative, a rich man,
wished it also. But why talk long of this? She is an honest
maiden, beautiful as a deer, and has a proper dowry. But it
could not take place. I wanted Yagenka, but I wanted
Danusia more, and I went to her in Mazovia; for I tell you
sincerely I could not live longer without her. You remember how you yourself loved — remember that! and you will
not wonder at me."

Here Zbyshko stopped while waiting for some word
from Yurand, but, as he remained silent, the young man
continued, —

"At the hunting-lodge God granted me to save the
princess and Danusia from a wild bull, and the princess
said immediately after: 'Now Yurand will not be opposed;
for how could he refuse reward for such a deed?' But even
then I had not thought of taking her without your parental
permission. Besides, I had no chance of doing so; for the
savage beast had so crushed me that he almost squeezed out
my soul. But afterward, you know, those people came for
Danusia, as if to take her to Spyhov, and I had not risen
from my bed yet. I thought that I should never see her
again; I thought that you would take her to Spyhov and
give her to some other man. In Cracow you were opposed
to me, you know. I thought that I should die. Hei, mighty
God, what a night that was! Nothing but suffering; nothing
but sorrow! I thought when she went away from me that
even the sun would not rise again. You understand people's
love and their sorrow."

For a moment tears quivered in Zbyshko's voice, but he had a brave heart, so he mastered himself, and continued, —

"Men came for her in the evening, and wanted to take her immediately, but the princess commanded them to wait till morning. Now, the Lord Jesus inspired me to implore the princess and beg of her Danusia. I thought that if I were to die I should have even that consolation. Remember that the girl was to go, and I was to remain there sick, almost dying. There was no time to beg for your permission. The prince was not at the hunting-lodge, so the princess hesitated; she had no one with whom to advise: At last she and Father Vyshonek took pity on me, and Father Vyshonek married us. God's might, God's justice."

"God's punishment," added Yurand, in a deep voice.

"Why punishment?" asked Zbyshko. "Only notice, they sent for her before the marriage, and whether it took place or not they would have carried her away."

Yurand said nothing, and rode on shut up in himself, gloomy and with such a stony face that Zbyshko, though he felt immediately that consolation which the confession of a long-hidden secret always produces, was frightened at last, and said to himself with increasing alarm, that the old knight had grown stubborn in his anger, and that thenceforth they would be as strangers to each other and enemies.

And a moment of great affliction came on him. Never had he been in such a plight since the day of leaving Bogdanets. It seemed to him that there was no hope of reconciling Yurand, and, what was worse, no hope of saving Danusia; it seemed that all was useless; that in future there would fall on him only increasing misfortune and increasing misery. But this oppression was brief, or rather, in accordance with his nature, it turned quickly into anger and a desire for quarrel and battle.

"He wants no agreement," thought Zbyshko, in reference to Yurand; "let there be disagreement, let come what may!" And he was ready to spring at the eyes of Yurand himself. He was seized with a desire for battle with some one about some question; he wished to do something if he could give escape to his regret, his bitterness and anger; if he could find some relief.

Meanwhile they halted on the cross-road at an inn called Svetlik, where Yurand, when on journeys from the prince's castle to Spyhov, usually gave rest to his men and horses. He stopped now unconsciously. After a time Yurand and

Zbyshko found themselves in a room apart. On a sudden Yurand halted before the young knight, and fixing a glance on him inquired, —

"And hast thou wandered in here for her?"

Zbyshko answered almost rudely, —

"Do you think that I shall hesitate to answer?"

And he looked straight into Yurand's eyes, ready to burst out with anger against anger. But in the old warrior's face there was no stubbornness; there was only sadness almost without limit.

"And didst thou save my child?" asked he after a while, "and dig me out of the snow?"

Zbyshko looked at him with wonder and fear lest his brain might have become unsettled; for Yurand repeated exactly the same questions which he had asked already.

"Sit down," said he; "for it seems to me that you are weak yet."

But Yurand raised his hands, placed them on Zbyshko's shoulders, and all at once he drew him with what strength he had to his heart. Zbyshko, when he recovered from momentary astonishment, seized him around the waist, and they held each other long; for common suffering and misfortune had bound them together.

When they let go of each other, Zbyshko grasped the old knight's knees, and then kissed his hand, with tears in his eyes.

"Then you will not be offended with me?" asked he.

To which Yurand answered, —

"I was opposed to you; for in my soul I had devoted her to God."

"You devoted her to God, and God to me. It is His will."

"His will!" repeated Yurand; "but now we need mercy."

"Whom should God aid if not a father looking for his child, or a husband seeking his wife? He will not assist bandits, be sure."

"Still they carried her away," answered Yurand.

"Then give them De Bergov for her."

"I will give them everything they ask."

But at thoughts of the Knights of the Cross old hatred was roused in him at once, and embraced him like a flame; for after a while he added through his set teeth, —

"And I will give that which they do not want."

"I, too, have made a vow," said Zbyshko; "but now we must be off to Spyhov!"

And he urged the saddling of the horses. In fact, when the horses had eaten oats and the people had warmed themselves in the rooms somewhat, they moved on, though it had grown dark out of doors. Since the road before them was long, and there were severe frosts at night, Yurand and Zbyshko, who had not regained all their strength yet, rode in a sleigh. Zbyshko told of his uncle, Matsko, for whom he was yearning in spirit. He grieved, too, that that uncle was not present; for his cunning might be of equal use with his valor, cunning which against such enemies was even more needed than valor. At last he turned to Yurand, and asked, —

"But are you cunning? For I am not able in any way to succeed in that."

"Neither am I," answered Yurand. "It was not with cunning that I warred against them, but with this hand and with the grief that is in me."

"Ah, that I can understand," said the young knight. "I understand because I love Danusia, and they carried her away. If they should — but God preserve — "

And he did not finish; for at the very thought he felt in his breast, not his own, but a wolf's heart. For some time they went forward in silence over the white road filled with moonlight, and then Yurand said as it were to himself, —

"Had they reason for revenge, I should not say anything. But, by the dear God, they have none. I fought with them in the field when I was going on an embassy from our prince to Vitold, but here I lived with them as neighbor with neighbor. Bartosh Nalench seized forty knights who were going to Malborg; he put them in chains and confined them underground in Kozmin. The Knights of the Cross had to pay half a wagon-load of money for them. As to me, when a German guest happened along who was going to the Knights of the Cross, I entertained him as one knight another, and gave him presents. More than once Knights of the Cross came across the swamp to me. I was not harsh to them in those days, and still they did to me that which even to-day I would not do to my greatest enemy."

And terrible recollections rent him with increasing force; the voice died in his breast for a time, then he continued, half groaning. —

"I had one dear lamb, the same to me as the single heart in my breast; they bound her with a rope as they might bind a dog, and she grew pale and died on that rope of theirs. Now they have taken my child—Jesus! O Jesus!"

Again there was silence. Zbyshko raised toward the moon his youthful face, in which was depicted amazement; then he looked at Yurand.

"Father," said he, "it would be better for the Knights to win the love of men and not their vengeance. Why do they work so much harm on all people and all nations?"

Yurand spread out his arms as if in despair, and said in a dull voice,—

"I know not."

Zbyshko meditated a time over his own question, but after a while his mind turned to Yurand,—

"People say that you have wreaked on them a praise-worthy vengeance."

Yurand choked down his pain, recovered, and said,—

"Yes, for I vowed it to them—and I vowed to God that if He would let me wreak that vengeance I would devote to Him the child which was left to me. For this reason I was opposed to thee. But now I know not if that was done by His will or if thou hast roused His anger by thy act."

"No," said Zbyshko. "Just now I have told you that if the marriage had not taken place, the dog brothers would have seized her anyhow. God accepted your wish, but Danusia He gave to me; for without His will we should not have done anything."

"Every sin is against the will of God."

"A sin is, but not a sacrament. A sacrament is a thing of God."

"For this reason there is no cure in thy case."

"Glory to God that there is not! Complain not, more-over; for no man could help you against these bandits as I shall. Look here! I will pay them for Danusia in my own way, but if there is even one of those alive who carried off your dead one, give him to me, and you will see!"

Yurand shook his head.

"No," answered he gloomily. "Of those, not a man is alive."

For some time nothing was audible but the snorting of horses and the dull tread of hoofs as they struck the beaten snow.

"Once, one night," continued Yurand, "I heard some voice, as if coming out of the wall, and it said to me, 'Vengeance enough!' but I did not obey; for that was not her voice."

"And what voice might it have been?" inquired Zbyshko, with alarm.

"I know not. Often in Spyhov some one speaks in the wall to me, and groans sometimes; for many of them have died in chains in the cellar."

"But what does the priest say?"

"The priest blessed the castle, and told me to stop taking vengeance; but that cannot be. I became too grievous to the Germans, and then they set out to take vengeance themselves. They formed ambushes and challenged me to the field. That was the case lately. Meinegger and De Bergov challenged me first."

"Have you ever taken ransom?"

"No. Of those whom I seized captive, De Bergov will be the first to go out alive."

The conversation stopped; for they turned from the broad highway to a narrow road, along which they advanced slowly; for it was steep, and in places changed into forest hollows full of snow-drifts difficult to cross. In spring or summer, in time of rains, this road must have been almost impassable.

"Are we near Spyhov now?" inquired Zbyshko.

"Yes," answered Yurand. "There is a large strip of pine wood yet, and then a swamp; in the midst of that swamp is my castle. Beyond are meadows and dry fields, but to the castle it is impossible to go except by a dam. More than once the Germans wanted to reach me, but they could not, and of their bones a great many are decaying along the forest edges."

"Then it is not easy to go there," said Zbyshko. "If the knights send people with letters, how will they find the way to you?"

"They send often; they have people who know the way."

"God grant us to meet them in Spyhov."

The wish was to be realized earlier than the young knight imagined; for when they had driven out of the wood to an open plain, on which stood Spyhov in the midst of a swamp, they saw two men on horseback, and a low sleigh, in which were sitting three dark figures. The night was very clear, so that on the white cover of snow they could see the whole company distinctly. The hearts of Yurand and Zbyshko beat more quickly at sight of it; for who would go to Spyhov at night except messengers from the Order?

Zbyshko directed the driver to go with more speed, and soon they approached so considerably that the people heard them, and the two horsemen, who were watching evidently over the safety of the sleigh, turned toward them, and raising cross-bows from their shoulders, cried, —

"Wer da (who is there)?"

"Germans," whispered Yurand to Zbyshko.

"Then he raised his voice, and said, —

"It is my right to inquire, thine to answer. Who are ye?"

"Wayfarers."

"What kind of wayfarers?"

"Pilgrims."

"Whence?"

"From Schytno."

"They are the persons!" whispered Yurand again.

The sleighs were now near each other, and at the same time in front of both appeared six horsemen. These were guards from Spyhov, who night and day watched the dam leading to the castle. In front of the horses ran dogs, dangerous and large, quite like wolves.

The guards, on recognizing Yurand, called out in his honor, but in the calls was heard wonder that the heir was returning so soon and unexpectedly; but he, occupied entirely with the messengers, turned to them a second time.

"Whither are ye going?" asked he.

"To Spyhov."

"What do ye wish?"

"We can only tell that to the master himself."

The words, "I am the master of Spyhov," were on Yurand's lips, but he restrained himself, understanding that the conversation could not take place before people. He gave command to go almost as fast as the horses could gallop.

Zbyshko was so impatient also for news from Danusia that he could turn attention to no other thing. He was all impatience when the guards stopped his way twice on the dam, impatient when they let down the bridge beyond which was an enormous palisade on the wall, and though formerly a desire had seized him often to see what sort of a look that castle of ominous repute had, at sight of which Germans made the sign of the cross on themselves, he saw nothing now save those messengers of the Order, from whom he might learn where Danusia was and when freedom would be restored to her. But he did not foresee that grievous disappointment was waiting for him in a moment.

Besides the horsemen given for defence and the driver, the embassy from Schytno was composed of two persons, one of whom was that same woman who had brought the healing balsam to the hunting-lodge; the other a young pilgrim. Zbyshko did not know the woman, for he had not seen her; the pilgrim seemed at once to him a disguised attendant. Yurand conducted both to the corner chamber. He stood before them, immense in size and almost terrible in the light which fell on him from the fire blazing in the chimney.

"Where is my child?" asked he.

They were frightened when they stood eye to eye with the terrible Yurand. The pilgrim, though his face was insolent, simply trembled like a leaf, and the woman shook in every limb. Her glance passed from Yurand's face to Zbyshko, then to the shining, bald head of Father Kaleb, and again returned to Yurand, as if with the question, What are those two doing here?

"Lord," said she at last, "we know not what your question means; but we are sent here to you on important business. He who sent commanded us expressly to talk to you without witnesses."

"I have no secrets before them," said Yurand.

"If you command them to remain, we shall pray you for nothing save permission to leave here to-morrow."

On the face of Yurand, who was unaccustomed to resistance, anger was evident. For a time his yellow moustache moved ominously, but he remembered that Danusia was in peril, and restrained himself. Zbyshko, for whom the first question was that the conversation should take place at the earliest, and who was certain that Yurand would repeat it to him, said, —

"Since it is to be so, remain alone."

And he went out with Father Kaleb, but he had hardly found himself in the main chamber, the walls of which were covered with shields and armor won by Yurand, when the Cheh approached him.

"Lord," said he, "this is the same woman."

"What woman?"

"From the Knights of the Cross, who brought the Hercynian balsam; I recognized her right away, and so did

Sanderus. She has come evidently to spy, and she knows surely where the young lady is."

"And we shall know," said Zbyshko. "Dost thou recognize the pilgrim too?"

"No," replied Sanderus. "But buy no indulgences from that man; for he is a false pilgrim. If he were put to torture, one might learn much from him."

"Wait," answered Zbyshko.

"Barely had the door of the corner room closed behind Zbyshko and the priest, when the woman pushed up quickly to Yurand, and whispered, —

"Bandits carried off your daughter."

"Bandits with crosses on their mantles?"

"No. But God blessed the pious brothers; so they rescued her, and now she is in their possession."

"Where is she?" I ask.

"She is under the protection of the pious brother, Schaumberg," answered the woman, crossing her hands on her breast and bowing with humility.

Yurand, when he heard the terrible name of the executioner of Vitold's children, grew as pale as linen. After a while he sat on a bench, closed his eyes, and began to wipe away the cold sweat which was in drops on his forehead.

Seeing this, the pilgrim, though unable just before to restrain his terror, put his hand on his hip, threw himself on a bench, stretched out his feet, and looked at Yurand with eyes full of pride and contempt. A long silence followed.

"Brother Markwart helps Brother Schaumberg to care for her," said the woman. "It is a diligent attention, and no harm will happen to the young lady."

"What am I to do to induce them to give her up to me?" asked Yurand.

"To become humble before the Order," answered the pilgrim, with pride.

Hearing this, Yurand rose, went to the man, and, bending over him, said, with a restrained and terrible voice, —

"Silence!"

The pilgrim was frightened again. He knew that he might threaten and might say something which would restrain and break Yurand, but he was afraid that before he could utter the word something terrible might happen him; so he was as silent, and turned on the terrible face of the master of

Spyhov eyes as round as if petrified from fear, and sat motionless, but his chin began to quiver.

Yurand turned to the sister of the Order.

" Have you a letter? "

" I have no letter. What we have to convey, we must, by command, convey through word of mouth."

" Then speak! "

She repeated once more, as if wishing that Yurand should beat it well into his memory, —

" Brothers Schaumberg and Markwart are guarding the young lady; therefore restrain your anger; for, though you have wronged the Order during many years, the brothers wish to pay you with good for evil, if you will satisfy their just wishes."

" What do they wish? "

" That you free Pan de Bergov."

Yurand drew a deep breath of relief.

" I will give them De Bergov."

" And other prisoners which you have in Spyhov?"

" There are two attendants of Meinegger and De Bergov, besides their servants."

" You must free them, and reward them for their captivity."

" May God not permit me to haggle over the freedom of my daughter."

" The pious Knights of the Cross expected this," said the woman; " but this is not all that they commanded me to say to you. People of some sort, undoubtedly bandits, stole away your daughter. They did so of course to receive a rich ransom. God permitted the brothers to rescue her for you, and now they ask nothing but that you render up their guest and comrade. But the brothers know, and you know, what a hatred there is toward them in this country, and how unjustly all suspect their most pious acts even. For this cause they are sure that if people here should learn that your daughter is among them, they would suspect that it was they who stole her, and in this way, in return for their virtue, they would receive nothing but complaints and slander. Oh, what I say is true! evil and malicious people of this country have paid them often in that way, by which the fame of the pious Order has suffered greatly, fame which the brothers must protect; and, therefore, they lay down one more condition, that you inform the prince of this country and all the stern knighthood how the truth is; that not the

---

Knights of the Cross, but bandits, carried off your daughter, and that you had to ransom her from robbers."

"It is true," said Yurand, "that robbers stole my child, and that I must ransom her from robbers."

"And you must not speak otherwise to any one; for if even one man should learn that you had negotiations with the brothers, if even one living soul, or even one complaint should go to the Master or the Chapter, serious difficulties would follow."

Alarm appeared on Yurand's face. At the very first it had seemed to him quite natural that the comturs wished secrecy because they feared responsibility and ill repute; now the suspicion rose in him that there might be some other cause; but since he was unable to understand this cause, such fear seized him as seizes the most daring men when danger threatens, not themselves, but those who are near and dear to them. He resolved, however, to learn something further from the woman.

"The comturs wish secrecy," said he, "but what secret is there to keep when I release De Bergov and those others in ransom for my daughter?"

"You will say that you took a ransom for De Bergov so as to have something with which to pay the bandits."

"People will not believe; for I have never taken ransom," answered Yurand, gloomily.

"Well, it has never been a question of your child," hissed back the woman.

Again came silence, after which the pilgrim, who had summoned boldness now, and judged that Yurand needed still more curbing, said, —

"Such is the will of Brothers Schaumberg and Markwart."

"You will say that this pilgrim, who has come with me, brought you a ransom," continued the woman. "We will go from here with the noble De Bergov and the other captives."

"How is that?" asked Yurand, frowning. "Do you suppose that I will yield up captives before you return me my daughter?"

"Then choose another way. You can go to Schytno for your daughter; the brothers will take her there to meet you."

"I? To Schytno?"

"Yes; for should bandits seize her on the road again, your suspicion and that of people here would fall upon the pious knights a second time; therefore they prefer to give your child into your own hands."

" But who will guarantee me a return after I have crawled into the wolf's throat?"

" The virtue of the brothers, their piety and justice."

Yurand walked up and down in the room; he began to foresee treason, and he feared it, but he felt at the same time that the Knights of the Cross had power to impose such conditions as pleased them, and that in presence of them he was powerless.

But evidently some plan came to his head; for stopping before the pilgrim on a sudden, he examined him quickly; then he turned to the woman, and said, —

" Well, I will go to Schytno. You and this man, who has on him the dress of a pilgrim, will await my return, after that you will go from here with De Bergov and the captives."

" You do not wish, lord, to believe the knights," replied the pilgrim; " how, then, are they to believe that when you return you will release us with De Bergov and the others?"

Yurand's face grew pale from indignation, and a terrible moment came, in which it seemed that he was just ready to seize the pilgrim by the breast and put him under his knees, but he throttled the anger in his bosom, drew a deep breath, and spoke slowly with emphasis, —

" Whoever thou be, bend not my patience over much lest it break."

But the pilgrim turned to the sister.

" Tell what is commanded thee."

" Lord," said she, " we would not dare to doubt your oath on the sword and the honor of a knight, but it would not be proper for you to take an oath before people of common position, and we were not sent here for your oath."

" For what did they send you?"

" The brothers told us that you are not to mention to any one that you must be in Schytno with De Bergov and the captives."

At this Yurand's arms began to push backward and his fingers to spread out like the talons of a bird of prey; standing before the woman, he bent, as if he wished to speak into her ear.

" Did they not tell you that I would give command to break you and De Bergov on the wheel in Spyhov?"

" Your daughter is in the power of the knights, and in the

care of Schaumberg and Markwart," replied the sister, with
emphasis.

"Bandits, poisoners, hangmen!" burst out Yurand.

"Who will be able to avenge us, and who told us at parting: 'If all our commands are not complied with, it would
be better that the girl died as did the children of Vitold.'
Take your choice!"

"And remember that you are in the power of the
comturs," added the pilgrim.   "They have no wish to
wrong you, and the starosta of Schytno sends word by
us that you will be free to go from his castle; but they
wish you to come to bow down before the mantle of the
knights, and beg the favor of the conquerors in return for
what you have done to them.   They wish to forgive you,
but they wish first to bend your proud neck.   You have
denounced them as traitors and oath-breakers, so they wish
you to give yourself up on faith in them.   They will return
freedom to you and your daughter, but you must beg for
it.   You have trampled them; you must swear that your
hand will never rise again in hostility to the white mantle."

"So wish the comturs," added the woman, "and with
them Schaumberg and Markwart."

A moment of deathlike silence followed.   It seemed only
that somewhere among the beams of the ceiling some muffled
echo repeated, as if in terror: "Schaumberg, Markwart."
From outside the window came also the cries of Yurand's
archers watching on the bastions of the wall.

The pilgrim and the sister of the Order looked for a long
time, now at each other, now at Yurand, who sat leaning
against the wall motionless, and with face sunk in the shadow
falling on it from a bundle of skins hung at the side of the
window.   In his head there remained one thought alone, that if
he would not do the knights' will, they would strangle his
daughter; if he should do their will, even then, perhaps, he
would not save either himself or Danusia.   And he saw no
help, no escape.   He felt above him a merciless superiority of
power which was crushing him.   He saw in spirit already the
iron hands of the knights on the neck of Danusia; for, knowing
them, he doubted not for an instant that they would kill her,
cover her up in the ditch of the castle, and then deny, swear
themselves out of it.   Who would be able then to prove that
they had kidnapped her?   Yurand had, it is true, the messengers in his hands; he might take them to the prince to
obtain a confession through torture, but the knights had

Danusia, and on their part might spare no torture on her. And for a time it seemed to him that his child was stretching her hands to him from a distance and imploring rescue. If even he knew certainly that she was in Schytno, he might move that same night to the boundary, fall upon the Germans who expected no attack, seize the castle, cut down the garrison, and free his child; but she, perhaps, was not in the castle, and surely not in the village of Schytno. Again it flashed through his head like lightning that if he should seize the woman and the pilgrim and take them straight to the Grand Master, perhaps the master would obtain from them a confession, and command the release of Danusia; but that lightning flash was quenched as quickly as it shone. Moreover, these people might say to the Master that they went to Spyhov to ransom De Bergov; that they had no knowledge of any girl. No! that road led to nothing — but what road led to anything? For he thought that if he should go to Schytno, they would put him in chains and thrust him into a dungeon; but Danusia they would not release anyhow, even for this reason, lest it be discovered that they had kidnapped her. Meanwhile death was above his only child; death was above the last life that was dear to him. And, finally, his thoughts grew confused, and his pain became so great that it strained itself and passed into numbness. He sat motionless, because his body had grown dead, as dead as if cut out of stone. Had he wished to stand up at that moment, he would not have been able to do so.

Meanwhile the others had grown tired of long waiting; so the woman rose and said, —

"Dawn is not distant, so, lord, permit us to withdraw; for we need rest."

"And refreshment after the long road," added the pilgrim.

Both bowed then to Yurand, and went out. But he continued sitting motionless, as if seized by sleep, or death. After a while, however, the door opened, and in it appeared Zbyshko, behind him the priest.

"Well, where are the messengers? What do they want?" inquired the young knight, approaching Yurand.

Yurand quivered, but did not answer immediately; he merely blinked greatly, like a man roused from sleep.

"Are you not sick, lord?" asked the priest, who, knowing Yurand more intimately, saw that something unusual was happening within him.

"No," answered Yurand.

" But Danusia," continued Zbyshko, — " where is she, and what did they tell you? What did they bring?"

" A ran-som," answered Yurand, slowly.

" A ransom for Bergov?"

" For Bergov."

" How for Bergov? What has happened to you?"

" Nothing."

But there was in his voice something so strange and, as it were, imbecile, that both men were seized with sudden fear, especially since Yurand spoke of a ransom, and not of the exchange of De Bergov for Danusia.

"By the dear God!" exclaimed Zbyshko, "where is Danusia?"

" She is not with the Knights of the Cross," answered Yurand, with a sleepy voice.

And he fell from the bench to the floor like a dead man.

CHAPTER XXVII.

THE messengers had a meeting with Yurand on the following day about noon; an hour later they drove away, taking with them de Bergov, two attendants, and a number of other captives. After that, Yurand summoned Father Kaleb, to whom he dictated a letter to Prince Yanush, with information that the Knights of the Cross had not stolen away Danusia, but that he had succeeded in discovering where she was hidden, and hoped in the course of a few days to find her. He repeated the same to Zbyshko, who since the night before had been wild from amazement and fear. The old knight would answer no question, but told him to wait patiently and undertake nothing toward freeing Danusia, because it would be superfluous. Toward evening he shut himself in with the priest, whom he commanded first of all to write his last will; then he confessed, and, after receiving communion, summoned Zbyshko and the old, ever-silent Tolima, who had been his companion in all expeditions and battles, and who in time of peace managed the lands in Spyhov.

" Here is," said he, turning to the old warrior and raising his voice as if speaking to a man hard of hearing, " the husband of my daughter, whom he married at the court of Prince Yanush, and for which he has received my consent. After my death he is to be therefore the owner and inheritor of this castle, the lands, the forests, the meadows, the people, and all kinds of property existing in Spyhov."

When he heard this, Tolima was greatly astonished, and turned his square head now toward Zbyshko, now toward Yurand; he said nothing, however, for he rarely said anything; he merely inclined before Zbyshko and clasped his knees lightly.

But Yurand spoke on, —

" Which will of mine Father Kaleb has written, and at the end of the writing my seal is placed in wax; thou art to testify that thou hast heard this from my lips, and that I have commanded thee to give the same obedience to this young knight as to me. Therefore, whatever plunder and money there is in the treasury thou wilt show him, — and thou wilt be faithful to him in peace and in war until death. Hast thou heard me?"

Tolima raised his hands to his ears and bowed his head; afterward, at a sign from Yurand, he bowed and withdrew. The knight turned to Zbyshko then, and said with emphasis:

"There is enough in the treasury to tempt the greatest greediness, and ransom not merely one, but a hundred captives. Remember this."

"But why dost thou give me Spyhov?" inquired Zbyshko

"I give thee more than Spyhov, for I give thee my child.'

"And the hour of death is unknown," said the priest.

"Indeed, it is unknown," repeated Yurand, as if with sadness. "For instance, not long ago the snow covered me, and, though God saved me, I have not my former strength."

"By the dear God!" cried Zbyshko, "what has changed in you since yesterday? — and you are more willing to mention death than Danusia! By the dear God!"

"Danusia will return," answered Yurand. "God's care is above her. But hear what I say; when she returns, take her to Bogdanets, and leave Spyhov in care of Tolima. He is a trusty man, and this is a difficult neighborhood. There they will not seize her on a rope from thee, — there it is safe."

"Hei!" cried Zbyshko, "but you are talking now as it were from the other world. What does this mean?"

"I have been more than half in the other world, and now it seems to me that some kind of sickness has laid hold of me. But my child is the question for me, for she is all that I have. Though I know that thou lovest her — "

Here he stopped, and drawing from its sheath a short sword of the kind called misericordia, he turned the hilt of it toward Zbyshko.

"Swear to me on this cross," said he, "that thou wilt never do her a wrong, and wilt love her always."

Zbyshko, with tears in his eyes, threw himself on his knees in a moment, and putting his finger on the hilt, exclaimed, —

"By the Holy Passion, I will do her no wrong, and I will love her always."

"Amen!" said the priest.

Yurand put the misericordia into its sheath and opened his arms to Zbyshko.

"Now thou art my child too!"

After that they separated, for deep night had come, and for some days they had had no good rest. Zbyshko, however, rose next morning at dawn, for the evening before he had been afraid that some sickness was coming on Yurand,

and he wished to learn how the old man had passed the
night.

Before the door of Yurand's room he stumbled on Tolima,
who had that moment come out of it.

"How is your master? Is he well?" inquired he.

Tolima bowed, and then surrounding his ear with his palm,
asked, —

"What does your Grace command?"

"I ask how is your master," repeated Zbyshko, in a
louder voice.

"He has gone away."

"Whither?"

"I know not.   He was in armor."

CHAPTER XXVIII.

DAYLIGHT had just begun to whiten the trees, the bushes, and the large blocks of limestone scattered here and there on the field, when a hired guide walking at the side of Yurand's horse stopped, and said, —

" Permit me to rest, lord knight, for I am out of breath. There is dampness and fog, but it is not far now."

" Lead me to the road, and return," said Yurand.

" The road is to the right beyond the pine wood, and from the hill you will see the castle directly."

The peasant fell now to slapping his hands crosswise under his arm-pits, for he was chilled from the morning dampness; then he sat on a stone, for he was still more out of breath after this exercise.

" And knowest thou if the comtur is in the castle?" asked Yurand.

" Where should he be, since he is sick?"

" What is the matter with him?"

" People say that the Polish knights gave him a dressing," answered the old peasant. And in his voice could be felt a certain satisfaction. He was a subject of the Order, but his Mazovian heart was delighted at the superiority of Polish knights. Indeed, he added after a while, —

" Hei! our lords are strong, though they have hard work with the others. But he glanced quickly at the knight, as if to be sure that nothing evil would meet him for his words, which had shot out incautiously.

" You speak in our way, lord," said he; " you are not a German?"

" No," answered Yurand; " but lead on."

The peasant rose, and walked again near the horse. Along the road he thrust his hand from time to time into his pouch, took out a handful of unground wheat, and turned it into his mouth. When he had appeased his first hunger in this way, he explained why grain was unground, though Yurand, occupied with his own misfortune and his own thoughts, had not noticed what he was doing.

" Glory to God even for this?" said he. " A grievous life under our German lords. They have put such taxes on grinding that a poor man must chew unskinned grain, like a beast; for if they find a mill in the house they punish the man, take away his cattle, and, more than that, do not spare even women or children. They fear neither God nor priest, as they did not when they carried off the parish priest of Velbor in chains because he blamed them. Oh, it is hard to live under the Germans! Whatever grain a man grinds between two stones he keeps the handful of flour from it for Easter week, and even on Friday people eat grain as birds do. But glory to God even for grain, because two months before harvest we have no grain. It is not permitted to fish or to kill wild beasts — not as in Mazovia."

Thus did the peasant subject of the knights complain, speaking partly to himself, partly to Yurand; meanwhile they had passed the open space, which was covered with fragments of limestone sheltered under the snow, and entered the forest, which in the early light seemed gray, and from which came a damp, severe cold. It had dawned completely, otherwise it would have been difficult for Yurand to pass along the forest road, which was rather steep, and so narrow that in places his immense war-horse was barely able to push past between the tree-trunks. But the wood ended soon, and a few "Our Fathers" later they found themselves on the summit of White Hill, through the middle of which passed a beaten highway.

"This is the road," said the peasant; "you will be able to go on alone now."

"I shall be able," answered Yurand. "Go back to thy house, man."

And reaching to a leather bag which was fastened to the front of his saddle, he drew out a silver coin and gave it to the guide.

The man, more accustomed to blows than to gifts from Knights of the Cross in that district, was almost unwilling to believe his own eyes, and, seizing the money, he dropped his head toward Yurand's stirrup, and embraced it.

"O Jesus and Mary!" cried he; "God reward your great mightiness."

"Be with God."

"May the might of God conduct you. Schytno is before you."

He inclined once more toward the stirrup and vanished. Yurand remained alone on the hill, and looked in the direction indicated by the villager; he looked at the gray, damp barrier of mist which screened the world before him. Behind the mist was concealed the castle, that evil enemy toward which ill fate and superior force were impelling him. It was near now, near! hence, what had to happen and be accomplished would happen and be accomplished soon. At thought of this, in addition to his fear and anxiety about Danusia, in addition to his readiness to ransom her, even with his blood, from the hands of the enemy, an unheard-of bitter feeling of humiliation was born in his heart, a feeling never felt by him up to that moment. He (Yurand), at the remembrance of whom the comturs of the boundary had trembled, was going now at their command with a penitent head. He, who had overcome and trampled so many of them, felt conquered and trampled at that moment. They had conquered him, not in the field, it is true, not with courage and knightly strength, but still he felt conquered. And for him, that was something so unheard-of that the whole order of the world seemed to him inverted. He was going to humiliate himself before the Knights of the Cross, — he, who, had it not been for Danusia, would have preferred to meet all the power of the Order single-handed. Had it. not happened that a single knight, having the choice between shame and death, had struck on whole armies? But he felt that shame might meet him also, and at that thought his heart howled from pain, as a wolf howls when he feels the shaft in his body.

But this was a man who had not only a body, but also a soul of iron. He was able to break others; he was able to break himself also.

"I will not move," said he, "till I have chained this angei which might ruin my child instead of saving her."

And immediately he seized, as it were by the shoulder, his proud heart, with its stubbornness and desire for battle. Whoso might have seen on that hill the man in armor motionless, on that immense horse, would have thought him some giant cast out of iron, and would not have suspected that that motionless knight there was fighting at that moment the hardest battle that ever he had fought in his life. But he wrestled with himself till he conquered and till he felt that his will would not fail him.

Meanwhile the mist grew thin, and, though it had not vanished entirely, there appeared dimly at the end of it something of deeper color. Yurand divined that that was the walls of the castle of Schytno. At sight of this he did not move from his place, but he began to pray as ardently and fervently as a man prays for whom there is nothing left in this world but God's mercy.

And when he moved forward at last, he felt that solace of some kind was entering his heart. He was ready now to endure everything that might meet him. He called to mind that Saint George, a descendant of the greatest family in Cappadocia, had endured various humiliating tortures, and still he not only did not lose his honor, but is seated on the right hand of God, and is named patron of all earthly knighthood. Yurand had heard frequent narratives of his adventures from pilgrims who had come from distant lands, and with the remembrance of them he strengthened his heart at that moment.

Gradually even hope itself was roused in him. The Knights of the Cross had, it is true, been noted for vengefulness; hence, he doubted not that they would work revenge on him for all the defeats which he had inflicted, for the shame which had fallen on them at every meeting, and for the terror in which they had lived so many years.

But it was this very thing which gave him courage. He thought that they had carried off Danusia only to get him; so when they had him what would they care for her? That was it! They would put him in chains, beyond doubt, and, not wishing to keep him in the neighborhood of Mazovia, would send him to some remote castle, where he would groan to the end of his life in a dungeon, but Danusia they would free. Even should it appear that they had taken him by deceit and were tormenting him, the Grand Master would not take it very ill of them, nor would the Chapter; for he (Yurand) had been really grievous to the Germans, and had squeezed more blood out of them than any other knight then alive. But that same Grand Master would punish them, perhaps, for imprisoning an innocent maiden, and, moreover, a ward of the prince of Mazovia, whose good-will he was trying diligently to win, in view of the threatening war with the King of Poland.

And hope was taking possession of Yurand with increasing force. At moments it seemed to him almost certain that Danusia would return to Spyhov under Zbyshko's strong protection. "He is a firm fellow," thought Yurand; "he will not let any man harm her." And he recalled with a certain emotion all that he knew of Zbyshko. "He had fought with the Germans at Vilno; he had met them in duels; the Frisians he and his uncle challenged to a battle of four, and he attacked Lichtenstein, also; he saved my child from the wild bull, and surely he will not spare those four Germans whom he challenged." Here Yurand raised his eyes, and said, —

"I give her to Thee, O God, and do Thou give her to Zbyshko!"

And he became still fresher, for he judged that if God gave her to the young man, he would not permit the Germans to trifle with him, and would wrest her from their hands, even though the whole power of the Order were detaining her. Then he thought of Zbyshko again: "Indeed, he is not only a firm fellow, but he is as true as gold. He will guard her, he will love her, and grant the child, O Jesus, what Thou mayest of the best. But it seems to me that with him she will regret neither the prince's court nor her father's love." At this thought Yurand's lids became moist on a sudden, and in his heart there sprang up immense yearning. He would like, of course, to see his child in life again, and sometime or another to die in Spyhov near them, and not in the dark dungeons of the Order. But God's will! Schytno was visible now. The walls were outlined with increasing clearness in the mist; the hour of sacrifice was near, hence he strengthened himself more, and said to himself, —

"Surely it is the will of God! The evening of life is near. A few years more, a few less, will come out all the same. Hei! I should like to look at the two children again, but in justice I have lived my time. What I had to experience I have experienced, what I had to avenge I have avenged. And now what? Rather to God than to the world, but since there is need to suffer, I must suffer. Danusia and Zbyshko, though in the greatest enjoyment, will not forget me. Surely, they will mention me more than once, and take counsel: "Where is he? Is he alive, or is he with God in the heavenly host?" They will inquire everywhere and learn where I am. The Knights are eager for vengeance, but they are eager also for ransom. And Zbyshko would not spare anything to ransom even my bones. And for a mass Danusia and Zbyshko will surely give money many a time. Both have honest and loving hearts, for which do Thou, O God, and Thou, O most Holy Mother, bless them."

The highroad not only increased in width, but numbers of people appeared on it. Peasants were drawing loads of

THE KNIGHTS OF THE CROSS.

wood and straw toward the town. Herdsmen were driving cattle. Men were drawing on sleighs frozen fish from the lakes. In one place four bowmen were leading a chained peasant to judgment, evidently for an offence, since his hands were bound behind his back and on his feet were fetters, which, dragging on the snow, hardly let him move forward. From his distended nostrils and open mouth the breath came forth as rolls of steam, but the bowmen sang as they urged him. When they saw Yurand they looked at him curiously, evidently amazed at the size of the knight and his horse, but at sight of his golden spurs and girdle they lowered their crossbows in sign of salutation and honor. In the town there were more people still, and it was noisier; they gave way to an armed man, however, hurriedly. He passed the main street and turned toward the castle, which, sheltered in the fog, seemed to be sleeping.

But not all were asleep round about; at least crows and rooks were not sleeping; whole flocks of them were whirling above the elevation which formed the approach to the castle, flapping their wings and cawing. When Yurand had ridden up nearer, he understood why those birds were circling there. At the side of the road leading to the castle gate stood a large gibbet; on it were hanging four bodies of Mazovian peasants, subjects of the Knights of the Cross. There was not the least breeze, so that the bodies, the faces of which seemed to be looking at the feet, did not swing, except when the dark birds perched on their shoulders and on their heads, quarrelling with each other, pulling at the ropes, and pecking the drooping heads. Some of the four must have hung for a long time, for their skulls were entirely bare, and their legs had stretched out beyond proportion. At the approach of Yurand the flock flew away with great noise, but soon made a turn in the air and alighted again on the crossbeam of the gibbet. Yurand passing by made the sign of the cross, approached the moat, and stopping in the place where the drawbridge was raised near the gate, blew the horn.

Then he sounded a second, a third, and a fourth time. There was not a living soul on the walls, and from inside the gate came no voice. But after a while a heavy slide, inside the grating evidently, was raised with a gritting sound in a loophole near the gate.

"Wer da (who is there)?" inquired a harsh voice.

"Yurand of Spyhov!" answered the knight.

After these words the slide was dropped again, and deep silence followed.

Time passed. Inside the gate not a movement was audible, but from the direction of the gibbet came the croaking of birds.

Yurand stood a long while yet before he raised the horn and blew in it a second series of times.

But he was answered by silence again.

He understood now that they were detaining him before the gate through the pride of the Knights, which knew no bounds in presence of the conquered. They desired to humiliate him, as if he had been a beggar. He understood, too, that he would have to wait perhaps till evening, or even longer. At the first moment the blood boiled in Yurand; the desire seized him all at once to come down from his horse, raise one of the large stones that lay before the moat, and hurl it against the gate. He would have acted thus at another time, and every other Mazovian or Polish knight also, and let them rush out afterward from behind the gate and fight with him. But recollecting why he had come, he recovered his mind and restrained himself.

"Have I not offered myself for my child?" said he in his soul.

And he waited.

Meanwhile something began to grow dark on the wall. Fur-covered heads showed themselves, dark cowls, and even iron helmets, from under which curious eyes gazed at the master of Spyhov. These figures increased in number every moment, for the terrible Yurand was waiting alone at the gate, — this for the garrison was an uncommon spectacle. Those who before that had seen him in front of them saw their own death, but now it was possible to look at him safely. Heads rose higher and higher till at last all the battlement near the gate was covered with serving-men. Yurand thought that surely those higher in rank must be looking at him through the grating of windows in the gate-tower, and he raised his glance upward, but the windows there were cut in deep walls, and through them one could see only distant objects. But the crowd on the battlement, which had looked first at him in silence, began to call out. This and that man repeated his name, here and there was heard laughter, hoarse voices called to him as to a wolf, more and more loudly, more and more insolently; and when evidently no one from inside forbade, they began at last to hurl lumps of snow at the knight without motion.

He, as if unconsciously, moved forward with his horse, then in one instant the lumps of snow ceased to fly, the voices stopped, and even some heads disappeared behind the wall. Terrible indeed must have been Yurand's name. But even the most cowardly recollected that a moat and a wall divided them from the terrible Mazovian, so the rude soldiery began again to hurl not only balls of snow, but ice, rubbish, and small stones, which rebounded with a noise from his armor and the horse-trappings.

"I have sacrificed myself for my child," repeated Yurand to himself.

And he waited. Then noon came; the walls were deserted; the soldiers were summoned to dinner. Not many were those whose duty it was to stand guard, but they ate on the wall, and after eating amused themselves again by throwing bare bones at the hungry knight. They began also to talk among themselves, and inquire one of the other who would undertake to go down and give the knight a blow on the neck with a fist or the shaft of a lance. Others, after returning from dinner, called to him, saying that if disgusted with waiting, he might hang himself; for there was one unoccupied hook on the gibbet and a rope with it. Amid such ridicule, cries, outbursts of laughter, and curses, the afternoon hours passed away. The short winter day inclined to its close gradually, but the bridge was ever in the air, and the gate remained fastened.

Toward evening the wind rose, blew away the fog, cleared the sky, and disclosed the brightness of evening. The snow became blue, and afterward violet. There was no frost, but the night promised clear skies. The people went down from the walls again, except the guards; the crows and rooks flew away from the gibbet to the forest. At last the sky became dark, and complete silence followed.

"They will not open the gate till sometime about night," thought Yurand. And for a while it passed through his head to return to the town, but immediately he rejected the idea. "They want me here," said he. "If I turn back they will not let me go to a house, but will surround me, seize me, and then say that they are not bound to me in anything; for they took me by force; and, though I should ride through them, I should have to return."

That immense power of Polish knights in enduring cold, hunger, and toil, admired by foreign chroniclers, allowed them frequently to perform deeds which more effeminate people in the West could not accomplish. Yurand possessed this endurance in a greater degree than others; so, though hunger had begun to twist him internally, and the cold of evening penetrated his coat covered with armor, he resolved to stay, though he were to die at that gate.

But suddenly, before night had set in completely, he heard steps behind him on the snow.

He looked around; six men were coming from the side of the town. They were armed with spears and halberds. In the middle of them went a seventh, supporting himself with a sword.

"Perhaps the gate will be opened, and I shall enter with them," thought Yurand. "They will not try to take me by force or kill me; for they are too few; but were they to strike me, that would be a sign that they do not wish to keep faith, and then — woe to them!"

Thus thinking, he raised the steel axe hanging at his saddle, an axe so large that it was even too heavy for both hands of a common man; and moved with his horse toward them.

But they had no thought of attacking him. On the contrary, the soldiers planted the ends of their spear-shafts and halberds in the snow, and, since the night was not dark altogether yet, Yurand noticed that the shafts trembled in their hands somewhat.

The seventh man, who seemed to be an officer, stretched forward his left arm hurriedly, and turning his fingers upward, inquired, —

"Are you the knight Yurand of Spyhov?"

"I am."

"Do you wish to hear why I have been sent here?"

"I am listening."

"The mighty and pious comtur Danveld commands me to declare that till you dismount the gate will not be opened to you."

Yurand remained a while motionless; then he came down from his horse, onto which one of the spearmen sprang immediately.

"And your arms are to be delivered to us," said the man with the sword.

The lord of Spyhov hesitated. "Will they fall on me while unarmed and thrust me through, like a wild beast? Will they seize me and throw me into a dungeon?" But then he thought that if that had been their intention, a greater number of men would have been sent. For were they to rush

at him, they would not be able to pierce his armor at once,
while he might wrest a weapon from the nearest German
and destroy them all before help could come.   Moreover,
they knew what manner of man he was.

"And even," said he to himself, "if they wish to let my
blood out, I have not come here for another purpose."

With this thought, he threw down his axe, then his sword;
next his misericordia, and waited.

They seized all these; then that man who had spoken to
him withdrew a few tens of paces, halted, and said in a voice
loud and insolent, —

"For all the wrongs which thou hast done the Order,
thou art, at command of the comtur, to put on thyself this
hempen bag which I leave thee, tie to thy neck on a rope the
scabbard of thy sword, and wait humbly at the gate till the
grace of the comtur gives command to open it."

And after a little Yurand was alone in darkness and
silence.   On the snow lay black before him the penitential
bag and the rope, but he stood there long, feeling that something in his soul was unhinging, something breaking, something coming to an end, something dying, and that soon he
would be no longer a knight, no longer Yurand of Spyhov,
but a wretch, a slave without name, without fame, without
honor.

So much time passed before he approached the penitential
bag, and said, —

"How can I act differently?   Thou, O Christ, knowest
that they will kill my innocent child unless I do what they
command.   And thou knowest also that I would not do this
to save my own life.   Shame is a bitter thing!   Oh, bitter!
but before Thy death men put shame on Thee.   Well, then,
in the name of the Father and the Son." .

He stooped down, put on the bag, in which there were
holes for his head and arms, then on the rope around his
neck he hung the sheath of his sword, and dragged himself to
the gate.

He did not find it open, but it was all one to him at that
moment whether they opened it earlier or later.   The castle
sank into the silence of night; the guards called to each other
now and then at the corners.   There was light in one little
window high up in the gate tower; the others were in
darkness.

The night hours passed one after another; on the sky rose
the sickle of the moon and lighted the castle walls gloomily.

There was such silence that Yurand might have heard the beating of his own heart, but he had grown benumbed and altogether stony, just as if the soul had been taken out of him, and he gave no account to himself of anything. Only one idea remained to the man, that he had ceased to be Yurand of Spyhov, but what he had become he knew not. At moments something quivered before him, it seemed, in the night; that Death was coming to him stealthily over the snow from those corpses on the gibbet which he had seen in the morning.

All at once he quivered and recovered completely.

" O merciful Christ, what is that?"

Out of the lofty little window in the gate tower came certain sounds of a lute, at first barely audible. Yurand, when going to Schytno, felt sure that Danusia was not in the castle, but those sounds of a lute in the night roused his heart. In one instant it seemed to him that he knew them, and that no one else was playing but his child, his love. So he fell on his knees, joined his hands in prayer, and listened, while trembling as in a fever.

With that a half-childish and immensely sad voice began:

> " Oh, had I wings like a wild goose,
> I would fly after Yasek;
> I would fly after him to Silesia!"

Yurand wanted to answer, to cry out the dear name, but the words stuck in his throat as if an iron hoop had squeezed them down. A sudden wave of pain, tears, sadness, misfortune rose in his breast; he threw himself on his face in the snow, and began with ecstasy to cry to heaven in his soul, as if in a thanksgiving prayer, —

"O Jesus! I hear my child yet! O Jesus!"

And sobbing rent his gigantic body. Above him the yearning voice sang on in the undisturbed silence of night:

> " I would sit on a fence in Silesia;
> Look at me, Yasek dear,
> Look at the poor little orphan."

Next morning a bearded, burly man at arms kicked the side of the knight who was lying before the gate.

" To thy feet, dog! The gate is open, and the comtur commands thee to stand before his face."

Yurand woke as if from sleep. He did not seize the man by the throat; he did not crush him in his iron hand;

Yurand's face was calm and almost submissive. He rose, and without saying one word followed the German through the gate.

He had barely passed it when he heard behind him the bite of chains; the drawbridge rose, and in the gateway itself dropped the heavy iron grating.

CHAPTER XXIX.

WHEN Yurand found himself in the courtyard of the castle
he knew not whither to go, for the servitor, who had conducted him through the gateway, left him and went toward
the stables. At the wall stood men at arms, it is true, some
singly, some in small groups, but their faces were so insolent and their glances so jeering that the knight could
divine easily that they would not show him the way, and
that were they to answer his question they would do so con-
temptuously or with rudeness. Some laughed and pointed
their fingers at him, others began to throw snow, as on the
day previous. But he, noting a door larger than others,
over which Christ on the Cross was carved in stone, made
toward it, thinking that if the comtur and officers were in
another part of the castle, or in other chambers, some one
would in every case have to turn him from the mistaken
way.

And that was what happened. At the moment when
Yurand was approaching the door the two halves of it
opened suddenly, and a youth stood before him tonsured like
a cleric, but wearing the dress of a layman.

" Are you Pan Yurand of Spyhov?" inquired he.

" I am."

" The pious comtur has commanded me to conduct you.
Follow me."

And he led on through a great arched entrance-chamber
toward a stairway. At the steps, however, he halted, and
casting his eyes on Yurand inquired, —

" Have you weapons on your person? They have ordered me to search you."

Yurand raised both arms so that the guide might see his
whole body clearly, and answered, —

" Yesterday I surrendered all."

Thereupon the guide lowered his voice and said almost in
a whisper, —

" Guard against breaking into anger, for you are under
power, and power which is superior."

" But I am under the will of God too," answered Yurand.

Then he looked at his guide more attentively, and finding in his face something in the nature of compassion and pity, he said, —

" Honesty is looking out of thy eyes, boy. Wilt thou answer me truly touching that which I ask?"

" Hurry, lord," answered the guide.

" Will they give me my child?"

The youth raised his brows in astonishment.

" Is that your child who is here?"

" My daughter."

" That damsel in the tower at the gate?"

" Yes. They promised to send her home if I would give myself up to them."

The guide made a motion in sign that he knew not, but his face expressed doubt and fear.

Yurand added another question, however, —

" Is it true that Schaumberg and Markward are guarding her?"

" Those brothers are not at this castle. But take your daughter away before Danveld, the starosta, recovers."

Yurand trembled on hearing this, but there was no time to make further inquiry, for they had come to a hall on the story where Yurand was to stand before the starosta of Schytno. The youth opened the door and withdrew to the stairway.

The knight of Spyhov entered, and found himself in a large chamber which was very dark, for the glass panes, fitted into leaden sash, admitted light scantily, and moreover the day was wintry and cloudy. In a great chimney at the farther end of the room a fire was burning, it is true, but the wood, being imperfectly seasoned, gave out little flame. Only after a time, when Yurand's eyes had grown accustomed to the gloom, did he see in the distance a table with knights sitting near it, and beyond their shoulders a whole company of armed attendants, also men at arms, among whom was the castle jester, who held a tame bear by a chain.

Yurand had fought with Danveld on a time, later he had seen him twice at the court of Prince Yanush in the character of envoy, but since those times some years had passed; still, in spite of the darkness he recognised him at once, by his corpulence, by his face, and finally by this, that he was sitting at a table, in the centre of the room, in an easy-chair, with his arm bound in splints and resting on the side of the chair. At his right sat old Siegfried de Löwe of Insburg, an implacable enemy of Poles in general, and Yurand of Spyhov in particular; at his left were the younger brothers Gottfried, and Rotgier. Danveld had invited them purposely to behold his triumph over the terrible enemy, and also to enjoy the fruits of that treachery which they had thought out together, and in the execution of which the other three had assisted him. So they sat comfortably arrayed in garments of dark material, with small swords at their sides — joyful, self-confident, looking at Yurand with pride and with that boundless contempt which they felt at all times for the weaker and the conquered.

Silence continued long, for they wished to sate themselves with looking at the man before whom they had simply been terrified, and who stood now with drooping head before them, arrayed in the hempen bag of a penitent, with a rope around his neck from which depended his scabbard.

They wished also, as was evident, the greatest number of people to witness the humiliation of Yurand, for through side doors leading to other chambers every one who wished had the entry, and the hall was almost half filled with armed spectators. All gazed with measureless curiosity on the captive; they spoke loudly and made remarks which referred to him. But while looking at them he only gained consolation, for he thought in his soul: "If Danveld had not wished to keep his promise he would not have summoned such a number of witnesses."

Danveld raised his hand and conversation ceased; thereupon he gave a sign to one of the shield-bearers, who approached Yurand and, seizing the rope which encircled his neck, drew him a number of steps toward the table. Danveld looked then in triumph on the spectators and said, —

"See how the power of the Order overcomes pride and malice!"

"God grant that it be thus at all times!" answered those present.

Now came a moment of silence, after which Danveld turned to the prisoner, —

"Like a mad dog thou hast bitten the Order, and God has brought thee to stand like a dog before us, with a rope around thy neck, waiting for pardon and favor."

"Compare me not to a dog, comtur," answered Yurand, "for thou art belittling the honor of those who have met me, and fallen by my hand."

At these words a murmur rose among the armed Germans; it is not known whether the daring of the answer roused their anger, or the truth of it struck them. The comtur was not rejoiced at such a turn of speech, so he added, —

"See, he spits into our eyes again by his pride and haughtiness."

But Yurand raised his hands like a man calling heaven to witness, and said, nodding his head, —

"God sees that my haughtiness has remained outside the gates of this castle. God sees, and will judge whether by insulting my knightly dignity you have not insulted yourselves. The honor of knighthood is one in all places. Every belted man is bound in duty to respect it."

Danveld frowned, but that moment the castle-jester rattled the chain on which he held the young bear, and called, —

"A sermon! a sermon! A preacher has come from Mazovia! Listen! A sermon!"

Then he turned to Danveld.

"Lord," said he, "Count Rosenheim, whenever the sexton roused him to a sermon too early by bell-ringing, commanded the man to eat the bell-rope from one knot to another; this preacher has a rope around his neck, command him to eat it before he reaches the end of his sermon."

After these words he looked with some fear at the comtur, for he was not sure whether Danveld would laugh, or give the order to flog him for untimely speech. But the Knights of the Cross, smooth, pliant, and even submissive when they did not feel themselves in power, knew no measure in presence of the conquered; hence Danveld not only nodded at the jester in sign that he permitted the indignity, but burst forth in rudeness so unheard of that astonishment was depicted on the faces of some of the younger armor-bearers.

"Complain not that thou art disgraced," said he; "even were I to make thee an under dog-keeper, a dog-keeper of the Knights of the Cross is superior to a knight of thy people!"

"Bring a comb," cried the buffoon, now emboldened, "and comb the bear; he will comb out thy shaggy locks with his paw!"

Laughter broke forth here and there, while a certain voice called from behind the brotherhood, —

"In summer thou wilt cut reeds on the lake!"

"And catch crawfish with thy carrion!" cried another.

"But begin now to scare away crows from the gallows!" added a third. "Thou wilt have no lack of work here."

Thus did they jeer at Yurand, who on a time was their terror. Joyousness seized the assembly gradually. Some, coming from behind the table, approached the prisoner to examine him from nearby, and to say: "Then this is the wild boar of Spyhov whose tusks are knocked out by our comtur; of course he has foam on his snout; he would gladly bite some one, but he cannot!" Danveld and other brothers of the Order, who wished at first to give a certain solemn semblance of judgment to the hearing, on seeing that the affair had taken a new turn, rose also from the benches and mingled with those who were approaching Yurand.

Old Siegfried of Insburg was not rejoiced at this, but the comtur said to him: "Smooth your wrinkles; our amusement will be all the greater." And they also fell to examining Yurand. That was a rare opportunity, for up to that day those of the knighthood, or men at arms who had seen him in such proximity, closed their eyes forever after. Hence some said: "His shoulders are immense, even if he has a skin coat under the bag; one might wrap pea straw around his body and exhibit him in market-places;" others called for beer, so that the day might be still more joyous.

In fact a moment later the sound of tankards was heard, and the dark hall was filled with the odor of foam falling from under covers. The comtur grew merry and said: "Thus precisely is it proper, he need not think that an insult to him is important." So they approached Yurand again, and said, punching him under the chin with their tankards: "Thou wouldst be glad to moisten thy Mazovian snout!" And some, pouring beer on their palms, plashed it into his eye; but he stood among them, howled at, insulted, till at last he moved toward old Siegfried, and feeling evidently that he could not restrain himself long, cried in a voice loud enough to drown the noise which prevailed in the hall, —

"By the passion of the Saviour, and your own soul's salvation, give my child to me as you promised!"

And he wished to seize the right hand of the old comtur, but Siegfried started back suddenly and said, —

"Away, slave! What art thou doing?"

"I have liberated Bergov, and come hither alone, because in return for this you promised to give back my child to me; she is here."

"Who promised?" inquired Danveld.

"Thou, comtur, in faith and in conscience."

"Thou wilt not find witnesses, but no witness is needed in a question of word and honor."

"On thy honor! on the honor of the Order!" cried Yurand.

"In that case thy daughter will be given thee!" answered Danveld.

Then he turned to those present and continued, —

"All that has happened him in this place is innocent play, not reaching the measure of his crimes and offences. But since we promised to return his daughter, should he come here and humiliate himself before us, know that the word of a Knight of the Cross must be like the word of God, sacred, and that girl whom we rescued from bandits we will present now with freedom, and after exemplary penance for his sins against the Order, Yurand may go home also."

This speech astonished some, for, knowing Danveld and his former feelings of offence against Yurand, they did not expect the like honesty. So old Siegfried and also Rotgier, with Brother Gottfried, looked at the man, raising their brows in amazement, and wrinkling their foreheads; he, however, feigned not to see their inquiring glances, and said, —

"I will send thy daughter away under escort, but thou wilt stay here till our escort returns safely, and till thou hast paid the ransom."

Yurand himself was somewhat astonished, for he had lost hope that even the sacrifice of his own life could serve Danusia; hence he looked at Danveld almost with gratitude, and answered, —

"God reward thee, comtur!"

"Recognize in me a Knight of Christ!" replied Danveld.

"All mercy comes from Him," answered Yurand. "But as it is long since I have seen my child, let me look at her, and give her my blessing."

"Yes, but in presence of us all, so that there should be witnesses of our good faith and favor."

Then he commanded an attendant youth to bring in Danusia, and moved himself up to Siegfried, Rotgier, and Gottfried, who, surrounding him, began to speak with animation and quickly.

"I oppose not, though thou hadst a different intention," said old Siegfried.

"How," asked the passionate Rotgier, who was noted for

cruelty and bravery, — " thou wilt free, not only the girl, but this hell hound to bite again?"

" He will not bite as before! " exclaimed Gottfried.

" Oh, he will pay the ransom," answered Danveld, carelessly.

" Though he were to give us all he has he would strip twice as much in one year from our people! "

" As to the girl I make no opposition," repeated Siegfried, " but the lambs of the Order will cry more than once because of that wolf."

" But our word? " inquired Danveld, with a laugh.

" Thou hast spoken differently on that point."

Danveld shrugged his shoulders.

" Have ye had too little amusement? " asked he. " Do ye want more? " Yurand was surrounded now by others, who, conscious of the glory which had come to all the brotherhood because of Danveld's act of honor, fell to boasting before the prisoner, —

" Well, bone-breaker! " said the captain of the archers to Yurand, " thy pagan brothers would not act thus with our Christian Knighthood! "

" Thou didst drink our blood."

" We give thee bread in return for a stone."

Yurand paid no heed to the pride or contempt in their words; his heart was full and his eyelids moist. He was thinking that in a moment he should see Danusia, and see her through their favor, hence he looked on the speakers almost with compunction, and finally he answered, —

" True, true! I have been stern against you — but not false."

Meanwhile at the other end of the hall a voice shouted: " They are leading in the girl! " and immediately there was silence. The men at arms stood apart on both sides. Though no man had seen Yurand's daughter, and the greater number, because of the mystery with which Danveld surrounded his acts, did not even know of her presence in the castle; those who did know hurried to whisper to others of her marvellous beauty. Every eye therefore turned with exceeding curiosity to the doorway through which she was to enter.

Now came the youth; after him the serving woman of the Order, who was known to all, she who had gone to the hunting-lodge; behind her entered a girl dressed in white, with hair let down at full length and then fastened above the forehead with a ribbon.

All at once an immense burst of thunder-like laughter was heard through the hall. Yurand, who at the first moment was ready to spring toward his daughter, drew back on a sudden and stood as pale as linen, gazing with astonishment at the pointed head, blue lips, and expressionless eyes of an idiot whom they were giving him as Danusia.

"That is not my daughter!" said he, with a voice of alarm.

"Not thy daughter?" cried Danveld. "By Saint Liborius of Paderborn! Then either we did not rescue thy daughter from the bandits, or some wizard has transformed her, for there is no other in Schytno."

Old Siegfried, Rotgier, and Gottfried exchanged swift glances filled with supreme admiration for the keenness of Danveld, but no man of them had time to speak, for Yurand cried in a terrible voice, —

"She is here! my daughter is in Schytno, I heard her sing! I heard the voice of Danusia."

Thereupon Danveld turned to the assembly and said, coolly and with emphasis, —

"I take all here present to witness, but especially thee, Siegfried of Insburg, and you pious brothers Rotgier and Gottfried, that, in accord with my word and pledged promise, I yield up this maiden whom bandits, vanquished by us, declared to be the daughter of Yurand of Spyhov. If she is not his daughter there is no fault of ours in this, but the will of God, who has given Yurand into our hands."

Siegfried and the two younger brothers inclined their heads in sign that they heard and would testify when needed. Then they exchanged swift glances a second time, for Danveld's work was more than they had been able to hope for: to seize Yurand, and not yield up his daughter, and still to keep promise apparently, — who else could have done that !

But Yurand cast himself on his knees and adjured Danveld by all the relics in Malborg, by the dust and the heads of his ancestors, to give him his daughter, and not to act as a trickster and a traitor who breaks oaths and promises. There was such sincerity and desperation in his voice that some began to divine the deceit; to others it occurred that a wizard might have changed the girl really.

"God is looking at thy treason!" cried Yurand. "By the wounds of the Saviour! by the hour of thy death, give my child to me!"

And rising from his knees he advanced, bent down double, toward Danveld, as if wishing to embrace his knees; his eye was gleaming with something like genuine madness, and his voice was breaking with pain, fear, desperation, and menace. Danveld, reproached in the presence of all with treachery and trickery, began to snort; at last anger broke forth on his face like a flame, so, wishing to trample the ill-fated prisoner to the lowest, he pushed up to him, and bending to his ear hissed through set teeth, —

" If I give her to thee, it will be with my bastard! "

That instant Yurand roared like a wild bull; he seized Danveld with both hands and raised him above his head. In the hall was heard one piercing cry: " Spare!! " then the body of the comtur struck the stone floor with such terrible impetus that the brains of his broken skull were spattered on Siegfried and Rotgier who were standing right there.

Yurand sprang to the side wall on which were weapons, and, seizing a great double-handed sword, rushed like a storm at the Germans, who were petrified with terror.

Those men were accustomed to battles, blood, and slaughter, still their hearts sank to that degree that even when their stupor had passed they began to withdraw and flee as sheep from a wolf which kills with one snap of his teeth. The hall was filled with screams of terror, with trampling of feet, with the crash of overturned vessels, with cries of attendants, with despairing calls for weapons, shields, swords, and crossbows, and with the howls of the bear which broke away from the jester and climbed to a lofty window. At last weapons gleamed, and the points of some tens of them were directed at Yurand, but he heeded nothing; half insane he sprang toward them himself, and a wild, unheard-of battle began, — a battle more like a slaughter than a conflict with weapons. The youthful and passionate Brother Gottfried was the first to bar the way to Yurand; but Yurand with the lightning swiftness of his sword edge hurled off his head, and with it an arm and shoulder; after him fell the captain of the archers and the steward of the castle, Von Bracht, and an Englishman who, though he did not understand well what the question was, took pity on Yurand and his suffering and drew his sword only after the slaying of Danveld. Others, beholding the terrible strength and rage of the man, gathered into a crowd to resist in company; but that method brought still more deplorable defeat, for Yurand, with his hair on end, with wild eye, bespattered with gore and breathing blood, enraged, out of his mind, broke, tore, and slashed that dense crowd with dreadful blows of his broadsword, hurling men to the floor with his reeking blade, as a tempest hurls limbs and trees to the earth.   And again came a moment of ghastly terror, in which it seemed that the awful Mazovian would cut down and slay every one, and that they, like a pack of howling dogs, could not finish the maddened wild boar unless men with muskets assisted them; and in such degree were those armed Germans inferior in strength and rage to Yurand that a battle with him was simply death and destruction.

"Scatter! Surround him! Strike from behind!" cried old Siegfried.

So they scattered through the hall like a flock of starlings in a field when a crooked-beaked falcon swoops down from the sky on them; but those men could not surround him, for in his rage of battle, instead of seeking a place from which to defend himself, he hunted them around the walls, and the man whom he reached died as by a lightning stroke. Humiliation, despair, deceived hope turned into the single desire for blood seemed to intensify his savage strength tenfold.   That sword, for which the strongest warriors of the Order needed both hands, he wielded like a feather with one. He was not seeking freedom or victory, he was not seeking to save his life; he was seeking vengeance; and like a conflagration, or like a river which has swept away obstructions and is destroying blindly everything that stands before its current, he, the awful, the blinded destroyer, rends, smashes, tramples, murders, extinguishes.

They could not strike him from behind, for they could not overtake him; besides, common warriors feared to approach the man, even from behind, knowing that if he turned no human power could save them.   Others were seized by perfect terror at the thought that no unaided mortal could have made such slaughter, and that they had to do with one to whom superhuman power gives assistance.

But Siegfried and Rotgier rushed to a gallery which projected above the great windows of the hall, and called on others to follow and save themselves.   They did so in haste, so that men crowded one another on the narrow staircase, wishing to be there at the earliest, and thence strike the giant with whom every hand-to-hand struggle had proved impossible.   Finally the last man slammed the door leading to the gallery, and Yurand was alone on the ground floor.

Shouts of delight and triumph were heard in the gallery; heavy oaken tables, benches, iron sockets of torches began to fly now at Yurand. One of the missiles struck him above the brow and covered his face with blood. That moment the door of the main entrance was burst open, and in rushed a crowd of soldiers, summoned through the upper windows; they were armed with darts, halberds, axes, crossbows, pointed stakes, hooks, ropes, or whatever weapon each one had seized in a hurry.

But with his left hand the raging Yurand wiped the blood from his face so that it might not darken his eyesight, collected himself, and rushed at the multitude. Again were heard in the hall groans, the clank of iron, the gritting of teeth, and the terrified voices of men in the midst of slaughter.

CHAPTER XXX.

In that same hall, in the evening, at a table sat old Sieg-fried, who after Danveld's demise had taken temporary charge of Schytno; near him sat Brother Rotgier, the knight de Bergov, Yurand's recent captive, and two noble youths, novices, who were soon to assume the white mantle. A winter whirlwind was howling outside the windows; it shook the leaden sashes, and caused the torches burning in iron sockets to quiver, and blew from time to time rolls of smoke down the chimney, and through the hall. Silence reigned among the brothers, though they had assembled to take counsel. They were waiting for Siegfried's words, but he, with elbows on the table and his palms against his droop-ing gray head, sat gloomy, with his face in the shadow, and grim thoughts in his soul.

" On what are we to take counsel? " asked Brother Rotgier, at last.

Siegfried raised his head, gazed at the speaker, and said, rousing himself from meditation, —

" On the misfortune and on this : What will the Grand Master and the Chapter say? Besides, we are to see that no harm come to the Order from our actions."

Then he was silent again, but after a time he looked around and moved his nostrils.

" There is still an odor of blood here."

" No," answered Rotgier, " I gave command to wash the floor, and smoke the place with sulphur. The smell is of sulphur."

Siegfried cast a strange glance on those present and said, —

" Have mercy, O God, on the soul of Brother Danveld and on the soul of Brother Gottfried! "

But they understood that he implored the mercy of God on those souls because the thought of hell had occurred to him at the mention of sulphur; hence a shiver ran through their bones, and all answered in chorus, —

" Amen, amen, amen! "

For a time the howling of the wind was heard and the shaking of the window-panes.

"Where are the bodies of the comtur and Brother Gott-fried?" asked the old man.

"In the chapel; the priests there are singing a litany over them."

"Are they in the coffins already?"

"In the coffins, but the comtur's head is covered, for his face and skull are broken."

"Where are the other bodies? — and the wounded?"

"The bodies are on the snow, so as to stiffen before the coffins are finished. The wounded are cared for in the hospital."

Siegfried joined his hands above his head a second time.

"And one man did all this! O God, have the Order in Thy care when it comes to a general war with this wolfish race!"

At these words Rotgier cast a glance upward as if recall-ing something, and said, —

"At Vilno I heard the Voit of Sambia say to his brother the Grand Master: 'Unless thou raise a great war and destroy them so that their name be not left — woe to us and our people.'"

"God give such a war and grant a meeting with them!" said one of the noble novices.

Siegfried looked at him fixedly, as if wishing to say: "Thou couldst have met one to-day," but seeing the slen-der and youthful figure of the novice, and remembering, perhaps, that he himself, though renowned for courage, would not court sure destruction, he omitted to reproach him, and only asked, —

"Has any of you seen Yurand?"

"I have," answered De Bergov.

"Is he alive?"

"Alive, but lying in the net in which they entangled him. When he regained consciousness the soldiers wished to finish him, but the chaplain would not permit."

"It is not permissible to kill him. He is a man of con-sideration among his own people, and there would be a terri-ble outcry," answered Siegfried. "It will be impossible too to conceal what has happened, for there were too many spectators."

"What are we to say then, and what must we do?" inquired Rotgier.

Siegfried meditated a while.

"You, noble Count de Bergov," said he at last, "go to the Grand Master at Malborg. You have groaned as a captive in Yurand's castle, and are a guest of the Order; being a guest, hence not obliged absolutely to speak in favor of the brothers, men will believe you all the more. Tell what you have seen. Say that Danveld captured a certain maiden from bandits on the boundary, and thinking her the daughter of Yurand, informed Yurand, who came to Schytno, and — what happened later you yourself know."

"Consider, pious comtur," said De Bergov, "I have suffered sore captivity at Spyhov, and as your guest I should be glad to testify at all times in your favor; but tell me, to satisfy my conscience, was not Yurand's daughter really in Schytno, and did not Danveld's treachery bring her dreadful father to that madness?"

Siegfried halted with the answer. In his nature lay profound hatred of the Poles, and also cruelty, in which he exceeded even Danveld, and rapacity whenever the Order was in question; and in it were pride and also greed, but falsehood was not there. Hence the great bitterness of his life and its deepest sorrow was this, that in recent times all interests of the Order had arranged themselves in such fashion, through self-will, disobedience, and debauchery, that falsehood had become a common weapon, and one of the most effective in the business of the Order. Therefore De Bergov's question touched the most painful side in his soul, and only after a long period of silence did he answer, —

"Danveld is standing before God, and God is judging him. If they ask you for opinions, tell what you please; if they ask what your eyes have seen, tell them that before we entangled the raging man in a net you saw nine corpses on the floor, besides the wounded, and among them those of Danveld, Brother Gottfried, Von Bracht, an Englishman, and two noble youths — God grant eternal rest to them. Amen!"

"Amen! Amen!" said the novices.

"And say also," added Siegfried, "that, though Danveld desired to quell the enemy of the Order, no one here drew the sword first on Yurand."

"I will only tell what my eyes have seen," replied De Bergov.

"Before midnight you will be in the chapel, where we also shall be, to pray for the souls of the departed," said

Siegfried. And he stretched forth his hand as a sign of thanks and dismissal, for till further consultation he desired to be alone with Brother Rotgier, whom he loved and in whom he had great confidence. In fact, after the departure of De Bergov he dismissed the two novices under pretext of hastening work on the coffins of the common soldiers slain by Yurand, but when the door closed behind them he turned to Rotgier quickly and said, —

" Listen to what I tell thee. There is only one salvation, — concealment; no living soul must ever know that Yurand's real daughter was with us."

" That will not be difficult," answered Rotgier; " no one knew that she was here except Danveld, Gottfried, us two, and that serving woman of the Order who has care of her. Danveld gave command to intoxicate the men who brought her hither from the hunting-lodge, and then he hanged them. There were persons in the garrison who suspected something, but they were confused through that idiotic maiden, and now they know not whether we mistook the girl, or some wizard really metamorphosed Yurand's daughter."

" That is well."

" I have thought, noble comtur, of this : Should we not throw all the blame on Danveld, since he is not alive?"

" And acknowledge before the whole world that we in time of peace and while negotiating with Prince Yanush of Mazovia bore off from his court a foster daughter of the princess, her favorite damsel? No, as God lives, that cannot be! People have seen us at the court with Danveld, and Danveld's relative, the Grand Hospitaller, knows that he and we undertook everything in company. If we accuse Danveld the Hospitaller will try to avenge his memory."

" Let us consider this point," said Rotgier.

" We must consider it well, or woe to us. If Yurand's daughter is set free she will say that we did not rescue her from bandits, but that the men who took her carried her to Schytno directly."

" That is true ! "

" And God is witness that I am thinking not of responsibility alone; the prince will complain to the King of Poland, and their ambassadors will not fail to cry out at all courts against our violence, our crime, our treachery. God alone knows how much harm may result to the Order from this matter. If the Grand Master himself knew the truth he would be bound in duty to secrete that maiden."

" If that be true, when she disappears they will not complain of us, will they?" asked Rotgier.

" No! Brother Danveld was very adroit. Dost thou remember that he laid this down as a condition to Yurand, that he was not only to present himself at Schytno, but before coming to declare, and to inform the prince by letter, that he was going to ransom his daughter from bandits, and knew that she was not in our possession?"

" True, but how justify that which has happened at Schytno?"

" We will say that as we knew Yurand to be searching for his daughter, and as we had rescued from bandits a girl who could not tell who she was, we notified Yurand, thinking that this might be his daughter; but when he came he fell into a rage at sight of the girl, and, possessed by the evil one, shed so much innocent blood that frequently more is not shed in a battle."

" Indeed," answered Rotgier, " reason and the experience of age speak through you. Danveld's evil deeds, even should we accuse him, would be laid on the Order, therefore on us all, on the Chapter, and the Grand Master himself; but when our innocence is evident all blame will fall upon Yurand, to the detriment of the Poles and their alliance with Satan."

" And after that let any one judge us who pleases: the Pope, or the Roman Cæsar!"

" Yes!"

A moment of silence followed, after which Rotgier inquired, —

" What shall we do with Yurand's daughter?"

" Let us think over this."

" Give her to me."

Siegfried looked at him and answered, —

" No! Listen, young brother! In a question of the Order spare neither man nor woman, but spare not thyself either. The hand of God touched Danveld, for he wished not only to avenge wrongs done the Order, but to gratify his own desires."

" You judge me wrongly!" said Rotgier.

" Indulge not yourselves," interrupted old Siegfried, " for ye will make both body and soul effeminate, and one day the knees of that stalwart race will press your breasts and ye will never rise afterward."

And for the third time he rested his gloomy head on his

hand, and evidently he was conversing with his conscience, and was thinking of himself solely, for he said after a while, —

" On me also much human blood is weighing, much pain, many tears — I, too, when it was a question of the Order and when I saw that I could not succeed through strength alone, had no hesitation in seeking other methods; but when I stand before the Lord I shall say to Him: ' I did that for the Order, but in my own case my choice was this.' "

And when he had spoken he opened the dark garment covering his bosom, under that garment a haircloth appeared.

Then he seized his temples with his two hands, turned his face and eyes upward, and cried, —

" Renounce luxury and dissoluteness, strengthen your hearts and bodies, for up there I see white eagle plumes in the air, and eagle talons with the blood of Knights of the Cross on them."

Further words were interrupted by a sweep of the tempest, which was so terrible that a window above the gallery opened with a crash, and the entire hall was filled with the howling and whistling of wind, bearing snowflakes.

" In the name of the Father, Son, and Holy Ghost! This is an evil night," said the old man.

" A night when foul spirits have power," answered Rotgier.

" But are there priests with Danveld's body?"

" There are."

" He left the world without absolution — O God, be merciful to him ! "

And both were silent. Then Rotgier called attendants and commanded them to close the window and trim the torches. When they had gone he inquired again, —

" What will you do with Yurand's daughter? Will you take her to Insburg?"

" I will take her to Insburg, and dispose of her as the good of the Order demands."

" Well, what am I to do?"

" Hast thou courage in thy soul?"

" What have I done to cause you doubt on that point?"

" I doubt not, for I know thee and I love thee as a son because of thy manfulness. Go then to the court of the Mazovian prince and relate to him all that has happened here, just as we have described it between us."

" I may expose myself to certain destruction."

"Should thy destruction be to the glory of the Cross and the Order thou art bound to go. But no! Destruction is not awaiting thee. They will not harm a guest unless some one may wish perhaps to challenge thee, as did that young knight who challenged all of us — He, or some other may challenge, but of course that is not terrible."

"God grant it to come! But they may seize me and cast me into a dungeon."

"They will not. Remember that Yurand wrote a letter to the prince, and moreover thou wilt go to complain against Yurand. Thou wilt tell truly what he did in Schytno, and they must believe thee. The case is this: we informed him first that there was a girl in our possession, we begged him to come and look at her; he came, he went mad, killed the comtur, slaughtered our people. Thus wilt thou speak, — but what can they say to thee in answer? The death of Danveld will be heralded throughout all Mazovia. In the face of that they will cease complaints. Evidently they will search for Yurand's daughter, but since Yurand himself wrote that she was not in our hands suspicion will not fall on us. We must be brave and shut their jaws, for they will think, if we do so, that were we guilty no man of us would dare go to them."

"That is true. After Danveld's funeral I will take the road immediately."

"May God bless thee, my son! If we do all that is proper, not only will they not detain thee, but they will perforce reject Yurand lest we say, 'See how they treat us!'"

"And we must complain thus at all foreign courts."

"The Grand Hospitaller will see to that for the good of the Order, and as a relative of Danveld."

"Yes, but if that Spyhov devil should recover and regain liberty?"

Siegfried glanced forward gloomily, then he answered slowly and with emphasis, —

"Even should he be free again he will not utter one word of complaint against the Order."

After that he began again to instruct Rotgier what to say and what to demand at the court of Mazovia.

CHAPTER XXXI.

But news of what had happened in Schytno preceded Brother Rotgier and roused astonishment and alarm in Tsehanov. Neither the prince himself nor any one of his court could understand what had happened. A little while earlier, just as Mikolai of Dlugolyas was starting for Malborg with a letter from the prince complaining bitterly that Danusia had been stolen by disorderly comturs of the boundary, and asking with a threat almost to send her back straightway, a letter came from the master of Spyhov, announcing that his daughter had not been taken by Knights of the Cross, but by ordinary bandits of the border, and that soon she would be freed for a ransom. The envoy did not start, for it did not occur to any one that Knights of the Cross had forced such a letter from Yurand under threat of killing his daughter. It was difficult to understand what had happened if one believed the letter, for marauders of the boundary, as subjects of the prince and the Order, attacked one another in summer, not in winter, when snow would show their traces. Usually they fell upon merchants, or robbed throughout villages, seizing people, and driving their herds away; but to attack the prince himself and bear off his foster child, the daughter of a powerful knight who roused terror everywhere, was a deed which seemed simply beyond human credence. But to that, as to other doubts, the answer was Yurand's letter with his seal, and brought this time by a man whom they knew to have started from Spyhov. In view of these facts no suspicion was possible, but the prince fell into such rage as no one had seen for a long time, and commanded his men to hunt down bandits along every border, inviting also the Prince of Plotsk to do likewise, and spare no punishment on the turbulent.

Just at this juncture came news of what had happened in Schytno.

And passing from mouth to mouth it arrived with tenfold increase. Yurand, it was said, had gone with five others to Schytno; he had rushed in through the open gate and committed such slaughter that few of the garrison were left among the living. It was said that they had to send for aid to neighboring castles, and summon the best of the knights and armed bodies of footmen, who only after a siege of two days had succeeded in bursting into the fortress and cutting down Yurand, together with his comrades. It was said too that very likely these troops would cross the boundary, and a great war come undoubtedly.

The prince, who knew how very anxious the Grand Master was that in case of war with the Polish king the forces of the two Mazovian principalities should be neutral, did not believe these reports, for to him it was no secret that if the Knights of the Cross began war against the Prince of Plotsk, or against him, no human power could restrain Poland; hence the Grand Master feared war. He knew that war must come, but being of peaceful nature he wished delay, and moreover he knew that to measure himself with the power of Yagello he needed forces such as the Order had never put forth up to that time; he needed besides to assure himself of aid from the princes and knighthood, not only of Germany, but of all Western Europe.

The prince had no fear of war, therefore, but he wished to know what had happened, what he was to think really of the event in Schytno, of the disappearance of Danusia, and of all those tidings brought in from the boundary; hence, though he could not endure the Order, he was glad when one evening the captain of the archers announced that a Knight of the Cross had come and requested an audience.

He received him haughtily, and, though he knew at once that the man was one of those brothers who had been at the hunting-lodge, he feigned not to remember him, and inquired who he was, whence he had come, and why he had visited Tsehanov.

"I am Brother Rotgier," answered he, "and had the honor not long since to bow down to the knees of your Princely Grace."

"Since you are a brother, why have you not the insignia of the Order on your person?"

The Knight explained that he had not put on a white mantle because had he done so he would have been captured or slain beyond doubt by the knights of Mazovia. "In all the world elsewhere," said he. "in all other principalities and kingdoms, the cross on a mantle wins good-will and hos-

pitality from people, in Mazovia alone does the cross expose
to certain destruction him who bears it — "

"Not the cross exposes you," broke in the prince, angrily,
"for we also kiss the cross, but your own criminality.   And
if somewhere else men receive you better than we do, it is
because you are less known to them."

Then seeing that the knight was greatly offended by these
words, he inquired, —

"Hast thou been in Schytno, or knowst thou what has
happened there?"

"I have been in Schytno, and I know what has happened
there," answered Rotgier, "and I have come hither not as
the envoy of any one, but for this reason only, that the
experienced and pious comtur of Insburg said to me:
'Our Grand Master loves the pious prince and confides in
his honesty, hence while I hasten to Malborg do thou go to
Mazovia and explain to him the wrongs and insults inflicted
upon us, — explain our misfortune.   Be sure that that just
ruler will not favor the disturber of peace, the savage attacker
who shed as much Christian blood as if he were serving
not the Saviour, but Satan.'"

And now he narrated how everything had happened in
Schytno.   How Yurand, invited by the brothers to see if
the girl taken from the bandits was his daughter, instead
of showing gratitude, had fallen upon them madly; killed
Danveld, Brother Gottfried, the Englishman Hugo, Von
Bracht, and two noble youths, not counting soldiers; how
the brothers, remembering God's commands, and not wishing
to kill any one, were forced at last to entangle in a net the
raging maniac, who then turned his weapons on himself
and wounded his own body dreadfully; finally how, not only
in the castle, but in the town, there were people who in the
midst of the winter storm heard on that night after the
battle laughter and hideous voices crying out in the air:
"Our Yurand!   The enemy of the Cross! the spiller of
innocent blood!   Our Yurand!"

The whole narrative, but especially the last words of it,
made a deep impression on all.   Terror simply seized them.
Has Yurand, thought they, really summoned unclean powers?
— and deep silence fell on them.   The princess, who was
present, and who, loving Danusia, bore in her heart an
incurable sorrow, turned to Rotgier with this sudden
query, —

"You say, Knight, that when you had rescued the idiot

you thought her Yurand's daughter, and therefore invited him to Schytno."

"True, Gracious Lady," answered Rotgier.

"But how could you think so, since you had seen Yurand's real daughter with me in the hunting-lodge?"

At this Rotgier was confused, for he was not prepared for the question. The prince rose and fixed a stern glance on him; Mikolai of Dlugolyas, Mrokota, Yasko, and other Mazovian knights sprang at once toward him, asking one after another in threatening voices, —

"How could you think so? Say, German! How was that possible?"

But Rotgier rallied.

"We brothers of the Order," said he, "do not raise our eyes on women. At the lodge there were damsels not a few in attendance on the Gracious Princess, but who among them was Yurand's daughter no man of us knew."

"Danveld knew her," said Mikolai. "He conversed with her even, at the hunt."

"Danveld is standing in the presence of God," answered Rotgier, "and I will say only this of him, that on the morning after his death blooming roses were found on his coffin. As the season is winter no human hand could have put them there."

Again silence followed.

"How did ye know that Yurand's daughter was stolen?" inquired the prince.

"The very godlessness and insolence of the deed caused it to be bruited about in all places. Hence on hearing of it we had a mass celebrated in thanksgiving that it was only an ordinary damsel and not one of your Grace's children that was stolen from the hunting-lodge."

"But it is a wonder to me that ye could consider an idiot girl to be the daughter of Yurand."

To this Brother Rotgier answered, —

"Danveld said, 'Satan often betrays his servants, so perhaps he transformed Yurand's daughter.'"

"But the bandits could not, as they are ignorant people, forge a letter from Father Kaleb and put Yurand's seal on it. Who could have done that?"

"The evil spirit."

Again no one was able to find an answer. Rotgier looked carefully into the eyes of the prince, and said, —

"In truth these questions are as swords in my breast, for

suspicion and doubt is contained in them. But confident
in the justice of God and the power of truth, I ask your
Princely Grace: Did Yurand himself suspect us of this
deed, and if he suspected us why did he, before we invited
him to Schytno, search the whole boundary for bandits so as
to ransom his daughter from them?"

"Well," said the prince, "as to truth, though thou hide
it from people, thou wilt not hide it from God. Yurand
held you guilty at first, but afterward — afterward he
had another idea."

"See how the brightness of truth conquers darkness,"
said Rotgier. And he looked around the ball with the glance
of a victor, for he thought that in the heads of the Knights
of the Cross there was more wit and keenness than in
Polish heads, and that the Polish race would serve always as
plunder and nourishment for the Order, just as a fly must
be plunder and nourishment for a spider. So, casting aside
his former pliancy, he approached the prince, and demanded
in a voice which was haughty and insistent, —

"Reward us, Lord, for our losses, for the injustice inflicted on us, for our tears and our blood! This son of hell
was thy subject, hence in the name of God, from whom
comes the power of kings and princes, in the name of justice
and the Cross, repay us for our wrongs and our blood!"

The prince looked at him with amazement.

"By the dear God," said he, "what dost thou wish? If
Yurand shed blood in his rage, must I answer for his rage?"

"He was thy subject, in thy principality are his lands, his
villages, and his castle in which he imprisoned servants of
the Order; hence let those lands at least and that godless
castle become henceforth the property of the Order. Of
course this will be no fitting return for the noble blood shed
by him, of course it will not raise the dead to life, but it
may even in part still God's anger and wipe away the
infamy which otherwise will fall on this whole principality.
O Lord! Everywhere the Order possesses lands and castles
with which the favor and piety of Christian princes have
endowed it, but it has not a hand's-breadth in your domin-
ions. Let the injustice done us, which calls to God for
vengeance, be redeemed even in this way, so that we may
say that here too live people who have in their hearts the
fear of God."

The prince was astonished still more on hearing this, and
only after long silence did he answer, —

" By the wounds of God! But if this Order of yours is seated here, by whose favor is it here if not by the favor of my ancestors? Have ye not enough yet of those towns, lands, and regions which belonged to our people formerly and which to-day are yours? Besides, Yurand's daughter is living yet, for no one has informed you of her death. Do ye wish then to seize an orphan's dowry and right with an orphan's bread some wrong done you?"

" Lord, thou recognizest the wrong," said Rotgier, " then give satisfaction as thy princely conscience and thy just soul dictates."

And again he was glad in heart, for he thought: " Now not merely will they not complain, they will take counsel how to wash their hands of the affair and squeeze out of it. No one will reproach us with anything, and our fame will be like the white mantle of the Order, stainless."

Meanwhile the voice of old Mikolai was heard unexpectedly, —

" They accuse thee of greed, and God knows with justice, for in this case thou carest more for profit than the honor of the Order."

" That is true!" answered the Mazovian knights in a chorus.

Rotgier advanced a number of steps, raised his head haughtily, and said, measuring them with a lofty glance, —

" I have not come here as an envoy, but as a witness in a cause, and as a Knight of the Cross, ready to defend the honor of the Order with my own blood to the last breath of life. Whoso dares then in the face of what Yurand himself has said to accuse the Order of taking part in the seizure of his daughter, let him take up this knightly challenge, and stand here before the judgment of God! "

Then he cast down before him his gauntlet of a knight, which fell on the floor. They stood in deep silence, for though more than one man would have been delighted to dint a sword on the shoulder of the German, they feared the judgment of God. It was a secret to no one that Yurand had testified explicitly that the Knights of the Order had not stolen his daughter, hence every man thought in his soul that truth. and therefore victory, would be on the side of Rotgier.

The knight grew more and more haughty, and, resting his hand on his hip, he inquired, —

" Is there a man who will take up this gauntlet? "

That moment some knight whom no one had seen enter,

and who at the door had been listening to the conversation, stepped into the middle of the room, took up the gauntlet, and said, —

"I am here!"

When he had spoken thus he cast his own gauntlet straight into Rotgier's face, and began in a voice which in the universal silence spread through the hall like thunder, —

"In the presence of God, in the presence of the worthy prince, and in presence of all the honorable knighthood of this land, I tell thee, Knight of the Cross, that thou liest like a dog against truth and justice — and I challenge thee into the lists to do battle on foot, or on horseback, with lances, with axes, with short swords or long ones — and not to loss of freedom, but to the last breath of life, to the death!"

In that hall one might have heard a fly on the wing. All eyes were turned to Rotgier, and to the challenging knight whom no one knew, for he had a helmet on his head, without a visor, it is true, but with round side pieces which went below his ears, covering the upper part of his face altogether and shading the lower part deeply. The Knight of the Cross was not less astonished than others. Confusion, pallor, and wild anger flashed across his face in succession, like lightning across a night sky. He seized the glove, which, slipping from his face, had caught on a link of his shoulder-piece, and inquired —

"Who art thou who callest on the justice of God?"

The other man unfastened the buckle under his chin, raised his helmet, from under which appeared a bright, youthful face, and said, —

"Zbyshko of Bogdanets, the husband of Yurand's daughter."

All were astounded, and Rotgier with the rest, for no one save the prince and princess, with Father Vyshonek and De Lorche, knew of Danusia's marriage. The Knights of the Cross felt certain that except her father, Danusia had no natural defender, but at that moment Pan de Lorche came forward and said, —

"On my knightly honor I testify to the truth of his words; whoso dares to doubt it to him I say: here is my gauntlet."

Rotgier was a stranger to fear, and in his heart anger was storming at that moment; he would perhaps have raised that gauntlet also, but remembering that the man who had cast it down was himself a great lord, and a relative of the Count of

Guelders, he restrained his anger; he did this all the more since the prince rose and said with a frown, —

" It is not permitted to raise the gauntlet, for I too testify that this knight has spoken truly."

When Rotgier heard this he bowed, and then said to Zbyshko, —

" If it be thy choice, then on foot, in closed barriers, with axes."

" I challenged thee the first time in that way," replied Zbyshko.

" God grant victory to justice!" cried the knights of Mazovia.

CHAPTER XXXII.

In the whole court, as well among the knighthood as
the women, there was alarm because of Zbyshko, for he
was loved universally. In view of Yurand's letter no
one doubted that right was on the side of the German.
They knew besides that Rotgier was one of the most
renowned brothers of the Order. The armor-bearer Van
Krist narrated, perhaps purposely, among the Mazovian
nobles that his lord, before becoming an armed monk, had sat
at the table of honor given by the Knights of the Cross, to
which table were admitted only knights famed throughout
Christendom, men who had made a pilgrimage to the Holy
Land, or who had battled victoriously against dragons, giants,
or mighty sorcerers. When the Mazovians heard these narratives of Van Krist, and also the assurances that his lord
had fought frequently single-handed against five, having a
misericordia in one hand and an axe or a sword in the other,
they were frightened, and some said, —

"Oh, if Yurand were here he could manage two of them,
no German ever escaped him; but woe to the youth! for that
knight exceeds him in strength, years, and training." Others
lamented that they had not taken up the gauntlet, declaring
that had it not been for the tidings from Yurand they would
have done so without fail — "but the fear of God's judgment." They mentioned also, when they could, and for
mutual consolation, the names of Mazovian, or in general
of Polish knights, who, either in court tournaments or in
meetings with lances, had gained numerous victories over
knights of the West. First of all, they mentioned Zavisha
of Garbov, whom no knight in Christendom had equalled.
But some were of good hope concerning Zbyshko also.
"He is no decked-out knight," said they, " and as ye have
heard he has hurled down German heads on trampled earth
worthily." But their hearts were strengthened specially by
Zbyshko's armor-bearer, Hlava, who, on the eve of the duel,
when he heard Van Krist exalting the unheard-of victories of
Rotgier, being an excitable young man, seized Van Krist by

the chin, pushed back his head, and said: "If thou art not ashamed to lie before people look up, because God too hears thee!" And he held him in that way as long a time as would be needed to say one "Our Father;" the other, when he was freed at last, inquired about Hlava's family, and learning that he came of nobles challenged him straightway to axes.

The Mazovians were pleased at this, and again more than one of them said: "Such men will not limp on the field of combat, and if truth and God are on their side the brothers of the Order will not bear away sound bones from this struggle." But Rotgier had cast sand in the eyes of all so successfully that many were alarmed touching this point: on which side is truth, and the prince himself shared the alarm with others. Hence on the evening before the combat he summoned Zbyshko to an interview, and inquired of him, —

"Art thou sure that God will be with thee? Whence knowest thou that they seized Danusia? Did Yurand tell thee anything? For, seest thou, here is Yurand's letter, written by Father Kaleb, and upon it is his seal. In this letter Yurand declares that to his knowledge the Knights did not carry off Danusia. What did he say to thee?"

"He said that it was not the Knights of the Cross."

"How canst thou risk life then and appear before the judgment of God?"

Zbyshko was silent; but after some time his jaws quivered and tears gathered in his eyes. "I know nothing, Gracious Lord," said he. "We went away from here with Yurand, and on the road I told him of the marriage. He began to complain that that might be an offence against Heaven, but when I told him that it was God's will he grew pacified, and forgave me. Along the whole road he said that no one had carried off Danusia but Knights of the Order. and after that I know not myself what happened. To Spyhov came that woman who brought some medicine for my use to the hunting-lodge, and with her one messenger. They shut themselves in with Yurand and counselled. What they said I know not, only after that conversation Yurand's own servants could not recognize him, for he was as if saved from a coffin then. He said to us: "Not the Knights of the Cross," but he let out of the dungeon Bergov and all the captives whom he had taken, God knows why; he went away himself without attendant or servant. He said that he was going to the bandits to ransom Danusia, and he commanded me to wait for him. Well, I waited till news came from Schytno that Yurand had murdered Germans and had himself fallen. O, Gracious Lord! the land of Spyhov was burning beneath me, and I came near running mad. I put men on horseback to avenge Yurand's death, but Father Kaleb said: 'Thou canst not take the castle, and do not begin war. Go to the prince; they may know something there of Danusia.' So I came, and happened in here just as that dog was barking about the wrong done the Order and the madness of Yurand. I took up his gauntlet because I had challenged him earlier, and though I know nothing, I know this one thing exactly, that they are hellish liars, without shame, faith, or honor. See, Gracious Prince, they stabbed De Fourcy and tried to cast the blame of that deed on my attendant. As God lives! they slaughtered De Fourcy like a bullock, and then came to thee, lord, for restitution and vengeance. Who will swear that they did not lie to Yurand, and have not lied now to thee? I know not where Danusia is, but I have challenged this man; for though I should have to lose my life, death is sweeter to me than is life without her who in all the world is my dearest."

When he had said this he forgot himself; he tore the net from his head and the hair fell over his shoulders; he seized it and sobbed grievously. Anna Danuta, afflicted to the depth of her soul by the loss of Danusia, placed her hand on his head in compassion for his sufferings, and said, —

"God will aid, bless, and comfort thee!"

CHAPTER XXXIII.

THE prince did not oppose the duel, for, according to the custom of the time, he had no authority to do so. He simply caused Rotgier to write to the Grand Master and to Siegfried de Löwe, stating that he had cast down the gauntlet first before the Mazovian knights, that because of this he was to meet in combat Yurand's son-in-law, who moreover had challenged him on an earlier occasion. Rotgier explained to the Grand Master that if he fought without permission he did so because the honor of the Knights was in question, and he had to avert foul suspicion which might bring shame to the Order, which he, Rotgier, was ready at all times to vindicate with his life-blood. This letter was sent straightway to the boundary by an attendant of the brother; beyond that it was to go to Malborg by post, which the Knights had invented many years before others, and introduced into the lands of the Order.

Meanwhile the snow in the courtyard of the castle was trampled and sprinkled with ashes, so that the feet of the combatants might not slip over its surface or sink in it. An uncommon movement reigned within the castle. Emotion had so seized the knights and damsels that no one slept the night before the combat. They said that a combat with lances on horseback, or even with swords, ended frequently with wounds, but on foot, and especially with the terrible axes, it was ever mortal. All hearts were on Zbyshko's side, and the greater the friendship for him or Danusia the greater the fear caused by reports of the skill and fame of the German. Many women passed that night in the church, where, after confessing to Father Vyshonek, Zbyshko himself performed penance. So women, when they saw his face, almost boyish, said to one another: "Why, he is a child yet! How can he expose his young head to the axe of the German?" And the more earnestly did they implore aid for him. But when he rose at dawn and went through the chapel to put on his armor their courage increased somewhat, for though Zbyshko's head and face were really boy-like, his body was bulky and stalwart beyond measure, so that he seemed to them a chosen man, who could fight his own battle even against the strongest.

The combat was to take place in the courtyard of the castle, which was surrounded by a portico. When day had dawned completely, the prince and princess with their children came and sat down in a central place between the pillars, whence they could see the whole courtyard in the best manner. At both sides of them were the foremost courtiers, noble ladies, and the knighthood. These filled all corners of the portico. The servants fixed themselves beyond an embankment formed of snow which had been swept from the courtyard. Some had mounted on window-sills, and even on the roof. On these places the common people muttered: "God grant our man not to falter!"

The day was damp and cold, but clear. The air was full of daws, which had settled on the roofs and bastion points, but, disturbed by unusual movements, they circled above the castle with great fluttering. In spite of the cold, people were sweating from emotion, and when the first trumpet sound announced the arrival of the combatants, all hearts beat like hammers.

The two men entered from opposite sides of the barriers and halted at the ends of them. Breath stopped in the breasts of all spectators. Each thought: Two souls will soon fly to the judgment threshold of God, and two corpses will be left on the snow! The lips and cheeks of women grew blue and pallid at thought of that; the eyes of men were fixed on the opponents as on a rainbow; each wished to predict in his mind from their forms and weapons the side to which victory would fall.

Rotgier was arrayed in a blue enamelled breastplate, with a similar armor for the thighs, and wore a helmet of the same material with raised visor, and lordly peacock plumes on the top of it. Zbyshko's breast, sides, and back were covered by that splendid Milan armor which he had won from the Frisians. On his head was a helmet not fastened under the chin, and without plumes; on his legs were raw bull-hides. On their left shoulders the men carried shields with their escutcheons: on the German's was a chessboard above, and below three lions rampant; on Zbyshko's, the "dull horseshoe." In their right hands they carried the broad, terrible axes with oaken handles, which had grown dark and were longer than the arm of a man full-grown. They were accompanied by their armor-bearers, Hlava and Van Krist, both in dark iron-plate mail, both with shields and axes. On his escutcheon Van Krist had a sprig of broom. The escutcheon of the Cheh was the bullhead, with this difference, that on the head, instead of an axe, a short sword was sunk in the eye half-way.

The trumpets sounded a second time; after the third the combatants were to begin, according to agreement. They were separated from each other by only a small space, over which gray ashes were sprinkled. Above that space death was hovering like a bird of ill-omen. But before the third signal was given Rotgier, approaching the pillars between which the prince and the princess were sitting, raised his steel-incased head, and called with a voice so resonant that it was heard in all corners, —

"I take to witness God, thee, worthy lord, and all the knighthood of this land, that I am guiltless of the blood which will be shed here."

At these words hearts were straitened again, because the German felt so sure of himself and of victory. But Zbyshko, who had an honest soul, turned to Hlava and said, —

"That boasting is foul in my nostrils; it would have meaning after my death, but not while I am living. That boaster has a peacock plume on his helmet, and I at the very first made a vow to get three such, and later, I vowed to get as many as I have fingers on my hands. God will give success!"

"My master," said Hlava, bending down and gathering some ashes from the snow, so that the axe handle might not slip along his palms, "perhaps Christ will grant me to finish quickly with this Prussian; will it be permitted me then, if not to touch the German, at least to put an axe handle between his legs and bring him to the earth with it?"

"God guard thee from doing that!" cried Zbyshko with vehemence; "thou wouldst cover thyself and me with dishonor."

With that the sound of the trumpet was heard for the third time. The attendants sprang forward quickly and with passion, but the knights approached each other more slowly and carefully, as their dignity and distinction demanded, till the first blows were given.

Few turned to the attendants, but those among men of experience and the servants who looked at them understood straightway that Hlava had on his side a tremendous advantage. Van Krist's axe moved slowly in his hand, and the motions of his shield were more labored. The legs seen beneath his shield were longer, but slender and less springy than the powerful limbs covered by the close-fitting dress of Hlava, who pressed on so passionately that Van Krist had to retreat almost from the first moment. People understood this immediately: one of those opponents rushes on the other like a storm, he pushes, presses, strikes like a thunderbolt, while the other, in the feeling that death is above him, defends himself only to defer the dread moment to the utmost. Such was the case in reality. That boaster, who in general went to combat only when he could not do otherwise, saw that insolence and thoughtless words had brought him to that struggle with a man of great strength, whom he should have avoided as he would destruction; hence, when he felt that each of those blows might have brought down a bullock, the heart fell in him utterly. He forgot almost that it was not enough to catch blows on a shield, but that he must return them. He saw above him gleams of an axe, and thought that each gleam was the last one. When holding his shield up he shut his eyes in terror, doubting whether he would open them another time. He gave a blow rarely, and hopeless of reaching his opponent, he merely raised his shield higher and higher above his head to protect it.

At last he was tortured, but Hlava struck on with increasing vigor. As from a great pine-tree immense chips fly under the axe of a peasant, so under the blows of the Cheh plates began to break and fall from the mail of the German attendant. The upper edge of his shield bent and broke, the shoulder-piece fell from his right shoulder, and with it the bloody, severed armor strap. The hair stood on Van Krist's head and mortal terror seized him. He struck still once and a second time with all the vigor of his arm against Hlava's buckler. Seeing at last that, in view of the terrible strength of his opponent, there was no rescue, and that nothing could save him except some uncommon exertion, he hurled himself suddenly at Hlava's legs with all the weight of his body and his armor.

Both fell to the earth and wrestled, turning in the snow and rolling. But the Cheh was soon the superior. He restrained for a time the desperate struggles of his opponent, till at last he pressed with his knee the iron network covering Van Krist's stomach, and drew from his own sword-belt a short, triple-edged misericordia.

"Spare!" whispered the German, raising his eyes to the eyes of Hlava.

But the latter, instead of an answer, stretched above him so as to reach with his hands more easily, and when he had cut the leather helmet strap under the chin of his enemy he stabbed the hapless man twice in the throat, directing the point downward toward the middle of his bosom.

Van Krist's eyes sank in his skull, his hands and feet rubbed the snow as if to clear it of ashes, but after a while he stretched and lay motionless, merely pouting his lips, covered now with red foam, and bleeding with uncommon profuseness.

The Cheh rose, wiped his misericordia on the clothing of the German, then raising his axe and leaning on the handle gazed at the more difficult and stubborn battle between Zbyshko and Brother Rotgier.

The knights of western Europe were in those days accustomed to luxury and comfort, while the "heirs" in Great and Little Poland, as well as in Mazovia, were severe in their lives and self-denying. Because of this they roused admiration even in enemies and strangers by their strength of body and endurance.

It turned out on this occasion that Rotgier was excelled by Zbyshko in strength of arms and legs no less than his attendant was excelled by Hlava, but it turned out also that Zbyshko being young was surpassed in knightly training by the German.

It favored Zbyshko in some degree that he had chosen to fight with axes, for parrying with that kind of weapon was impossible. With long or short swords a man had to know blows and thrusts and be skilled to parry them; in such combat the German would have had a notable advantage. As it was, both Zbyshko himself and the spectators knew by the movements and handling of his shield that they had before them in Rotgier a man of experience, and dangerous, who, as they saw, was not engaged for the first time in that sort of combat. To every blow given by Zbyshko the German presented his shield, and as the blow fell he withdrew it a little; by this move the blow, though most violent, lost some effect, and could not cut or even crack the smooth surface. At moments he withdrew, at moments he pushed forward, though so swiftly that the eye could barely take note of his movements. The prince feared for Zbyshko, and men's faces grew gloomy, since it seemed to them that the German was playing with his opponent as if purposely. More than once he did not even present his shield, but at the instant when Zbyshko delivered the blow he made a half turn to one side, and thus Zbyshko's axe cut vacant air. That was for Zbyshko most perilous, as he might lose his balance and fall, in which case his ruin would be inevitable. Seeing this, Hlava, who stood over the slaughtered Van Krist, was alarmed also, and said in spirit:

"As God is dear to me, should my lord fall I will give the German a blow between the shoulders and let him tumble also."

But Zbyshko did not fall; he had immense strength in his legs, and, spreading them widely, was able to sustain on each one the whole weight of his blow and his body.

Rotgier noticed this straightway, and the spectators were mistaken in thinking that he despised his opponent. On the contrary, after the first blow, when in spite of all skill in withdrawing his shield his arm was benumbed almost, he understood that a sore struggle with that youth was awaiting him, and that if he could not fell him luckily, the battle might be protracted and dangerous. He had calculated that after Zbyshko's blow in the air he would fall on the snow, and when that did not happen he grew alarmed immediately. From under his visor Rotgier beheld the fixed nostrils and lips of his opponent, and his gleaming eyes also, at instants, and thought that his ardor would bear him away, that he would forget himself, lose his head, and in blindness think more of giving blows than defending his person. But in this too he was mistaken. Zbyshko had not skill to dodge blows by half turns, but he minded his shield, and when raising his axe did not expose himself more than was needful. His attention was evidently redoubled, and noting the accuracy and experience of Rotgier, not only did he not forget, but he collected himself, grew more cautious, and in his blows there was a calculation to which not heated, but cool resolution, may bring a man.

Rotgier, who had been in many wars and had fought battles not a few, both single-handed and in company, knew from experience that some men, like birds of prey, are created for combat, and gifted specially by nature, — men who, as it were, divine what others acquire by whole years of experience, — and straightway he saw that with one of these he was now doing battle. This youth had that certain something which is in the falcon, which considers an opponent as

mere prey, and thinks of naught else save to grasp that
prey in its talons. In spite of all his strength he noticed
that in strength too he was no match for Zbyshko, and that if
he became exhausted before he could give the settling blow,
the combat with that terrible though less prepared youth
would be fatal. Considering this, he resolved to fight
with the least labor possible : he drew the shield toward
his body ; he did not advance too much, he did not withdraw
too much ; he limited his motions ; he collected his whole
strength of mind and arm for one decisive blow, and watched
for the moment.

The fierce battle was protracted beyond usual duration.
A deathlike silence had settled down on the portico.   Nothing was heard save blows on the shields from the edges and
backs of the axes, now dull, and now piercing.   To the
prince, princess, knights, and damsels such sights were not
novel ; still a feeling akin to terror pressed all hearts as
with vices.   They knew that there was no question then of
showing strength, skill, or bravery, but that there was a
greater rage in that combat, a deeper despair, a harder, a
keener resolve, and a deadlier vengeance.   On one side was
a feeling of dreadful injustice endured, and with it love and
grief beyond limit ; on the other, the honor of a whole Order
and with it concentrated hate.   These two had met on that
place of conflict to receive God's decision.

Meanwhile the pale winter morning had brightened, the
gray obstruction of mist had been broken, and a sun-ray now
lighted Rotgier's blue armor and the silvery Milan mail worn
by Zbyshko.   In the chapel the bell rang for the mid-forenoon
prayer, and at sound of it flocks of daws flew again from
the peaks of the castle, flapping their wings and croaking
noisily, as if from delight at the spectacle of bloodshed
and that corpse lying motionless there on the snow.   Rotgier
had cast his eyes at it more than once in the course of the
battle, and felt now a great loneliness all on a sudden.
Every eye which looked at him was the eye of an enemy.
Every prayer, wish, and silent vow made by women were in
favor of Zbyshko.   Besides, though the brother of the Order
felt perfectly sure that Hlava would not rush from the rear
and fall on him treacherously, the presence and proximity of
that terrible figure filled him with that kind of fear which
people feel at sight of a bear, wolf, or buffalo from which
they are not separated by a grating.   And he could not
ward off that feeling, all the more since Hlava, while follow-

ing the course of the battle, moved and changed places, approaching the combatants, now from behind, now from the front, now from one side, inclining his head meanwhile and looking at the German with ominous gaze through the opening in the iron visor of his helmet, and raising somewhat at moments the bloody point of his sword, as though not noting that he did so.

Weariness began at last to seize Rotgier. He gave two short but fierce blows in succession, directing them against the right arm of Zbyshko. Zbyshko, however, repulsed them so forcibly with his shield that the axe turned in Rotgier's hand and he had to push back suddenly to escape falling, and thenceforth he pushed back continually. At last not only his strength but his patience and coolness of blood were exhausted. From the breasts of the spectators, at sight of his withdrawal, a number of shouts were rent, as if in triumph. These shouts roused in him desperation and anger. The blows of the axes grew more and more frequent. Sweat flowed from the foreheads of both combatants; from between the parted teeth of both the hoarse breath of their breasts escaped. The spectators had ceased to bear themselves calmly, and from moment to moment were heard cries, at one time of men, at another of women: "Strike!" "At him!" "The judgment of God!" "The punishment of God!" "God aid thee!" The prince raised his hand a number of times to enforce silence, but he could not. The noise became louder, children began to cry here and there on the portico, and at last, right at the side of the princess, some young, sobbing voice of a woman called, —

"For Danusia, Zbyshko!"

Zbyshko knew without this reminder that he was there doing battle for Danusia. He was sure that that Knight of the Cross had assisted in stealing her, and that in fighting with him he was fighting to redress the wrong done her. But, as he was young and eager for struggle, in the moment of combat he thought only of combat. All at once that cry, brought before him his loss and her suffering. Love, sorrow, and vengeance put fire in his veins. The heart whined in him from suddenly roused pain, and the rage of battle seized him directly. Rotgier could not catch now the terrible blows which were like those of a tempest, nor could he avoid them. Zbyshko struck his shield against the shield of the German with such force that the German's arm was benumbed that instant, and dropped without control. He retreated in terror and bent back, but the glitter of an axe flashed in his eyes, and its edge fell on his right shoulder like a thunderbolt. To the ears of the spectators came the single piercing shriek: "Jesus!" Rotgier withdrew one step more and fell backward to the centre.

Immediately there was an uproar, a movement on the balcony, as in a hive where bees, warmed by sun-rays, buzz and move. Knights ran down the steps in crowds, serving-men sprang over the wall of snow to look at the bodies. Everywhere were heard shouts of: "Here is the judgment of God!" "Yurand has an heir!" "Glory and thanks to him!" "He is a man for the axe!" Others cried: "Look at him and wonder!" "Yurand himself could not have cut better!" In fact a crowd of curious people formed around the body of Rotgier. He lay on his back with a face white as snow, his mouth widely open, and his bloody shoulder divided from the neck to the armpit so terribly that it held by some filaments only. Then a few men remarked: "He was alive a little while ago and walked over the earth proudly, but he moves no finger now!" And thus speaking, some wondered at his stature, for he occupied a great space on the field of combat, and seemed larger after death than before; others fixed the price of his peacock plumes as they changed colors marvelously on the snow, and a third group his armor, which was held to be worth a good village. But Hlava had just come up with two of Zbyshko's attendants to strip that armor from the dead man, and the curious surrounded Zbyshko, praising him to the skies and extolling him, for it seemed to them proper that his glory should fall on the whole knighthood of Mazovia and Poland. Meanwhile they removed his shield and axe to relieve him, and Mrokota unbuckled his helmet and covered his sweat-moistened hair with a cap of scarlet. Zbyshko, as if in a maze, stood, breathing heavily, with the fire in his eyes still unquenched, with face pale from resolve and exertion, trembling somewhat from excitement and struggle. They took him now by the arm and led him to the prince and princess, who were waiting, in a heated room, near the chimney. The young knight knelt before them and, when Father Vyshonek had blessed him and repeated eternal rest for the souls departed, the prince embraced Zbyshko.

"The Most High God has judged between him and thee," said he, "and guided thy hand, for which praised be His name

— Amen!" Then turning to De Lorche and others, he added,
"Thee, as a knight, and all of you here present, I take to
witness that which I myself testify, that they fought according to rule and custom, in the way that the judgments of
God are sought for in all places; hence this man has acted
in knightly fashion and in obedience to God."

The warriors shouted in a chorus of agreement, and when
the prince's words were interpreted to De Lorche he rose and
announced that not only did he testify that all had been
done in accordance with the law of knighthood and of God,
but also that if any one from Malborg or the court of any
prince should dare to call that in question, he, De Lorche,
would challenge him straightway to meet within barriers on
foot or on horseback, not only if he were an ordinary knight,
but even a giant, or some sorcerer surpassing Merlin himself
in magic.

Now Princess Anna Danuta, when Zbyshko was embracing her feet, asked, bending toward him, —

"Why art thou not glad? Rejoice and thank God, for if
the Lord in His mercy has freed thee from this net He will
not desert thee hereafter, and will bring thee to happiness."

"How can I rejoice, gracious lady?" answered Zbyshko.
"God has given victory and avenged me on this brother of
the Order, but Danusia, as she has not been found, is not
recovered yet, and I am no nearer her now than I was
before the battle."

"Her most inveterate enemies, Danveld, Gottfried, and
Rotgier, are no longer alive," replied the princess, "and as
to Siegfried, they say that he is juster than the others,
though more cruel. Praise God's mercy then for even this.
De Lorche has promised also that if the Knight of the Cross
fell he would take the corpse to Schytno, and go immediately to Malborg and defend Danusia before the Grand
Master of the Order. They will not dare, be assured of
that, to disregard the Grand Master."

"God give health to Pan de Lorche," said Zbyshko, "and
I will go with him to Malborg."

But the princess was as much frightened at these words
as if Zbyshko had said that he would go unarmed among
wolves, which gather in packs during winter in the great
pine forests of Mazovia.

"Why!" exclaimed she. "To certain destruction? Immediately after the duel neither De Lorche can assist thee,

nor the letters which Rotgier wrote before the combat.
Thou wilt not save any one, and wilt destroy thyself."

"So help me God," said Zbyshko, rising and crossing his
palms, "I will go to Malborg, and if need be beyond the
sea. So bless me, O Christ, as I shall seek her with the last
breath in my nostrils, I will not stop unless I perish. It is
easier for me to beat Germans and fight in armor, than for
the orphan to groan in a dungeon. Oi, easier! easier!"

And he spoke, as indeed he did whenever he mentioned
Danusia, with such excitement and in such pain that at
moments the words were wrested from him, as if some one
were grasping his throat. The princess saw that it would
be vain to seek to dissuade him, and that to hold the
man back one would have to thrust him manacled into a
dungeon.

But Zbyshko could not set out immediately. Knights of
that period disregarded all obstacles, but they were not permitted to break knightly custom, which commanded every
victor in a duel to pass the day of his triumph on the field of
combat and stay there till the following midnight. This was
done to prove that he was master of the field, and to show that
he was ready for combat in case a relative or friend of the
vanquished wished to challenge. This custom was observed
by whole armies, who thus lost frequently the advantage
which promptness after victory might have brought them.
Zbyshko did not even try to escape this unbending ordi-
nance, and, after strengthening himself to some degree and
putting on his armor, he remained beneath a gloomy winter
sky within the courtyard of the castle till midnight, waiting
for an enemy who could not come from any side whatever.

Only at midnight, when the heralds announced by sound
of trumpet his victory decisively, did Mikolai summon him
to supper, and immediately after to a consultation with
Prince Yanush.

CHAPTER XXXIV.

THE prince opened the consultation.

" It is unfortunate," said he, " that we have no letter or testimony against the comturs; our suspicion seems just, it is true, and I myself believe that they and no one else seized Yurand's daughter, — but what of that? They will deny. And when the Grand Master demands proof what shall we show him? Nay, more! Yurand's letter is proof in their favor." Here he turned to Zbyshko. "Thou sayst that they extorted the letter from Yurand by threats. Perhaps that is really true, for if justice were on their side God would not have aided thee against Rotgier. But since they extorted one letter perhaps they extorted two. They may have a testimony from Yurand that they are innocent of seizing the unfortunate maiden. In that case they will show it to the Grand Master — what will happen then?"

" But they themselves stated that they rescued Danusia from bandits, and that they have her."

" I know. But now they will say that they were mistaken and that it was another girl, the best proof of which is that Yurand himself rejected her."

" He did, for they showed him a different person; through this they enraged him."

" That is true indeed, but they can say that this is merely guess work on our part."

" Their lies," said Mikolai, " are like a forest. Something may be seen from the edge of a forest, but the farther a man goes the denser it becomes, till he gets astray and loses himself altogether."

Then he repeated in German his words to De Lorche, who said, —

" The Grand Master is better than they, and better than his brother; though insolent in spirit he is sensitive to knightly honor."

" True," answered Mikolai. " The Grand Master is humane, but has not power to restrain comturs or the

Chapter, and he cannot help this, that everything in the Order is built on injustice; but he does not rejoice in the injustice. Go, go, Knight de Lorche, and tell him what has happened here. Those monks fear foreigners more than us, they fear lest people should tell at foreign courts of their treasons and dishonest deeds, but if the Grand Master asks you for proofs say this : ' To know the truth is God's work, to seek for it is man's. If thou wish proofs, lord, search for them ; give command to stir up the castles, examine people ; let us seek, for it is folly and a fable to say that bandits of the forest seized the orphan."

"Folly and a fable," repeated De Lorche.

"Bandits would not have raised their hands against the prince's court, nor against Yurand's daughter. And even had they taken her it would have been to get a ransom ; and they themselves would have declared that they had her."

"I will tell all this," said the man of Lorraine, "and I will find De Bergov also. We are from the same country, and, though I do not know him, people say that he is a relative of the Count of Guelders. He has been in Schytno; let him tell the Grand Master what he has seen."

Zbyshko understood something of these words, and Mikolai interpreted what he did not understand. Then Zbyshko seized De Lorche by the body and pressed him to his bosom with such vigor that the knight was forced to groan.

"But dost thou wish to go in every case?" asked the prince of Zbyshko.

"I do, Gracious Lord. What else am I to do? I wished to take Schytno, even if I had to gnaw the walls through, but how can I begin war without permission?"

"The man who should begin war without permission would repent under the sword of an executioner," said Prince Yanush.

"Of course law is law," answered Zbyshko. "I wanted to challenge all who were at Schytno, but people said that Yurand had slaughtered them like bullocks ; I could not tell who were living and who were dead. So help me God and the Holy Cross, I will not desert Yurand till my last breath."

"Thou speakest honorably and pleasest me," said Mikolai. "But as thou didst not fly alone to Schytno it is clear that thou hast wit, for even a dull man would guess that they have not kept there either Yurand or his daughter, but taken both to other castles. God has given thee Rotgier because thou camest hither."

" Yes! " said the prince, " as we have learned from
Rotgier, of those four only old Siegfried is alive; God has
punished the others already, either with thy hand or Yurand's.
As to Siegfried, he is less a scoundrel than the others, but
is perhaps more cruel. It is unfortunate that Yurand and
Danusia are in his power; there is need of swift rescue in
their case. But lest an evil fate befall thee I will give a
letter to the Grand Master. Only listen well, and understand
that thou art not going as an envoy, but a confidant, and I
will write to the Grand Master as follows: Since on a time
they attacked us, the descendants of their benefactors, it is
likely that they seized Yurand's daughter for the reason
specially that they were angry at Yurand. I will ask the
Grand Master to command a diligent search for her, and if
he desires my friendship to deliver her into thy hands
immediately."

On hearing this Zbyshko cast himself at the feet of the
prince, embraced his knees, and said, —

" But Yurand, Gracious Lord, what of Yurand? Take his
part too! If he be wounded mortally, let him die in his own
house at least, and near his children."

" There is something touching Yurand also," replied the
prince with kindliness. " The Grand Master is to send two
judges and I two, who will judge the comtur's acts and those
of Yurand according to the rules of knightly honor. And
those four will choose a fifth to be their head, and as all
decide so will it be."

The consultation ended there. Zbyshko took farewell
now of the prince, for they were to start upon the road
immediately. But before parting Mikolai, who was experienced and knew the Knights of the Cross, took Zbyshko
aside and asked, —

" But that young man, the Cheh, wilt thou take him with
thee among the Germans? "

" It is sure that he will not leave me. But why the
question? "

" I am sorry for him. He is a splendid fellow, and do
thou note what I say: thou wilt bring away a sound head
from Malborg unless thou meet a better man in a duel, but
Hlava's death is certain."

" Why? "

" Because the dog brothers complained that he stabbed
De Fourcy. They must have written of his death to the
Grand Master, and to a certainty they wrote that the Cheh

shed his blood. The Knights at Malborg will not forgive
that. Judgment and vengeance await him, for how wilt
thou convince the Grand Master of Hlava's innocence?
Moreover he crushed Danveld's arm, and Danveld was a
relative of the Grand Hospitaller. I am sorry for Hlava,
and I repeat that if he goes he will go to his death."

"He will not go to his death, for I shall leave him in
Spyhov."

But it did not happen thus, for other causes intervened
and prevented the Cheh from remaining in Spyhov.

Zbyshko and De Lorche set out on the morrow with their
escorts. De Lorche, whom Father Vyshonek freed from his
vow touching Ulrika de Elner, was happy and devoted
altogether to remembering the charms of Yagenka of Dlugolyas; hence he travelled in silence. Zbyshko, unable to
talk with him of Danusia, for the men did not understand
each other well, talked with Hlava, who so far knew nothing
of the intended expedition to the realms of the Order.

"I am going to Malborg," said Zbyshko, "but the time
of my return is in the power of God. Perhaps it will be
soon, perhaps in the spring, perhaps a year hence, perhaps
never. Dost understand?"

"I understand. Your Grace is going surely to challenge
the Knights there. And glory to God, for every knight of
them has an attendant."

"No, I am not going there to challenge unless the challenge comes of itself. Thou wilt not go at all, but remain
at home, at Spyhov."

On hearing this Hlava was terribly mortified, he fell to
complaining piteously, and implored his young master not to
desert him.

"I have sworn not to abandon your Grace. I have sworn
on the Cross and my honor. Should any misfortune befall
you how could I appear before my lady in Zgorzelitse? I
have taken an oath, therefore spare me so that I may not
disgrace myself in her eyes."

"Hast thou not given her a vow to obey me?"

"Of course! In all things, but not to leave you. If
your Grace sends me away I shall follow at a distance and
be at hand when needed."

"I have not dismissed thee," answered Zbyshko, "and I
shall not; but it would be slavery for me if I could not send
thee whithersoever I pleased, even over the longest road, and
if I could not relieve myself of thy presence even for a day.

Thou wilt not stand above me, of course, like a headsman above an innocent person! And as to fighting, how art thou to assist me? I will not say in war, for in war people fight together, but in a duel thou wilt not fight for me. If Rotgier had been the stronger his armor would not be on our wagon, but mine on his. And know besides that it will be worse for me there with thy company; thou mayst put me in danger."

"How so, your Grace?"

Zbyshko told how he had heard from Mikolai that the comturs, unable to acknowledge the murder of De Fourcy, had accused Hlava, and would pursue him vindictively.

"If they seize thee," said Zbyshko at last, "I shall of course not leave thee to them as to dogs, and for this cause I may lay down my own head."

The Cheh became gloomy on hearing these words, for he recognized truth in them; still he tried further to turn the affair according to his wishes.

"Those men who saw me are no longer in this world, for people say that the old master of Spyhov killed some, and your grace has slain Rotgier."

"Thou wert seen by attendants who dragged on at some distance in front, and Siegfried, that old Knight of the Cross, is still living and is surely in Malborg; or if he is not there he will go there, for the Grand Master will certainly summon him."

There was no answer to this, so they rode on in silence as far as Spyhov. They found perfect readiness for war in the castle, since old Tolima expected that either the Knights of the Cross would make an attack, or that Zbyshko would summon them forth to save the old master. The guards watched everywhere at passages through the swamp; they watched in the castle also. The people were armed; and, as war was nothing new to them, they waited for the Germans with willingness, promising themselves famous booty. Father Kaleb received Zbyshko and De Lorche, and immediately after supper showed them the parchment with Yurand's seal, on which parchment he himself had written the last will of the master of Spyhov.

"He dictated it to me," said the priest, "that night when he started for Schytno. Well—he did not expect to return."

"Why did you say nothing?"

"I said nothing because he declared under the secret of confession what he intended to do. The Lord grant him endless rest, and let eternal light shine on him."

" Say no *Our Father* for him. He is living yet. I know
that from Rotgier, with whom I fought in the courtyard of
the prince's castle. The judgment of God was between us,
and I killed him."

" All the more for that reason will Yurand not return —
unless by the power of God."

" I will go with this knight here to wrest him from their
hands."

" Then thou knowest not their hands, that is clear. I
know them, for before Yurand received me into Spyhov I
was a priest fifteen years in their country. God alone can
save Yurand."

" And He can help us too."

" Amen ! "

Then the priest unrolled the parchment and read it.
Yurand had bequeathed all his land and property to Danusia
and her descendants, and in case of her death without posterity to her husband, Zbyshko of Bogdanets. To conclude
he confided this his testament to the care of the prince, "so
that should there be anything not in accordance with law,
the favor of the prince would make law of it." This conclusion was added since Father Kaleb knew only canon law,
and Yurand himself, occupied exclusively with war, knew
only the law of knighthood. After reading the document to
Zbyshko the priest read it to the older men of the garrison ;
these acknowledged the young knight at once as heir and
promised obedience. They thought besides that Zbyshko
would lead them straightway to rescue the old master,
and they rejoiced, because stern hearts eager for battle
were beating in their bosoms, hearts attached to Yur-
and ; therefore great gloominess seized them on learning
that they must remain at home, and that their lord with
a small retinue was going to Malborg not to offer battle,
but to make complaint. The Cheh shared their gloom,
though on the other hand he rejoiced at the notable
increase of Zbyshko's property.

" Ei," said he, " who will rejoice if not the old lord of
Bogdanets? He would know how to manage in this place !
What is Bogdanets if compared to an inheritance like
Spyhov ! "

But Zbyshko was seized at that moment by a sudden
yearning for his uncle, such a yearning as seized him often,
especially in grievous and difficult junctures ; so turning to
the attendant he said without hesitation, —

"What hast thou to do sitting here in idleness? Go to Bogdanets; thou wilt take a letter."

"If I am not to be with your Grace I should prefer to be there," answered he, delighted.

"Call Father Kaleb to me; let him write, as is proper, of all that has happened; the priest of Kresno will read the letter to uncle, or the abbot will read it if he is in Zgorzelitse."

But the next moment he struck his palm on his youthful mustaches, and added, speaking to himself, —

"Oh! the abbot!"

And Yagenka passed before his vision blue-eyed, dark-haired, shapely as a deer, and with tears on her eyelids. He felt awkward, and for a time rubbed his forehead.

"Indeed the girl will feel sad, but not sadder than I," said he.

Meanwhile Father Kaleb appeared and sat down to write. Zbyshko dictated to him minutely all that had happened from the time of his coming to the hunting-lodge. He kept back nothing, for he knew that old Matsko when he looked into those matters carefully would be glad at last. Indeed it was not possible to compare Bogdanets with Spyhov, which was a broad and rich property, and Zbyshko knew that Matsko valued such things immensely.

When, after long effort, the letter was finished and closed with a seal, Zbyshko called his attendant a second time and delivered it, saying, —

"Perhaps thou wilt return with uncle; if so I shall rejoice greatly."

But Hlava's face was full of evident anxiety; he hesitated, stood on one foot, then on the other, and did not start till the young knight spoke, —

"If thou hast more to say, say it."

"I should wish to know this. If people ask how shall I answer?"

"What people?"

"Not those in Bogdanets, but in the neighborhood, — for certainly they will wish to know."

At this Zbyshko, who had determined to make no concealment of anything, looked at Hlava quickly, and answered, —

"With thee it is not a question of people, but only of Yagenka."

Hlava blushed, then he grew somewhat pale and said, —

"Of her, lord."

"But how dost thou know that she has not been given in marriage to Stan of Rogov or Vilk of Brozova?"

"The young lady has not married any one," said Hlava, with emphasis.

"The abbot may have commanded her."

"The abbot obeys the young lady, not she the abbot."

"What dost thou wish then? Tell the truth to her, as to others."

Hlava bowed and went away somewhat angry.

"God grant," said he to himself, thinking of Zbyshko. "God grant her to forget thee. God grant her a better man. Thou art married but wifeless, and mayest thou be a widower before the marriage is finished."

Hlava had grown attached to Zbyshko, he had compassion on Danusia, but Yagenka he loved beyond everything, and from the time that he had heard of Zbyshko's marriage before the last battle at Tsehanov he carried pain in his heart, and bitterness.

"God grant that thou be a widower before thy marriage is real!"

But later other thoughts, evidently sweeter, came to his head, for coming to his horses he said, —

"God be praised for even this, that I shall embrace her feet."

Meanwhile Zbyshko was impatient for the journey, and a fever tormented him. Since he could not occupy himself with other matters he endured real torture, thinking always of Danusia and Yurand. But he had to remain in Spyhov one night at least, for Pan de Lorche, and for the preparations which such a long journey demanded. Besides he was wearied beyond every measure by the battle, by watching, by the journey, by lack of sleep, by grief. That night, very late, he cast himself on Yurand's hard bed in the hope that even a short slumber would visit him. But before he fell asleep Sanderus knocked at the door and entered.

"Lord, you saved me from death," said he, bowing down; "with you I have lived more pleasantly than I have lived for a long time. God has given you a great estate; you are richer than ever, and the treasury of Spyhov is not empty. Give me a purse of some sort; I will go from castle to castle in Prussia, and though it is not very safe for me there, perhaps I may serve you."

Zbyshko, who at the first moment wished to push him out of the room, stopped at these words, and after a while drew from a traveling-bag at the bedside a large purse, threw it to him, and said, —

"Take this; go! If thou art a rogue thou wilt deceive, if honest thou wilt serve me."

"I will deceive cunningly," said Sanderus, "but not you; you I will serve truthfully."

CHAPTER XXXV.

SIEGFRIED DE LÖWE was just ready to start for Malborg
when the post-boy brought him unexpectedly a letter from
Rotgier with news from the court of Mazovia. This news
moved the old Knight of the Cross to the quick. First of
all it was evident from the letter that Rotgier had presented
and managed the case against Yurand with excellent skill
before Prince Yanush. Siegfried smiled while reading how
Rotgier had made a further demand that the prince should
give Spyhov in feudal tenure as satisfaction for wrongs done
the Order. But the second part of the letter contained
unexpected and less desirable tidings. Rotgier wrote in
addition that, to show more convincingly that the Order was
innocent of seizing Yurand's daughter, he had thrown down
his gauntlet before the knights of Mazovia, challenging every
doubter to the judgment of God; that is to a combat before
the whole court. "No one took up the gauntlet," continued
Rotgier, "for all knew that Yurand's own letter testified in
our favor, hence they feared the justice of God, but just then
appeared a young man whom we saw at the hunting-lodge;
he took up the gauntlet. Therefore be not astonished, wise
and pious brother, that I delay in returning, for, since I gave
the challenge myself, I must accept combat. And, since I
did this for the glory of the Order, I hope that the Grand
Master will not take the act ill of me, and that you will not,
— you whom I honor and love as with the heart of a son.
My opponent is a mere stripling, and combat to me, as you
know, is no novelty, hence I shall shed this blood easily to
the glory of the Order, and especially with the aid of Christ
the Lord, who is surely more concerned for those who bear
his cross than for some Yurand, or for the wrongs of one
paltry wench from Mazovia."

The news that Yurand's daughter was married astonished
old Siegfried most of all. At the thought that a new enemy,
terrible and vengeful, might settle in Spyhov, a certain alarm
seized even that aged comtur. "It is clear," said the old
man to himself, "that he will not forego revenge; all the

more will he not if he finds his wife and she tells him that we took her away from the hunting-lodge. It would appear at once that we invited Yurand just to destroy him, and that no one had a thought of restoring the daughter to her father." Here it occurred to Siegfried that in answer to the prince's letters the Grand Master would probably order a search in Schytno, even to clear himself before that same prince of Mazovia. It was important to him and the Chapter, in case of war with the powerful King of Poland, that the princes should be neutral. Omitting those princes' troops, which were not among the fewest, it was proper, in view of the number of Mazovian nobles and their valor, not to despise Prince Yanush and his brother; peace with them secured the boundary along great spaces, and permitted the Order to concentrate its forces better. They had mentioned this frequently in Malborg before Siegfried, and comforted themselves with the hope that after conquering the King they would find later on some pretext against Mazovia, and then no power could snatch that land from the grasp of the Order. That was a great and certain reckoning, hence it was positive in that juncture that the Grand Master would do everything to avoid irritating Prince Yanush, who, married to Keistut's daughter, was more difficult to please than Ziemowit of Plotsk, whose wife, for undiscovered reasons, was thoroughly devoted to the Order.

In view of these thoughts old Siegfried, with all his readiness for every treachery, crime, and cruelty, and though he loved the Order, and its glory began to reckon with his conscience. "Would it not be better to liberate Yurand and his daughter? Treason and foulness weighed down the name of Danveld, but he was not living. And even," thought he, "if the Grand Master should punish me and Rotgier severely, since we were in every case participants, will not that be better for the Order?" But here his vengeful, cruel heart began to storm within him at the thought of Yurand. Liberate him, that oppressor and executioner of people of the Order, a victor in so many conflicts, the author of so many defeats and so much shame, the conqueror, and later the murderer, of Danveld, the captor of De Bergov, the slayer of Meinegger, Gottfried, and Hugo, of him, who in Schytno itself shed more German blood than is shed in a good engagement in time of warfare. "I cannot, I cannot!" repeated Siegfried in spirit. And at the very thought the grasping fingers of the old man contracted in a cramp, and his dried-up breast caught its breath with effort. "And still, if that were for the greater profit and glory of the Order? If the punishment, which in that case would fall on those authors of the crime who are still living, should win Prince Yanush, hostile thus far, and facilitate a treaty, or even a truce, with him? They are passionate," continued the old comtur with himself, "but if one shows them a little kindness they forget their wrongs easily. The prince, for instance, was seized on his own territory, and still he takes no active vengeance."

Here the old man began to walk through the hall in great internal conflict, and finally he stopped before the crucifix, which opposite the entrance door occupied almost the height of the wall between both windows, and kneeling at the foot of it he began: "Enlighten me, O Lord, teach me, for I know not what to do! If I liberate Yurand and his daughter our deeds will be discovered in all their nakedness. People will not say: 'Danveld did this,' or 'Siegfried did this;' they will say, 'the Knights of the Cross did this,' and infamy may fall on the whole Order, and hatred in that prince's heart will become still greater. If I do not liberate them, but hide or kill them, suspicion will remain on the Order, and I must defile my lips with lying in the presence of the Grand Master. What shall I do, O Lord? Teach me and enlighten! If vengeance is urging me on, then judge me according to Thy justice; but teach me now, enlighten me, for it is a question of Thy Order, and whatever Thou commandest I will do, even though I were to wait for death and liberation in a dungeon and manacled."

And, resting his forehead on the wood of the Cross, he prayed a long time, for it did not flash through his head for an instant that that prayer of his was blasphemous and crooked. Then he rose more at peace, believing that favor from the tree of the Cross had sent him a simpler and a clearer thought, and that something from above said: "Rise and await the return of Rotgier." "Yes! it was necessary to wait. Rotgier would slay that youth without fail, and then he would have either to secrete or liberate Yurand and his daughter. In the first case the prince would not forget them, it is true, but having no proof as to who seized the girl, he would search for her, he would send letters to the Grand Master, not with a complaint, but inquiring — and the case would go on in unending deferment. In the second case, delight at the return of Yurand's daughter would be greater than desire of vengeance for having carried her away. And besides, we can always say that we found her after Yurand inflicted the slaughter." This last thought pacified Siegfried thoroughly. As to Yurand, Siegfried had long since, in company with Rotgier, invented a method through which, if they should liberate him, he would have no power for complaint or vengeance. Siegfried rejoiced now in his savage soul as he remembered that method. He rejoiced also at thought of the judgment of God which was to take place at the castle of Tsehanov. As to the outcome of that mortal struggle no alarm troubled him. He called to mind a certain tournament in Krolevets where Rotgier had finished two knights of renown, who in their native Anjou were held to be invincible. He remembered also a battle at Vilno with a certain Polish knight, a follower of Spytko of Melstyn; this knight was slain by Rotgier. His face brightened and his heart swelled with pride, for though Rotgier was a renowned knight already, he, Siegfried, was the first to lead him in expeditions to reduce Lithuania and to teach him the best methods of warfare against the people of that country; hence he loved him as a son, with that deep love of which only those men are capable who have been forced to confine in the heart for a long time the desire of love and the power of it. And now this dear son will shed once again that hated Polish blood and will return clothed in glory. That is the judgment of God, and the Order will be cleansed of suspicion at the same time. "The judgment of God!" For one twinkle of an eye the old man's heart was straitened with a feeling like fear. Rotgier had to stand up in mortal struggle to defend the innocence of the Knights of the Order — but they were guilty; he will fight for a lie then. But if a misfortune should happen? After a moment, however, that seemed to Siegfried impossible. "Yes! Rotgier writes truly. Surely Christ will care more for the men who bear his cross than for Yurand and the wrongs of one paltry wench from Mazovia. Yes, in three days Rotgier will return — and return a victor."

When he had pacified himself in this way the old knight meditated longer: "Would it not be better meanwhile to send away Danusia to a more remote castle, which in no case would yield to an attack by Mazovians?" But after meditating a moment he dropped even this thought: Only the husband of Yurand's daughter could plan an attack and stand at the head of it; but he was about to perish at the hand of

Rotgier. After that there would be on the part of the prince and the princess merely correspondence, questions, efforts, complaints, but just through these the affair would be blurred and effaced, not to mention delays well-nigh endless. "Before they reach a result," added Siegfried, "I shall be dead, and perhaps Yurand's daughter herself will grow old in the prisons of the Order."

But he gave command to have everything ready for defence in the castle and also for the road, since he knew not precisely what might result from his conference with Rotgier; and he waited.

Two days, then three and four, passed beyond the date at which Rotgier had promised at first to return; still no retinue appeared before the gate of Schytno. Only on the fifth day, just before dark, was heard the sound of a horn before the bastion of the gatekeeper. Siegfried, who had just finished his evening prayers, sent a boy at once to learn who had come.

The boy returned after a while with confused face, but Siegfried could not note the change, since the fire in the room burned in a deep chimney and lighted the gloom only a little.

"Have they come?" asked the old knight.

"Yes," answered the boy. But in his voice there was something which alarmed Siegfried immediately, so he said, —

"But Brother Rotgier?"

"They have brought Brother Rotgier."

At this Siegfried rose from his armchair. For a long time he held the arm with his hand as if fearing to fall, then he said in a suppressed voice, —

"Give me my mantle."

The boy placed the mantle on his shoulders. He had regained his strength evidently, for he drew the cowl over his head and walked out of the chamber.

He soon found himself in the courtyard of the castle, where it had grown dark completely. He walked over the squeaking snow with slow step toward the retinue, which had halted near the gate after passing it. A dense crowd of people had gathered already, and a number of torches held by soldiers of the garrison were gleaming there. At sight of the old brother of the Order the soldiers stood apart from one another. By the light of the torches alarmed faces were visible, and in the darkness low voices were whispering, —

" Brother Rotgier — "

" Brother Rotgier is slain."

Siegfried pushed up to the sleigh in which on straw lay a body covered with a mantle, and raised the mantle.

"Bring a light," said he, pushing his cowl aside.

One of the soldiers brought forward a torch, by the light of which Siegfried saw Rotgier's face pale as snow, frozen, surrounded by a dark kerchief with which they had bound his chin, so that his mouth might not open. The whole face was contracted, and thereby so changed that one might think him some other person. The eyes were covered with their lids, blue spots were around the eyes and on the temples. The cheeks were glazed with frost.

Siegfried gazed for a long time amid unbroken silence. Others looked at him, for they knew that he was as a father to the dead man, and that he loved him. But no tear flowed from his eyes; on his face there was merely a sterner expression than usual, and a certain icy calm.

"They sent him hither in that form!" said he at last.

But the next moment he turned to the castle steward and said, —

"Have a coffin made before midnight, and place the body in the chapel."

"There is one coffin left of those made for the men slain by Yurand; I will have it covered with cloth."

"And have a mantle placed over it," said Siegfried, covering Rotgier's face; " not one like this, but a mantle of the Order."

After a moment he added, —

" Do not close the lid."

The people approached the sleigh, Siegfried pulled the cowl over his head again, but called to mind something before going, for he asked, —

"Where is Van Krist?"

"Slain also," answered one of the men, " but they buried him in Tsehanov, for he had begun to decay."

"That is well."

Then he walked away slowly, and returning to the chamber sat down in the same armchair in which the news had found him; and he sat motionless, with a stony face, and sat so long that the boy grew alarmed and pushed his head in through the door more and more frequently. Hour followed hour; the usual noise ceased in the castle; only from the direction of the chapel came the dull, undefined blows of the hammer, and then nothing disturbed the silence save the calling of sentries. It was near midnight when the old knight woke as if from sleep and called the boy, —

" Where is Brother Rotgier? " asked he.

The boy, startled by the silence, the events, and sleeplessness, did not understand evidently, for he looked at him with alarm, and answered with a quivering voice, —

" I do not know, lord."

The old man smiled as if heart-broken and said mildly, —

" I asked, child, if he is in the chapel."

" He is, lord."

" That is well. Tell Diedrich to be here with a lantern and wait till I come. Let him have also a kettle with coals. Is there a light now in the chapel?"

" There are candles burning at the side of the coffin."

When Siegfried entered he surveyed the chapel from the door to see if any one was present, then he closed the door carefully, approached the bier, put aside two candles from the six which were burning in great brass candlesticks, and knelt at the coffin. His lips made no movement whatever, hence he was not praying. For some time he looked only at the stiffened but still comely face of Rotgier, as if wishing to find traces of life in it. Then amid the quiet of the chapel he called in low tones, —

" O son! O son! "

He was silent again. It seemed that he was waiting for an answer.

Then he stretched forth his hands, thrust his dried talon-like fingers under the mantle which covered Rotgier's bosom, and began to feel beneath it. He sought everywhere, at the middle, at the sides, below the ribs and along the shoulder-blades; at last he felt through the cloth the cleft which extended from the top of the right shoulder to a point below the armpit; he pressed in his fingers, pushed them along the whole length of the wound, and again he spoke with a voice in which complaint seemed to tremble, —

" Oo — what a merciless blow! But thou didst say that he was just a stripling! The entire shoulder! The whole arm ! How often thou didst raise that arm against Pagans in defending the Order! And now a Polish axe has hewn it from thee, — and this is thy end! This is the close of thy career! Christ did not bless thee, for it is evident that He cares more for one wrong done to man than for our whole Order. In the name of the Father, and the Son, and the Spirit: thou hast defended the wrong, thou hast died for injustice, without absolution — and maybe thy soul — "

The words broke in his mouth, his lips began to quiver, and in the chapel deep silence set in a second time.

" O son! O son! "

In Siegfried's words there was entreaty now, and at the same time he called in a still lower voice, as do people who are making inquiry touching some awful and terrible secret, —

" O merciful Christ! If thou art not damned, my son, give a sign, move thy hand, or open thy eyes for one instant, the heart is whining within my old bosom. Give a sign; I loved thee — speak ! "

And resting his hands on the edge of the coffin he fixed his vulture-like eyes on Rotgier's closed lids.

" Oh, how couldst thou speak ! " said he finally; " cold and the odor of death issues forth from thee. But since thou art silent I will tell thee something, and let thy soul fly hither between the burning candles and listen."

Then he bent to the face of the corpse.

" Thou rememberest how the chaplain would not let us kill Yurand, and how we gave an oath to him. That is well; I will keep the oath, but I will comfort thee wherever thou art, though I be damned myself for it."

Then he withdrew from the coffin, put back the candlesticks which he had set aside, covered the body and the face with the mantle, and went forth from the chapel.

At the door of his chamber the wearied boy slept a deep sleep. Diedrich was waiting according to Siegfried's command. He was a short, strong man with bow-legs, and a square face which was partly concealed by a dark, jagged cowl which dropped to his shoulders. He wore a kaftan made from untanned hide of buffalo; above his hips was a belt of the same hide; behind this a bunch of keys and a short knife were thrust. In his right hand he held an iron lantern with membrane; in his left hand was a small brass kettle and a taper.

" Art ready? " inquired Siegfried.

Diedrich inclined in silence.

" I commanded thee to have coals in the kettle."

A second time the strong man made no answer; he merely pointed to sticks blazing in the chimney, took an iron shovel which was standing at the side of the chimney, and began to take from under the sticks coals for the kettle, then he lighted the lantern and waited.

" Listen to me now, thou dog," said Siegfried. " Once thou didst babble out what Comtur Danveld commanded thee to do, and the comtur had thy tongue cut out. But since thou art able to show the chaplain on thy fingers whatever pleasest thee, I declare that if thou show with a single movement what thou doest at my order I will command to hang thee."

Diedrich bowed again in silence, but his face was distorted ominously by a terrible recollection, because the tongue had been torn from him for a reason entirely different from that given by Siegfried.

" Move ahead now, and lead to Yurand's dungeon."

The executioner seized the bale of the kettle with his gigantic hand ; he raised the lantern, and they left the room. Outside the door they passed the sleeping boy, and descending the steps went, not to the main door, but to the rear of the steps, behind which was a narrow corridor which extended along the whole width of the building, and ended at a heavy gate hidden in a niche of the wall. Diedrich pushed in the gate, and they found themselves beneath the open sky in a small courtyard, which was surrounded on four sides by stone storehouses, in which grain was kept for use in the castle during sieges. Under one of these storehouses on the right were subterranean dungeons for prisoners. There was no guard there, for should a prisoner be even able to break out of the dungeon he would find himself in the court out of which the only issue was through that gate.

" Wait," said Siegfried.

And resting his hand against the wall he halted, for he felt that something of no good import was happening to him, and that breath was failing him, as if his breast had been confined in armor that was too narrow. In simple fact, that through which he had passed was beyond his failing strength. He felt also that his forehead under the cowl was covered with sweat-drops, and he halted to regain the breath that was failing him.

After a gloomy day the night had grown unusually bright. The moon was shining in the sky, and the whole yard was filled with clear light, in which the snow appeared green. Siegfried drew the fresh and somewhat frosty air into his lungs greedily. But he recalled at the same time that on such a clear night precisely Rotgier went to Tsehanov, whence he was now brought back a corpse.

"But now thou art lying in the chapel," muttered he in a whisper.

Diedrich, thinking that the comtur was speaking to him, raised the lantern and lighted his face, which was terribly pale, almost corpse-like, and also resembling the head of an aged vulture.

"Lead on!" said Siegfried.

The yellow circle of light from the lantern trembled again on the snow, and they went farther. In the thick wall of the storehouse was a recess where a few steps led to a great iron door. Diedrich opened the door and began to descend along steps into the depth of a black passage, raising the lantern with effort to light the way for the comtur. At the foot of the steps was a passage; on the right and left sides of it were the exceedingly low doors of cells for prisoners.

"To Yurand," said Siegfried.

After a while the bolts squeaked and they entered. It was perfectly dark in that hole, therefore Siegfried, not seeing clearly by the dim light of the lantern, commanded to light the torch, and soon in the strong gleam of its flame he saw Yurand lying on straw. The prisoner had fetters on his feet, and on his arms a chain, which was long enough to let him reach food to his mouth. He was dressed in the same penitential bag in which he had stood before the comturs, but it was covered now with dark traces of blood; for on that day in which an end had been put to his fight, when mad from rage and pain they had entangled the knight in a net, the soldiers, wishing to kill the man, had stabbed him a number of times with their halberds. The local chaplain of Schytno had prevented the killing; the halberd thrusts had not proved mortal, but so much blood had left Yurand that he was taken half-dead to the prison. It was thought by all at the castle that he might die any hour, but his great strength had conquered death, and he lived though his wounds were not dressed, and he was thrust into that dreadful dungeon, where moisture dropped for whole days from the ceiling, and where in time of frost the walls were covered with a thick, snow-like coating and with ice-crystals.

He lay enchained on the straw, powerless, but so immense that, especially when prostrate, he produced the impression of a piece of a cliff cut into human form. Siegfried gave command to turn the light straight to his face, and for some time the old man gazed on it in silence, then, turning to Diedrich, he said,—

"Thou seest that he has sight in one eye only; burn that one out of him."

There was in the old comtur's voice a certain weakness and decrepitude, but precisely because of that the dreadful order seemed still more dreadful. The torch trembled somewhat in the hand of the executioner, but he inclined it, and soon great flaming drops of pitch began to fall on the eye of the captive, and finally they covered it completely from his brow to his prominent cheek-bone.

Yurand's face writhed, his yellow mustaches turned upward and disclosed his set teeth, but he uttered no word, and whether it was through exhaustion, or the innate force of will in his tremendous nature, he groaned not.

"They promised to let thee go forth free," said Siegfried, "and thou wilt go, but thou wilt not be able to blame the Order, for the tongue with which thou hast blasphemed against it will be taken from thee."

Again he made a sign to Diedrich, who gave forth a strange guttural sound and indicated by winks that he needed both hands and wished the comtur to hold the light for him.

The old man took the torch and held it with outstretched, trembling hand, but when Diedrich pressed Yurand's bosom with his knees, Siegfried turned his face away and looked at the wall, which was lined with hoar-frost that night.

For a while the clatter of chains was heard, next the panting breaths of human breasts, after that something like a deep, dull groan, and then silence followed.

At last the voice of Siegfried was heard again, —

"Yurand, thy punishment had to meet thee in this way, but besides the punishment already suffered, I have promised Brother Rotgier, now slain by thy daughter's husband, to lay thy right hand in his coffin."

Diedrich, who had raised himself, when he heard these words bent anew over Yurand.

After a certain time the old comtur and Diedrich found themselves again in that yard which was filled with moonlight. While advancing through the corridor Siegfried took the lantern from the executioner, and also a dark object with a rag round it.

"Now back to the chapel," said he to himself aloud, "and then to the watch-tower."

Diedrich looked at him quickly, but the comtur commanded him to sleep, and, swinging the lantern, dragged on himself

toward the space lighted by the chapel windows. Along
the road he pondered over what had happened. He felt
a certain conviction that his end was now approaching,
that these were his last deeds on earth, that for them he
would have to answer before God alone; still his soul of
a Knight of the Cross, though less false by nature than
cruel, had, under the influence of implacable necessity,
become so accustomed to the evasions of cheating, and to
shielding the bloody deeds of the Order, that even now he
thought involuntarily of casting the infamy · of the torture
and the responsibility for it both from himself and from the
Order. Diedrich was dumb, he could make no confession,
and though he could explain to the chaplain he would not do
so from very terror. Then what? Then who could learn
that Yurand had not received all those wounds in battle?
He might easily have lost his tongue from a spear thrust
between the teeth; a sword or an axe might have cut his
right hand off; and he had only one eye, hence what wonder
that that eye was knocked out when he hurled himself in
madness on the whole garrison of Schytno? Ah, Yurand!
The last delight of his life shook up for a moment the heart
of old Siegfried. "Yes, Yurand, should he recover, must
be freed!" Here Siegfried recalled how he had counselled
with Rotgier touching this, and how the young brother said,
with a smile, "Let him go then whithersover his eyes lead,
and if he cannot find Spyhov let him inquire the way to it."
For what had happened had been partly determined between
him and Rotgier. But now, when Siegfried entered the
chapel a second time, and, kneeling down at the coffin, laid
Yurand's bloody hand at the feet of Rotgier, the joy which
had quivered in him a moment earlier was reflected on his
face for the last time.

"Seest thou," said he, "I have done more than we
decided, for King Yan of Luxemburg, though blind, appeared
in battle, and died with glory, but Yurand will not rise again;
he will perish like a dog near some fence."

Here again he felt the lack of breath, just as before, when
he was going to Yurand's prison, and on his head the weight
as it were of an iron helmet; this lasted, however, but one
twinkle of an eye. He breathed deeply, and continued, —

"Ei, and now comes my time. I had only thee, now I
have no one. But if it is destined me to live longer, I vow
to thee, my son, that on thy grave I will place the hand
which slew thee, or die myself. Thy slayer is living yet—"

Here his teeth gritted; such a mighty spasm seized him that the words stopped in his mouth, and only after some time did he begin anew to speak, with broken voice, —

"Yes, thy slayer is living yet, but I will reach him — and before I reach him I will inflict on him another torture worse than death itself."

And he was silent.

After a moment he rose, and approaching the coffin said in a calm voice, —

"Now I will bid thee farewell; I will look on thy face for the last time; I shall know, perhaps, if thou rejoice at my vow. This is the last time!"

And he uncovered Rotgier's face, but drew back on a sudden.

"Thou art smiling," said he, "but thy smile is terrible."

The body had thawed in fact under the cloak, and perhaps from the warmth of the candles; as a result of this it had begun to decay with uncommon rapidity, and the face of the young comtur had become indeed terrible. His swollen, immense, blackened ears had in them something monstrous, and his blue puffed-out lips were twisted as if smiling.

Siegfried covered that ghastly human mask in all haste. Then taking the lantern he went out. On the road breath failed him a third time, so returning to his chamber he threw himself on his hard couch and lay for a while motionless. He had thought to fall asleep, but suddenly a strange feeling seized him. It seemed to the aged knight that sleep would never come again to him, but that if he remained in that chamber death would come directly.

Siegfried had no fear of death. In his measureless torture and without hope of sleep he saw in it a kind of boundless rest, but he had no wish to yield to death on that night.

"Give me time till morning," said he, rising on the couch.

With that he heard clearly a certain voice whispering in his ear, —

"Go forth from this chamber. To-morrow will be too late, and thou wilt not accomplish that which thou hast promised. Go forth from this chamber!"

The comtur, raising himself with effort, went forth. The sentries were calling on the battlements at the corners. Near the chapel a yellow gleam fell on the snow through the windows. In the middle of the square, near the stone well, two black dogs were playing, pulling some cloth from each other; except them the court was empty and silent.

"Then to-night absolutely," said Siegfried. "I am wearied beyond measure, but I will go — all are sleeping. Yurand conquered by torture sleeps also, perhaps, but I shall not sleep. I will go, I will go, for death is in my chamber, and I have promised thee — let death come after that, since sleep is not to come. Thou art smiling there; but strength fails me. Thou art smiling; it is evident then that thou art pleased. But thou seest my fingers have grown numb, strength has left my hand, I cannot finish that alone — the servant woman who sleeps with her will finish it — "

While speaking thus he went on with heavy step toward the tower which stood at the gate. Meanwhile the dogs which were playing at the stone well ran up and began to fawn around him. In one of them Siegfried recognized the mastiff which was an inseparable comrade of Diedrich; people said in the castle that the dog served the man at night for a pillow.

After greeting the comtur, the mastiff gave a low bark once or twice, then bounded toward the gate as if divining Siegfried's thought.

Soon the comtur found himself before the narrow door of the tower, which at night was bolted from the outside. Pushing back the bolt he felt for the stairway railing, which began right there inside the door, and ascended. He had forgotten his lantern through mental distraction; he felt his way, stepping carefully, and searched for the steps with his feet.

On a sudden, after some advance, he halted, for higher up, but straight above, he heard something like the panting of a man, or a beast.

"Who is there?"

No answer was given, but the panting grew more rapid.

Siegfried was fearless; he had no dread of death, but his courage and self-command were exhausted to the last on that night of terror. Through his brain flashed the thought that Rotgier, or perhaps the evil spirit, was barring the way to him. The hair rose on his head, and his forehead was covered with cold perspiration. He withdrew almost to the very entrance.

"Who is there?" inquired he, with a choked voice.

But that moment something struck him in the breast with such terrible force that he fell backward through the open door without uttering a syllable.

Silence followed.   Then a dark figure pushed from out the
tower and moved stealthily toward the stable which stood
next to the arsenal on the left side of the courtyard.   Diedrich's
mastiff rushed after it in silence.   The second dog sprang
after that one and vanished in the shadow of the wall, but
soon appeared with head toward the earth, coming back
slowly and as it were sniffing the tracks of the man.   In this
manner it approached Siegfried, who was lying motionless;
sniffed him carefully, then sat near his head, raised its jaws,
and began to howl.

The howling was heard for a long time, filling that dole-
ful night as it were with new sadness and terror.   At last a
door hidden in the niche of the great gate squeaked and the
gatekeeper stood in the court with a halberd.

"A plague on the dog!   I will teach thee to howl at
night," said he.

And thrusting out the halberd point he wished to pierce
the beast with it, but that moment he saw some one lying
near the open door of the tower.

"Herr Jesus! what is this?"

Bending forward he looked into the face of the prostrate
person and cried, —

"Hither!   Hither!   Rescue!"

Then he sprang to the gate and pulled the bell-rope with
all his might.